Emerging Economies and Firms in the Global Crisis

Also by Marin A. Marinov

INTERNATIONALIZATION IN CENTRAL AND EASTERN EUROPE

MARKETING IN THE EMERGING MARKETS OF CENTRAL AND EASTERN EUROPE: The Balkans

MARKETING IN THE EMERGING MARKETS OF ISLAMIC COUNTRIES

MARKETING IN THE EMERGING MARKETS OF LATIN AMERICA

Also by Marin A. Marinov and Svetla T. Marinova

FOREIGN DIRECT INVESTMENT IN CENTRAL AND EASTERN EUROPE

IMPACTS OF EMERGING ECONOMIES AND FIRMS ON INTERNATIONAL BUSINESS

INTERNATIONAL BUSINESS (*with Michael Czinkota, Ilkka Ronkainen and Michael Moffett*)

INTERNATIONALIZATION OF EMERGING ECONOMIES AND FIRMS

THE CHANGING NATURE OF DOING BUSINESS IN TRANSITION ECONOMIES

Emerging Economies and Firms in the Global Crisis

Edited by

Marin A. Marinov
University of Gloucestershire, Cheltenham, Gloucestershire, UK

and

Svetla T. Marinova
Aalborg University, Aalborg, Denmark

palgrave
macmillan

First published 2013 by
PALGRAVE MACMILLAN

Palgrave Macmillan in the UK is an imprint of Macmillan Publishers Limited, registered in England, company number 785998, of Houndmills, Basingstoke, Hampshire RG21 6XS.

Palgrave Macmillan in the US is a division of St Martin's Press LLC, 175 Fifth Avenue, New York, NY 10010.

Palgrave Macmillan is the global academic imprint of the above companies and has companies and representatives throughout the world.

Palgrave® and Macmillan® are registered trademarks in the United States, the United Kingdom, Europe and other countries.

ISBN 978–1–137–27746–6

This book is printed on paper suitable for recycling and made from fully managed and sustained forest sources. Logging, pulping and manufacturing processes are expected to conform to the environmental regulations of the country of origin.

A catalogue record for this book is available from the British Library.

Library of Congress Cataloging-in-Publication Data
Emerging economies and firms in the global crisis / edited by Marin Marinov and Svetla Marinova.
p. cm.
Includes bibliographical references.
ISBN 978–1–137–27746–6
1. International business enterprises—Developing countries. 2. Investments, Foreign—Developing countries. 3. Industries—Developing countries. 4. Developing countries—Commerce. 5. Industries—Developing countries. 6. Financial crises—Developing countries. 7. Global Financial Crisis, 2008–2009. 8. Developing countries—Economic conditions—21st century. I. Marinov, Marin, 1948– II. Marinova, Svetla Trifonova.
HD2932.E43 2013
338.8′881724—dc23 2012034967

10 9 8 7 6 5 4 3 2 1
22 21 20 19 18 17 16 15 14 13

Printed and bound in Great Britain by
CPI Antony Rowe, Chippenham and Eastbourne

Contents

Illustrations

Tables

Figures

Contributors

Fabio Bertoni is Tenured Assistant Professor in the Department of Management, Economics and Industrial Engineering of Politecnico di Milano, Italy. He has a doctorate in management. His research interests include venture capital and private equity, sovereign wealth funds, financial constraints, and firm investments. He has contributed chapters to books and published articles in journals including *Small Business Economics, Research Policy, Management International Review,* and *European Financial Management.*

Katarina Blomkvist is Assistant Professor of International Business in the Department of Business Studies, Uppsala University, Sweden. She has a doctoral degree from Uppsala University, Sweden. Her main research interest is the development and transfer of technology within multinational firms, with a specific focus on the evolution of subsidiary technological capabilities and the drivers of innovation. Her research includes the internationalization of Chinese firms. She has published papers in academic journals such as *Journal of International Business Studies.*

Thomas Borghoff is Senior Lecturer in the School of Marketing and International Business at Victoria University of Wellington, New Zealand. He obtained his doctorate from the University of Dortmund, Germany, in 2004. He has had numerous visiting appointments at a number of universities in Germany and Indonesia. His research focuses on the globalization of firms in general and of small and medium-sized enterprises in particular. His most recent project explored the influence of information and communication technologies on the globalization of firms. His research interests are in international management, evolutionary theories of firms, dynamic organization theories, international strategy, organizational structure, and culture.

Louis Brennan is Professor in the School of Business and Director of the Institute for International Integration Studies at Trinity College Dublin, Ireland. He is Proposer and Chair of EU COST Action IS0905, which encompasses a 23-nation research network addressing the emergence of non-triad multinational firms and their impact on Europe. He has published extensively and recently edited the volume *Emergence of Southern Multinationals: Their Impact on Europe.*

Rian Drogendijk is Associate Professor of International Business in the Department of Business Studies at Uppsala University, Sweden. She received her doctoral degree from Tilburg University, the Netherlands. Her research interests include international expansion strategies of multinational firms and the impact of cultural differences on international management. Currently she is studying the internationalization of Western firms in Africa, the internationalization by Chinese firms, and the communication of expansion opportunities within multinational organizations. She has published her research in many well-established periodicals, such as *Journal of International Business Studies, International Business Review, Advances in International Management,* and *International Journal of Intercultural Relations.*

Stefano Elia is Assistant Professor at Politecnico di Milano, Italy. His main research interests are foreign direct investments from emerging to advanced economies, with a special focus on firm entry strategies and the impact of market entry on host economies. His other research interests include labor effects of outward foreign direct investments on the home countries, the drivers of the location choices of multinational firms, and the governance mode and performance implications of offshoring. He has published papers in academic journals such as *Journal of Economic Geography, Management International Review, International Business Review,* and *European Journal of International Management.*

Sergey Filippov is Assistant Professor of Innovation Management at Delft University of Technology, the Netherlands. In 2010 he was awarded a doctorate in economics and policy studies by Maastricht University. His research focuses on technology and innovation management, corporate innovation strategies, the rise of emerging multinationals, and their operations in advanced economies. He has published a number of articles in refereed periodicals as well as book chapters.

Françoise Hay has a PhD in Economics with research interests in Asian economies, focusing on their national development and integration within the global economy. Recently, her research has focused on the internationalization of Chinese firms worldwide as well as their internationalization drivers and strategies in Europe.

Andreja Jaklič is Assistant Professor and Researcher in the Centre for International Relations at the University of Ljubljana, Slovenia, where she obtained her PhD. Her interests are in the internationalization of transition economies and their firms, outward foreign direct investment, and innovations in multinational enterprises. She has published papers in journals, has co-edited books and has written chapters for edited volumes.

Jorma Larimo is Professor of International Marketing in the Faculty of Business Studies, University of Vaasa, Finland, and a Part-Time Professor in the Faculty of Economics and Business Administration, University of Tartu, Estonia. He is also Director of the Finnish Graduate School of International Business. His main research areas are the internationalization of small and medium-sized firms, firms' foreign direct investment strategies and performance, and entry and marketing strategies in Central and Eastern European countries. He is an active member of several academic associations, and his research has been published in a number of edited books and academic journals, including *Journal of Business Research, Journal of International Business Studies, Journal of International Marketing, Journal of World Business, International Business Review, Management International Review,* and *Journal of Global Marketing.*

Marina Latukha is Associate Professor in the Graduate School of Management, St. Petersburg State University, Russia. She has graduated from several postdoctoral programs in leading European and US business schools (Harvard Business School, Haas School of Business, University of California at Berkeley, London Business School, and HEC-Paris School of Business). Dr Latukha is the author of a large number of case studies and academic articles. Her academic work focuses on international human resource management, personnel education and development, talent management, human resource evaluation, and professional skills development.

Marin A. Marinov is Professor of International Business and Management at the University of Gloucestershire, UK, and Visiting Professor at Aalborg University, Denmark. He has held a number of professorial appointments worldwide, including Germany, Sweden, Denmark, Bulgaria, the US, Finland, France, Portugal, China, Austria, and Spain.

His research encompasses internationalization of businesses, multinational corporations, and business development in emerging economies; business policy and strategy; and curricula development for business education. Dr Marinov has consulted numerous multinational firms and national governments on topics related to country and firm strategies in the process of their internationalization, mostly via foreign direct investment. He has published nine books, three of which are on marketing in emerging markets, numerous book chapters, and more than 70 articles in refereed academic journals.

Svetla T. Marinova has an MBA from the University of Warwick, UK, and a doctorate from Copenhagen Business School, Denmark. She is Associate Professor of International Business at the Aalborg University, Denmark. She has taught and conducted extensive research in many countries on both sides of the Atlantic and in Asia. Her research interests include business internationalization as well as the role of institutions, strategy of multinational firms from emerging economies, and changes in management and marketing of firms undergoing intensive internationalization. Dr Marinova has published five books, numerous book chapters, and papers in refereed academic journals including *International Marketing Review, Research in Marketing,* and *European Journal of Marketing.*

Geraldine McAllister is Visiting Scholar at the Institute for Social and Economic Research and Policy, Columbia University, US. Her research is currently focused on regulation of the financial sector in the US.

Christian Milelli has a PhD in Economics. His research interests include growth regime, globalization, and foreign direct investment with a focus on North-East Asia. Lately his research has also focused on the internationalization of multinational firms originating from China and India. He has published frequently on these topics in various periodicals.

Krzysztof Obłój is Distinguished Professor of Strategic Management and holds chairs of the Strategic Management Departments in the School of Management of the University of Warsaw and Kozminski University in Poland. He has a doctoral degree in Management and was President of the European International Business Academy. Dr Obłój has had many visiting professorships worldwide. He has extensively published. He published two books in the US and co-authored several in Europe, the most recent being *Contemporary Corporate Strategy: Global*

Perspective. He has published articles in many international journals, including *Entrepreneurship: Theory and Practice, Journal of Management Studies, European Management Journal, International Small Business Journal,* and several Polish journals. He is president of three supervisory boards of large international firms in Poland.

Andrei Panibratov is Professor of Strategic and International Management in the Graduate School of Management, St. Petersburg University, Russia. He holds a PhD in Economics from St Petersburg State University and an MBA from the University of Wales, UK. He has participated in training programs and development workshops in Haas School of Business, University of California at Berkeley and Texas A&M University (both in the US), HEC-Paris (France), Aalto University School of Management (Finland), ECCH (France, Singapore), and WACRA (UK, Canada). Andrei has also participated in consulting and research projects for the World Bank (US), UMIST (UK), Aalto University School of Economics and Tampere University of Technology (both in Finland) and European and Russian companies. He is Visiting Professor at Lappeenranta University of Technology School of Business, Finland. His research interests include Western multinationals' strategy in Russia, firms' marketing decisions when internationalizing, internationalization of firms from emerging economies, and Russian outward foreign direct investment. He is author/co-author of several monographs, case studies, and many articles published in Russia and abroad.

Larissa Rabbiosi is Assistant Professor in the Department of Strategic Management and Globalization, Copenhagen Business School, Denmark. Her research interests include knowledge transfer within multinational corporations, internationalization of emerging economy firms, organizational design, and performance of firms/individuals. She has published in international journals such as *Industrial and Corporate Change, Human Resource Management, Management International Review,* and *Journal of International Management,* and chapters in several books.

Karl P. Sauvant is Founding Executive Director of the Vale Columbia Center on Sustainable International Investment, Senior Research Scholar and Lecturer in Law at Columbia Law School, Co-Director of the Millennium Cities Initiative, and Guest Professor at Nankai University, China. He received his PhD from the University of Pennsylvania in 1975. Until July 2005, Dr Sauvant was Director of the United Nations

Conference on Trade and Development Division on Investment, Technology and Enterprise Development, the focal point in the UN system for matters related to foreign direct investment and technology, as well as a major interface with the private sector. While at the UN, he created, in 1991, the prestigious annual *World Investment Report*, of which he was the lead author until 2004. He is the author of, or responsible for, a substantial number of publications on issues related to economic development, foreign direct investment, and services. In 2006 he was elected Honorary Fellow of the European International Business Academy, and in 2011 he was elected Fellow of the Academy of International Business.

Yunnan Shi has a PhD in economics. His research interests are in the internationalization of the Chinese economy, development of Chinese firms, and Chinese foreign economic relations.

Marjan Svetličič is Professor in the Faculty of Social Sciences, University of Ljubljana, awarded Ambassador of Science of the Republic of Slovenia, Fellow of the European Academy of International Business of which he was also president, a member of the Trans European Policy Study Association board, Vice Chair of the COST project 'The Emergence of Southern Multinationals', and a member of the FP7 Advisory Group for International Scientific Cooperation. His areas of research interest and expertise are foreign direct investments, transnational firms, European Union integration, internationalization of small countries, globalization, and internationalization. Dr Svetličič has authored more than 300 articles and many books, among which are *Enhanced Transition by Outward Internationalization: Outward FDI by Slovene Firms* (co-authored with A. Jaklič); *Small Countries in a Global Economy* (co-edited with D. Salvatore and J.P. Damijan); and *The World Economy: Challenges of Globalization and Regionalization* (co-edited with H. Singer).

Rakhi Verma is a doctoral candidate in International Business in the School of Business, Trinity College Dublin, Ireland. She researches foreign direct investment from emerging economies to the developed world and, more specifically, business strategies of emerging economy multinationals and the impact of outward foreign direct investment on emerging economies in general and India in particular.

Tiia Vissak is Senior Researcher in International Business in the Faculty of Economics and Business Administration at the University of Tartu, where she obtained her PhD. Her main research interests are in different forms of linear and nonlinear internationalization (the pace, country and market entry/operation mode selection, success factors, reasons for de- and re-internationalization), international entrepreneurship issues (the role of managers and other actors in internationalization, the role of subsidiaries in foreign owners' networks and the factors impacting that role), networks and strategic alliances (the roles of different actors and factors, the reasons of relationship dissolution), transition economies, and case studies as a research methodology. She has published a number of papers and book chapters.

Aleksandra Wąsowska is Assistant Professor in the School of Management, University of Warsaw, Poland. Her research focuses on the strategies of emerging economy multinational firms. She has published a number of papers in the area of strategy and international business and has worked as a business consultant in Poland, France, and Portugal.

Witold Wilinski is Lecturer in the World Economy Faculty in the Warsaw School of Economics, Poland. His current research focuses on internationalization and outward foreign direct investment from post-communist countries, strategies of multinational companies, and corporate finance. He received his PhD from Warsaw School of Economics and a post-master diploma from the University Paris Dauphine, France. He has 12 years' professional experience in corporate finance.

Xiaotian Zhang is Lecturer in the Faculty of Economics and Business Administration, University of Tartu, Estonia, and in the Department of Management and International Business at the University of Oulu, Finland. His main research areas include internationalization processes of firms, global firms, and international entrepreneurship.

1

The Global Crisis and the World: The Cases of Emerging and Developed Economies

Marin A. Marinov and Svetla T. Marinova

Introduction

The global crisis represents a worldwide economic downturn that started with the financial crash of the US housing market. The price of housing reached unprecedented heights in 2005 then all of a sudden started crashing in 2006 (Perkins, 2009). The collapse was accompanied by deterioration in other sectors of the US economy. In a matter of months the financial breakdown spread throughout the entire US economy. Due to the interrelated and interdependent functioning of the world economy, within a year the crisis impacted to varying degrees the national economies of all countries around the globe (Krugman, 2009). The effect of the global crisis started to appear in the macroeconomic indicators of most countries, reaching its across-the-board climax soon afterwards.

The current global economic crisis has huge significance and has been compared to the Great Depression (see e.g. Harman, 2009; Wessel, 2010) that began in 1929 and lasted for at least a decade (Garraty, 1986). The cyclical nature of the functioning of the economy has accounted for its ups and downs or regional economic collapses. Thus in 1997 the countries of Southeast Asia experienced a colossal financial blow instigated by global banks and investors, determining that this region was an insecure context on which to capitalize and hastily withdrawing their financial assets (Rodrik, 2011). Consequently, the economies of the region were hit hard, prompting the Asian crisis, which rapidly engulfed the then weak Russian economy and eventually bringing economic dismay to Latin America.

The causes of the current global economic crisis are being investigated by many scholars. It is a common belief that US public monetary policy and the functioning of private financial institutions have impelled the crisis. US mortgage practices had been decentralized, lacked control, and were based on ever declining standards and the application of high-risk lending (Faiola *et al.*, 2008). The uncompromising competition among mortgage lenders for market share and possible profits represented the spark that ignited the fire of the crisis. The cause of the crisis is also attributed to the debt inflicted in an exorbitant manner on the US economy.

The crisis resulted in the worsening of a series of macroeconomic indicators, which pointed to deteriorating economic performance first in one country and then on a global level. The real gross domestic product (GDP) started diminishing on a global scale in 2008, and in 2009 its fall was so significant that it matched the decline that was characteristic of the world economy during the Great Depression of the 1930s. Capital investment in domestic and foreign markets declined substantially, especially in the key investing countries from the developed world. Demand was plummeting and customer confidence evaporating. In the period 2006–2008 about US$15 trillion of the value of global firms from the Western world was wiped out.

In an attempt to stabilize the financial situation in 2008 and 2009, a number of banks were partially and temporarily privatized. Providing rescue plans for the national banking systems in particular, and the entire financial system in general, massive bailouts were implemented in most developed countries and to a lesser extent by several emerging economies.

Among the first victims of the crisis, apart from the US, was Iceland, which was followed by many other countries. Over time the global crisis brought financial instability and unpredictability to the US and also to most of the advanced economies. A clear example is the European Union (EU), where the crisis caused real problems in the Eurozone, in which 17 EU Member States share a currency (the Euro), which is the second most important currency after the US dollar. Hence, financial institutions in most of the Eurozone countries were downgraded. Some countries, such as Greece, are in a disastrous financial state having defaulted on their external debt.

While Poland has been the only EU Member State to circumvent shrinking of its GDP, many countries started experiencing economic recession even in 2008, including Estonia and Latvia. From the largest world economies, only China and France experienced a positive GDP change in 2008. Meanwhile at the beginning of 2009, the National Bank of Ukraine announced a 20 per cent decline in national GDP due to the excessive dependency of the Ukrainian economy on export revenue.

The global economic crisis has caused political volatility and unpredictability. The heads of states or governments in many Western countries have either been ousted from power or lost elections. Thus, in November 2011 the Greek prime minister, Papandreou, was overthrown from power as a result of the extremely negative consequences of the global crisis on Greece, and the former French president, Sarkozy, lost the confidence of the electorate in the second tour of presidential elections to victorious Hollande in May 2012.

The global crisis has caused huge protests in many countries as a reaction to the negative effects of the worsening economic and social conditions. Events such as the Arab Spring and the Occupy Wall Street Movement are clear indicators of the economic and social consequences of the global crisis. Countries such as Libya, Syria, and Bahrain have been through mass protests. In Libya these resulted in a regime change and the killing of the former leader of the country, Colonel Qaddafi. Having started in the autumn of 2011, the Occupy Wall Street protest was renewed in 2012. Such protests have not been confined to the developed world. Communist supporters and other opposition members gathered in Moscow in 2011 and 2012 to protest against the economic policy of the government, as well as the lack of orderliness and legality of the parliamentary and presidential elections in Russia. Due to a drastic fall in exports to the developed world, a significant increase in unemployment in some parts of China has resulted in massive social unrest since 2010.

Developed and emerging economies in the global crisis

A solution to the negative trends of economic performance caused by the global crisis has proved to be difficult to find and implement. There is a view that dealing successfully with the large macro imbalances and altering the downward trend of demand on the developed economies represent the greatest challenges in overcoming the global crisis. After a period of insubstantial and irregular recovery, growth of the world economy has presaging and dubious growth perspectives. Economic feebleness in key developed countries causes slogging worldwide economic recovery, which jeopardizes future recovery prospects. It seems that there are no fast and efficient solutions for the economic complications in the advanced economies, especially due to the devastating aftermath of their financial crises.

The largest developed economy, that of the US, has been struggling to get out of the longest and most severe recession that it has experienced since the Great Depression. The rate of its recovery has been much slower than anticipated and marred by inconsistencies. Registering a mere 2.6 per cent growth rate in 2010, the US economy growth rate was still lower in 2011. At such indeterminate recovery rates, the level of GDP is still struggling to return to its pre-crisis level. The economic performance in the crisis period of another key developed economy, that of the UK, is significantly more worrying. Being in recession in 2008 and 2009, the UK economy had a very tiny positive GDP growth in 2010. However, in the last quarter of 2011 it contracted by 0.3 per cent and in the first quarter of 2012 by 0.2 per cent, indicating that the country is in a double-dip recession.

It is uncertain whether the fiscal consolidation plans that have been announced so far by governments of developed countries will impact positively on GDP growth in the period 2012–2015. The picture becomes less clear cut when considering the strong GDP growth in many emerging economies (see Figure 1.1) despite the crisis. Figure 1.1 presents the annualized GDP growth rates in percentage terms for three groups of economies for the period 2007–2011. The first group consists of the four largest emerging economies (Brazil, Russia, India, and

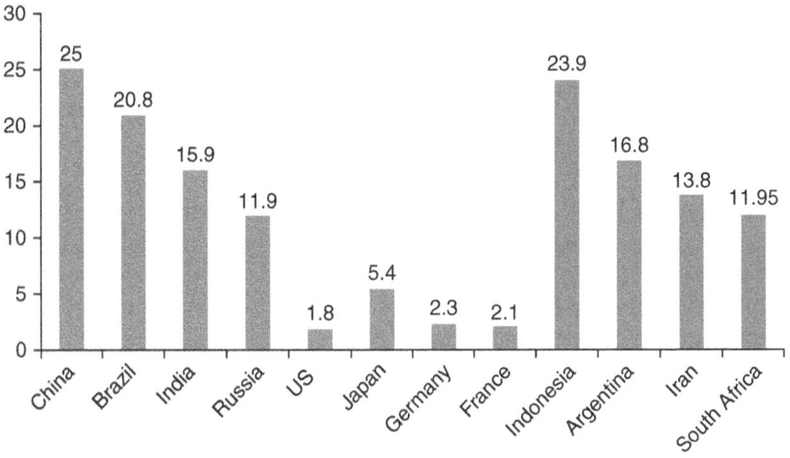

Figure 1.1 Annualized GDP growth rate, 2007–2011 (%)
Source: Authors, using raw data from the statistics of International Monetary Fund.

China, known as the BRIC countries). The second group comprises the four most significant developed economies (the US, Japan, Germany, and France). The third group includes four sizable emerging economies (Indonesia, Argentina, Iran, and South Africa) with good growth rates of their annualized GDP during this period.

As Figure 1.1 illustrates, the move toward economic recovery has been led by the BRIC economies and some other populous economies of Asia, Latin America, and Africa. Increasing domestic demand and well-performing exports have facilitated an appropriate response to and a quick recovery from the global economic downturn by many emerging economies.

With a fast rebound since the second quarter of 2009, resilient emerging economies have pioneered the recovery of international trade (see Figure 1.2), building on trade ties between themselves and with other parts of the world through global value chains. As seen in Figure 1.2, by the end of 2010, trade originating from emerging economies had surpassed the pre-crisis level. The same was true for their manufacturing

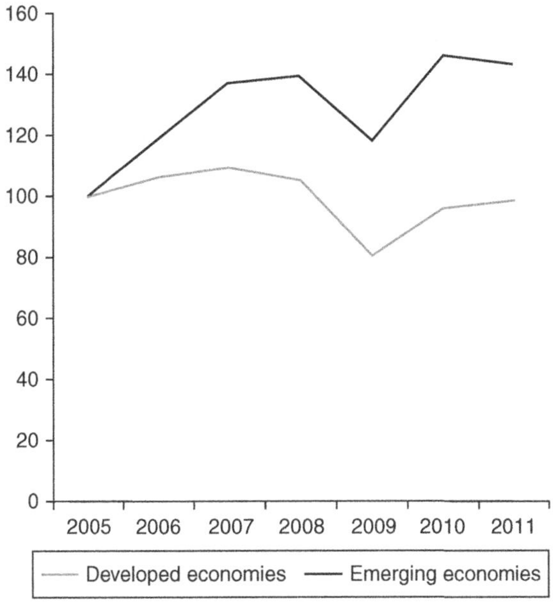

Figure 1.2 Volume of world trade by developed and emerging economies, 2005–2011 (volume of trade in 2005 = 100%)

Source: Authors, using data from Bureau for Economic Policy Analysis, CIB, the Netherlands.

production. It is, however, uncertain whether the emerging economies will be able to sustain their vigorous growth rate in the future. The intensified trade ties among these countries are not sufficient to guarantee sustainability. The emerging economies are still very reliant on demand in the developed parts of the world to realize their exports. If emerging economies fail to continue their robust economic development, this will jeopardize prospects for economic recovery in the developed world as well as globally. It is, however, expected that the large and prosperous economy of China with its ever-growing domestic demand can take the lead in getting the world out of the current economic slump.

Initially, the global economic crisis had a negative impact on emerging economies' outward investment. Thus in 2009, foreign direct investment (FDI) originating from emerging economies fell by 28 per cent after having reached a record level of US$207 billion in 2008. On a comparative scale, this deterioration was considerably less than the almost halved FDI outflows from the developed economies in 2009 vs. its level in 2008. Being major providers of FDI, the BRIC economies remain indisputable leaders, having provided, by the end of 2011, more than 70 per cent of the cumulative FDI from emerging economies (UNCTAD, 2011). Considering the FDI location of cross-border mergers and acquisitions (M&As) and greenfield investment, more than 60 per cent of the outward foreign direct investment (OFDI) flows from emerging economies has ended up in other emerging economies, mainly via greenfield investment, whereas emerging economy FDI into the developed world is primarily in the form of M&As (UNCTAD, 2011). As a consequence of the severe drop in OFDI originating from developed economies since the start of the global crisis, the prominence of OFDI from other emerging economies and mostly the so-called South–South FDI has become more than a third of the total investment flow in 2010 (UNCTAD, 2011).

Despite the continuing economic turmoil, the global FDI in 2011 rose by 17 per cent in comparison with its level in 2010 (UN New Centre, 2012). The dynamics in the fluctuation of OFDI originating from developed and developing countries using year-on-year change in percentage terms in the period 2007–2011 is presented in Figure 1.3.

In a pre-crisis introduction to a special issue of the *Journal of International Business Studies*, Luo and Tung (2007) present the solid foundations, motives, strategies, external and internal forces, and challenges and remedies for the internationalization of firms from emerging economies. Many authors (e.g. Enderwick, 2009; Gammeltoft,

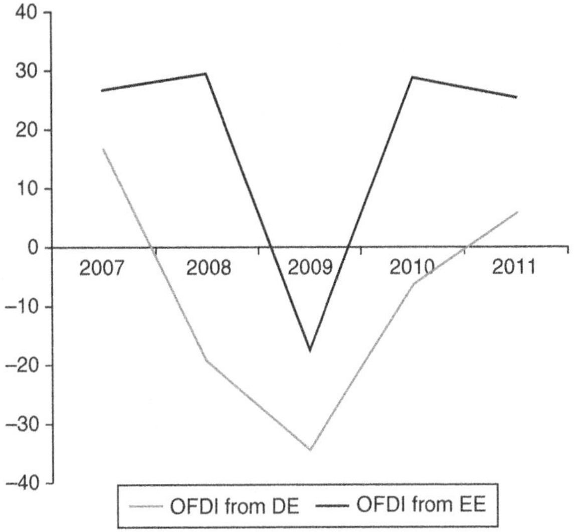

Figure 1.3 Year-on-year percentage change in OFDI from developed and emerging economies, 2007–2011
Source: Authors, based on data from UNCTAD.

2010; Marinova and Marinov, 2011) express their belief that emerging economies and their firms will provide a trigger to economic advancement and provide key assistance in exiting from the global crisis.

Overview of this book

Chapter 2 by Geraldine McAllister and Karl P. Sauvant presents an analysis of OFDI by emerging economy multinationals, putting in focus the way in which they deal with the challenges that the global crisis presents to them. Revealing the changing cross-border patterns of investment flows, the authors bring to our attention key issues, such as the formation of a 'New Triad' and the new sectoral composition of foreign investment. The coping strategies of emerging economies in the global crisis are investigated, placing emphasis on the specifics of the BRIC economies. Furthermore, the authors deal with the future challenges concerning strategic issues as well as issues of home and host country policy, facing global firms from emerging economies amid the insecurity of economic upheaval. The chapter ends with recommendations concerning the aspects of sustained OFDI by emerging economy multinational firms.

In Chapter 3, Fabio Bertoni, Stefano Elia, and Larissa Rabbiosi address the trends and patterns of OFDI by BRIC economies via M&As in developed economies. They present the characteristics from 417 acquisitions in developed countries, made by Brazil, Russia, India, and China. Various investment strategies and motives of market-seeking, asset-seeking and resource-seeking nature are uncovered, and underlying horizontal, vertical, related, and conglomerate investments have been identified. The authors have conducted a detailed analysis of a sub-sample of 115 Western European firms acquired by multinationals from BRIC economies, which reveals that Chinese multinational firms tend to follow aggressive acquisition strategies by taking over poorly performing firms. Moreover, target firms involved in conglomerate and horizontal investments appear to be the largest among those studied, whereas horizontal and vertical investments are on average aimed at better-performing targets than conglomerate and related investments. By exploring the specifics and the motives of BRIC acquisitions in developed economies, this chapter concludes that acquisitions by BRIC economies of firms in developed countries are expected to increase significantly in the future, spurred by the effect of the global crisis on foreign investment patterns.

In Chapter 4, Witold Wilinski focuses his attention on the internationalization of countries and firms in Central and Eastern Europe during the global crisis. He reveals the main financial and investment aspects of the internationalization of national economies and their multinational firms from the region. Micro level strategies and internationalization drivers are put under scrutiny. The chapter concludes by showing that the global crisis has affected investment strategies of multinationals from Central and Eastern Europe in terms of volume and location of investments, whereas investing firms from Asian emerging economies have benefited from the crisis by intensifying their OFDI, spreading their international expansion aggressively.

In Chapter 5, Thomas Borghoff reveals the role of globalization in building up international activities, including four sub-processes in the globalization of small and medium-sized enterprises (SMEs) from China, India, New Zealand, and Singapore in the crisis. The first sub-process has been identified as 'global foundation', covering the emergence of global firms from the start of their going overseas. The second has been defined as 'internationalization' in terms of changing the scope and spread of international activities by the firms from emerging economies. The third sub-process is named 'global network development' and relates to the integration and co-ordination of activities on a global level. The fourth reflects global evolutionary dynamics that are driving the entire globalization process of SMEs from China, India, New Zealand, and Singapore. Some 20 case studies from the Asia/Pacific region are presented and serve to explore the role of information and communication technologies in the globalization of SMEs from this vibrant region referring to the context of emerging economy firms in the global crisis.

Chapter 6 by Rakhi Verma and Louis Brennan represents a comprehensive analysis of the macroeconomic determinants of Indian OFDI. Hypotheses are brought forward to test and explain the patterns of Indian overseas investments. An analysis of empirical results is presented, leading to a discussion and conclusions. Conducting a longitudinal study in the period from 1981 to 2009 of international investments from India, the role of macroeconomic determinants in the period including the crisis is revealed. The authors conclude that the role of macroeconomic determinants is strengthened by the domestic policy of the Indian government and potential accumulation of ownership advantages in the process of their internationalization.

In Chapter 7, Rian Drogendijk and Katarina Blomkvist address the issues of how cultural distance impacts OFDI from China. They point out that starting in the second part of the 2000s, Chinese OFDI has exposed a clear ascending trend, making the country currently one of the key foreign investors in culturally distant countries. This fact has prompted augmenting attention to recognize this development. Filling in the gap in research on how cultural differences influence the direction of Chinese OFDI, the authors conduct a comprehensive analysis of Chinese OFDI and cultural distance in foreign investment. Testing hypotheses, they find that the cultural distance between China and host countries negatively influences Chinese OFDI. The chapter's findings suggest that cultural differences between China and investing destinations influence investment decisions by Chinese firms.

Chapter 8 by Sergei Filippov sheds light on the way in which merging multinational firms from Russia deal with the challenges of the global crisis. The author addresses the internationalization specifics of Russian multinationals and comes to the conclusion that it has become a distinctive phenomenon. Newly emerged Russian firms have recently expanded their international presence, initially to the nearest former Soviet republics but soon by an aggressive expansion into the advanced economies of Western Europe and the US and beyond. Like all firms, the Russian multinationals have been forced to face the global economic meltdown. The chapter analyzes the impact, effects, and consequences of the global economic crisis on international activities and internationalization strategies of emerging Russian multinationals by combining quantitative and qualitative methods. To broaden the insight gained through these quantitative analyses, the chapter presents qualitative data about ways in which Russian multinationals have responded to the crisis. The study reveals an interplay between the foreign expansion of Russian multinational firms and the policies and internationalization of the strategic priorities of the Russian government.

In Chapter 9, Françoise Hay, Christian Milelli, and Yunnan Shi analyze critically the internationalization of Chinese car-producing firms. Taking a retrospective stance, they present various time periods of the analyzed phenomenon. Various modes of market entry are highlighted and evaluated. The critically important policy of the Chinese government in the internationalization of the car manufacturing industry is given separate attention. The process is presented in diverse models. The chapter concludes that the car manufacturing sector has become a global industry functioning in a global marketplace, including new latecomers from emerging economies, with Chinese car-producing firms at the forefront. They have earned their place lately. This trend for gaining ground has been significantly accelerated by the global economic crisis, which has meanwhile adversely affected developed countries and their industrial bases. The main reasons for bringing Chinese car manufacturing to the forefront of globally performing firms are highlighted.

In Chapter 10, Aleksandra Wąsowska and Krzysztof Obłój have conducted a study of location determinants of Polish OFDI considering the impact of the global crisis. Their research objectives are twofold. The first represents an investigation of the host-country-specific factors impacting the attractiveness of Polish overseas investment in order to test whether the patterns of OFDI from the Polish emerging economy can be explained with the extant typology of key motives for investing abroad. The second research aspect relates to the significance of the impact of the global crisis on investment location decisions by Polish multinational firms. Supported by empirical evidence, the study holds the view that existing international investment theories can explain the investment behavior of emerging economies, such as Poland. Concerning certain specifics, the current FDI theories may need further development and/or refinement when the emerging economy context is addressed. In line with the overall trend of foreign investment provided by emerging economies, empirical evidence suggests that the current impact of the global crisis on the pattern of Polish OFDI is limited, and that the strategic investment choices by international Polish firms are on a large scale predictable. It can also be pointed out that the global crisis forces Polish multinationals to reconsider the pace and scale of their internationalization.

The ways in which Slovene multinational firms deal with the challenges of the global crisis are investigated in Chapter 11. Here, Marjan Svetličič and Andreja Jaklič define the objective of their chapter as an evaluation of how the global crisis impacts Slovene firms operating abroad and what their reaction to the crisis has been so far. Firms' performance during the crisis has been evaluated by focusing on the dynamics of Slovene OFDI in general, and the response of top Slovene multinationals to the crisis. More specifically, the performance of the best Slovene multinationals since 2008 has been demonstrated in various ways. Some disappeared from the top-ranking firms due to takeovers by foreign investors, anguish selling or poor dynamics in their development. The authors have found that the largest group, which disappeared due to governance and internal managerial problems, also manipulated leveraged management buyouts and increased financial constraints on their functioning during the crisis period. Another group of firms, which disappeared from the top ranking, experienced significant pre-crises stagnation and slow or non-implemented restructuring. At the same time a number of new firms entered the list of top Slovene multinationals. On the whole, four types of response of firms to the crisis have been identified. Consequently, firms have been named accordingly. Thus, dinosaurs have been firms failing to find a proper response to the crisis, disintegrating, and makings losses. Hedgehogs have been firms with predominantly defensive reactions to the crisis. The endangered koalas have been firms under real threat of insolvency, whereas cheetahs have been firms with proactive, dynamic internationalization after first conducting relevant cost reduction. The study provides clear evidence that the reactions of Slovene multinational firms to the global crisis have been deeply embedded in the local context.

In Chapter 12, Tiia Vissak investigates the impact of the global crisis on the internationalization of Estonian firms using a case study approach. She explores both the positive and the negative consequences of the global crisis in the period 2008–2009 on the international activities of four Estonian firms. The research is based on the cases of two textile manufacturers and two firms from the casino industry. It concludes that the global crisis affected these firms in dissimilar ways. The effects of the crisis have depended on not only external but also internal factors. Thus, it has been shown that strategic decisions before and during the crisis affected the firms' situations during the crisis period. Consequently, due to various impacts of the crisis on the studied firms and their differences in strategic responses to the crisis, two of them had positive performance indicators and continued to grow, one faced serious problems and unstable performance, and one firm went bankrupt.

In Chapter 13, Marina Latukha and Andrei Panibratov present a study of the reasons for and approaches of Russian information technology (IT) firms toward internationalization. They explore the issues of servicing local customers for entering foreign markets. The study suggests that the internationalization motives of these firms may be primarily explained with the highly skilled labor force and low labor cost opportunities. Considering the fact that the technological sophistication of Russian case companies and that of their foreign competitors in the high-tech sector is almost the same, partnership internationalization strategies seem appropriate. The study shows that the strategic priorities of the internationalizing Russian IT firms are focused on the acquisition of customers rather than on the acquisition of technologies. This strategic orientation proved successful during the global crisis. The authors have shown that internationalized Russian IT firms experience less influence from the home government, their internationalization being shaped mainly by economic rather than political factors; hence their internationalization succeeded in the turbulent times of crisis when they prioritized exploration of investment opportunities rather than escaping for home context specifics.

In Chapter 14, Xiaotian Zhang and Jorma Larimo investigate the longitudinal internationalization processes of three Chinese cases of born global firms. They point out that in recent decades, scholars have studied various forms of internationalization of born global firms, focusing on how they initiated their activities abroad. Hence the main research focus has been on the earlier stages of born global internationalization, whereas the internationalization pattern development of these firms taking a longitudinal perspective has drawn inadequate attention. The empirical part of the presented study focuses on Chinese cases of rapid internationalization followed by radical changes in the firms caused by the global crisis. They have been in the form of de-internationalization and subsequent re-internationalization. The study contributes to the scarce longitudinal investigation of the international development of born global firms from the home context of an emerging economy, China.

References

Enderwick, P. (2009). Responding to the global crisis: The contribution of emerging markets to strategic adaptation, *International Journal of Emerging Markets*, 4(4): 358–374.

Faiola, A., Nakashima, E., and Drew, J. (2008). What went wrong. *Washington Post*, 15 October, http://www.washingtonpost.com/wp-dyn/content/article/2008/10/14/AR2008101403343.html?hpid= topnews&sid= ST2008101403344&s_pos=, Accessed May 8, 2012.

Gammeltoft, P. (2010). Emerging multinationals: Home and host country determinates and outcomes, *International Journal of Emerging Markets*, 5(3/4): 254–265.

Garraty, J.A. (1986). *The Great Depression*. New York, NY: Harcourt Brace Jovanovich.

Harman, C. (2009). *Zombie Capitalism: Global Crisis and the Relevance of Marx*. London: Bookmarks Publications.

Krugman, P. (2009). The crisis and how to deal with it. *New York Review of Books*, June 11: 73–76.

Luo, Y. and Tung, R.L. (2007). Introduction – International expansion of emerging market enterprises: A springboard perspective, *Journal of International Business Studies*, 38(4): 481–498.

Marinova, S. and Marinov, M. (2011). New challengers in the global game: Reflections on the internationalization of emerging economies and firms, in M. Marinov and S. Marinova (Eds.) *Internationalization of Emerging Economies and Firms*, Basingstoke: Palgrave Macmillan: 367–380.

Perkins, J. (2009). *Hoodwinked*. New York, NY: Broadway Books.

Rodrik, D. (2011). *The Globalization Paradox*. Oxford: Oxford University Press.

UN New Centre. (2012). Despite global economic turmoil, foreign direct investment increased in 2011 – UN, January 24, http://www.un.org/apps/news/story.asp?NewsID= 41029&Cr= economy&Cr1=, Accessed May 11, 2012.

UNCTAD. (2011). *World Investment Report*. Geneva; New York, NY: UNCTAD.

Wessel, D. (2010). Did 'Great Recession' live up to its name. *The Wall Street Journal*, April 8: 16–17.

2

Foreign Direct Investment by Emerging Economy Multinationals: Coping with the Global Crisis*

Geraldine McAllister and Karl P. Sauvant

Introduction

Even before the onset of the global crisis, the global market for foreign direct investment (FDI) had undergone significant changes. Foremost amongst these changes was the increasing importance of emerging market[1] multinationals (MNEs). While outward foreign direct investment (OFDI) from these markets is, in itself, not new, the magnitude that this phenomenon achieved prior to the crisis and its resilience in the face of the global crisis suggest that this is not a temporary occurrence but rather a sign of a fundamental change that is taking place in the global OFDI market. However, emerging markets are not homogenous: in addition to the rise in OFDI from emerging markets, the formation of new regional groupings has led to the emergence of fresh investment patterns. This chapter examines changes taking place in global FDI flows and looks at the impact of the crisis in the context of profound structural changes; it also focuses on the response of emerging markets and the enormous risks and challenges that lie ahead. It is vital to note that this crisis is ongoing, and it is too early to predict the final contours it will leave in its wake on the FDI landscape.

Changing patterns of OFDI: Beyond the global crisis

Changing patterns of OFDI

The rise of global OFDI over the past three decades has been remarkable. Prior to the crisis, global OFDI flows had grown by a factor of

*This text builds on Sauvant *et al.* (2010).

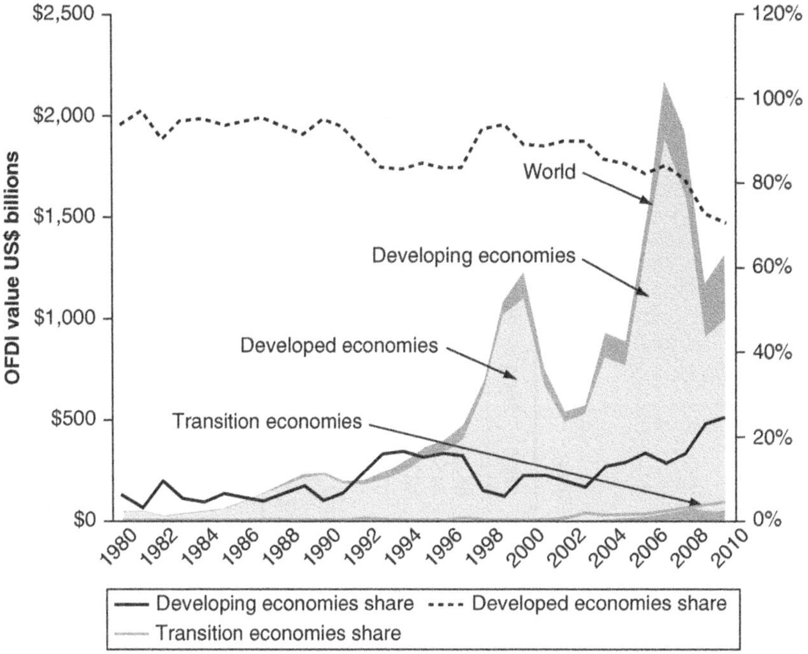

Figure 2.1 FDI outflows, globally and by group of economies, 1980–2010 (US$ billions)
Source: Authors, based on data from unctadstat.unctad.org.

40 in less than three decades, from a yearly average of US$47 billion in 1980–1985, to US$2.2 trillion in 2007 (Figure 2.1 and Table 2.1). Since peaking in 2007, OFDI flows have declined significantly. Nevertheless, at US$1.2 trillion, average OFDI flows for the five-year period 2003–2007 were almost 40 per cent higher than in the period 1998–2002, when they averaged US$860 billion.

Even more remarkable has been the rise in OFDI from emerging markets in recent years,[2] and its ability to withstand the worst of the global crisis. From less than 5 per cent of OFDI flows in 1990, emerging markets accounted for almost 30 per cent of OFDI flows in 2010 (Figure 2.2), a trend that showed no sign of changing in 2011 too. (UNCTAD, 2011a). In terms of inward foreign direct investment(IFDI), the performance of emerging markets has been equally impressive. The share of inward investment flows rose from 17 per cent in 1990, to no less than 50 per cent each year until 2009, reflecting an average annual growth of 12 per cent since 2000 (UNCTAD, 2012b).

Table 2.1 FDI outflows by home region and BRIC economy, 1980–2010 (US$ billion)

Region	1980	1990	2000	2001	2002	2003	2004	2005	2006	2007	2008	2009	2010
World	51.6	241.5	1,232.1	752.7	537.2	573.8	930.1	882.1	1,405.4	2,174.8	1,910.5	1,170.5	1,323.3
Developed economies	48.4	229.6	1,094.7	667.4	482.8	517.0	794.6	745.7	1,155.0	1,829.0	1,541.2	851.0	935.2
Developing economies	3.2	11.9	134.2	82.5	49.7	46.0	121.4	122.1	226.7	294.2	308.9	270.7	327.6
Brazil	0.4	0.6	2.3	−2.3	2.5	0.2	9.8	2.5	28.2	7.1	20.5	−10.1	11.5
China	–	0.8	0.9	6.9	2.5	2.9	5.5	12.3	21.2	22.5	52.2	56.5	68.0
India	0.0	0.0	0.5	1.4	1.7	1.9	2.2	3.0	14.3	17.2	19.4	15.9	14.6
Transition economies	–	0.0	3.2	2.7	4.7	10.8	14.1	14.3	23.7	51.6	60.4	48.8	60.6
Russian Federation	–	–	3.2	2.5	3.5	9.7	13.8	12.8	23.2	45.9	55.6	43.7	51.7

Source: Authors, based on data from unctadstat.unctad.org.

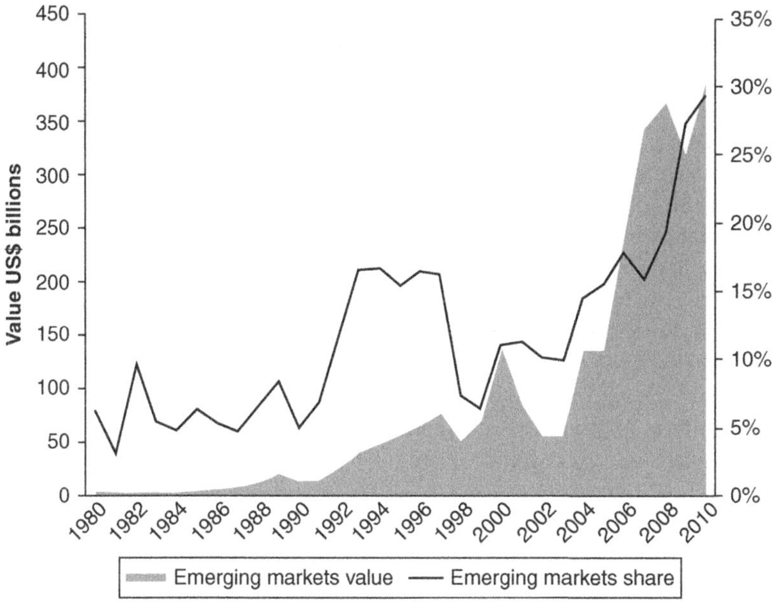

Figure 2.2 Emerging markets OFDI, value and share, 1980–2010 (US$ billions %)
Source: Authors, based on data from unctadstat.unctad.org.

The changing FDI landscape: Beyond the global crisis

To date, the focus has been on the immediate impact of the crisis, as measured by the value of OFDI flows. The dramatic increase in these flows till 2007 and their subsequent decline, however, is one of the visible aspects of the fundamental changes that are reshaping the global market for FDI. A number of these changes were perceptible prior to 2007–2008; the main impact of the crisis has been on their rate of change. Other changes stem directly from the crisis, but are likely to continue even when the world economy returns to robust health.

Number of MNEs

The ongoing economic crisis has halted or even reversed years of economic growth in many countries and slowed the rate of growth in others. Its impact on the trend toward an increasingly integrated world economy has been more limited, however, and, in many instances, the domestic downturn has spurred firms to seek growth opportunities abroad. The significant increase in the number of MNEs, despite the recent years of economic turmoil, reflecting this trend. From about 70,000 MNEs in 2004, with about 690,000 foreign affiliates, there are over 100,000 MNEs in existence today, with more than 890,000 foreign affiliates (UNCTAD, 2005: xix; UNCTAD, 2011, annex table 34).

The geographical distribution of these MNEs and their foreign affiliates underlines the increasing integrated and competitive nature of the world economy, requiring MNEs everywhere to develop a portfolio of locational assets if they are to compete successfully in the global economy. In 2010, over 30,000 parent corporations were based in emerging markets, a whole 30 per cent of the total (UNCTAD, 2011, annex table 34). Emerging markets were host to over 500,000 foreign affiliates (58 per cent of the total), a 17 per cent increase on 2004 (ibid., UNCTAD, 2005: xix). Developed economies were host to more than 370,000 foreign affiliates (42 per cent of the total), a figure that has grown by over 50 per cent since 2004 (ibid.).

A new Triad?

The increasing importance of OFDI by emerging market MNEs is the latest discernible pattern in global OFDI. In a global market once dominated by the US and the European Union (EU), this duopoly gave way to the Triad of the US, EU, and Japan. This Triad declined, as Japan entered a prolonged period of economic stagnation, and is often referred to as 'Old Triad.' The rise in OFDI from emerging markets has contributed to the appearance of a 'New Triad' consisting of the US, the EU, and emerging markets (see Figure 2.3). Yet, Figure 2.3 reveals that this New Triad's share of global OFDI stocks was, in fact, higher in the early 1980s, underlining the frequently short-lived nature of such trends. Moreover, we may well move beyond a world of Triads. Economou and Sauvant (2011) look to the possible emergence of a 'multi-polar FDI world ... in which smaller poles coexist with the dominant members of the former Triad,' (2011: 2). The World Bank envisions 'a new world order with a more diffuse distribution of economic power ... the shift toward multipolarity' (The World Bank, 2011: xi).The changing origins of OFDI is only one part of the picture; the sectors into which OFDI flows is also undergoing change.

Sectoral change

The sectoral composition of global OFDI stock has changed considerably over recent decades and the service sector has assumed greater importance, aided by innovation and deregulation, as well as advances

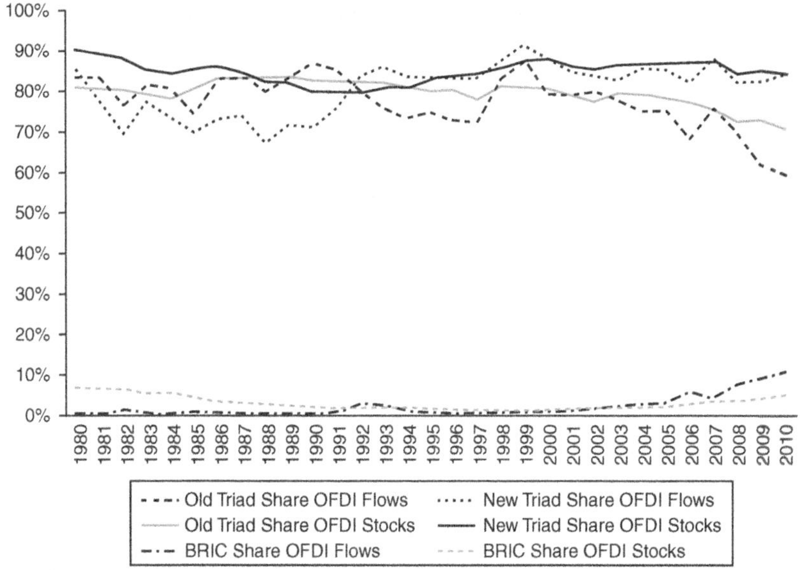

Figure 2.3 Old and New Triad, and BRICS share of global OFDI, 1980–2010 (%)
Source: Authors, based on data from unctadstat.unctad.org.

in information communications technology (ICT). In 1990, the service sector accounted for almost half of global OFDI stock, a share that had risen to two-thirds by 2009. Interestingly, over this period the share of finance within the service sector remained relatively constant, at 24 per cent in 1990 to 26 per cent in 2009 (UNCTAD, 2011, annex table 25). Almost all of the growth recorded, occurred within business activities, and was the result of a shift in management practices toward core activities, and technological advancements that facilitated the off shoring and outsourcing of various business support functions. The share of the primary sector in global OFDI stock declined only slightly over this period, from 9 per cent in 1990 to 8 per cent in 2009, as MNEs continued to seek secure access to finite reserves of natural resources (ibid.). Manufacturing, however, declined significantly, from 43 per cent of global OFDI stock in 1990, to only 24 per cent in 2009 (ibid.).

This picture is repeated across developed economies, where the share of the primary sector fell from 9 per cent in 1990 to 8 per cent in 2009 (ibid.). The services sector rose from 48 per cent to 64 per cent over this period, the result of increase in business services (ibid.). At the global level, the share of manufacturing declined from 43 per cent in 1990 to 26 per cent in 2009 (ibid.).

The picture for emerging market OFDI is very different, and rather surprising. Both the primary and manufacturing sectors shrank significantly over the period 1990–2009, from 13 per cent to 6 per cent, and from 36 per cent to 11 per cent, respectively (ibid.). The service sector, which was the principal sector in 1990 accounting for 51 per cent of total OFDI stock, was dominating the scene by 2009, accounting for 79 per cent of OFDI stock, driven by growing OFDI in business services (ibid.). This is explained largely by significant investment in business activities in Hong Kong and China.[3,4]

The dramatic impact of the financial crisis and the ongoing global crisis continue to affect the investment choices and decisions of MNEs. For some, the need to reduce their debt burden has forced them to dispose whole divisions, creating an opportunity for others to capitalize on. Nevertheless, the sheer scale of the financial crisis and uncertainty over the shape of ongoing reform has resulted in the decline of investment in the service sector (Figure 2.4), and, in 2010, manufacturing accounted for almost 50 per cent of total investment in FDI projects.

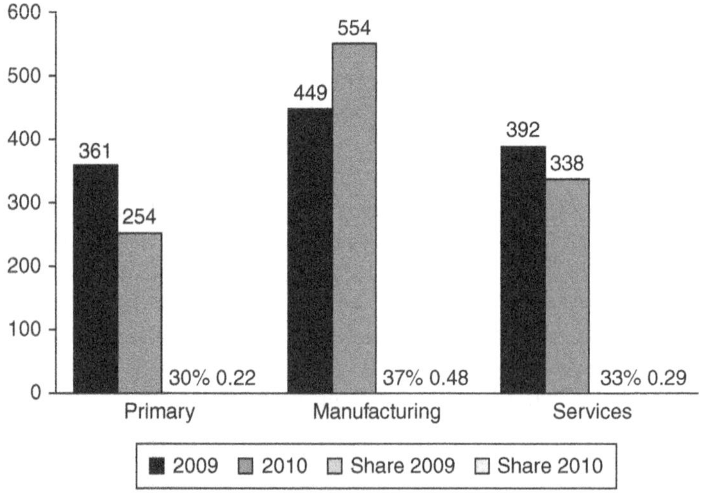

Figure 2.4 Sectoral distribution of FDI projects, 2009–2010 (US$ billions, %)
Source: UNCTAD (2011: 9).

Mode of investment

Levels of mergers and acquisitions (M&As) and greenfield investment, the principal vehicles for FDI, highlight the dramatic changes taking place in the global FDI market (Figure 2.5).

Total M&A activity peaked in 2007 at US$1 trillion, more than double the average of the previous decade (Figure 2.6). From 2008, however, as markets became illiquid and firms adopted a 'wait and see' approach to investment, M&A activity declined sharply, to US$250 billion in 2009, one quarter of the previous high. A gradual recovery took place in 2010, but at US$339 billion, total M&A activity was only one-third the level of 2007.

The decline in M&As was most pronounced in developed economies. From a high of US$842 billion in 2007, the total value of M&As had fallen 80 per cent, to US$161 billion by 2009 (UNCTAD, 2011, annex table 10). Growth resumed in 2010, but at US$216 billion, the total value of M&As undertaken by developed countries was one quarter of its 2007 high (ibid.).

Emerging markets have weathered the crisis better. From a high of US$167 billion in 2007, the total value of M&As declined 51 per cent to US$81 billion in 2009 (ibid.). As in developed countries, growth resumed in 2010, and by the end of the year the total value of M&As was almost two-thirds of its 2007 high, at US$106 billion (ibid.).

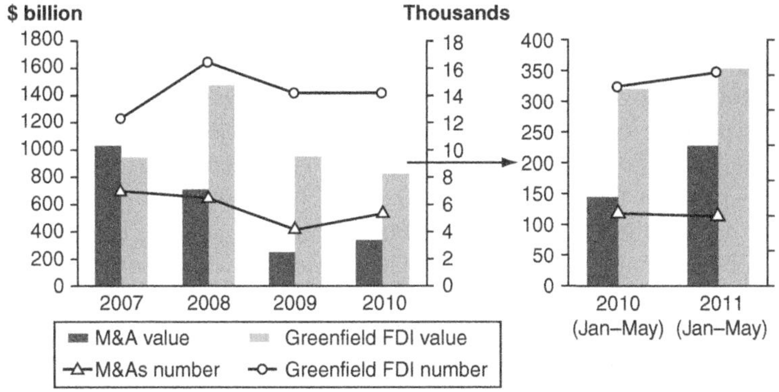

Figure 2.5 Value and number of cross-border M&As, and greenfield FDI projects, 2007–2011 (May)

Note: Data for value of greenfield FDI projects refer to estimated amounts of capital investment.

Source: UNCTAD (2011: 11).

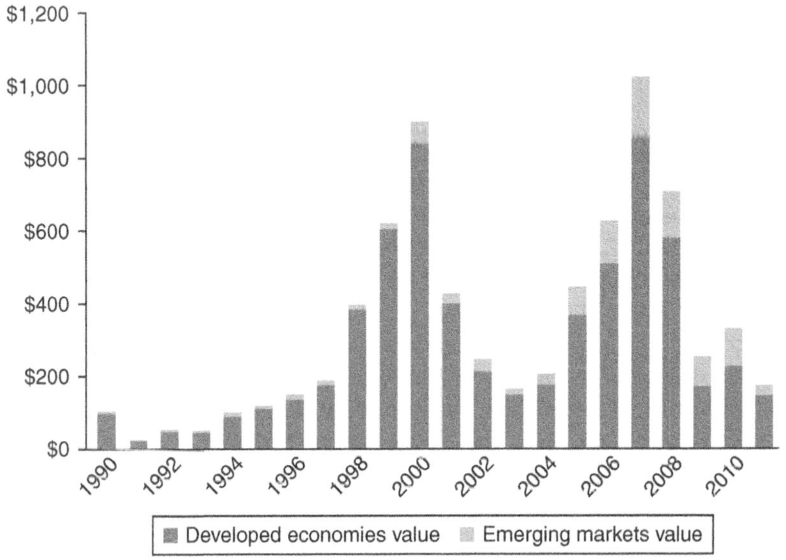

Figure 2.6 Total M&A value by purchase region, 1990–2011 (May) (US$ billions)
Source: Authors, based on data from UNCTAD (2011, annex table 10).

In terms of M&As, the shift in activity from developed economy MNEs to emerging market MNEs has gained momentum since the beginning of the crisis. Emerging markets accounted for only 10 per cent of all M&A activity in the 1990s, a share that rose to 17 per cent in the 2000s (ibid.). By 2010, one-third of all M&A activity was taken over by emerging market MNEs (ibid.).

Greenfield investments, which was by nature slower to react to changing economic circumstances, continued to grow through 2008, and reached a high of US$1.5 trillion, an 80 per cent increase on the average of the previous five years (Figure 2.7) (UNCTAD, 2011, annex table 18). They declined in 2009 and 2010, but the decline was less dramatic to that of M&As; at US$807 billion in 2010, the levels of greenfield investments were at 55 per cent in 2008, and in line with the average for the period 2003–2007, at US$801 billion.

The pattern of total greenfield investments since 2003 reflected also in the levels in both developed economies and emerging markets. Developed economies' greenfield investments peaked in 2008 at US$1 trillion, a rise of 60 per cent on 2007, before falling back to US$569 billion in 2010, a drop of 45 per cent (UNCTAD, 2011, annex table 18). Emerging markets' greenfield investment rose by 58 per cent in 2008 to reach a high of US$434 billion, and declined to 45 per cent over the next two

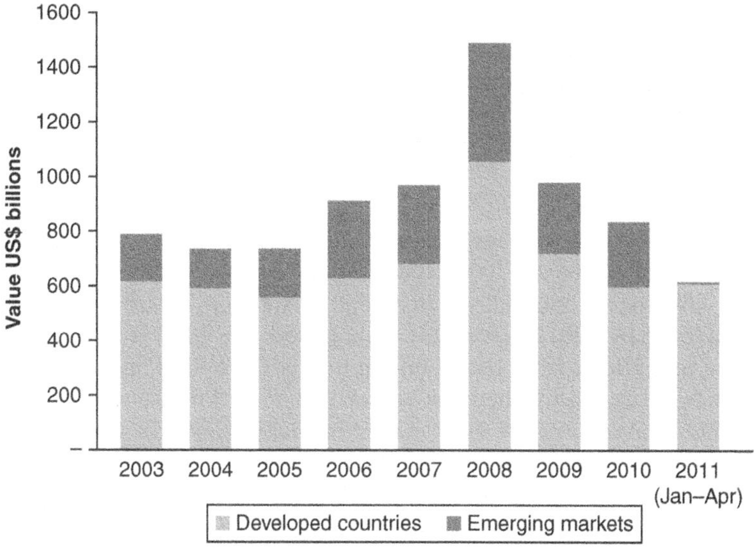

Figure 2.7 Value of greenfield projects by source, 2003–2011 (May) (US$ billions)
Source: Authors, based on data from UNCTAD (2011, annex table 18).

years to US$238 billion (ibid.). Nevertheless, over the course of the past decade, the share of emerging markets has increased gradually: From 23 per cent in 2003, it stood at 29 per cent by 2010 (ibid.).

Emerging markets: Coping with the crisis

The crisis that began in the banking and financial systems of the US and Europe in 2007, spread rapidly and spared few economies. Emerging markets have not escaped the crisis, but most have displayed greater resilience than developed economies, emerging earlier from the downturn, thereby strengthening their relative position in the global economy. That this has occurred less than a decade after a crisis had swept through Asia, Russia, Latin American, and Turkey, a decade that saw these economies become more closely integrated into the global economy, raises the question of how this group of economies has achieved this.

Coping strategies

The term 'emerging markets' encompasses a large, diverse group of economies, affected in different ways and to different degrees by the global crisis. In this section, we will examine the impact of the global crisis on four key emerging markets: Brazil, Russia, India, and China, and examine how they have responded to, and coped with, it. We will consider the state of the economy at the onset of the crisis; the impact of the crisis on the economy and outward investment of MNEs; policy measures adopted in response to the crisis; and their success to date.

Brazil

Brazil, the largest economy in Latin American, enjoyed strong annual growth from 2000 to 2008, averaging 3.7 per cent, driven, in large part, by high commodity prices and increasing exports to China (UNCTADSTAT, 2012). Over this same period, the OFDI stock of Brazil more than tripled from US$54 billion to US$ 156 billion (ibid.).

The global crisis touched first on Brazil's financial markets. By the end of 2008, the value of the stock market had halved, and the real value of stocks depreciated as investors sought safe havens (Trading Economics, 2012). The crisis moved quickly to the broader economy. Foreign investment declined, commodity prices fell, and exports volumes declined as growth in Brazil's export markets, particularly its largest export market, China, slowed.

The Brazilian Government responded quickly to the crisis. In December 2008, it had launched a US$20 billion stimulus package, equivalent to 1.2 per cent of GDP, extending the Growth Acceleration Program of 2007 (Congressional Research Service, 2009: 75). The program included investments in infrastructure, tax cuts and measures to maintain household income, intended to shore up domestic demand. It was largely successful, and the large domestic market and stronger demand helped mitigate the effects of the global crisis on the economy. After contracting by 0.2 per cent in 2009, the economy grew by 7.5 per cent in 2010, one of the highest annual rates of growth since 1986 (OECD, 2010: 195).

OFDI activity by Brazilian MNEs was also curtailed during the crisis, and flows fell from US$20 billion in 2008, to minus US$10 billion in 2009, as intra-company loans were repaid, in order to shore up parent companies during the height of the crisis (ECLAC, 2009; UNCTAD, 2011). Growth resumed in 2010, and at US$11.5 billion, OFDI flows were just over half of their 2008 high (ibid.). However, the outlook for 2011 looks less positive, with concerns that high levels of intercompany loan repayment by foreign affiliates will result in negative outflows once again (see UNCTAD, 2011: 60). The higher than usual levels of intercompany-loan repayment may be the result of efforts to shore up parent companies, or it may be one solution to limited access to financing domestically. Unusual, as it is to see affiliates helping the activities of their parent companies, this underlines the importance of OFDI to the continued success of Brazilian MNEs.

Russia

The 1980s and 1990s were a particularly turbulent period for the Russian economy, but that appeared to change in 1999, when Russia entered a decade of dynamic growth averaging 8 per cent per annum, driven largely by rising energy prices and a domestic lending boom (UNCTADSTAT). By 2007, Russia's foreign-held debt, including inherited Soviet-era debt, was paid down and the government debt to GDP ratio was only 7 per cent (The World Bank, 2012).Total financial assets were equivalent to only 68 per cent of GDP); there was a regular budget surplus, and foreign reserves totaled US$597 billion by mid-2008 (Nanto, 2009: 96). Over this period, Russian OFDI grew dramatically, from US$2 billion in 1999 to US$56 billion in 2008 (UNCTADSTAT). OFDI stock rose from US$9 billion in 1999, to US$370 billion by 2007 (ibid.).

The global crisis brought this decade of growth to an abrupt end. The fall in global demand caused commodity exports to fall and prices to collapse—extremely damaging for an economy in which ten of the twenty largest non-financial outward investors[5] are in the oil and gas, or metal industries (IMEMO-VCC, 2011: 2). More than half the value of the Russian stock exchange was wiped out between July 2008 and July 2009, as nervous investors withdrew (Financial Times, 2008: 13), and a weak banking system and tighter credit reduced domestic demand (Filippov, 2011). From growth of 8.5 per cent in 2007, the economy shrank by 7.8 per cent in 2009 (UNCTADSTAT). Over this same period, Russian OFDI stock also declined. Having grown 18-fold between 2000 and 2007 to a total of US$370, it fell by 44 per cent in 2008 to US$206 billion (UNCTADSTAT), reflecting a fall in the value of foreign assets, and firms pulling back after a period of rapid expansion (Panibratov and Kalotay, 2009). However, the downturn in 2008–2009 did not signal the beginning of an extended period of economic decline: The economy and OFDI both returned to growth in 2010, growing 4 per cent and 50 per cent, respectively (UNCTADSTAT).

How has Russia succeeded in coping with this global crisis, only a decade after a more-limited crisis forced the government to devalue its currency and default on its debt? One of the critical differences is that this was not a crisis solely of Russia's making and, as a result, its economy was less directly impacted than the economies of developed countries in whose banking systems the crisis had its roots. Strong global growth before the crisis kept commodity prices high, allowing Russia to accumulate almost US$600 billion in currency reserves (Nanto, 2009: 96), including US$130 billion in the Stabilization Fund of the Russian Federation, created in 2004 (Ministry of Finance of the Russian Federation, 2012). As a result, the authorities enjoyed much greater 'space' in which to develop emergency policies in response to the crisis. The IMF estimates at 10.5 per cent of GDP the loosening that occurred in Russia's primary balance over 2008–2009 (IMF, 2010: 29), used to shore up the domestic economy through loans to banks, government purchase of stocks, emergency loans to strategically important firms, and a lowering of the corporate tax rate. Yet, not all efforts were successful: Attempts to support the ruble failed, at an estimated cost of US$200 billion (IMF, 2010: 28) and, finally, it was allowed to devalue.

The crisis highlighted structural weaknesses in the Russian economy: an over-reliance on the oil and gas and metal industry, and a weak banking sector. Yet, the government has done little to diversify economic activity; focusing resources on a small number of state-controlled firms further hampers private firms' access to capital (Nanto, 2009; Filippov, 2011). Finally, the government response has been criticized for its opacity (Jellinek, 2009; Wisniewska *et al.*, 2010; Filippov, 2011) with concerns that support went primarily to firms deemed strategically important, while failing to develop clear policies to support OFDI by Russian MNEs.

India

The years 2000 to 2010 saw India enjoy average annual growth of 7.9 per cent, its highest decade of growth since 1970 (UNCTADSTAT), driven largely by growing domestic demand. With the gradual liberalization of the economy from the 1990s onward, India became more closely integrated into the global economy through trade and capital flows, a trend that is reflected in the rapid growth of OFDI by Indian MNEs.[6] From US$1.4 billion in 2001, OFDI flows exceeded US$19 billion in 2008 (UNCTAD, 2011). In 2009, seven Indian MNEs featured among the top-100 non-financial MNEs of emerging markets (UNCTAD, 2011, annex table 30), in industries as diverse as metal and metal products and consulting services. Only one of the seven firms, Oil and Natural Gas Corporation Limited, is state-owned, reflecting the dominant role of the private sector in Indian OFDI.

As the home-country policy framework changed, so have the patterns of Indian OFDI. From an early concentration in manufacturing and an emphasis on south–south investments prior to 1991, Indian OFDI shifted toward investment in services, increasingly in developed economies (Kumar, 2007). Deregulation spurred growth in the domestic economy, underlining the importance of securing access to natural resources. Between 2000 and 2007, 25 per cent of Indian OFDI was in the primary sector, with 40 per cent in manufacturing, and 35 per cent in services (Pradhan, 2011b). Hand in hand with this shift, OFDI by Indian MNEs increasingly took place through M&As in developed economies. Between 2000 and 2009, 58 per cent of all OFDI by Indian MNEs was in developed economies: Europe received 41 per cent of OFDI flows and North America 10 per cent, with 21 per cent in South-Eastern Asia (Pradhan, 2011a: 125, 127).

The greater openness of the Indian economy, with globalization acting as an accelerator in good economic times, lessened its resistance to the global crisis. From 9.6 per cent in 2007, the rate of growth of the Indian economy almost halved to 5.1 per cent in 2008, as exports fell and capital flows declined (UNCTADSTAT). The credit freeze limited access to overseas borrowing, a critical source of funding for cross-border M&As, and OFDI flows declined significantly. From a high of US$19 billion in 2008, OFDI flows from India fell by 18 per cent, to US$16 billion in 2009 (UNCTAD, 2011).

The Government responded swiftly to the global crisis through a combination of fiscal and monetary policy measures; its efforts focused on shoring up aggregate demand and maintaining liquidity. With domestic demand driving growth in the Indian economy, the downturn was short-lived (Pradhan, 2011b). The rate of growth picked up in 2009, reaching 7.7 per cent that year, and 8.5 per cent in 2010 (UNCTADSTAT). Yet, as the global downturn continued with developed economies worst affected, OFDI registered a further 8 per cent decline in 2010, falling to US$14.6 billion (UNCTAD, 2011).

China

China is the largest emerging market and, since 2011, the world's second largest economy, following three decades of average annual growth approaching 10 per cent, driven by the industrialization of the economy and its increasing openness to trade and foreign investment. Between 2000 and 2007 alone, annual growth averaged 10.5 per cent (UNCTADSTAT). OFDI by Chinese MNEs has also grown rapidly. From less than US$40 million in 1981, OFDI stocks totaled US148 billion in 2008, a 54 per cent increase on 2007 (UNCTAD, 2011). OFDI flows more than doubled from 2007 to 2008, to US$52 billion (ibid.). As a result of its growing trade surpluses and FDI, China's holdings of foreign reserves have increased dramatically, totaling US$1.6 trillion (excluding gold) before the crisis (end 2007) and US$2.8 trillion at the end of 2010 (The People's Bank of China, 2008, 2010).

Despite its record of strong growth, the importance of trade and FDI to the Chinese economy exposed it to the recession in its largest export markets, the European Union and the US. By May 2009, exports were less than three-quarters of their level of the previous year (Congressional Research Service, 2009: 75). Inward FDI flows (IFDI), having doubled since the beginning of the decade, fell by 12 per cent in 2009 (UNCTADSTAT). The rate of growth of OFDI flows fell rapidly, from 132 per cent in 2007–2008, to 8 per cent in 2008–2009 (ibid.), but in a context in which world FDI flows halved. The impact on unemployment was swift, with the government estimating that 20 million migrant workers had lost their jobs in 2008 because of the crisis (Congressional Research Service, 2009: 75).

The Chinese authorities acted swiftly to mitigate the effects of the crisis on the domestic economy, launching a US$586 billion stimulus package in November 2008, equivalent to 12 per cent of GDP (Congressional Research Service, 2009: 75). The scale of the stimulus package and the speed with which it was announced, ahead even of the US announcement of a US$787 stimulus package in February 2009 (Recovery.gov), indicated the authorities' level of concern over the impact of the crisis on the Chinese economy. Their aim was to maintain aggregate demand through increased spending on infrastructure and social welfare, and tax deductions on capital spending by firms (Nanto, 2009). Monetary policy measures were also adopted: after a period of strengthening, the RMB was allowed to depreciate, interest rates and reserve requirements were lowered, and lending by state banks was eased (De Beule and Van Den Bulcke, 2010). Furthermore, the government sought to support OFDI by Chinese firms, by simplifying the approvals process, for example, and reducing restrictions on firms' lending to their affiliates (ibid.).

The measures adopted by the Chinese authorities in response to the global crisis were largely successful, sparing the economy from its worst effects. Growth, which had fallen from 14 per cent in 2007 to 9.2 per cent in 2009, exceeded 10 per cent in 2010 (World Bank Indicators). The rate of growth of OFDI picked up: From 8 per cent in 2008–2009, it reached 20 per cent in 2009–2010 (UNCTAD, 2011). By 2010, China's OFDI stock totaled US$298 billion, double their 2008 level (ibid.), as Chinese firms, unhindered by the credit crisis and taking advantage of lower asset prices, made a large number of acquisitions. Despite the apparent success of the policies implemented in mitigating the impact of the crisis on the economy, concerns remain. While the measures implemented have helped Chinese firms weather the storm in the short term, will state-control hamper their ability to pursue policies based on economic objectives in the longer term? (De Beule and Van Den Bulcke, 2010).

The BRIC economies

The BRIC group of economies and the OFDI activities of their MNEs have shown great resilience in the face of the global crisis. As the crisis hit, MNEs responded by scaling back their OFDI: From a high of US$148 billion in 2008, OFDI flows fell by 14 per cent in 2009, to US$126 billion (UNCTADSTAT). Nevertheless, by 2010, activity had returned to pre-crisis levels and the combined OFDI flows from the BRIC economies totaled US$146 billion, 99 per cent of their record 2008 level (ibid.). In 2010, they accounted for 11 per cent of global OFDI flows, a dramatic increase on their 1 per cent share in 2000 (ibid.). For the first time, the combined OFDI stock of the BRIC group exceeded US$1 trillion in 2010, 5 per cent of the global OFDI stock (ibid.). This represented an almost tenfold increase on 2000, when their OFDI stock totaled slightly more than US$100 billion (ibid.).

There are a number of reasons for the resilience of these emerging markets and the OFDI activities of their MNEs in the face of the worst global crisis since the 1930s. The global crisis began in the financial markets of developed economies, where more than two decades of deregulation had reduced considerably levels of oversight and control at a time of great innovation in financial products. This was not the case in emerging markets, where the harsh lessons learned from the emerging markets crisis of the 1990s were still fresh. Governments in these economies have maintained a much greater role in the operation and supervision of financial markets. In addition, total levels of debt, especially foreign currency denominated debt, were low, and sustained budget surpluses combined with high levels of FDI, enabled governments to accumulate significant foreign currency reserves. Despite some initial weakening, therefore, emerging market currencies generally remained strong, limiting the impact of the crisis on the domestic economy.

High levels of growth in emerging markets are often attributed to the important role of exports in their economies. Exports are indeed important but their relative importance is declining. Instead, it is their strong domestic demand, with high levels of consumption and investment that has supported high growth rates in most emerging markets, and insulated them from the worst of the crisis. High savings rates and bank deposits have supported domestic lending; critically, bank lending did not decline at the onset of the crisis. The authorities did not raise interest rates, and in a number of economies, including India, interest rates were lowered.

Emerging markets have benefited from the dominance of FDI in their private capital flows, generally considered a more stable form of capital than portfolio investment or other forms of debt finance such as loans and bonds. However, even FDI is not quite as stable a form of capital as it once was considered to be, as its composition also shifts from mainly equity to debt in the form of intra-company loans. The risks associated with this are seen in the OFDI from Brazil, which is expected to decline or become negative in 2011, the result of higher than usual levels of intra-company loan repayment (UNCTAD, 2011: 60). There are a number of possible explanations for this: Weaker performance in the home market may have reduced profitability, or access to capital may have become more limited; but the fact that foreign affiliates are shoring up their parent companies further underlines the importance of OFDI.

OFDI by emerging market MNEs has taken the form of greenfield investment for the most part, while developed country MNEs have relied more on M&As. The latter are more vulnerable to shocks to the financial system and, as liquidity and funding dried up, the number of M&As undertaken by developed economy MNEs fell rapidly. Emerging market MNEs, especially relatively young firms, have not enjoyed the same access to international capital markets, and they and their OFDI activities consequently suffered less. In those instances in which emerging market MNEs do engage in cross-border M&As, they are more likely to pay for them in cash rather than in shares (World Bank, 2011: 83–84), a decision linked to the ownership nature of these firms and the limitations of their domestic capital markets. Emerging market firms are more likely to be family or state-controlled entities that seek to avoid any dilution of their control, and so prefer to pay for acquisitions in cash (ibid., Resende *et al.*, 2010).

Finally, the strong performance of emerging markets and their MNEs highlights how critical it is to maintain strong economic fundamentals. Thanks to their sound economic management pre-crisis, with large foreign exchange reserves and low levels of national debt, these governments had the necessary 'policy space' to implement emergency measures to shore up their economies during turbulent economic times.

Global players from emerging economies: challenges ahead

In the immediate aftermath of the crisis, the attentions of key actors were focused on responding to its most pressing challenges and, to date, these efforts have proven relatively successful. By the end of 2010, OFDI flows from emerging market MNEs had reached a new high of US$388 billion (UNCTADSTAT). Inward investment to emerging markets has also made a strong recovery, reaching US$753 billion in 2011, 97 per cent of its 2008 high (UNCTAD, 2012). However, numerous other challenges persist, some inherent in the rise of these new global players, others resulting from the ongoing economic crisis. This section addresses a number of these risks and challenges, and considers the path ahead.

Key strategic challenges for emerging market MNEs

Perhaps the single most important challenge that emerging market MNEs face relates to their human resources. Building a successful, integrated international production network is a formidable challenge, to do so through the successful integration of acquired firms amplifies the difficulties. It places considerable demands on their human resources, in particular on their managerial skills and capacity. Moreover, the scale of the challenge is relatively higher for emerging market MNEs: Internationalizing often at an early stage in their development (and more recently), they have had less time to develop such skills and capacities. Those emerging markets that have a longer and greater experience with OFDI have distinct advantages in this area, having been able to develop management skills, expertise, and an understanding of international markets (Jaklič and Svetličič, 2010).

Emerging markets MNEs that have undertaken OFDI more recently are less likely to have built up expertise and capacity in integrating acquisitions and managing foreign affiliates, a gap that may be further compounded by an unwillingness to hire non-national managers. An example is Brazil, where the level of foreign managerial employment among leading MNEs is almost half that of the 100 largest developing country MNEs (Resende *et al.*, 2010: 104). Family-controlled MNEs seek to avoid any dilution of their control and high levels of 'in-group collectivism' (ibid.), and such practices complicate further the building of international management networks and do not bode well for the ability of those MNEs to create integrated international production networks.

There are also broader challenges to be met. MNEs face the continuous challenge of balancing opportunities and risks. The rapid pace of globalization and industry consolidation has led in many cases to a mind-set of 'hunt or be hunted' (Price Waterhouse Coopers, 2007: 5). One illustrative industry in this respect is mining, where record commodity prices facilitated the paying down of debt incurred to pursue acquisitions. Industry players saw consolidation as essential to achieving economics of scale and synergies in operations. Today, however, the dominance of resource-based firms in the OFDI of a number of emerging markets brings its own set of challenges (Kalotay, 2010). Natural-resource-based firms account for four-fifths of the foreign assets of the top 25 Russian MNEs, for example (ibid.). Their rapid expansion took place on the back of high commodity prices. While commodity prices have recovered, high levels of debt make for an uncertain future, in which divestiture and further industry consolidation may be the only options available.

Sustainable FDI is another area that presents potential challenges for emerging market MNEs, looking at the importance of FDI along four dimensions: 'economic development, environmental sustainability, social development, good governance' (VCC-WAIPA, 2010: 4) rather than in dollar and employment terms. Just as emerging markets become important players in global FDI markets, the scale against which importance is measured is shifting from quantity to quality (Filippov and Guimón, 2009). This represents a challenge for all MNEs—but the scale of the challenge is perhaps greater for emerging market MNEs. In the case of these MNEs, importance to the domestic economy is still measured in terms of dollars and employment created. In addition, emerging market MNEs are important investors in natural resources, a sector in which until recently the focus has been on short-term contributions measured in dollar terms. The ability of emerging market MNEs to adapt to these new standards is critical to their continued growth and success—and may ultimately have spillover effects in the home country, leading, in the longer term, to a harmonization of standards upwards.

Challenges for home country policies

Today, while the landscape of home country OFDI policies is very uneven, the vast majority of emerging markets do not provide a supportive environment for the OFDI activities of their firms, placing them at a competitive disadvantage vis-à-vis their developed country counterparts. The principal challenge for home country policy in emerging markets is, within the constraints of limited resources and widespread needs, to create an environment and policy framework that supports domestic firms. This framework should enhance their competitiveness, enable them to compete effectively in the global arena and, ultimately, secure the benefits of OFDI for their home countries. Certainly, the substantial rise in outward investment from emerging markets is a relatively new phenomenon, and national policy is not written or rewritten overnight. On the one hand, if emerging market firms are disadvantaged by a continued lack of supportive policies, and thus are hampered in their competition on the world market, they may, in extreme cases, shift their base to another country in order to stay competitive. On the other hand, the scope of government action and policy-making is constrained by economic reality—limited resources, scarce foreign reserves, and potential concerns over the export of capital and jobs.

The lack of a supportive policy framework in many emerging markets[7] stands in contrast to developed countries, which have built an extensive and comprehensive policy framework over decades, policies that have evolved in tandem with, and complement, their economic situation. The result has been a gradual but persistent shift in home country policy from restricting and controlling OFDI, to permitting it, and finally to promoting OFDI actively, reflecting the recognition that, in a global market, firms must be globally competitive, with OFDI being one source of such competitiveness.

The experience of developed countries in building a policy framework for OFDI offers lessons for policy-makers in emerging markets. In the aftermath of World War II, early restrictions on OFDI focused on capital and foreign exchange controls. Gradually phased out by the early 1980s, these controls were eliminated, finally, as a global capital market became a reality. From restrictions on OFDI, developed countries adapted policies to shape and, ultimately, promote OFDI[8] (Buckley *et al.*, 2010). However, even with a detailed understanding of the policies implemented in developed countries, challenges remain for emerging markets. While the lack of a clear policy framework leaves domestic firms at a competitive disadvantage, changing the situation is not without its own challenges, given the lack of domestic experience and competence in this area, the risks of regulatory capture, and the absence of a significant social safety net (ibid.).

Coming through the crisis with their relative position in the global economy strengthened has done little to reduce the policy dilemma facing emerging markets. The need for firms to acquire a portfolio of locational assets in order to retain and maximize their competitiveness in a global setting must be balanced against the broad macroeconomic interests of home country needs. Concerns over the export of jobs are as relevant in emerging markets as in developed economies (Broadman, 2010). Where national champions or state-owned enterprises (SOEs) from emerging markets undertake FDI, this poses potential political challenges for the home country as much as for the host country. Whilst a relatively small share of total OFDI in most emerging markets, as SOEs move abroad and 'grow up,' they may well seek greater independence in determining their own economic future, free from political constraints (ibid.). Furthermore, critics argue that SOEs crowd out more efficient private companies in markets for financial and human capital (The Economist, 2012: 11). How do home country policy-makers retain control, without hindering the competitiveness of their SOE-MNE? This question remains unanswered; but to hope that as they mature and expand, SOEs will simply throw of their political shackles is unrealistic.

Information on the experiences of developed countries and the different policy options available is useful for emerging markets, but how applicable is it? Furthermore, even with this information, the challenge of sequencing shifts in policy remains. The fact that emerging market MNEs may be 'born global,' or may skip stages of development and internationalization does nothing to lessen the complexity of the policy makers' task (De Beule and Van Den Bulcke, 2010). Rapid globalization and the early internationalization of emerging market MNEs render redundant some of the policy lessons from developed countries. It is more likely that emerging markets will instead combine elements of policy from different stages of development—the selective promotion of OFDI, for example, with retaining elements of control (ibid.).

China is an example of how one particularly important emerging market has addressed the challenges for home country policy and, in particular, the shift from OFDI restriction to promotion. China's OFDI policy evolved in three phases from 1984 to 2008 (Xue and Han, 2010). Adopted largely out of economic necessity in 1984, early policy involved strict controls on OFDI. By 1991, the domestic policy environment had liberalized gradually, and OFDI's role in economic growth was endorsed. From 1991, OFDI policy focused on large SOEs until, in 2000, funds were established to encourage the internationalization of small and medium-sized firms. The year 2000 also saw the unveiling of China's 'Going Global' policy and the differentiation of OFDI policies into policies of regulation, guidance and support (ibid.). China offers a particularly interesting example: It embraced 'Open-Door' policies only three decades ago but, in a relatively short period, OFDI flows have grown considerably, from only US$44 million in 1982 to US$68 billion in 2010 (UNCTADSTAT). Furthermore, the continued and prominent role of SOEs in the Chinese economy and the country's OFDI allows the government a degree of direct influence, impossible for most other national policy-makers.

Challenges for host country policies

In spite of the global economic turmoil, the investment climate for FDI remains overwhelmingly welcoming, and virtually all countries seek to attract inward investment (Figure 2.9). While a certain number of restrictive and adverse measures have been introduced even before the onset of the global crisis, they should be considered in the context of an investment environment that is already largely open. Furthermore, the vast majority of the regulatory measures introduced were limited to specific sectors, including land ownership and investment in natural resources (Economou and Sauvant, 2012), particularly sensitive sectors even in the best of economic times. The OECD's FDI Restrictiveness Index for 2010, measuring the restrictiveness of FDI policies across 48 countries (Figure 2.8) shows that on a scale from 0 (open) to 1 (closed)

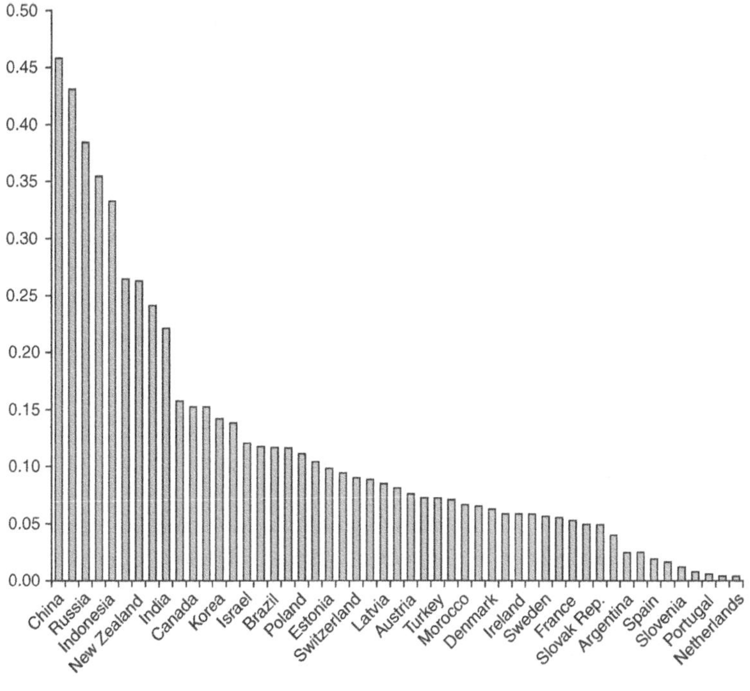

Figure 2.8 OECD's FDI Restrictiveness Index, 2010
Source: Authors, based on OECD (2010).

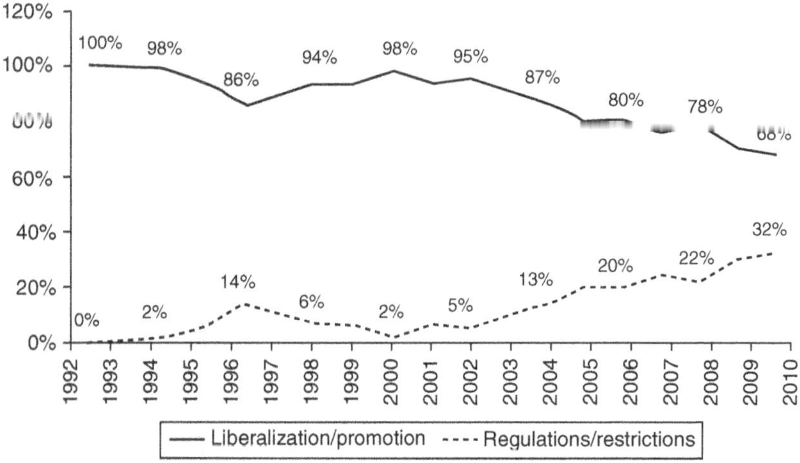

Figure 2.9 National regulatory measures, 1992–2010 (%)

all major economies are rated below 0.46, and most are rated below 0.15 (OECD, 2010).

Yet, a distinct trend toward a more restrictive investment climate has emerged over the past decade (Figures 2.9 and 2.10) and, in 2010, one-third of all national regulatory measures imposed greater regulation or restrictions on FDI.[9]

In a regulatory environment that has become more restrictive, the rise of outward investment from emerging markets presents its own set of challenges for host country policies, particularly for developed host countries. As noted above, investment by emerging market MNEs in developed economies generally takes the form of acquisitions, often considered less attractive by the host country because of the limited contribution to increased economic output. That the firms being acquired may be deemed part of a 'strategic sector,' raises further concerns over national security. When the acquiring firm is a state-owned enterprise or a sovereign wealth fund, this only amplifies host country concerns. In the US, the share of inward investment notices that progressed to investigations rose from 15 per cent in 2008 to 38 per cent in both 2009 and 2010 (Table 2.2) (Committee on Foreign Investment in the United States, 2011: 3).

The rapid rise in OFDI from China in the past decade and the dominant role played by SOEs in this outward investment represents a particular challenge to host country policy for the US (Sauvant, 2010a,b).

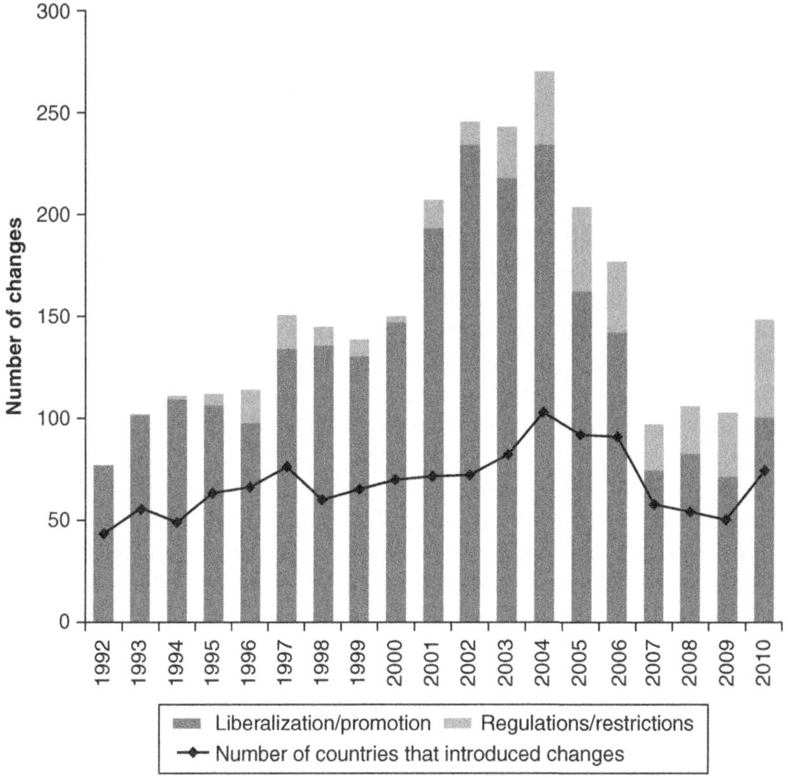

Figure 2.10 National regulatory measures, 1992–2010

Source: The authors, based on UNCTAD 2008 (13) and UNCTAD (2011) (94).

Table 2.2 CFIUS: Covered transactions, withdrawals, and presidential decisions, 2008–2010

Year	Number of Notices	Notices Withdrawn During Review	Number of Investigations	Notices Withdrawn During Investigation	Presidential Decisions
2008	155	18	23	5	0
2009	65	5	25	2	0
2010	93	6	35	6	0
Total	313	29	83	13	0

Source: Based on the Committee on Foreign Investment in the United States, Annual Report to Congress (2011: 3).

By the end of 2010, China had invested almost US$298 billion abroad, a near ten-fold increase since 20000 (UNCTADSTAT). China is the US government's largest creditor: It holds US$1.6 trillion of US securities and foreign exchange reserves of US$3.2 trillion (Morrison and Labonte 2011: i). The fact that the vehicle of choice for most of this OFDI has been mergers and acquisitions only exacerbates tensions. Policy in the US has become more cautious in recent years, especially with regard to Chinese firms. National security concerns play a more important role in shaping this policy, fed by fears that Chinese investment decisions are driven as much (if not more) by strategic and political motivations rather than by economic motivations. This situation is not completely new, however: Japanese investment once stirred up similar fears, which were successfully allayed when Japanese firms worked closely with the different stakeholders in order to become 'insiders' (ibid., Milhaupt, 2010).

Host country apprehension—founded or not—that certain acquisitions are driven by political rather than commercial objectives will do nothing to reduce restrictions on FDI. Unchecked, this could evolve into FDI protectionism, inflicting damage on the recovery, continued integration, and smooth functioning of the global economy. Protectionism on the part of developed countries, traditionally the main proponents of liberalization, in response to the emergence of new players would border on hypocrisy, and would deprive host (developed) economies of the widely recognized benefits of FDI. Restricting the access of these new players to developed markets would deny their firms vital access to new skills, technologies, and markets, preventing them from building the portfolio of locational assets so essential to their global competitiveness. Ultimately, opportunities for both growth and development, for the firm, home and host economy, would be lost.

The path ahead

Two decades ago, outward investment from emerging markets accounted for less than 8 per cent of the world's outward investment stock (UNCTADSTAT). The Soviet Union had only recently reintroduced the right of private ownership in an attempt to stimulate its economy. Fifteen years ago, the Asian financial crisis devastated economies across the region and beyond. Today, as global players from emerging markets move toward the center of the world stage, the world is in the grip of the worst economic crisis since the 1930s, a crisis that broke over four years ago and that shows little sign of ending in a number of countries. Looking ahead, what are the main challenges facing FDI and the main actors in this process? Will the current economic downturn require them simply to ride out this crisis, with normal business resuming as soon as possible? Alternatively, will the combination of the rise of global players from emerging markets and the global crisis require the rules of FDI to be rewritten?

Perhaps the single most important challenge that emerging market MNEs face relates to their ability to address the heightened levels of political risks resulting from the ongoing global crisis. The relative youth of many emerging market MNEs serves to increase the scale of the challenge. Broadly defined as 'the probability of disruption of the operations of companies by political forces and events' (MIGA, 2011: 21), until recently, the challenges presented by political risk have been viewed largely in the context of MNEs from developed countries investing in emerging markets. The global crisis has shattered this assumption.

It is important to recognize that, having developed in riskier political and economic environments, emerging market MNEs' notions of risk can be very different from those of developed countries' MNEs. Generally, the greater the levels of political risk in the home country, the greater the tolerance for risk that MNEs develop (MIGA, 2010). Location, sector, size of investment, and home country environment and earlier experience with outward investment all shape their perception of political risk (ibid.). Interestingly, in terms of entry mode, while greenfield investments are considered economically more desirable and less politically risky in developed countries, emerging market MNEs consider them more risky in other emerging markets where 'the presence of a domestic partner tends to reduce risk perceptions' (MIGA, 2010: 228). Fortunately, governments—alone or in conjunction with the private sector—have the ability to minimize the impact of political risk on investment decisions through the provision of insurance, a policy tool that should become an increasingly important element of home country policy in emerging markets.

However, since the onset of the global crisis, emerging market MNEs are most concerned by changes in the regulatory framework (Figure 2.11) and more concerned about such changes to the investment climate than they are about the state of the global economy and access to financing (MIGA, 2011). In particular, it is 'the instability of the regulatory regime ... rather than the regime itself' that concerns investors (MIGA, 2011: 22). The dramatic growth and strong performance of emerging markets and their MNEs mitigated the scale of the global downturn. The recovery of the global economy is patchy and remains

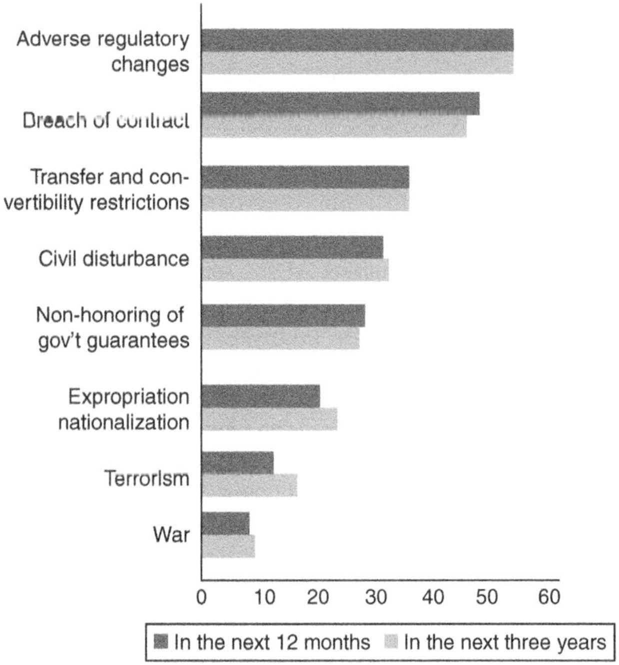

Figure 2.11 Types of political risk of most concern to investors in developing countries (% respondents)

Source: MIGA-EIU Political Risk Survey, reproduced in MIGA (2011) World Investment and Political Risk Report, 20.

fragile. It is vital that efforts are made to keep the global economy open to outward investments from emerging markets.

The financial crisis and subsequent government rescue programs have increased previously high public debt to unsustainable levels in several developed economies—in excess of 100 per cent of gross domestic product (GDP) in Ireland, Portugal, Greece, and Italy (Eurostat, 2012). Not since the 1930s has a Western European country defaulted on its debt, but there is real concern today that, orderly or disorderly, Greece cannot avoid a sovereign default. Greece's creditors are at immediate risk, and investors are wary of an economy that is in its fifth year of contraction. The greatest risk, however, is that this sovereign debt crisis will spread beyond Greece to other highly in debt Eurozone economies: Ireland, Portugal, Spain, and (of most concern given the size of its economy) Italy. The potentially disastrous consequences for the European economy should fears of contagion become reality, make this one of the most pressing risks of the day. Moreover, the EU is a key pillar of the global economy, a vital source of, and destination for FDI, with the Euro a global reserve currency that accounts for close to 27 per cent of the world's currency reserves (The Economist, 2011). Whatever happens within the Eurozone and the European Union, therefore, will have dramatic implications for the global economy and FDI. Rising levels of civil unrest hinder the economic reform efforts of national governments and raise concerns about the stability and predictability of future policies. The crisis in Greece has laid bare the slow and unwieldy nature of EU policy-making and, more worryingly, the divisions that exist among member nations, exacerbated in these tough economic times. Further uncertainty in this region could well tip the global economy back into recession.

Conclusions

This chapter has sought to place the rise of emerging market MNEs in context, examining the role of these new global players in global FDI flows, how they have responded to the global crisis, and the challenges inherent in their rise for MNEs themselves as well as for home and host countries. Whatever the tensions and temporary setbacks, the great number of firms undertaking FDI will build an ever more interconnected and integrated international production system.

All this, finally, needs to be seen against one basic fact: Countries do not look at FDI as an end in itself. Rather, it is seen as a tool to advance their development, be it as a home country or host country. As part of that, FDI is a powerful means to help countries in their integration into the world economy. In addition, economic development through integration into the world economy is one of the means by which countries lift themselves out of poverty. Despite the global crisis, much progress has been made in recent years, yet much remains to be done—and the greater the number of firms involved in this process the better it is for all of us.

Finally, efforts to build a multilateral investment framework must be stepped up. The need to address and allay concerns that feed growing economic nationalism and FDI protectionism is not limited to MNEs, home and host country governments: This situation highlights the important role that international organizations must play if the international investment regime is to remain relatively open, transparent, and stable. An international framework, establishing best practices and minimum standards, and bringing greater transparency to the now truly international investment regime are to the benefit of all.

Notes

1. According to UNCTAD terminology, the group of 'developed economies' comprises the 27 Member States of the European Union, plus Australia, Bermuda, Canada, Gibraltar, Iceland, Israel, Japan, New Zealand, Norway, Switzerland, and the US. 'Emerging markets' comprise both 'developing countries' and 'transition economies.' The 'transition economies' group consists of the six countries of Southeast Europe (Albania, Bosnia and Herzegovina, Croatia, The FYR of Macedonia, Montenegro, and Serbia) as well as the twelve countries of the Commonwealth of Independent States (CIS): Armenia, Azerbaijan, Belarus, Georgia, Kazakhstan, Kyrgyzstan, the Republic of Moldova, Russian Federation, Tajikistan, Turkmenistan, Ukraine, and Uzbekistan. All other countries are 'developing countries'.
2. For a full discussion, see Sauvant *et al.* (2010); Sauvant (2010); Ramamurti and Singh (2009); Ramamurti (2008); Sauvant *et al.* (2008).
3. See UNCTAD (2011, annex table 25), note [a].
4. UNCTAD (2011, annex table 25) Notes states that 'Data should be interpreted with caution. The world total was extrapolated on the basis of data covering 29 countries in 1990 and 54 countries in 2009, or latest year available. They account for 82 and 89 per cent of world outward FDI stock, respectively, in 1990 and in 2009. Only countries for which data for the three main sectors were available were included. The distribution shares of industries of these countries were applied to estimate the world totals of sectors and industries. As a result, the sum of the sectors for each group of economies is different from the totals shown in annex table 2. Approval data were used for India (2005 instead of 2007) and Taiwan Province of China. For 1990, the world total includes the countries of South-East Europe and the CIS although data by sector and industry are not available for that region. Moreover, as major home developing economies were not covered due to lack of data, the respective shares for developing economies were underestimated in that year,') http://www.unctad.org/sections/dite_dir/docs/WIR11_web%20tab%2025.pdf, last visited March 9, 2011).
5. Measured by foreign assets.
6. For a discussion of the rise of Indian MNEs, see Sauvant *et al.* (2010).
7. The term 'emerging markets,' the grouping together of developing countries and transition economies, risks giving the impression, falsely, of a homogenous group of countries. It should also remind us of the limitations inherent in any attempt to construct one policy framework that fits all emerging markets. The key to successful policy is to ensure that it is appropriate to the stage of development of the national economy.
8. The authors group these measures into seven categories: '(i) the provision of information and technical support, (ii) financial support, (iii) fiscal incentives, (iv) investment insurance and guaranteed, (v) support of national champions, (vi) international investment related concordats and agreements,

and (vii) official development assistance (ODA) programs' (Buckley *et al.*, 2010: 259).

9. Available data for 2011 (January–September 15), appear to show a slight shift toward a more relaxed investment climate, with almost three-quarters of all the measures adopted liberalizing or promoting FDI, but it is perhaps too soon to draw any definitive conclusions.

References

Broadman, H.G. (2010). Multinational enterprises from emerging markets: Implications for the North and the South, in K.P. Sauvant, G. McAllister, and W.A. Maschek (Eds) *Foreign Direct Investments from Emerging Markets: The Challenges Ahead*, New York, NY: Palgrave MacMillan: 325–334.

Buckley, P.J., Clegg, J.L., Cross, A.R., and Voss, H. (2010). What can emerging markets learn from the outward direct investment policies of advanced countries? in K.P. Sauvant, G. McAllister, and W.A. Maschek (Eds) *Foreign Direct Investments from Emerging Markets: The Challenges Ahead*, New York, NY: Palgrave Macmillan: 243–276.

Clover, C. and Belton, C. (2008). Retreat from Moscow, investors take flight as global fears stoke Russian crisis. *The Financial Times*, September 17, 2008: 13.

Committee on Foreign Investment in the United States. (2011). *Annual Report to Congress*, Washington, DC: CFIUS.

Congressional Research Service. (2009). *The Global Financial Crisis: Analysis and Policy Implications*, July 10, 2009, fpc.state.gov/documents/organization/127296.pdf.

De Beule, F. and Van Den Bulcke, D. (2010). The global crisis, foreign direct investment and China, *Brussels Institute of Contemporary China Studies*, 5(6): 1–31.

ECLAC. (2009). *Foreign Direct Investment in Latin America and the Caribbean: Briefing Paper*, Santiago: ECLAC.

Economou, P. and Sauvant, K.P. (2011). From the FDI Triad to multiple FDI poles? *Columbia Perspectives 418*, New York, NY.: Vale Columbia Center on Sustainable International Investment.

Economou, P. and Sauvant, K.P. (2012). Recent trends and issues in foreign direct investment, 2010, in K.P. Sauvant (Ed.) *Yearbook on International Investment Law & Policy*, New York, NY: Oxford University Press: 3–36.

Eurostat. (2012). *Eurostat News Release 20/2012*. Brussels: Eurostat.

Filippov, S. (2011). Russia's emerging multinational companies amidst the global economic crisis. *UNU-MERIT Working Paper Series 2011–003*.

Filippov, S. and Guimón, J. (2009). From quantity to quality: Challenges for investment promotion agencies. *UNU-MERIT Working Paper Series 2009–057*.

IMEMO and VCC. (2011). *Investment from Russia Stabilizes After the Global Crisis*. Moscow and New York, NY: IMEMO and VCC.

International Monetary Fund. (2010). *How Did Emerging Markets Cope in the Crisis?* Washington, DC: International Monetary Fund.

Jaklič, A. and Svetličič, M. (2010). Unknown multinational enterprises: Top MNEs from Slovenia, in K.P. Sauvant, G. McAllister, and W.A. Maschek (Eds) *Foreign Direct Investments from Emerging Markets: The Challenges Ahead*, New York, NY: Palgrave Macmillan: 197–226.

Jellinek, R. (2009). *Russia and the Global Meltdown: Domestic and Foreign Policy Responses to the International Financial Crisis, Carnegie Moscow Center Report*, Moscow: Carnegie Moscow Center.

Kalotay, K. (2010). Takeoff and turbulence in the foreign expansion of Russian multinational enterprises, in K.P. Sauvant, G. McAllister, and W.A. Maschek (Eds) *Foreign Direct Investments from Emerging Markets: The Challenges Ahead*, New York, NY: Palgrave Macmillan: 113–144.

Kumar, N. (2007). Emerging TNCs: Trends, patterns and determinants of outward FDI by Indian enterprises, *Transnational Corporations*, 16(1): 1–26.

MIGA. (2010). South–south foreign direct investment and political risk insurance: Challenges and opportunities, in K.P. Sauvant, G. McAllister, and W.A. Maschek (Eds) *Foreign Direct Investments from Emerging Markets: The Challenges Ahead*, New York, NY: Palgrave Macmillan: 227–242.

MIGA. (2011). *2011 World Investment and Political Risk*. Washington, DC: MIGA.

Milhaupt, C.J. (2010). Is the U.S. ready for FDI from China? Lessons from Japan's experience in the 1980s, in K.P. Sauvant (Ed.) *Investing in the United States: Is the U.S. Ready for FDI from China?* Cheltenham: Edward Elgar: 185–208.

Ministry of Finance of the Russian Federation. (2012). Aggregate amount of the reserve fund. *Ministry of Finance of the Russian Federation*.

Morrison, W.M. and Labonte, M. (2011). *China's Holdings of U.S. Securities: Implications for the U.S. Economy*, Washington, DC: Congressional Research Service.

Nanto, D.K. (2009). *The Global Financial Crisis: Analysis and Policy Implications*, Washington, DC: Congressional Research Service.

OECD. (2010). *OECD Economic Outlook Volume 2010/2*. Paris: OECD.

Panibratov, A. and Kalotay, K. (2009). Russian outward FDI and its policy context. *Columbia FDI Profiles, Vale Columbia Center on Sustainable International Investment, No. 1*. http://www.vcc.columbia.edu/files/vale/documents/FDI_Profile-_Russia.pdf, Accessed on February 6, 2012.

Pradhan, J.P. (2011a). Emerging multinationals: A comparison of Chinese and Indian outward foreign direct investment, *International Journal of Institutions and Economies*, 3(1): 113–148.

Pradhan, J.P. (2011b). Firm performance during global economic slowdown: A view from India, *Economics, Management, and Financial Markets*, 6(1): 57–81.

Price Waterhouse Coopers. (2007). Mine: Riding the wave.

Ramamurti, R. (2008). *What Have We Learned About Emerging Market MNEs?* Cambridge: Cambridge University Press.

Ramamurti, R. and Singh, J.V. (Eds) (2009). *Emerging Multinationals in Emerging Markets*. Cambridge: Cambridge University Press.

Resende, P., Almeida, A., and Ramsey, J. (2010). The transnationalization of Brazilian companies, in K.P. Saivant, G. McAllister, and W.A. Maschek (Eds) *Foreign Direct Investments from Emerging Markets: The Challenges Ahead*, New York, NY: Palgrave Macmillan: 97–112.

Sauvant, K.P. (Ed.) (2010a). *Investing in the United States: Is the U.S. Ready for FDI from China?* Cheltenham: Edward Elgar.
Sauvant, K.P. (2010b). Is the United States ready for foreign direct investment from emerging markets? The case of China, in K.P. Sauvant, G. McAllister, and W.A. Maschek (Eds) *Foreign Direct Investments from Emerging Markets: The Challenges Ahead*, New York, NY: Palgrave Macmillan: 359–380.
Sauvant, K.P., Maschek, W.A., and McAllister, G. (2010). Foreign direct investment by emerging market multinational enterprises, the impact of the financial crisis and recession, and challenges ahead, in K.P. Saivant, G. McAllister, and W.A. Maschek (Eds) *Foreign Direct Investments from Emerging Markets: The Challenges Ahead*, New York, NY: Palgrave Macmillan: 3–30.
Sauvant, K.P., McAllister, G., and Maschek, W.A. (Eds) (2010). *Foreign Direct Investments from Emerging Markets: The Challenges Ahead*, New York, NY: Palgrave Macmillan.
Sauvant, K.P., Mendoza, K., and Ince, I. (Eds) (2008). *The Rise of Transnational Corporations from Emerging Markets: Threat or Opportunity?* Cheltenham: Edward Elgar.
Sauvant, K.P., Pradhan, J.P., Chatterjee, A., and Harley, B. (Eds) (2010). *The Rise of Indian Multinationals*, New York, NY: Palgrave Macmillan.
The Economist. (2011). Climbing greenback mountain, September 24.
The Economist. (2012). The rise of state capitalism, January 21.
The People's Bank of China. (2008). Gold and foreign exchange reserves.
The People's Bank of China. (2010). Gold and foreign exchange reserves.
The World Bank. (2011). *Global Development Horizons: Multipolarity – The New Global Economy*, Washington, DC: The World Bank.
Trading Economics. (2012). Brazil stock market.
UNCTAD. (2005). *World Investment Report 2005: Transnational Corporations and the Internationalization of R&D*. New York, NY; Geneva: UNCTAD.
UNCTAD. (2011a). *World Investment Report 2011, Annex Table 10. Value of Cross-Border M&As by Region/Economy of Purchaser, 1990-May 2011*. New York, NY; Geneva: UNCTAD.
UNCTAD. (2011b). *World Investment Report 2011: Non-Equity Modes of International Production and Development*, New York, NY; Geneva: UNCTAD.
UNCTAD. (2011c). Global Investment Trends Monitor No. 5.
UNCTAD. (2011d). Global Investment Trends Monitor No. 6.
UNCTAD. (2011e). Global Investment Trends Monitor No. 7.
UNCTAD. (2012a). Global Investment Trends Monitor No. 8.
UNCTAD. (2012b). Inward and outward foreign direct investment flows, annual, 1970–2010, *UNCTADSTAT*.
UNCTAD (2012c). Real GDP growth rates, total and per capita, annual, 1970–2010, *UNCTADSTAT*. http://unctadstat.unctad.org/TableViewer/tableView.aspx?ReportId=109, Accessed on February 6, 2012.
Vale Columbia Center on Sustainable International Investment and World Association of Investment Promotion Agencies. (2010). *Investment Promotion Agencies and Sustainable FDI: Moving Toward the Fourth Generation of Investment Promotion*. New York, NY: VCC-WAIPA.
Wisniewska, I., Dubas, A., and Rogova, J. (2010). *Russia in Crisis: Year One*, Warsaw: Centre for Eastern Studies.

The World Bank. (2012). *World Development Indicators*, March, New York, NY: The World Bank, World Development Indicators.

Xue, Q. and Han, B. (2010). The role of government policies in promoting outward foreign direct investment from emerging markets: China's experience, in K.P. Sauvant, G. McAllister, and W.A. Maschek (Eds) *Foreign Direct Investments from Emerging Markets: The Challenges Ahead*, New York, NY: Palgrave Macmillan: 305–324.

3

Outward FDI from the BRICs: Trends and Patterns of Acquisitions in Advanced Countries

Fabio Bertoni, Stefano Elia, and Larissa Rabbiosi

Introduction

In the last few decades, emerging markets have been characterized by liberalization of foreign direct investment (FDI) regimes, governance reforms, deregulation, and the general adoption of market-oriented policies. This major process has posed a number of challenges for emerging firms, which have been increasingly exposed to competition from foreign firms and to the pressure of global economic integration. In this scenario, outward foreign direct investments (OFDIs) from emerging countries grew rapidly and assumed a strategic role, representing 16 per cent of global OFDI flows in 2008 and 28 per cent in 2010 (UNCTAD, 2011). OFDIs are also earning increasing attention in the International Business (IB) literature (Luo and Tung, 2007; Sauvant, 2008; Athreye and Kapur, 2009) for three reasons. Firstly, they are a recent and growing phenomenon that still has to be fully described and understood (Hoskisson *et al.*, 2000; Sauvant, 2005). Secondly, they originate from countries and firms that do not easily fit into the traditional theoretical frameworks adopted to explain OFDIs from advanced countries (Mathews, 2006; Li, 2007; Rugman, 2007; Kalotay, 2008). Thirdly, their impact on the host and home countries still needs to be fully investigated (UNCTAD, 2005b; Goldstein, 2007).

The issue that the OFDIs from emerging economies require a special internationalization theory is one of the most debated subjects in IB literature at the moment. Great effort has been spent in examining the features that emerging multinational corporations (EMNCs) share with, and the ones that distinguish them from, traditional MNCs.

In fact, EMNCs may have firm-specific ownership advantages which differ from those of traditional MNCs (Dunning and Lundan, 2007), such as the ability to leverage their linkages with those MNCs from advanced economies which previously invested in their home country (Wu and Chen, 2001; Mathews, 2006; Pananond, 2007; Petrou, 2007). Nevertheless, firm-specific ownership advantages may be grounded in country-specific resources and capabilities (Rugman, 2007; Kalotay, 2008). On the other hand, EMNCs may overcome their lack of ownership advantages by engaging in strategic asset-seeking FDIs (Dunning *et al.*, 2008). Hence, EMNCs 'may have been both pushed and pulled "out of the nest" well before their own firm-specific advantages might have propelled them into becoming transnational corporations (TNCs)' (Eden, 2008: 334).

Within OFDIs from emerging countries, acquisitions from emerging to developed economies are becoming an increasingly relevant phenomenon. Firms from emerging countries, which traditionally acted as targets rather than acquirers in cross-border acquisitions, are now becoming progressively more active in taking over firms in developed economies (UNCTAD, 2006, 2007). The significant recent rise of acquisitions from emerging markets to advanced countries is attracting a great deal of attention (as well as some concerns) from policy-makers, practitioners and academics.

It has been argued that entering more advanced economies exposes acquiring firms from emerging countries to more sophisticated markets, increasing the need to upgrade their capabilities (Guillén and García-Canal, 2009). Specifically, acquisitions are used by EMNCs 'to simultaneously overcome the liability of foreignness in the country of the partner/target and to gain access to their competitive advantages with the aim of upgrading their own resources and capabilities' (Guillén and García-Canal, 2009: 28). EMNCs use OFDIs, and in particular mergers and acquisitions (M&As), to overcome their relatively limited competence base and increase their competitiveness by fulfilling the need for a portfolio of locational assets (Sauvant, 2006; Cantwell and Barnard, 2008). Therefore, OFDIs in developed countries represent an important way for emerging market firms to expand their activities, and to acquire and develop tangible and intangible resources (Luo and Peng, 1999; Hitt *et al.*, 2005; Wright *et al.*, 2005; Thomas *et al.*, 2007).

Nevertheless, in investigating OFDIs, and specifically M&As, researchers have often considered the similarities more than the differences among EMNCs. Conversely, in determining whether firms from developing countries benefit from investing abroad, Cantwell and

Barnard (2008) highlight the important role played by the home country's locational advantages, such as resource abundance and market size. Accordingly, we might expect that different emerging markets, though usefully analyzed as a group, are in fact likely to have quite different acquisition patterns. Moreover, we argue that the nature of the benefits that acquiring firms derive from acquired companies differs not only across different countries' resource abundances and sizes, but also across different types of acquisitions. In other words, what EMNCs can learn through acquisitions in developed countries is likely to differ from the acquirer-to-target relatedness—that is, the degree of association between an acquirer and its target (Haunschild, 1994; Capron, 1999; Haleblian and Finkelstein, 1999).

Our aim is to contribute to the growing literature on OFDIs from emerging countries through an exploratory investigation of what characterizes the acquisition strategy undertaken by EMNCs firms. Specifically, in this chapter, we focus on acquisitions in advanced economies made by firms from the developing economies of Brazil, Russia, India, and China (hereafter the BRICs). Based on a dataset consisting of 417 acquisitions that were undertaken by the BRICs in Western Europe, Japan, North America, Canada, and the US) between 2000 and 2007, we provide micro-level evidence of different trends and patterns of internationalization expansion. Accordingly, the questions this chapter seeks to answer are the following: What are the characteristics of the BRICs' acquisitions in developed economies? To what extent should the BRICs be considered as a homogeneous category with respect to M&As? What are the main characteristics of acquirer and acquired firms? What strategies do EMNCs follow when acquiring companies in developed countries?

To contribute toward answering these questions, we first describe how the acquisition behaviour of BRIC EMNCs varies along different dimensions such as: Time, home and host countries, industries, and acquirer-to-target relatedness (i.e. horizontal, related, vertical, or conglomerate acquisition). Moreover, using the acquirer-to-target relatedness classification, we investigate the BRIC firms' rationales behind entering advanced country markets and we relate our findings to the various internationalization theories. We analyze acquirer and target pre-acquisition accounting information on a subsample of 115 acquisitions in which the target company is European. This allows us to compare acquirer and target firms' characteristics such as size and profitability across different dimensions of the acquirer-to-target relatedness. Empirically, we contribute by conducting a fully-fledged, micro-level study comparing acquisitions from the BRICs and highlighting differences and similarities. We expect our micro-level study to be extremely useful in disentangling the drivers and the characteristics of foreign investments of BRIC EMNCs.

In the next section, we present our sampling procedure and show the sample distribution across the key dimensions. It has been argued that EMNCs use OFDIs mainly to acquire strategic assets and proprietary technology (Luo and Tung, 2007). We address this issue in the section 'BRIC acquisitions in developed countries: trends and patterns', by elaborating on the rationale and motives of BRIC acquisitions in developed countries that build on acquirer-to-target relatedness. The section 'Rationale and motives of BRIC acquisitions in developed countries' contains a more in-depth analysis on the characteristics of acquirer and acquired firms, complemented by accounting information, on a subsample of 115 acquisitions undertaken in Western Europe. Lastly, the section 'The characteristics of BRIC acquisitions in Western Europe' provides some conclusions and suggests future lines of research.

The research setting: Data and sample

For the purposes of our analysis, we identified firms located in Brazil, the Russian Federation, India, and China that completed cross-border acquisitions in Western Europe, North America, and Japan in the eight-year period from 2000 to 2007. Target firms operate in any industry, from agriculture to construction, from manufacturing to service. We defined 'acquisition' to mean a transaction that gives the acquiring firm a majority stake—more than 50 per cent—in the target company, provided that acquiring firm previously held either no shares or a minority stockholding in the target company. The final sample consists of 417 BRIC outward acquisitions.

As main source of data, we used the Zephyr merger and acquisition (M&A) database from Bureau van Dijk Electronic Publishing. Zephyr has global coverage of M&A activity and it allows the analysis of acquisitions irrespective of the transaction size, since there is no minimum transaction value. Furthermore, transaction information is theoretically quite reliable since, according to Bureau van Dijk, all new transaction records are checked by a senior researcher before they are published and, wherever possible, all transactions are verified against a primary source. Since Zephyr ultimately gathers and classifies publicly-disclosed information (e.g. from official company statements, press releases, newspaper articles), the following considerations should be noted. Firstly, we are more likely to include large acquisitions rather than small ones, which might not receive much media attention and, secondly, we are unlikely to include acquisitions that are carried out using opaque investment vehicles, thus keeping the identity (and nationality) of the ultimate acquirer hidden. The extent to which our results can then be generalized across the whole population of BRIC acquisitions depends on how different the smaller and more secretive transactions are from the (presumed) larger and disclosed transactions in our sample. While this is an interesting research question per se, there is little that can be done to address it using existing public information and commercial databases.

The representativeness of our sample suffers from the absence of reliable and consistent statistics on cross-border acquisitions of majority stakes from the BRICs. Firstly, most available databases do focus on the more general phenomenon of OFDIs, of which majority acquisitions represent a percentage that is likely both to vary substantially from one country to another and also to change considerably over time (this is, e.g. the case of Chinese M&A, as reported in Organization for Economic Cooperation and Development (OECD), 2008). Secondly, available statistics are often flawed by the difficulty in accurately gauging investments carried out abroad, especially from developing countries. Attempts to profit from fiscal and legal cross-border arbitrage opportunities and the fear of wealth expropriation in the home country may lead to round-tripping—that is, 'the channelling by direct investors of local funds to SPEs (special purpose entities) abroad and the subsequent return of the funds to the local economy in the form of direct investment' (IMF, 2004: 70). These flows are usually recorded as both an outward and an inward FDI, and therefore distort and inflate the official statistics by creating 'spurious' FDIs. Notably, it is quite interesting that two of the most celebrated examples of round-tripping are China and Russia (see for instance UNCTAD, 2006). It should be stressed that our database does not include the aforementioned 'spurious' FDIs and therefore is, in this aspect at least, more representative of the population than most official statistics. Lastly, some datasets, which are more comparable to ours, focus on a single BRIC country and accordingly do not allow us to check if we have over- or under-representation among the BRICs. Our discussion of representativeness therefore must be primarily speculative. Nevertheless, we believe that the sample used in this work is quite large and heterogeneous, allowing us—despite the shortcomings mentioned earlier—to conduct a fairly accurate exploratory investigation of the drivers and characteristics of BRIC acquisitions in developed economies. As suggested by Cantwell and Barnard (2008), acquisition data are expected to provide a more fine-grained analysis of global competitiveness of firms than FDI data alone and, although acquisition data cannot capture all economic activities of the relevant firms, 'it is likely that such data are a reasonable proxy for the main cross-country and industry patterns of activity' (Cantwell and Barnard, 2008: 62).

BRIC acquisitions in developed countries: Trends and patterns

Table 3.1 illustrates the distribution of the sample of 417 acquisitions across time and acquirer country. Brazilian firms were responsible for 27 (6.47 per cent) of the sampled acquisitions, while 251 (60.19 per cent) were undertaken by Indian multinationals, 67 (16.07 per cent) by Chinese and 72 (17.27 per cent) by Russian firms. Since 2003, the data reveal a rapid rise of acquisitions from India and China, while Russia has only registered a similar trend since 2005. Although Brazil is one of the largest sources of OFDIs among the emerging markets, its acquisition activity in developed countries is still quite limited in comparison with the other BRICs. These results give the impression of a certain amount of country-specificity among the BRICs, some of which may be due to different government policies that support or hinder OFDIs. The Government of Brazil, for instance, does not seem to give significant attention to promoting OFDIs (Sauvant, 2005; UNCTAD, 2005a). The Russian government, on the other hand, is supportive of the internationalization strategy pursued by its EMNCs, which incidentally is often aggressive and pursued by means of acquisitions (Skolkovo, 2007). Also Indian and Chinese EMNCs count on a wide range of policies to support their investments (Sauvant, 2005; UNCTAD, 2005a; Kumar, 2007). For

Table 3.1 BRIC acquisitions by acquisition's year and acquirer's country

Year	Brazil	Russia	India	China	Total
2000	2	2	6	2	12
2001	3	3	11	3	20
2002	3	2	11	2	18
2003	3	5	25	6	39
2004	3	3	27	11	44
2005	3	13	36	12	64
2006	5	22	52	16	95
2007	5	22	83	15	125
Total	27	72	251	67	417

instance, since the early 2000s, the Chinese government has promoted a 'go global' policy in order to encourage Chinese firms to invest in foreign operations and expand their international market shares (OECD, 2008). And in India, firms have been able to invest in foreign markets without prior approval since 2003.

Other reasons, besides dissimilar OFDI policy, explain the inter-BRICs differences illustrated in Table 3.1. Brazil's position can be partially explained, if we consider that the Latin American region remains the major destination for Brazil's OFDIs, and greenfield projects are the generally preferred mode of entry (Sauvant, 2005). A similar consideration holds in the case of China: It is the seventh-largest investor among emerging markets (Sauvant, 2005), yet Chinese OFDIs are largely located in developing countries. On the other hand, Chinese OFDIs appear to be increasingly pursued via M&As. The OECD (2008) reports that the fraction of M&As out of the total of OFDI flows averaged at 16.7 per cent in the 1990s as against 66.4 per cent between 2000 and 2006. Based on our data, there is no doubt that India is most active in acquisitions in developed economies, at least in terms of number of transactions. The number of acquisitions undertaken by Indian firms in advanced countries has increased more than twelve-fold between 2000 and 2007, which implies a compound annual growth rate of 45.5 per cent. The figures for Russia, China, and Brazil are 35.0 per cent, 28.6 per cent and 12.13 per cent per year, respectively.

Table 3.2 shows that amongst developed countries, Japan is the least likely destination of BRIC outward acquisitions. On the other hand, BRIC acquisitions are fairly equally distributed among Western Europe (56.35 per cent) and North America (41.73 per cent), with the notable exception of Russian acquisitions, which are mainly directed toward Western European countries. This result is in line with previous evidence showing that the preferred host countries for Russian EMNCs are in both Western and Eastern Europe (Kalotay, 2008).

The most attractive European countries are, in descending order, Great Britain (17.03 per cent), Germany (10.07 per cent), France (6.47 per cent), and Italy (4.32 per cent). However, it is notable that this picture may differ if we consider the value of the transactions. Unfortunately, the lack of data limits our analysis in this respect.

BRIC acquisitions in advanced countries are equally distributed between manufacturing (45.56 per cent) and service industries (51.32 per cent), while only 3.12 per cent of the acquisitions occurred in primary industries, as illustrated in Table 3.3. However, some specificity exists when we consider the four BRICs separately. The sectorial

Table 3.2 BRIC acquisitions by acquirer's country and target's country

	Acquirer's Country				
Target's Country	**Brazil**	**Russia**	**India**	**China**	**Total**
Western Europe	12	60	131	32	235
Austria	0	2	2	0	4
Belgium	0	1	5	1	7
Denmark	1	1	2	1	5
Finland	0	6	2	0	8
France	2	10	10	5	27
Germany	1	6	25	10	42
UK	0	14	49	8	71
Ireland	0	2	3	0	5
Italy	2	7	8	1	18
Luxembourg	1	1	0	0	2
Netherland	0	3	8	4	15
Norway	1	0	0	1	2
Portugal	1	0	2	0	3
Spain	1	1	6	1	9
Sweden	1	2	4	0	7
Switzerland	1	4	5	0	10
Japan	1	0	3	4	8
North America	14	12	117	31	174
Canada	3	2	11	3	19
US	11	10	106	28	155
Total	27	72	251	67	417

Table 3.3 BRIC acquisitions by acquirer's country and target's industry

Industry	**Brazil (%)**		**Russia (%)**		**India (%)**		**China (%)**		**Total (%)**	
Primary	2	(7.41)	7	(9.72)	1	(0.40)	3	(4.48)	13	(3.12)
Secondary	15	(55.56)	31	(43.06)	100	(39.84)	44	(65.67)	190	(45.56)
Tertiary	10	(37.04)	34	(47.22)	150	(59.76)	20	(29.85)	214	(51.32)
Total	27	(100)	72	(100)	251	(100)	67	(100)	417	(100)

distribution of outward acquisitions from China is skewed toward secondary industries (65.67 per cent), while acquisitions from India occur more often in the services sector (59.76 per cent). Since 2003, India has reported an increase in the number of acquisitions in both secondary and tertiary industries, while acquisitions from China in tertiary industries have begun to rise only since 2005.

Table 3.4 analyzes the industry distribution of BRIC acquisitions in more detail. Following Dunning (1996) and Cantwell and Barnard

Table 3.4 BRIC acquisitions by acquirer's country and technological intensity of target's industry

	BR	(%)	CN	(%)	IN	(%)	RU	(%)	Total	(%)
Resource-based industry	2	(7.41)	3	(4.48)	1	(0.40)	7	(9.72)	13	(3.12)
General services	5	(18.52)	6	(8.96)	22	(8.76)	20	(27.78)	53	(12.71)
Knowledge-intensive services	5	(18.52)	14	(20.90)	125	(49.80)	10	(13.89)	154	(36.93)
Low research-intensive manufacturing	5	(18.52)	7	(10.45)	16	(6.37)	9	(12.50)	37	(8.87)
Medium research-intensive manufacturing	8	(29.63)	17	(25.37)	49	(19.52)	18	(25.00)	92	(22.06)
High research-intensive manufacturing	2	(7.41)	20	(29.85)	38	(15.14)	8	(11.11)	68	(16.31)
Total	27	(100.0)	67	(100.0)	251	(100.0)	72	(100.0)	417	(100.0)

(2008), the industries in the sample have been categorized in terms of technological intensity, based on the average R&D spending in each industry. Specifically, the following categories are considered: (i) resource-based firms; (ii) general service firms; (iii) knowledge-intensive service firms; (iv) low research-intensive manufacturing firms; (v) medium research-intensive manufacturing firms; (vi) high research-intensive manufacturing firms.[1]

The BRICs have made acquisitions in developed countries especially in knowledge-intensive services (36.93 per cent) and in medium research-intensive manufacturing (22.06 per cent). However, reflecting the sectorial composition of national industries, most BRIC acquisitions are confined to a few key industries. Most of the acquisitions made by Brazilian and Russian companies involve general services and medium research-intensive manufacturing firms. Although fewer in absolute terms, the frequency of Brazilian and Russian acquisitions is higher than the average frequency of BRIC acquisitions, and this is also true for resource-based industries. For instance, recently—with considerable acquisitions in the EU and the US—Russian firms have been increasing their investment activity in communication services (6.94 per cent) and in retail industries (11.11 per cent). It is interesting to note that although Brazil's OFDIs in business services have proved to be significant both in terms of value and number of transactions (Sauvant, 2005), this type of investment must generally be directed toward other developing countries. In fact, we do not observe, Brazilian acquisitions in the business service industry in developed countries during the period 2000–2007. The five Brazilian acquisitions of knowledge-intensive service firms concern the banking industry.

Indian acquisitions are mostly in knowledge-intensive services (49.80 per cent), followed by investments in medium (19.52 per cent) and high (15.14 per cent) research-intensive manufacturing firms. It can be seen that Indian investments are concentrated in chemical and allied products (13.55 per cent). Out of India's 34 acquisitions in this industry, 66 per cent are in drugs and pharmaceuticals (see the Appendix). Although investments in manufacturing industries remain relevant, service sectors are taking the lead in the internationalization process of Indian firms in developed countries, accounting for about 60 per cent of total acquisitions, if we also consider acquisitions in general services. More than 40 per cent of India's acquisitions are concentrated in business services, in particular in computer programming services, pre-packaged software, and computer integrated system design.

As clearly represented by the percentage of acquisitions in medium (25.37 per cent) and high (29.85 per cent) research-intensive manufacturing firms, China's acquisitions are prominent in manufacturing, particularly in industrial and commercial machinery and computer equipment (16.42 per cent), and also in electronic and other electrical equipment and components (11.94 per cent), with a strong presence in the white goods sector. However, acquisitions in services are catching up, and this is partly driven by Chinese firms that are increasingly active in acquiring targets in the business services sector (16.42 per cent) in order to compete for larger contracts from MNCs (Niosi and Tschang, 2009). The incidence of acquisitions in sectors such as food and kindred products, chemical and allied products, and transportation equipment is also substantial (see the Appendix).

Considering the two dimensions, market size and availability of natural resources, of each BRIC country (Tolentino, 2000; Cantwell and Barnard, 2008), our findings confirm that EMNCs from (large) resource-rich countries (i.e. Brazil and Russia) are much more active in acquiring firms in resource-based industry and low research-intensive manufacturing than are EMNCs from (large) resource-scarce countries (i.e. India and China). However, only India seems to show a clear pattern of specialization, exhibiting a concentration of acquisitions in developed countries in knowledge-intensive service firms. In general, the industrial profile of Chinese acquisitions in developed economies is more widely distributed. Interestingly, general services have been relatively more important for large and resource-rich countries, in particular for Russia (27.78 per cent). Finally, the high relative incidence of Chinese acquisitions in high research-intensive manufacturing (29.85 per cent) suggests an ongoing industrial upgrading of Chinese EMNCs.

Rationale and motives of BRIC acquisitions in developed countries

Since the seminal work of Hymer (1960), the IB literature has highlighted the importance of distinguishing between vertical and horizontal foreign direct investments in order to disentangle the economic reasons that underlie MNC activities. Transaction cost economics argues that vertical acquisitions occur when uncertainty regarding the supply and/or asset specificity is high (Buckley and Casson, 1976; Hennart, 1982). In this situation, firms will engage in backward or forward vertical expansion to reduce transaction costs and uncertainty. Conversely, firms expand horizontally to protect their firm-specific ownership advantages, such as technology, brands, and know-how (Dunning, 1992). From an industrial organization perspective, horizontal investments are typically employed by firms to increase their market power through economies of scale, while related investments are used to pursue a strategy of diversification through economies of scope, and vertical investments are implemented to increase cost efficiency through backward or forward industrial integration (Singh and Montgomery, 1987; Buckley and Ghauri, 2002; Hopkins, 2002).

Acquisitions have often been categorized in literature according to their nature—vertical vs. horizontal—by looking at the acquirer-to-target relatedness, which refers to the degree of association between an acquirer and its target. Accordingly, we argue that understanding the nature of the relationship between acquirer-to-target relatedness and BRIC acquisitions is a key step in the investigation of why EMNCs acquire firms located in developed countries and what the nature of EMNCs' learning is.

We apply a well-established measure of acquirer-to-target relatedness (see, among others, Haunschild, 1994; Capron, 1999; Haleblian and Finkelstein, 1999) to distinguish between four different types of acquisitions, namely: Horizontal, related, vertical, and conglomerate. Specifically, an acquisition in which the acquiring and the target firms have at least one 3-digit SIC code (line of business by sales) in common among those in which they operated at the time of the acquisition is classified as horizontal, while the acquisition is coded as related if the two firms have at least one 2-digit SIC code in common. According to Haunschild (1994) and Haleblian and Finkelstein (1999), those acquisitions that are not classified as horizontal or related are classified as forward vertical acquisitions when the industry of the acquiring firm sold more than 5 per cent of its output to the industry of the acquired firm, and backward vertical acquisition when the industry of the acquiring firm received more than 5 per cent of its input from the industry of the acquired firm.[2] To operationalize this measure we used the input–output tables published annually by the Bureau of Economic Analysis of the Department of Commerce for the US.[3] To exemplify this categorization, we consider some acquisitions made by Indian pharmaceutical companies (4-digit SIC code 2834, Pharmaceutical Preparations). The acquisition made by Wockhardt of Laboratoires Negma (a French pharmaceutical company) is classified as horizontal, since the target's SIC code is 2834. The acquisition of the Italian Diaspa (SIC code 2899, Chemicals and Chemical Preparations) made by Strides Arcolab is classified as related (2 digits in common). The acquisition made by Dr Reddy's of Laboratorios Litaphar, a Spain-based genetic research company, is classified as backward vertical since the industry of the acquirer (i.e. Pharmaceutical Preparations) receives more than 5 per cent of its input from the industry of the target (SIC code 8731, Services/Commercial physical and biological research). Finally, acquisitions that are not classified as horizontal, related, or vertical are classified as conglomerate.

Horizontal expansion represents the most extreme form of relatedness: Related acquisitions can be seen as a lateral expansion, which is a quick way of complementing the business portfolio. Vertical expansion is typified by one firm engaged in different activities in the value chain while, at the other extreme, conglomerate acquisitions represent an unrelated diversification strategy.

Horizontal acquisitions

As shown in Table 3.5, most of the BRICs' expansion in developed countries took place through horizontal acquisitions (58.51 per cent). Horizontal acquisitions are often the only possible way for EMNCs to quickly enter structured developed markets and compete more effectively against their global rivals (Kalotay, 2008). Within the period 2000–2007, about 63 per cent, 54 per cent, 49 per cent, and 44 per cent of (respectively) Indian, Russian, Chinese, and Brazilian acquisitions, respectively, have been classified as horizontal. Most horizontal acquisitions in developed countries occur in knowledge-intensive services (26.38 per cent), and in medium (11.27 per cent) and high

Table 3.5 Horizontal BRIC acquisitions by acquirer's country and industry as a percentage of total transactions by country[a]

	BR	CN	IN	RU	Total
Resource-based industry	–	1.49	–	6.94	1.44
General services	3.70	–	1.59	8.33	2.64
Knowledge-intensive services	7.41	14.93	36.25	9.72	26.38
Low research-intensive manufacturing	11.11	2.99	2.39	6.94	3.84
Medium research-intensive manufacturing	18.52	10.45	9.56	15.28	11.27
High research-intensive manufacturing	3.70	19.40	13.94	6.94	12.95
Total	44.44	49.25	63.75	54.17	58.51

[a]We have been able to classify only 404 observations out of 417, because for 13 observations either we have no information about the SIC code of the acquirer or the acquirer is an individual. Therefore the percentages displayed in Tables 5–8, which have been computed over the whole sample of 417 observations, include only 404 observations. By adding the 13 missing observations to the totals displayed in Tables 5–8 we obtain 100%.

(12.95 per cent) research-intensive manufacturing industries. The only country which seems to be significantly active in horizontal acquisitions in resource-based industry is Russia, for which 6.94 per cent of all acquisitions fall into this category against an overall mean of 1.44 per cent. Notably, no horizontal acquisition in resource-based industry has been conducted by Brazilian or Indian companies.

Horizontal investments are usually driven by market-seeking and scale economies motivations. For instance, the majority of the acquisitions undertaken in high research-intensive manufacturing, such as the pharmaceuticals sector, aimed at accessing new markets and strengthening cost-effective production. The recent investments made by Wockhardt in the EU are a typical example. The acquisitions gave the Indian firm 'a larger footprint in Europe spread over the UK, Ireland and Germany. European business will now exceed US$200 million, accounting for almost half of Wockhardt's total sales,' according to the company's chairman, Habil Khorakiwala (The Economic Times, 2006).

Similarly, several Indian computer programming and data processing firms (i.e. knowledge-intensive services) are experiencing the benefit of acquiring established companies in developed countries to expand their markets and client bases. In 2001, Indian firm Cyberspace's acquisition of UII, a US software company, brought with it an impressive client base, including many Fortune 500 customers, to the Indian company. Other acquisitions of firms, such as the German AD Solutions by India's leading computer skills trainer and software firm NIIT Ltd, and Alcatel SA's fraud management software unit and Azure Solutions Ltd by Subex, were carried out to gain access to European markets and significantly expand the Indian companies' client bases across key geographical locations. Similarly, Chinese firms in software industries are engaging in horizontal acquisitions to scale up faster and penetrate new markets (Niosi and Tschang, 2009). Also, Chinese firms operating in industrial and commercial machinery, consumer electronics, and household appliances are mostly driven by the desire to transform the local product into a global brand by exploiting the markets, networks, and experience gained through horizontal acquisitions of globally-advanced firms.

Horizontal acquisitions may also facilitate access to strategic resources and assets available overseas. These characteristics can be illustrated, for instance, by considering the horizontal acquisitions that have occurred in the primary metal industry (medium research-intensive manufacturing). A group of horizontal acquisitions was driven by the increasing demand for steel, aluminum, iron ore, and similar from emerging markets. The acquisitions are therefore resource-seeking projects aimed at easing the BRICs' shortage of metals and mining products. On the other hand, horizontal acquisitions are also an important step toward increasing production scale and seeking strategic assets. Regarding the latter, although the primary metal industry is a mature sector and most of the basic technologies are available off-the-shelf, some process technologies still require specific and tacit know-how.[4] Horizontal acquisitions become, therefore, a strategic means of accessing upgraded technology, and also a way to internalize skilled labor resources.

Related acquisitions

With the exception of Russia, for which only 2.78 per cent of acquisitions are classified as related, the other BRICs have made quite a number of these transactions, as shown in Table 3.6. Specifically, our findings show that about 19 per cent, 9 per cent, and 12 per cent, respectively, of Brazilian, Indian, and Chinese acquisitions have been the related type.

Related acquisitions share common features with horizontal ones as they are usually undertaken in order to pursue market-seeking projects. However, related investments are usually also an important way for an acquiring firm to extend its activities to similar and/or complementary products and/or markets. EMNCs engage in related acquisitions to simultaneously benefit from market-seeking and strategic asset-seeking projects. Through related acquisitions, investing firms augment and

Table 3.6 Related BRIC acquisitions by acquirer's country and industry as a percentage of total transactions by country

	BR	CN	IN	RU	Total
Resource-based industry	7.41	1.49	–	1.39	0.96
General services	–	2.99	–	–	0.48
Knowledge-intensive services	3.70	–	3.59	–	2.40
Low research-intensive manufacturing	3.70	2.99	1.99	1.39	2.16
Medium research-intensive manufacturing	3.70	2.99	1.59	–	1.68
High research-intensive manufacturing	–	1.49	1.99	–	1.44
Total	18.52	11.94	9.16	2.78	9.11

complement their portfolio of physical assets and human skills in order to strengthen their long-term strategic objectives (Buckley and Ghauri, 2002; Dunning and Lundan, 2007). This type of investment is more likely in low and medium research-intensive manufacturing, in particular in sectors such as chemical and allied products, metal mining and the primary metal industry.

The above-mentioned acquisition of the Italian Diaspa made by Strides Arcolab Group is a good case for illustrating the characteristics of related acquisitions. Commenting on the acquisition, Mr Arun Kumar, vice chairman and managing director of Strides Arcolab Group, said that 'the acquisition of Diaspa will give Strides immediate access to a USFDA (US Food and Drugs Administration) and EU approved facility with strong history of technology and fermentation skills. [...] We are also delighted with the strong technology and management bandwidth Diaspa brings along with this acquisition' (The Economic Times, August 6, 2007).

Vertical acquisitions

Table 3.7 shows that vertical investments count for 12.71 per cent of the total number of acquisitions. Brazil, Russia, and India report 22.22 per cent, 12.50 per cent, and 13.15 per cent, respectively, of vertical acquisitions, while the incidence is slightly less in the case of China (7.46 per cent). It is also interesting to observe the distinction between backward and forward vertical acquisitions. Almost all vertical investments from Brazil and Russia are classified as forward vertical acquisitions. At the other extreme, 80 per cent of Chinese vertical investments are backward, with only one acquisition, in the primary metal industry (i.e. medium research-intensive manufacturing), being classified as forward. The situation is more balanced in the case of India,

Table 3.7 Vertical BRIC acquisitions by acquirer's country and industry as a percentage of total transactions by country

	BR	CN	IN	RU	Total
Resource-based industry	3.70	1.49	–	4.17	1.20
General services	3.70	2.99	1.20	1.39	1.68
Knowledge-intensive services	–	–	1.99	1.39	1.44
Low research-intensive manufacturing	–	–	1.59	1.39	1.20
Medium research-intensive manufacturing	11.11	2.99	5.18	2.78	4.80
High research-intensive manufacturing	3.70	0.00	3.19	1.39	2.40
Total	22.22	7.46	13.15	12.50	12.71

Table 3.8 Backward vertical BRIC acquisitions by acquirer's country as a percentage of total vertical transactions by country

	BR	CN	IN	RU	Total
Resource-based industry	–	1.49	–	–	0.24
General services	3.70[a]	2.99	0.80[b]	1.39[a]	1.44
Knowledge-intensive services	–	–	1.59[c]	1.39[a]	1.20
Low research-intensive manufacturing	–	–	0.80[c]	–	0.48
Medium research-intensive manufacturing	3.70[a]	1.49	2.79	1.39	2.40
High research-intensive manufacturing	–	–	1.99	–	1.20
Total	7.41	5.97	7.97	4.17	6.95

[a] 1 out of 1 observation has been classified as both backward and forward vertical acquisitions.
[b] 1 out of 2 observations has been classified as both backward and forward vertical acquisitions.
[c] 2 out of 4 observations have been classified as both backward and forward vertical acquisitions.

with slightly more than 50 per cent of the vertical investments being classified as backward.[5]

Forward vertical acquisitions (Table 3.8) are likely to be driven by strategic market-seeking motives, designed to advance the global interests of the acquiring firm by securing control of distribution centers and retailers where their goods or services are sold. Through cross-border acquisitions, downstream markets are reached more effectively and EMNCs establish a physical presence in the leading markets served by their competitors (Dunning and Lundan, 2007). This has been done not only by buying local distributors and wholesalers, but also by acquiring production facilities from which direct access to local markets is gained. These types of cross-border investments are well illustrated in our dataset, such as the forward vertical acquisitions of three European producers and wholesalers of generic medicines undertaken by Indian pharmaceutical firms. This result is in line with Athreye and Godley's (2009) analysis showing that Indian pharmaceutical investments in developed countries are mainly in downstream capabilities, such as distribution networks and brand development.

Other relevant examples are the acquisitions undertaken by the Russian firm Lukoil operating in oil and gas extraction. Lukoil management commented that the main effect of the acquisitions conducted in advanced countries will be to allow the company to become a new entrant in retail and non-retail sales of refined petroleum products to end customers. A similar situation is represented by the recent expansion in developed countries of Bharat Forge, a major global supplier of automotive engine and suspension components based in Pune. Its acquisitions in developed countries contributed to furthering its customer base and technological capacity. B.N. Kalyani, Bharat Forge's chairman and managing director, described the acquisition of Federal Forge Inc., a car parts manufacturer based in Michigan, as a 'significant step towards implementing Bharat Forge's strategy of expanding our global footprint and establishing a manufacturing presence in one of our largest markets—the USA' (The Times of India, June 25, 2005).

Backward vertical investments (Table 3.9) can be used to reduce the negative effects of inadequate upstream markets. In other words, EMNCs engage in backward vertical acquisitions in developed countries to circumvent the lack of an adequate supply base at home, such as of critical raw materials, supplies and services (Li *et al.*, 2006). Accordingly,

Table 3.9 Forward vertical BRIC acquisitions by acquirer's country as a percentage of total vertical transactions by country

	BR	CN	IN	RU	Total
Resource-based industry	3.70	–	–	4.17	0.96
General services	3.70[a]	–	0.80[c]	1.39[a]	0.96
Knowledge-intensive services	–	–	1.20[d]	1.39[a]	0.96
Low research-intensive manufacturing	–	–	1.20[b]	1.39	0.96
Medium research-intensive manufacturing	11.11[b]	1.49	2.39	1.39	2.64
High research-intensive manufacturing	3.70	0.00	1.20	1.39	1.20
Total	22.22	1.49	6.77	11.11	7.67

[a] 1 out of 1 observation has been classified as both backward and forward vertical acquisitions.
[b] 1 out of 3 observations has been classified as both backward and forward vertical acquisitions.
[c] 1 out of 2 observations has been classified as both backward and forward vertical acquisitions.
[d] 2 out of 3 observations have been classified as both backward and forward vertical acquisitions.

backward acquisitions can be motivated by resource-seeking reasons but they can also be considered a short-cut to gain strategic assets. Our findings suggest a similar behavior, particularly when Indian and Chinese acquisitions are considered. Backward vertical acquisitions are quite common in the transportation equipment sector, where acquisitions of target companies operating in sectors like fabricated metal products, metal forgings, and stampings secure the supply of steel for the production of automobiles. In other cases, backward acquisitions allow investing firms not only to assure a certain quality of input products and materials, but also to strengthen their technical and managerial assets and skills, and without incurring large R&D investments to boot. Examples are the acquisitions undertaken by pharmaceutical firms that have gained firm-specific technological advantages by buying targets with highly qualified R&D departments.

Conglomerate acquisitions

Quite surprisingly, as shown in Table 3.10, 16.55 per cent of the sampled acquisitions are conglomerate, with percentages increasing to 23.61 per cent and 25.37 per cent for Russia and China, respectively. Brazilian EMNCs concentrate on the use of this type of acquisition in resource-based industry and in low research-intensive manufacturing. Chinese conglomerate acquisitions are relatively more common in general services and medium research-intensive manufacturing. Conglomerate acquisitions are generally the outcome of an unrelated diversification strategy, and therefore they are not explicitly aimed at seeking specific resources, assets, or product markets. Rather, the focus is more on how the acquired firm can enhance the overall balance of the acquiring firm's total product portfolio, and on reaping economies of scope.

Table 3.10 Conglomerate BRIC acquisitions by acquirer's country and industry as a percentage of total transactions by country

	BR	CN	IN	RU	Total
Resource-based industry	3.70	1.49	0.80	4.17	1.68
General services	–	5.97	2.39	5.56	3.36
Knowledge-intensive services	–	1.49	4.38	4.17	3.60
Low research-intensive manufacturing	7.41	1.49	–	4.17	1.44
Medium research-intensive manufacturing	–	10.45	3.59	5.56	4.80
High research-intensive manufacturing	–	4.48	1.59	–	1.68
Total	11.11	25.37	12.75	23.61	16.55

The reason for such a high number of conglomerate acquisitions from the BRICs to developed countries is that recent liberalizations and changes in the regulations covering inward and outward FDIs in emerging markets have increasingly exposed BRIC firms to stiffer global competition, trimming profit margins in their local markets. Consequently, improvements in product quality and brand awareness, the expansion of product ranges and production capacities have become the new imperative strategies to pursue. The acquisition by the Indian Wipro (operating in computer programming services) of Quantech Global Services LLC, a US engineering company, is an example of this. Mr A. L. Rao, Wipro's COO, stated that '[...] customers are increasingly looking at us to provide them complete Product Engineering services. Quantech's key strength in Mechanical Design services complements Wipro's core strength of Embedded Software and System Design capabilities and helps us strengthen our position as an Original Design Engineering (ODE) solutions provider. This acquisition strengthens our offering and enables us to be a more strategic partner to our customers' (Business Wire, May 15, 2006).

We might expect that seizing opportunities in unrelated but promising areas in high-income countries is a relatively easy route to becoming globally-established EMNCs (Luo and Tung, 2007; Duysters *et al.*, 2009). Conglomerate firms can more easily leverage privileged access to internal pools of risk capital and tangible and intangible assets. Thus, conglomerate acquisitions offer EMNCs the flexibility needed to readjust and reorganize their domestic and international operations. An example of this is the acquisition of Tacpro Inc., a manufacturer of medical devices, by Essel Propack Ltd, an Indian producer of laminated plastic plate, sheet, and profile shapes. The rationale for the transaction is, according to Mr Ashok Goel, Managing Director of Essel Propack, the fact that '[m]edical devices is a new arena and our plan is to leverage our knowledge of polymers and polymer processing in this sector' (The Economic Times, March 20, 2006). Moreover, BRIC firms can better exploit their relationships with government bodies, since high degrees of product and geographical diversification are attributes of conglomerate firms that are likely to positively affect their influence on public policies (Siegfried and Barr Sweeney, 2002).

Discussion

To sum up, the following patterns emerged from the above discussion. Backward vertical expansion offers benefits of long-term supply security, providing access to more stable suppliers and higher-quality input products and raw materials. Forward vertical acquisitions facilitate access to a ready and robust distribution network to exploit new product opportunities in the future. Advanced countries therefore have a strong locational advantage, since their firms are likely to have both strategic assets and markets. We know about EMNCs undertaking vertical acquisitions in advanced countries. These acquisitions are typically made by EMNCs operating in sectors such as the primary metal industry, chemicals and pharmaceuticals, oil, and automotive. On the one hand, the acquiring firms must possess some kind of ability to develop cost-effective processes and products that can be effectively combined with acquired strategic resources such as brand names, access to customers and updated production processes (Kumar, 2007; Kumar and Chadha, 2009). On the other hand, large firms with monopolistic advantage in their domestic markets tend to enhance their monopolistic rents through backward vertical acquisitions—seeking raw materials—and forward vertical acquisitions—securing control of distribution centers and retailers (Cuervo-Cazurra, 2007; Kalotay, 2008). We might expect that their large scales of operations and accumulated expertise are the source of their ownership advantage.

EMNCs often suffer from latecomer or newcomer deficiencies in areas such as consumer base and brand recognition (Luo and Tung, 2007). This shortage is partially alleviated through horizontal acquisitions. Accordingly, we observe EMNCs acquiring firms operating in the same product markets in order to implement a growth strategy in the area of high value-added products. This is aimed at achieving market-share gain in developed countries, acquiring scale and global footprints and achieving sustainable value enhancement. However, often technological and organizational restructuring are also required to enhance competitiveness. Therefore horizontal acquisitions may offer access to better managerial and technical skills, key R&D skills, intellectual property, and complementary products and technologies.

Similarly, related acquisitions allow investing firms to seek both market and strategic asset projects. Related acquisitions are likely to facilitate the combination of similar and/or complementary know-how of the acquiring and target firms and therefore accomplish the goal of seeking opportunity (Luo and Tung, 2007). This process should create and provide a strong platform for sustainable growth and long-term strategies to establish a global presence across various businesses. However, knowledge obtained through previous international acquisitions is a critical factor in determining the extent to which firms will pursue exploitative acquisitions, which are most often related and horizontal in nature. The higher the experience in acquisitions in developed markets an EMNC has, the better will be its ability to evaluate the strategic fit of a target company and to realize its potential after the deal, which are critical elements of success in exploitative investments (Rabbiosi *et al.*, 2012).

The analysis of conglomerate acquisitions has shown that this type of investment is quite often used among BRIC firms and in particular by Russian and Chinese firms. This result may suggest the following observations. On the one hand, following the distinction between asset-specific ownership advantages (Oa) and transaction cost-minimizing advantages[6] (Ot) such as advantages of common governance, learning experiences and organizational competence (Dunning and Lundan, 2007), the relevance of conglomerate acquisitions may indicate a greater role played by Ot advantages compared to Oa advantages, when the internationalization of firms of less-advanced countries is analyzed (Kalotay, 2008). In particular, given that Russian and Chinese firms are less technology-based but more related to the oligopolistic or monopolistic advantages previously accumulated, conglomerate acquisitions are the opportunity to export a successful 'home-business model' (BCG, 2006; Kalotay, 2008). On the other hand, conglomerate investments might be the results of overseas expansion to capture the benefit of risk diversification, often encouraged by national governments especially keen to see the development of state-owned MNCs (OECD, 2008).

Lastly, it is interesting to observe that we find significant differences between large resource-rich countries (i.e. Brazil and Russia) and large resource-scarce countries (i.e. China and India) in terms of horizontal investments, and this seems to underlie well-defined market-seeking and asset-seeking strategies that are linked to the characteristics of the respective home countries. The internationalization strategies of EMNCs, especially for the BRICs, should therefore also include considerations about not only the firm-specific but also the country-specific advantages of EMNCs (Rugman and Li, 2007; Kalotay, 2008; Rabbiosi *et al.*, 2012). Indeed, Russia and Brazil, which are resource-abundant and which have developed traditional sectors for the transformation of such resources, aim at accessing markets and acquiring assets through horizontal investments in low and medium research-intensive sectors and in general services. Nevertheless, Russia is also upgrading its industries by investing in knowledge-intensive sectors, particularly in telecommunications (Kalotay, 2008). India, which has invested massively in education in recent years, is undertaking horizontal investments to access markets and assets in high research-intensive sectors and in knowledge-intensive services. Finally, China, which is labor-abundant, is undertaking market-seeking and asset-seeking horizontal investments both in medium research-intensive sectors and in high research-intensive industries and knowledge-intensive services, meaning that it is probably upgrading its industrial apparatus and, therefore, its skills and its investments.

This argument seems to be less clear-cut when we look at related acquisitions. China and India still undertake related investments in high research-intensive manufacturing industries, with India also being active in knowledge-intensive services together with Brazil. A fair number of related investments are also undertaken in low and medium research-intensive manufacturing industries, without displaying strong differences between the BRICs, unlike with horizontal investments. The only noticeable exception is Brazil, which seems to be willing to consolidate its position in resource-based industries through related investments as well.

The characteristics of BRIC acquisitions in Western Europe

In the previous sections we presented some evidence of the geographic and industrial distribution of the BRICs' acquisitions in developed countries by means of in-depth study of the drivers of these investments on micro-level data. A deeper analysis on the characteristics and performance of the acquiring and target firms can shed further light on the patterns of acquisitions from the BRICs and on the strategies of EMNCs.

For this purpose, for the subsample of acquisitions concerning Western European target companies, we supplemented transaction information from Zephyr with balance sheet and income statement information from the Amadeus database (Bureau van Dijk Electronic Publishing) which stores financial and market data for more than nine million European firms. Where available, we selected consolidated accounts to more accurately reflect a firm's fundamentals. Our final sample consists of 115 transactions.

The distribution of this subsample across home and host countries is broadly consistent with the Western European portion of the global sample shown in Table 3.2. In fact, the two χ^2 tests do not reject, at conventional confidence levels, the hypothesis that this subsample and the Western European population of target companies from the initial sample have the same distribution across home and host countries

Table 3.11 BRIC acquisitions in Western Europe by acquirer's country and transaction type

Country	Conglomerate	Horizontal	Related	Vertical	Total
Brazil	0	2	0	2	4
Russia	7	11	1	9	28
India	6	39	10	16	71
China	5	5	1	1	12
Total	18	57	12	28	115

($\chi^2(3) = 2.26$ and $\chi^2(15) = 13.37$, respectively). Despite this, our subsample is not likely to be a random draw from the underlying population according to other dimensions. In particular, it is quite likely that, all other things being equal, it is easier for larger target firms to be in the Amadeus database than smaller ones.

Table 3.11 shows the transaction distribution across home country and type of acquisition.

Tables 3.12 and 3.13 show the means and medians of key accounting figures broken down, respectively, by acquirer's home country and type of acquisition.

The first two columns in Table 3.12 show, respectively, the mean and median of the natural logarithm of the target's total assets (in thousands of Euro) as reported in the firm's balance sheet in the year prior to the acquisition. A significant difference across the BRICs is found in the means, and a close-to-significant difference is found in the medians. In particular, firms acquired by Brazilian and Chinese corporations are substantially larger than those acquired by Indian or Russian companies. In terms of total assets, the target firms of Brazilian and Chinese acquirers have a log(size) of around 11.2 against an average log(size) of around 10.0. This 1.2 difference in log(size) translates to a 1:2.4 proportional difference, meaning that the target firms of Brazilian and Chinese companies are larger than the average target by a factor of 2.4 (or, if we normalize the average target size to 1, their average size is 3.4).[7] The relatively fewer transactions carried out by Brazil and China are, therefore, on average much larger. This might be an indication of higher investment barriers faced by Brazilian and Chinese acquirers toward Western Europe, possibly deriving from relatively higher cultural or geographical distances. Incidentally, Table 3.2 shows that both countries appear to be more active in other developed countries (e.g. the US) rather than in Western Europe. In other words, the investment threshold for Chinese and Brazilian firms acquiring European firms may be

Table 3.12 Selected accounting indicators for acquirer and target firms for BRIC acquisitions in Western Europe by home country

Country	Log Assets Target		Log Assets Acquirer		Solvency Ratio Target		Current Ratio Target		Profitability Target
	Mean	Median	Mean	Median	Mean	Median	Mean	Median	Mean
Brazil	11.219	11.219	14.125	15.318	37.048	37.048	1.107	1.107	0.500
Russia	10.334	10.590	12.720	12.234	25.542	29.109	2.538	1.148	0.591
India	9.600	9.889	11.975	12.079	28.188	31.387	1.626	1.215	0.617
China	11.222	11.342	12.812	12.825	2.448	9.500	1.667	1.353	0.143
Total	9.994	9.943	12.308	12.212	25.778	27.198	1.874	1.217	0.564
Ho:	**Mean const.**	**Median const.**	**Mean const.**	**Median const.**	**Mean const.**	**Median const.**	**Mean const.**	**Median const.**	**Mean const.**
p-value	0.023	0.113	0.046	0.640	0.000	0.042	0.046	0.877	0.025

Table 3.13 Selected accounting indicators for acquirer and target firms for BRIC acquisitions in Western Europe by transaction type

Type	Log Assets Target		Log Assets Acquirer		Solvency Ratio Target		Current Ratio Target		Profitability Target
	Mean	**Median**	**Mean**	**Median**	**Mean**	**Median**	**Mean**	**Median**	**Mean**
Conglomerate	10.262	9.904	10.419	12.121	2.204	8.969	1.133	1.097	0.400
Horizontal	10.087	10.220	12.334	11.935	29.495	30.088	1.995	1.410	0.649
Related	9.297	9.376	11.737	12.011	24.037	25.288	1.168	0.944	0.429
Vertical	9.855	9.923	13.428	12.793	36.635	35.662	2.459	1.346	0.579
Total	9.994	9.943	12.308	12.212	25.778	27.198	1.874	1.217	0.564
Ho:	**Mean const.**	**Median const.**	**Mean const.**	**Median const.**	**Mean const.**	**Median const.**	**Mean const.**	**Median const.**	**Mean const.**
p-value	0.204	0.570	0.061	0.533	0.016	0.008	0.031	0.022	0.367

higher simply because Europe is not necessarily their most natural target candidate.

The second variable we inspect is (the natural logarithm of) the acquirer's total assets (translated into thousands of Euro using the year average exchange rate, when needed) in the year of the acquisition. The information is collected directly from Zephyr for each acquirer. Considering the diversity in accounting rules between the BRICs and Western European countries and between the BRICs themselves, we should be quite cautious in relying excessively on the accuracy of these figures. Some comments are however worth making. Apart from Brazilian acquirers, which are larger by far (1:1.8) than others, the difference between the Russian, Chinese, and Indian companies in terms of size is much smaller here than the difference found when we look at the target companies. In particular, Indian and Chinese acquirers do not seem to be significantly smaller than Russian ones.

It is also interesting to compare acquirer size with target size. Again, we can translate the difference in logarithmic size in terms of proportional difference. Acquirers are, as expected, much larger than targets and the logarithmic difference in size based on averages is 2.314 (i.e. 12.308–9.994), which means acquirers are around 10 times the size of targets. However, the logarithmic difference is only 1.5 for Chinese acquirers (i.e. they are only around 5 times larger in size than their targets) and, therefore, these acquisitions appear to be much more aggressive. Lastly, we observe that the null hypothesis, in which acquirer size is equally distributed across the BRICs, is rejected when we look at the means (p-value < 0.046), while it is not rejected when we look at the medians (p-value < 0.64). This is due to the distributional characteristics of this variable and, in particular, to the large size variation which we find in Russia as a consequence of the presence of giant players like Lukoil.

Interestingly, the last three variables in Table 3.12 give us further confirmation of the fact that Chinese companies are pursuing a different, more aggressive, penetration strategy in Europe. To gauge a firm's liquidity, for each target company we compute two ratios, the solvency ratio (i.e. the ratio between operating cash-flows and long and short term liabilities) and the current ratio (i.e. the ratio between firm's current assets and liabilities). We also build in a dummy variable, which equals 1 when the target company is operating at profits and 0 otherwise. These figures are all based on balance sheet and income statement information in the year before the acquisition. The choice of these somewhat superficial, yet fundamental, accounting indicators is driven by the need to use figures that can be compared across industries without introducing severe biases.

Recent work has suggested that Chinese firms undertake OFDIs to compensate their competitive disadvantages by leveraging the assets of target firms, and to overcome institutional constraints or to augment the institutional advantage they have in terms of strong economic support from the government (Morck *et al.*, 2008; Rui and Yip, 2008). This explains why they make use of a large amount of acquisitions as an entry strategy: Specifically, Chinese acquirers are mainly large EMNCs that buy firms in advanced countries, even with financial and strategic difficulties, in order to acquire their assets and enter their markets (Rui and Yip, 2008). Table 3.12 shows that the targets of Chinese companies rank fairly low along each of the three accounting ratios. This supports the anecdotal evidence that Chinese firms often acquire ill-performing targets in order to turn them around (e.g. by moving operations to China) or simply to gain access to complementary resources such as the distribution network.

The same variables are shown in Table 3.13 broken down by type of acquisition. In terms of total assets, the largest target companies are those acquired in conglomerate (mean) or horizontal (median) transactions. The difference between means and medians suggests that mega-transactions tend to be of conglomerate type (often in the primary industry). When comparing the target's size with the acquirer's, we observe that related and vertical transactions are usually associated with significantly higher differences. However, size in horizontal transactions is more leveled.

If we compare the accounting performance of target firms along different transaction types we find some degree of regularity: Targets of horizontal and vertical transactions are on average better-performing than targets of conglomerate and related transactions, meaning that they have sounder financials (solvency and current ratios) as well as profitability. The poorest performers are the targets of conglomerate transactions, of which only 40.0 per cent have positive profits and for which the solvency ratio is slightly more than a tenth of that of other target companies. Apparently, the more acquirers and targets are linked by industrial ties (e.g. as competitors in a horizontal transaction, as client-supplier in a vertical transaction) the higher the 'quality' (in terms of market success) of the firm at which the acquirer aims. If we believe that worse-performing companies are also the 'cheapest' ones to buy, then conglomerate transactions seem to be driven by the search for inexpensive targets.

Conclusions and implications

This chapter contributes to the existing literature on EMNCs by exploring the characteristics and the motivations of BRIC acquisitions in developed economies. The BRIC countries have become important players, along with the leading foreign direct investors, among emerging markets in the past decade. Outward acquisitions from the BRICs are expected to increasingly become a global phenomenon, with a particular relevance for those investments directed toward advanced countries.

We have provided a detailed analysis on the BRICs' acquiring activities in developed countries and we have elaborated on the motives which underpin them. We have done so by considering acquisition type based on acquirer-to-target relatedness. Our analysis has shown that although pull factors, such as the desire to secure stable production inputs and materials, acquire updated technology, and gain access to skilled human capital, are general drivers of EMNC acquisitions in developed countries (Luo and Tung, 2007), the choice of the type of acquisition to undertake is expected to depend on other aspects, such as the sector in which the acquiring firm operates (e.g. oligopolistic, monopolistic, knowledge-intensive, low research-intensive) and the nationality of the acquiring firm (e.g. the Chinese follow an aggressive strategy to overcome their strong cultural distance and competitive disadvantages).

For the subsample of acquisitions undertaken in Western Europe, our study sheds some further light on the characteristics of BRIC acquisitions by analyzing pre-transaction target and acquirer accounting information. We have found some noticeable aspects which distinguish BRIC acquisitions. Overall we have discovered that both the home country of the acquirer and the relatedness between the target and the acquirer are factors that influence the target's characteristics in terms of size and performance.

Our results are exploratory and several other significant issues remain to be examined. However, they provide a first insight that acquisitions in developed countries are often an important means to access markets and acquire established brands and proprietary technology. Such acquisition activity may indicate that BRIC investments in advanced economies are in fact undertaken to compensate a number of ownership disadvantages. Rabbiosi *et al.* (2012), for instance, provide evidence that emerging market firms' international experience is, indeed, a core source of learning and that the lack of country-specific advantages drives emerging firms to undertake related acquisitions to compensate for their shortcomings.

Nevertheless, Western countries, in encouraging or preventing investments from the BRIC countries, need to promote an understanding of the effects of acquisition, due to country-specific aspects and also to factors related to the specificity of the investment. For instance, if we consider differences in the acquisition behavior between acquirers' countries, our analysis suggests that, in Europe, Chinese EMNCs have engaged in more risky investments by acquiring large and, in particular, ill-performing firms. Although these acquisitions are indicative of aggressive penetration strategies (e.g. local production rationalization, transfer of activities to the home country, etc.), it should also be recognized that they have created new opportunities for the underperforming, troubled incumbents.

Policy considerations should also take into account differences in business and non-business reasons for internationalization strategies, as often the BRICs' governments, in particular China's and Russia's, play an important role in facilitating acquisition opportunities through strong economic and financial support. The high percentage of conglomerate acquisitions undertaken by Russian and Chinese firms can be seen as a possible manifestation of this phenomenon.

When factors related to the type of acquisitions are considered, our results indicate that targets of horizontal and vertical transactions are on average better-performing at time of acquisition than targets in conglomerate and related transactions, while the largest targets are those acquired in conglomerate or horizontal transactions. Since more than 50 per cent of the sampled acquisitions undertaken in advanced economies by India, Russia, and China are horizontal, some repercussions may be observed in the host countries. As horizontal transactions are often acquisitions of rivals that lead to rationalization and increase in concentration of the industry, further investigation is needed to sustain policy-makers' decisions when systematically larger and better-performing firms are acquired, suggesting a cherry-picking phenomenon. On the other hand, vertical investments can help geographic diversification and lessen BRIC firms' dependence on their own domestic market. This trend should encourage a more long-term strategic behavior of BRIC firms, with a positive effect on their competitive advantage and ultimately providing a net benefit to both home and host countries.

However, our conclusions are still preliminary and rely on cross-sectorial data, while panel data accounting for activities and performance of the target firm after the acquisition are required to confirm our insights and, in particular, to further develop implications for policy.

Appendix: BRIC acquisitions by acquirer's country and target's industry (2-digit SIC code)

SIC Industry Classification		BR	(%)	CN	(%)	IN	(%)	RU	(%)	Total	(%)
Primary											
01	Agriculture products	0	–	0	–	1	(0.40)	0	–	1	(0.24)
10	Metal mining	2	(7.41)	0	–	0	–	3	(4.17)	5	(1.20)
13	Oil and gas extraction	0	–	3	(4.48)	0	–	4	(5.56)	7	(1.68)
Secondary											
20	Food and kindred products	2	(7.41)	5	(7.46)	2	(0.80)	5	(6.94)	14	(3.36)
22	Textile mill products	0	–	0	–	8	(3.19)	0	–	8	(1.92)
23	Apparel and other finished products made from fabrics and similar material	0	–	0	–	2	(0.80)	0	–	2	(0.48)
24	Lumber and wood products, except furniture	0	–	0	–	0	–	1	(1.39)	1	(0.24)
25	Furniture and fixtures	0	–	1	(1.49)	0	–	0	–	1	(0.24)
26	Paper and allied products	0	–	0	–	0	–	1	(1.39)	1	(0.24)
27	Printing, publishing, and allied industries	0	–	1	(1.49)	2	(0.80)	1	(1.39)	4	(0.96)
28	Chemical and allied products	2	(7.41)	6	(8.96)	34	(13.55)	2	(2.78)	44	(10.55)
29	Petroleum refining and related industries	1	(3.70)	1	(1.49)	0	–	4	(5.56)	6	(1.44)
30	Rubber and miscellaneous plastic products	0	–	2	(2.99)	4	(1.59)	2	(2.78)	8	(1.92)
31	Leather and leather products	0	–	0	–	1	(0.40)	0	–	1	(0.24)
32	Stone, clay, glass, and concrete products	3	(11.11)	0	–	1	(0.40)	1	(1.39)	5	(1.20)
33	Primary metal industries	3	(11.11)	2	(2.99)	10	(3.98)	6	(8.33)	21	(5.04)

34	Fabricated metal products, except machinery and transportation equipment	1	(3.70)	1	(1.49)	11	(4.38)	1	(1.39)	14	(3.36)
35	Industrial/commercial machinery & computer equipment	2	(7.41)	11	(16.42)	3	(1.20)	3	(4.17)	19	(4.56)
36	Electronic and other electrical equipment and components, except computer	0	–	8	(11.94)	8	(3.19)	0	–	16	(3.84)
37	Transportation equipment	1	(3.70)	5	(7.46)	11	(4.38)	3	(4.17)	20	(4.80)
38	Measuring, analyzing/controlling instruments	0	–	0	–	3	(1.20)	1	(1.39)	4	(0.96)
39	Miscellaneous manufacturing industries	0	–	1	(1.49)	0	–	0	–	1	(0.24)
Tertiary											
42	Motor freight transportation and warehousing	1	(3.70)	0	–	0	–	0	–	1	(0.24)
44	Water transportation	1	(3.70)	0	–	0	–	2	(2.78)	3	(0.72)
45	Transportation by air	1	(3.70)	1	(1.49)	0	–	0	–	2	(0.48)
47	Transportation services	0	–	0	–	3	(1.20)	0	–	3	(0.72)
48	Communications	0	–	1	(1.49)	5	(1.99.)	5	(6.94)	11	(2.64)
49	Electric, gas, and sanitary services	0	–	1	(1.49)	1	(0.40)	1	(1.39)	3	(0.72)
50	Wholesale trade & durable goods	1	(3.70)	0	–	1	(0.40)	4	(5.56)	6	(1.44)
51	Wholesale trade & nondurable goods	1	(3.70)	0	–	5	(1.99)	4	(5.56)	10	(2.40)
54	Food stores	0	–	0	–	0	–	1	(1.39)	1	(0.24)
59	Miscellaneous retail	0	–	0	–	2	(0.80)	0	–	2	(0.48)
60	Depository institutions	5	(18.52)	0	–	0	–	5	(6.94)	10	(2.40)

(Continued)

	SIC Industry Classification	BR	(%)	CN	(%)	IN	(%)	RU	(%)	Total	(%)
61	Non-depository credit institutions	0	–	0	–	0	–	1	(1.39)	1	(0.24)
62	Security/commodity brokers, dealers, exchanges, services	0	–	1	(1.49)	2	(0.80)	1	(1.39)	4	(0.96)
64	Insurance agents, brokers, and service	0	–	0	–	2	(0.80)	0	–	2	(0.48)
65	Real estate	0	–	1	(1.49)	0	–	0	–	1	(0.24)
67	Holding and other investment offices	0	–	2	(2.99)	0	–	2	(2.73)	4	(0.96)
70	Hotels, rooming houses, camps, and other lodging places	0	–	0	–	3	(1.20)	4	(5.55)	7	(1.68)
73	Business services	0	–	11	(16.42)	104	(41.43)	3	(4.17)	113	(28.30)
78	Motion pictures	0	–	0	–	3	(1.20)	0	–	3	(0.72)
79	Amusement and recreation services	0	–	0	–	0	–	1	(1.39)	1	(0.24)
82	Educational services	0	–	0	–	1	(0.40)	0	–	1	(0.24)
83	Social services	0	–	0	–	1	(0.40)	0	–	1	(0.24)
87	Engineering, accounting, research, management, and related services	0	–	2	(2.99)	17	(6.77)	0	–	19	(4.56)
	Total	27		67		251		72		417	

Notes

1. The industries included in each category are the following: (i) Resource-based firms: agriculture, forestry, fishing, mining. (ii) General service firms: provision of electricity, gas, water etc., construction, wholesale and retail trade, hotels and restaurants, transportation and storage, property rental and business activities. (iii) Knowledge-intensive service firms: financial intermediation, banking, insurance and pension funding, business services, computing, research and development. (iv) Low research-intensive manufacturing firms: food products, beverages, textiles, clothing, leather and leather-type products, wood and wood products, rubber and plastic products, furniture and recycling. (v) Medium research-intensive manufacturing firms: refined petroleum products, chemicals and chemical products, rubber and plastic products, building materials, base metals and metal products, motor vehicles and other transportation equipment. (vi) High research-intensive manufacturing firms: machinery and equipment, office, accounting and computing machinery, electrical machinery, communication equipment, medical, precision and optical instruments, pharmaceuticals.
2. When both conditions are verified, the transaction is classified as a backward vertical and forward vertical acquisition.
3. By using the US input–output tables on a sample that does not include transactions within the US only, we implicitly make the assumption that sectorial ties are not country-specific but, rather, that they reflect fundamental characteristics of the production technology. This assumption is, incidentally, quite common in empirical studies of international trade (such as Bowen *et al.*, 1987).
4. For an overview and detailed analysis of Indian and Chinese OFDIs in the steel industry, see the work of Kumar and Chadha (2009).
5. It should be observed that in 4 cases the acquisition is classified as both forward and backward.
6. Transaction cost-minimizing advantages 'arise from the ability of a firm to coordinate multiple and geographically dispersed value-added activities and capture the gains of risk diversification' (Dunning and Lundan, 2007: 100).
7. Let $s_1 = \log(S_1)$ and $s_2 = \log(S_2)$ be the two log(size) measures. It is easy to see that the proportional difference, i.e. $(S_2 - S_1)/S_1$, is simply given by $\exp(s_2 - s_1) - 1$. Only for small values of $(s_2 - s_1)$ is the difference in natural logarithms very close (asymptotically equal) to the proportional difference itself.

References

Athreye, S. and Godley, A. (2009). Internationalization and technological leapfrogging in the pharmaceutical industry, *Industrial and Corporate Change*, 18: 295–323.

Athreye, S. and Kapur, S. (2009). Introduction: The internationalization of Chinese and Indian firms – trends, motivations and strategy, *Industrial and Corporate Change*, 18: 209–221.

BCG. (2006). *The New Global Challengers. How 100 Top Companies from Rapidly Developing Economies are Changing the World.* Boston Consulting Group. www.bcg.com.

Bowen, H.P., Leamer, E.E., and Sveikauskas, L. (1987). Multicountry, multifactor tests of the factor abundance theory, *The American Economic Review*, 77: 791–809.

Buckley, P.J. and Casson, M. (1976). *The Future of Multinational Enterprise*, London: Palgrave Macmillan.

Buckley, P.J. and Ghauri, P.N. (2002). *International Mergers and Acquisitions: A Reader*, London: Thomson Learning.

Cantwell, J.A. and Barnard, H. (2008). Do firms from emerging markets have to invest abroad? Outward FDI and the competitiveness of firms, in K.P. Sauvant (Ed.) *The Rise of Transnational Corporations from Emerging Markets. Threat or Opportunity?* Cheltenham, UK; Northampton, MA: Edward Elgar: 55–85.

Capron, L. (1999). The long-term performance of horizontal acquisitions, *Strategic Management Journal*, 20: 987–1018.

Cuervo-Cazurra, A. (2007). Sequence of value-added activities in the multinationalization of developing country firms, *Journal of International Management*, 13: 258–277.

Dunning, J.H. (1992). *Multinational Enterprise and the Global Economy*, Wokingham: Addison-Wesley.

Dunning, J.H. (1996). The geographical sources of the competitiveness of firms: Some results of a new survey, *Transnational Corporations*, 5: 1–29.

Dunning, J.H., Kim, C., and Park, D. (2008). Old wine in new bottles: A comparison of emerging-market TNCs today and developed-country TNCs thirty years ago, in K.P. Sauvant (Ed.) *The Rise of Transnational Corporations from Emerging Markets. Threat or Opportunity?* Cheltenham, UK; Northampton, MA: Edward Elgar: 158–172.

Dunning, J.H. and Lundan, S. (2007). *Multinational Enterprises and the Global Economy*, 2nd ed, Cheltenham: Edward Elgar.

Duysters, G., Jacob, J., Lemmens, C., and Jintian, Y. (2009). Internationalization and technological catching up of emerging multinationals: A comparative case study of China's Haier group, *Industrial and Corporate Change*, 18: 325–349.

Eden, L. (2008). The rise of TNCs from emerging markets: Threat or opportunity? in K.P. Sauvant (Ed.) *The Rise of Transnational Corporations from Emerging Markets. Threat or Opportunity?* Cheltenham, UK; Northampton, MA: Edward Elgar: 365–378.

Goldstein, A. (2007). *Multinational Companies from Emerging Economies. Composition, Conceptualization and Direction in the Global Economy*, New York, NY: Palgrave Macmillan.

Guillén, M.F. and García-Canal, E. (2009). The American model of the multinational firm and the 'new' multinationals from emerging economies, *Academy of Management Perspectives*, 23: 23–35.

Haleblian, J. and Finkelstein, S. (1999). The Influence of organizational acquisition experience on acquisition performance: A behavioral learning perspective, *Administrative Science Quarterly*, 44: 29–56.

Haunschild, P.R. (1994). How much is that company worth? Interorganization relationships, uncertainty and acquisition premiums, *Administrative Science Quarterly*, 39: 391–411.

Hennart, J.-F. (1982). *A Theory of Multinational Enterprise*, Ann Arbor: University of Michigan Press.

Hitt, M.A., Li, H., and Worthington, W.J. (2005). Emerging markets as learning laboratories: Learning behaviors of local firms and foreign entrants in different institutional contexts, *Management and Organization Review*, 1: 353–380.

Hopkins, H.D. (2002). Cross-border mergers and acquisitions: Global and regional perspectives, in P.J. Buckley and P.N. Ghauri (Eds.) *International Mergers and Acquisitions*, London: Thomson Learning.

Hoskisson, R.E., Eden, L., Lau, C.M., and Wright, M. (2000). Strategy in emerging economies, *Academy of Management Journal*, 43: 249–267.

Hymer, S.H. (1960). *The International Operations of National Firms: A Study of Direct Investment*, Cambridge: MIT (published by MIT Press under same title in 1976).

IMF. (2004). *Revision of the Balance of Payments Manual (Annotated Outline)*, 5th ed, Washington, DC: IMF.

Kalotay, K. (2008). Russian transnational and international investments paradigms, *Research in International Business and Finance*, 22: 85–107.

Kumar, N. (2007). Emerging multinationals: Trends, patterns and determinants of outward investment by Indian enterprises, *Transnational Corporations*, 16: 1–26.

Kumar, N. and Chadha, A. (2009). India's outward foreign direct investments in steel industry in a Chinese comparative perspective, *Industrial and Corporate Change*, 18: 249–267.

Li, P.P. (2007). Toward an integrated theory of multinational evolution: The evidence of Chinese multinational enterprises as latecomers, *Journal of International Management*, 13: 296–318.

Li, M., Ramaswamy, K., and Péscerot Petitt, B.S. (2006). Business groups and market failures: A focus on vertical and horizontal strategies, *Asia Pacific Journal of Management*, 23: 439–452.

Luo, Y. and Peng, M.W. (1999). Learning to compete in a transition economy: Experience, environment, and performance, *Journal of International Business Studies*, 30: 269–296.

Luo, Y. and Tung, R.L. (2007). International expansion of emerging market enterprises: A springboard perspective, *Journal of International Business Studies*, 38: 481–498.

Mathews, J.A. (2006). Dragon multinationals: New players in 21th century globalization, *Asia Pacific Journal of Management*, 23: 5–27.

Morck, R., Yeung, B., and Zhao, M. (2008). Perspectives on China's outward foreign direct investment, *Journal of International Business Studies*, 39: 337–350.

Niosi, J. and Tschang, T F. (2009). The strategies of Chinese and Indian software multinationals: Implications for internationalization theory, *Industrial and Corporate Change*, 18: 269–294.

OECD. (2008). *OECD Investment Policy Reviews. China: Encouraging Responsible Business Conduct*, Paris: OECD Publishing.

Pananond, P. (2007). The changing dynamics of Thai multinationals after the Asian economic crisis, *Journal of International Management*, 13: 356–375.

Petrou, A. (2007). Multinational banks from developing versus developed countries: competing in the same arena? *Journal of International Management*, 13: 376–397.

Rabbiosi, L., Elia, S., and Bertoni, F. (2012). Acquisitions by EMNCs in developed markets: An organisational learning perspective, *Management International Review*, 52(2): 193–212.

Rugman, A.M. (2007). Multinational enterprises from emerging markets. *Paper presented at Berlin Roundtable meeting on the Role of the G8 in an Endangered Global Economic and Political Climate*, Berlin.
Rugman, A.M. and Li, J. (2007). Will China's multinationals succeed globally or regionally? *European Management Journal*, 25: 333–343.
Rui, H. and Yip, G.S. (2008). Foreign acquisitions by Chinese firms: A strategic intent perspective, *Journal of World Business*, 43: 213–226.
Sauvant, K.P. (2005). New sources of FDI: The BRICs. Outward FDI from Brazil, Russia, India and China, *Journal of World Investment and Trade*, 6: 639–709.
Sauvant, K.P. (2006). Inward and outward FDI and the BRICs, in S.C. Jain (Ed.) *Emerging Economies and the Transformation of International Business*, Cheltenham, UK; Northampton, MA: Edward Elgar: 313–409.
Sauvant, K.P. (2008). *The Rise of Transnational Corporations from Emerging Markets. Threat or Opportunity?* Cheltenham, UK; Northampton, MA: Edward Elgar.
Siegfried, J.J. and Barr Sweeney, J.M. (2002). The social and political consequences of conglomerate mergers, in P.J. Buckley and P.N. Ghauri (Eds.) *International Mergers and Acquisitions*, London: Thomson Learning: 347–368.
Singh, H. and Montgomery, C. (1987). Corporate acquisition strategies and economic performance, *Strategic Management Journal*, 8: 377–386.
Skolkovo. (2007). Russian multinationals bullish on foreign markets. *Release of the SKOLKOVO – CPII 2007 Ranking of Multinational Enterprises by the Moscow School of Management and the Columbia Program on International Investment*, Moscow and New York.
Thomas, D.E., Eden, L., Hitt, M.A., and Miller, S.R. (2007). Experience of emerging market firms: The role of cognitive bias in developed market entry and survival. *Management International Review*, 47: 845–867.
Tolentino, P.E. (2000). *Multinational Corporations: Emergence and Evolution*, London: Routledge.
UNCTAD. (2005a). Case study on outward foreign direct investment by Russian enterprises. *TD/B/COM.3/EM.26/2/Add.4.*
UNCTAD. (2005b). Internationalization of developing country enterprises through outward foreign direct investment. *TD/B/COM.3/EM.26/2/Add.4.*
UNCTAD. (2006). *World Investment Report. FDI from Developing and Transition Economies: Implications for Development?*, New York, NY; Geneva: United Nations Conference on Trade and Development.
UNCTAD. (2007). *World Investment Report 2007: Transnational Corporations, Extractive Industries and Development.* New York, NY; Geneva: United Nations, United Nations Conference on Trade and Development.
UNCTAD. (2011). *Global Investment Trends Monitor*, New York, NY; Geneva: United Nations Conference on Trade and Development.
Wright, M., Filatotchev, I., Hoskisson, R.E., and Peng, M.W. (2005). Strategy research in emerging economies: Challenging the conventional wisdom, *Journal of Management Studies*, 42: 1–33.
Wu, H.L. and Chen, C.H. (2001). An assessment of outward foreign direct investment from China's transnational economy, *Europe-Asia Studies*, 53, 1235–1254.

4

Internationalization of Central and Eastern European Countries and their Firms in the Global Crisis

Witold Wilinski

Introduction

The global crisis has had varying regional impacts. The damaging impact of this crisis has for the most part been observed in the US and the European Union (EU) whereas its impact elsewhere has been smaller, the least of which has been observed in the Asian emerging economies. The crisis was initiated in and left a significant negative impact on the private financial sector in the US; while, in the EU, it affected mainly the public financial sector.

This study concentrates on the impact of the global crisis on the emerging economies and firms from the region of Central and Eastern Europe (CEE). It addresses two issues. The first concerns the macroeconomic environment as a determinant of the internationalization of firms and the second relates to the actual approaches to internationalization as practiced by the firms during the crisis.

The study is organized as follows. The research problems are initially identified, followed by a review of the macroeconomic situation during the crisis in the new EU Member States from CEE. This is done by taking into consideration public finance conditions as well as competitive advantages that can be specifically attributed to some emerging economies from this region, namely corporate tax rates and the floating exchange rate to the Euro. Finally, an attempt is made to clarify certain aspects related to the strategies applied by firms from emerging economies.

Conceptual framework

The new EU Member States differ significantly from the old EU Member States in terms of the level of economic development, measured in per capita GDP. This disproportion can be traced to the ineffective economic system implemented in CEE after the Second World War as a consequence of the political system imposed on them. For more than 40 years these countries functioned as central planned economies which lacked private ownership and market orientation. Based on democratic principles, West European countries created a balanced economic structure and infrastructure based on advanced technologies. These countries have also gone through an intensive process of internationalization leading to global business adherence. Similar processes, based on economic transformation, were initiated in CEE at the beginning of the 1990s to make up for the economic disparities dividing the European continent.

Considering the economic specifics of Western vs. Central and Eastern Europe, the following questions need to be addressed. Firstly, do the new EU Member States from CEE have macroeconomic advantages in the present global crisis, indicating better public finance stability in comparison with the old EU Member States? Secondly, could the possible macroeconomic advantages have positive impacts on the internationalization process of the emerging economies from CEE? Thirdly, are there differences in the internationalization strategies of firms from emerging economies in general and firms from CEE emerging economies in particular?

The initial studies on internationalization of the firms from emerging economies were carried out many years ago. Early studies concerning the internationalization of emerging economy firms were those carried out by Lecraw (1977), Wells (1983), and Lall (1983). The most recent ones are investigations by Luo and Tung (2007), Buckley *et al.* (2008), Cuervo-Cazurra and Genc (2008), Sauvant (2008), Goldstein (2009), Ramamurti and Singh (2009), Narula (2010), and Marinov and Marinova (2011). The internationalization of CEE firms outside the former Soviet Bloc started after the fall of the Berlin Wall in 1989 when political systems in this part of Europe began to change. Significant studies concerning the internationalization process of the entire CEE region comprise those by Svetličič and Rojec (2003), Andreff (2003), Kalotay (2003), Boudier-Bensebaa (2008), Rugraff (2010), Panibratov (2011), and Wilinski (2011). However, there are only a few studies investigating the internationalization strategies of the CEE firms. Thus, Lisitsyn *et al.* (2007) focus on strategies of Russian telecommunication firms, Malo and Norus (2009) on biotechnological firms in the Baltic countries and Poland, and Ang and Michailova (2008) analyze internationalization specifics of firms from Brazil, Russian, India, and China providing suggestions concerning internationalization strategies of Russian firms.

Wilinski (2012) analyzes specifics of the internationalization strategies of Polish firms concentrating on the impact of the current global crisis.

The studies dealing with the impacts of the crisis on the internationalization of firms from emerging economies include the research by Hill and Jongwanich (2009) dealing with the impact of the financial crisis on outward foreign direct investment (OFDI) from East Asia and that of Salidjanova (2011) focusing on the international expansion of Chinese firms in the period 2008–2010. Most of the studies on the impact of the global crisis focus on financial aspects of the impact. Arratibel *et al.* (2011) study the effect of nominal exchange rate volatility on real macroeconomic performance of CEE countries, Takagi and Shi (2011) estimate the impact of exchange rate movements on foreign direct investment (FDI) by using Fpanel data of Japanese FDI flows to nine dynamic Asian economies during 1987–2008, and Lee and Min (2011) study the influence of the exchange rates on OFDI strategies of Korean multinational firms. Haidar (2012) shows the mechanism of a currency crisis transmission through international trade in European Monetary Union (EMU) member countries.

Some authors focus on the impact of the crisis on the stock market. Samarakoon (2011) provides empirical evidence of the degree of interdependence and contagion between the US economy on the one hand and the emerging and the frontier markets during the US financial crisis on the other. He highlights that emerging and frontier markets have increased their importance as an asset class for investors in international portfolio diversification. Regarding European emerging economies, he analyzes the US crisis impact on the stock markets in Hungary, the Czech Republic, Poland, and Russia. In his study, European frontier markets are Bosnia and Herzegovina, Bulgaria, Croatia, Estonia, Latvia, Lithuania, Montenegro, Romania, Serbia, Slovakia, Slovenia, and the Ukraine.

Main economic indicators of CEE countries in the global crisis

There is no doubt that the crisis in the US was a specific catalyst, which highlighted the risks existing in the Eurozone, previously unnoticed or ignored. In 2011, the crisis had an impact on most of the Eurozone countries as well as on other EU Member States, mainly through:

- a sudden and sharp decrease of confidence in financial markets across the EU;
- the resulting cost of debt service in the EU;

- the more difficult access to financing firms via issuing new shares on the stock exchanges;
- instability of exchange rates in the non-Eurozone countries;
- at the same time, instability of Euro exchange rate compared to main world currencies;
- slowdown or decrease in the rate of growth of domestic demand in the EU as a result of uncertainty concerning the future economic situation in the EU.

It can be suggested that the long-term financing of budget deficits of some Eurozone countries by world financial institutions was one of the key causes of the crisis in the Eurozone. The credit institutions had initially assumed that the countries where they financed public debt would be able to repay it on a timely basis, despite the fact that the levels of their debt exceeded for certain periods of time the convergence conditions adopted in the Eurozone.[1] In 2010, the Eurozone government gross debt amounted to 85.3 per cent of the Eurozone gross domestic product. Five Eurozone countries, namely Ireland, Portugal, Belgium, Italy, and Greece exceeded this debt ceiling (see Figure 4.1). In 2011, the negative image of the countries with the highest debt in the

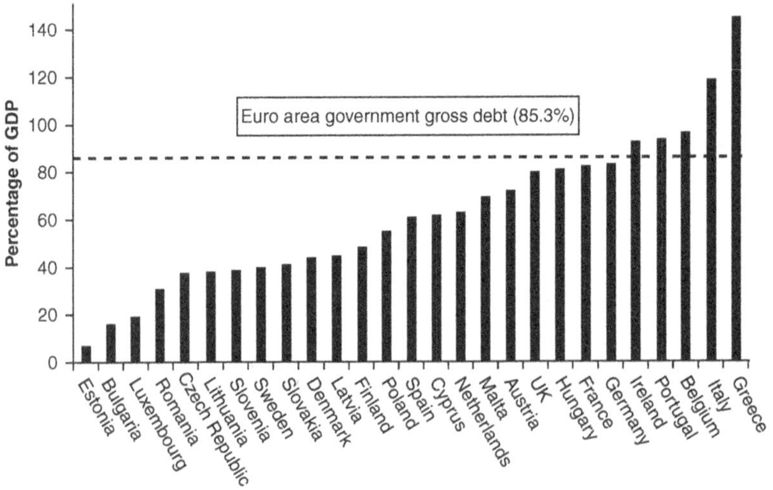

Figure 4.1 Government gross debts in EU countries, 2010, as a percentage of GDP
Source: Author using data on Eurostat data.

Eurozone worsened, causing a situation in which issuing government bonds involved increased costs of their service. Ultimately, the above resulted in the situation where the debt service costs (with the necessity to increase simultaneously the profitability of government bonds) was so high that proper debt service in the Eurozone countries with the highest debt was under threat.

Consequently, two main issues arise. Firstly, what caused the excessive debt levels in the Eurozone states? Secondly, what is the debt level of the new EU Member States from the CEE region? Addressing the first question, one should have in mind the dependence between the government debt and the percentage of public expenditures in relation to GDP. The higher the budget in relation to country GDP is, the higher the risk that such budget will need to be financed through further borrowing. Without taking into account considerations of the advocates and opponents of the economic policy based on Keynesian theory, it is worth paying attention to the fact that in the case of at least five Eurozone economies the policy of financing government expenditures with public debt has not become a fly wheel of their economies, on the contrary—it has caused a situation where, even with a positive economic growth, debt servicing could became a very big burden for the budget.

Nine out of 12 EU countries in which the debt level has been lower than 60 per cent of their GDP, are CEE EU Member States. This means that due to fact that these countries accessed the EU at a later stage of its existence, they avoided excessive debt accumulation that was normally generated in the West European states by the disproportionately developed welfare system (see Figure 4.1). It should be emphasized that in some CEE countries the level of debt expressed in percentage terms in relation to their GDP has been incredibly low when compared to the situation in Western Europe. Thus in 2011, this percentage was for Estonia 6.7 per cent, for Bulgaria—16.3 per cent, and for Romania 31 per cent. These figures indicate a fundamental difference between the old and the new CEE EU Member States. The difference indicates a significantly lower degree of debt levels in the CEE countries compared to debt of the West European countries.

GDP redistribution by means of state budget should be an effective tool not only to equalize development opportunities for the population and businesses in less developed regions, but also to stimulate quick economic growth. Afonso *et al.* (2010) found out that public sector expenditure efficiency across the new EU Member States was rather diverse especially when compared to its uniformity in the group of top performing emerging economies in Asia. Their findings show that countries with lean public sectors and public expenditure ratios not above 30 per cent of their GDP tend to be most efficient. The results of their study also confirm that countries in the crisis deliver around two-thirds of the output they could deliver if they were on the efficiency frontier. To understand the nature of the dependence between the level of GDP redistribution using the state budget and the economic growth rate in certain EU Member States reference can be made to the data presented in Figure 4.2. The chart in this figure presents statistical data based on ten-year time series and relates in two dimensions. The X-axis stands for average percentage of government expenditures in relation to GDP, whereas the Y-axis represents the average GDP growth in percentages. None of the old EU Member States achieved average economic growth rate higher than 3 per cent over the ten-year period. Only the CEE countries achieved GDP growth rate higher than 3 per cent as in the cases of the following countries: Slovakia, Lithuania, Romania, Bulgaria, Latvia, Poland, Estonia, and the Czech Republic. Attention should be drawn to the fact that in this group of countries the average level of the redistribution of GDP by means of the state budget was less than 45 per cent over the ten year period.

The high economic growth rate in CEE EU countries during the ten-year period was one of the key factors that prevented a quick running

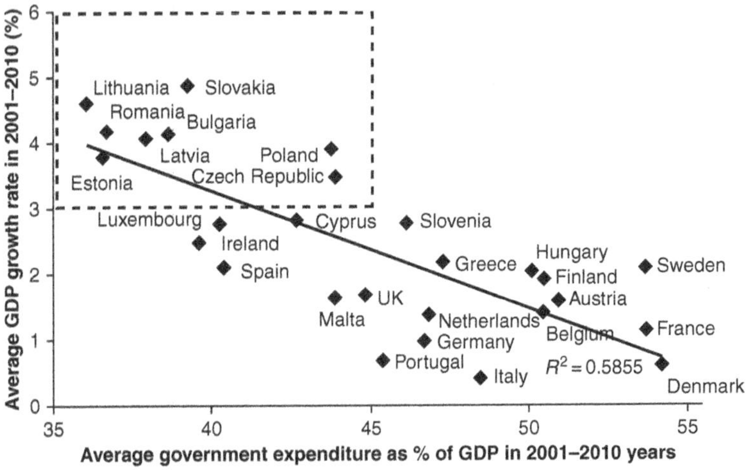

Figure 4.2 Government expenditure as a percentage of GDP and average GDP growth rate, 2001–2010, for the 27 EU countries
Source: Author calculation on Eurostat data.

of these economies into debt. If in the long run the government expenditure growth is less than the economic growth (which is possible with high economic growth rate), such a country should not increase its debt. Alternatively, in the group of the EU countries where the level of the budget redistribution was higher than 45 per cent over the last ten years, in most of the cases the economic growth rate was less than 2 per cent. In order to maintain full objectivism, it should also be noted that a high rate of economic growth of the CEE countries was also due to a relatively low level of GDP per capita in these countries. It should be pointed out that the data from all 27 EU countries clearly showed the dependence between the level of government expenditures in relation to GDP and the economic growth rate, R^2 amounted to 0.59.

To sum up the above data analysis of debt to GDP and the relation between the economic growth rate and the level of GDP redistribution through the state budget, it should be pointed out that according to both parameters more favorable values are found in the case of CEE EU economies. The present crisis showed that in the long-term, financing of the state activities with public debt may be the case. The debt crisis affected much strongly the EU Western and Southern European countries. This fact brought the whole EU in disarray. Tanzi and Schuknecht (1997) wrote that:

> Pressures for more spending are now clearly recognized as coming from vested interests rather than from the public interest. Many now realize that higher public spending is not necessarily the cure to many societal problems and does not necessarily contribute to higher well-being. On the other hand, it is better appreciated that serious macroeconomic problems often originate from the fiscal deficits and the high public debts created by high spending levels.

Although written a quarter of a century ago these words are now as valid as they were then.

Location competitiveness of old and new EU member states

At the beginning of the market transformation process, FDI inflow was of crucial importance to the CEE countries, mainly due to the then technological gap between the CEE countries and the highly developed countries, the lack of capital and the particular role that foreign multinational firms could play in the process of the overall internationalization of the economy and also due to their significant importance in the market transformation process. Thus, the attraction of foreign investors to the CEE region was of utmost importance for these countries. According to Dunning's eclectic paradigm (1981, 1993, 1996) one of the important factors that impacts the internationalization process is the location advantage. When analyzing the location advantages of the CEE countries during the economic crisis, the factors on which the governments of particular countries were unable to have quick impact (e.g. qualification level of workforce, labor cost level) were intentionally left out. The two location advantages of CEE EU economies, which have played the most important role during the crisis are the possibility of CEE countries to compete with old EU Member States by means of corporate tax rates and the possibility to mitigate the negative effects of the crisis through floating exchange rate of their currencies independent of Eurozone in the countries without currency boards.

The globalization process has increased capital and the tax payers' mobility worldwide. Therefore, the states have to compete through the quality of their institutions, including the level of applicable tax rates. In this context, it is interesting to compare the changes in corporate tax rates in the EU countries over the last 11 years. Figure 4.3 presents

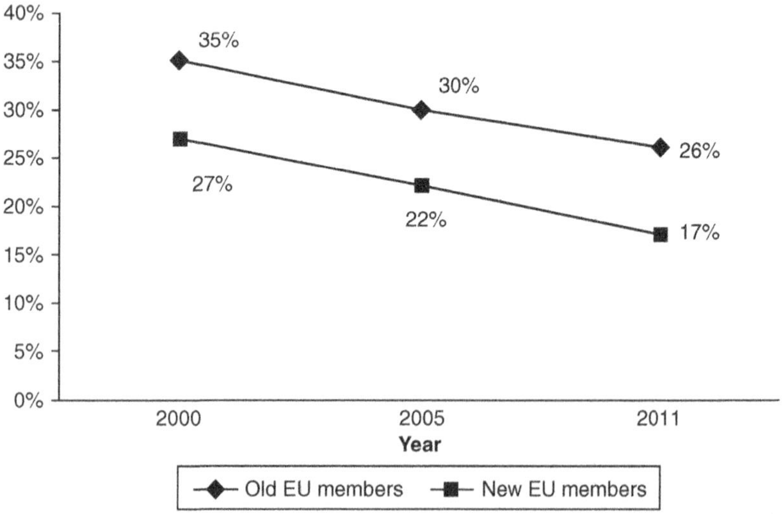

Figure 4.3 Average corporate tax rates in the old and new EU countries (%)
Source: Author, based on OECD and Eurostat data.

corporate tax rates during the years 2000–2011. The upper chart shows the levels of the rate in the old EU countries, whereas the lower chart shows the rates in the new EU Member States. The figure shows that the average tax rate in the CEE EU countries reduced during the last 11 years from 27 per cent to 17 per cent. During the same period, the tax rate in the old EU Member States reduced from 35 per cent to 26 per cent. Reduction of tax rates in the old EU countries was related not only to the worldwide trend of reducing direct taxes and increasing indirect taxes but also due to the competition coming from the CEE EU countries that were attempting to create additional competitive advantage through the reduction of their tax rates. Competitive pressures from the point of view of corporate tax could be quite easily observed by the example of the Austrian economy bordering with four CEE EU countries. Thus, the tax rates in Austria gradually decreased from 34 per cent to 25 per cent and this fact is not surprising if we consider that the present tax rates in the Czech Republic, Slovakia, and Hungary amount to 19 per cent and in Slovenia to 20 per cent. Maintaining tax rate at the previous level of 34 per cent would mean a partial loss of competition.[2] Fuest *et al.* (2011) indicate another important aspect related to the tax rate levels and their effect on operation of multinational firms from developed countries. Their studies confirm that the developing countries are more prone to tax-induced profit shifting by multinational firms, which means that corporate tax level is of particular importance in developing countries. Thus the higher the tax level, the more frequent the transfer of profit by multinational firms from emerging economies to their headquarters.

Another factor affecting the competitiveness of the CEE EU Members States has been the possibility to mitigate external effects of the crises due to the fact that most of these countries remain outside the Eurozone. During the crisis, the highest currency depreciation among the non-Eurozone EU countries took place in Poland, Romania, Hungary, and the UK and to a lesser extent in the Czech Republic and Latvia.

The depreciation of the Polish and Romanian currencies against Euro stimulated export growth through mitigation of its external effects of the crisis. However, in the UK and Hungarian economies, the weakening of their currencies only reduced the negative effects of the crisis but did not protect them against significant decreases in the value of their export. Stating the data concerning export dynamics of all EU countries during the period 2008–2010 is worth here. Among the old EU member states, only Ireland was able to achieve in 2010 the value of its export to the level before the crisis. As shown in Figure 4.4 the CEE EU

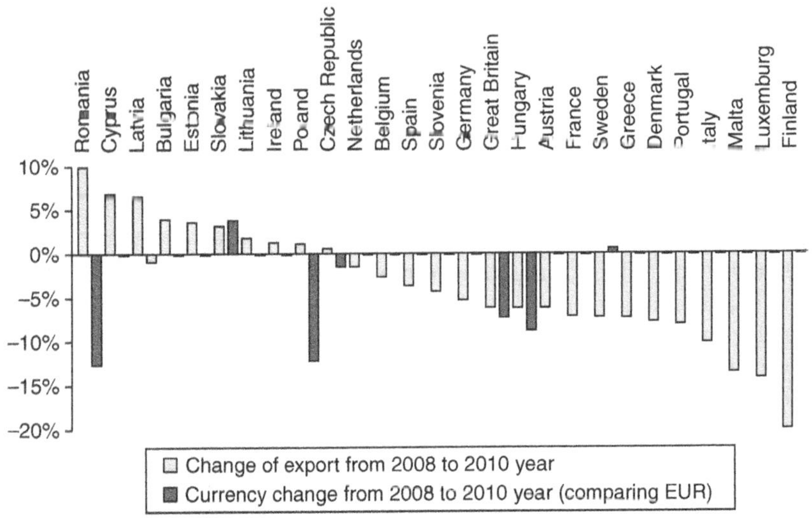

Figure 4.4 Export and currency changes in EU countries, 2008–2010 (%)
Source: Author, based on Eurostat data.

countries managed to overcome the negative effects of the crisis and in most of the cases to increase considerably the value of their export. This was the case of Slovakia, which quickly overcame the negative effects of the crisis, although it adopted the Euro in 2009. While analyzing the positive impact of the floating exchange rate on the export of the CEE EU countries one should have in mind that the floating exchange rate, especially during a global crisis, may produce negative effects on the economy.

Figure 4.5 illustrates the change in the level of debt of selected CEE countries between 2001 and 2008. The data clearly shows that the percentage of debt in foreign currencies in these countries increased noticeably after their accession to the EU. High percentage of borrowing in foreign currencies in a given country, at the moment of strong depreciation of its currency, which took place in all CEE countries that are not Eurozone members and have not adopted currency boards, could result in:

- difficulties with repayment of the government bonds issued in foreign currencies, which could lead to increase in current budget deficit;

- difficulties with repayment and rapid increase in the level of debt of the businesses, which may result not only in a decrease in their profitability for but also, quite frequently, in their actual bankruptcy;
- difficulties in the repayment of mortgage loans denominated in foreign currencies by individuals, characteristic of CEE countries that in many cases lead to real estate market collapse.

However, it should be noted that in most cases the economies of the CEE countries depend on export of industrial products, the value of which is contingent on the exchange rate of local currency vis-à-vis other currencies.

Strategies of emerging economy firms during the crisis

According to Rugman and Hoon (2011), throughout the economic crisis, multinational firms from developed economies use their networks of subsidiaries as a source of competitive advantage. Thus, they indirectly, benefit from intra-regional international diversification. Such a diversification should allow multinational firms from developed economies effective usage of arbitration among various markets. On the other hand, Rugman and Hoon (2011) point out that multinationals from

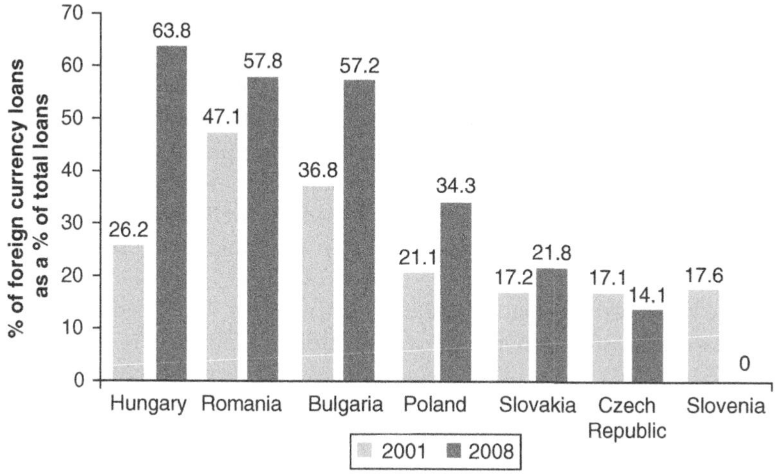

Figure 4.5 Foreign currency loans to selected CEE countries as a percentage of total loans, change between 2001 and 2008

Source: Author, based on Raiffeisen Bank research cited in Smith and Swain (2010: 19).

developed economies have more centralized organizational structures which impedes diversification in international markets. Theoretically, multinational firms from developed economies, as opposed to multinational firms from emerging economies, should not depend on government assistance due to the fact that their domestic economies are based on liberal free market principles. However, the analysis of government actions in both the US and in the developed EU countries during the period 2008–2011, shows that even in liberal free market economies the states assisted considerably their multinational firms. For instance, two well-known examples of government support in developed countries are the massive government administration support for the automotive industry in the US and the other, the colossal government support via bailing out the private banking sector in the EU.

As stated above the economic crisis did not have a similar affect on all regions worldwide. Most Asian countries have managed to stay in a good economic condition whereas the crisis hit heavily almost all highly developed countries. This is confirmed not only by the changes in GDP during the crisis, but also by the data concerning the functioning of the largest multinational firms. Table 4.1 presents the changes in the number of large firms by region between 2008[3] and 2011. The data clearly show a considerable decrease in the importance of the businesses originating from the classic Triad, namely the US, Europe, and Japan. The decrease was somewhat smaller concerning businesses originating from North America. The decrease of business originating from Russia is due to the decreased valuation of raw material firms because of the crisis. Moreover, it can be noted that the majority of firms from emerging economies remained unaffected by the crisis; in fact, during the crisis they managed to strengthen their pre-crisis position by expanding international operations. Asian firms (with the exception of those from Japan) have coped particularly well during the crisis. Their number increased from 60 to 87 in the ranking as presented in Table 4.1.

The weakened international stance of firms from developed countries and fast increasing importance of firms from Eastern Asia is confirmed in the UNCTAD report (2011). The value of OFDI from East Asian countries in the period 2007–2009, grew by more than 25 per cent, whereas the value of OFDI from developed countries dropped by 54 per cent during the same period. Hill and Jongwanich (2009) specify a number of motives for foreign investments made by Asian emerging economy firms during the crisis. The most important ones include large capital

Table 4.1 Changes in the number of global MNEs by region during the period 2008–2011

Region/Country	2008	2011	Percentage Change
Russia	13	11	−15
Developed Europe	152	129	−15
Japan	39	34	−13
North America	195	188	−4
New CEE EU countries	3	3	0
South America	17	17	0
Africa	5	6	20
Asia (excluding Japan)	60	87	45
Australia	11	16	45
The Middle East	5	10	100

Source: Author, based on FT Global 500 rank.

surpluses of Asian businesses and decrease in value of the assets of the firms in other regions, which created attractive buying opportunities for resource-flush investors. Salidjanova (2011) gives 148 examples of share purchasing by Chinese firms in the period 2008–2010, of which 53 per cent were investments in raw material firms.

OFDI from CEE countries decreased its value in the period 2007–2009 (UNCTAD, 2011). This fact signifies that the global crisis caused a slowdown in the internationalization of CEE firms. Additionally, due to the decline in GDP during that period in all CEE countries, except for Poland, the internationalizing firms could not get support from the government for their overseas activities.

Despite the negative trends it is worth giving some positive examples. For instance, Poland was the only EU country and also the only country in CEE, which did not record any decrease in GDP during the global crisis. Wilinski (2012) has studied the internationalization motives of Polish firms listed on the Warsaw Stock Exchange (WSE) as an important source for raising capital for investment abroad. The study analyzes 400 Polish firms, out of which 96 engaged in international activities. The most important motives for internationalization of the Polish firms listed on the WSE are market-seeking, followed by efficiency-seeking and strategic-asset seeking. The motive related to raw material exploration has been rare, whereas relocation to low cost production bases, secured Polish firms cost advantage. Polish firms have invested mainly in countries that are geographically close and are primarily concerned with efficiency-seeking investments.

The internationalization strategies of Polish firms during the global crisis are illustrated by the case studies of two companies listed on the WSE (see Box 4.1 and Box 4.2).

Box 4.1 The internationalization strategy of Asseco Poland

Asseco Poland (ACP) is a company operating in the information technology industry, which succeeded to consolidate a big part of the Polish IT sector during the period 2000–2009, simultaneously getting the highest share in the domestic IT services market. Consolidating the Polish market, the company started to acquire foreign firms before the global crisis, establishing Asseco DACH (operating in Germany and Austria), Asseco Central Europe (operating in Slovakia and the Czech Republic), Asseco South-Western Europe (operating in Spain). There were two reasons for these acquisitions. First, diversification of the risk of previous activities, related mainly to big government contracts. Second, the use of accumulated funds (as a result of earlier execution of the contracts on the Polish market) led to purchasing foreign assets.

During the global crisis, ACP succeeded to carry out two large projects related to the acquisitions of foreign companies. In 2009, the company carried out the issuing of new shares on the WSE, creating Asseco South Eastern Europe (ASEE), a company operating in Albania, Bosnia and Herzegovina, Bulgaria, Croatia, FYR of Macedonia, Moldova, Montenegro, Romania, Serbia, Slovenia, and Turkey—that is, in the countries with a very high growth potential, which predominately are not members of the EU. ASEE was established as a result of a series of acquisitions of several small entities. While creating ASEE, ACP built on its experience gained in the Polish market in the execution of large IT contracts, transferring operations to the Balkan market where the company competes successfully with firms from developed countries (originating from the old EU members and the US). Another project related to the internationalization of the company was the acquisition of Formula Systems from Israel in 2010 that was listed not only on Israel Stock Exchange but also on NASDAQ. In doing so the company diversified its activities based on the acquisition of the Israeli company operating in America and Asia, and also gained access to unique technologies. In other words, according to Dunning's classification of the motives for internationalization, this was an asset-seeking investment.

To summarize, the company accumulates funds based on government contracts and the issue of new shares on the WSE, successfully finances acquisitions of IT firms diversifying the risk of conducting activities in one market only and has gained access to unique information technologies.

Box 4.2 Internationalization strategy of Boryszew

Boryszew is a company listed on the WSE, operating in the electric engineering industry. During the global crisis, the company has adopted internationalization strategy that is typical for firms from East Asia, namely purchasing of a foreign company in poor financial condition. Thus, Boryszew acquired the Italian company Maflow, a subsupplier for the automotive sector. While acquiring this company, Boryszew also acquired all its subsidiaries located in France, Spain, Brazil, and China. The purpose of the acquisition was to increase the market share and gain new customers in the automotive industry, using the brand name of Maflow with the assumption that the company would be considerably restructured post acquisition.

The common features of the two companies presented in Boxes 4.1 and 4.2 are that, despite the global crisis they became two Polish global firms via foreign acquisitions. Another important aspect to note is that despite the severity of the crisis in the banking sector the two firms managed to raise finances for their internationalization projects by issuing shares on the WSE.

Conclusion

The global crisis affected all EU countries differently. The differences of the impact on the new and old EU members result from a relatively low level of GDP redistribution through the state budget in CEE countries. Such a low level of GDP redistribution through the budget makes the level of debt in CEE countries measured, as general government gross debt is less than in old EU member countries. This fact should have positive effect on the assessment of financial credibility of these countries by global financial institutions.

CEE countries possess two important location advantages. Firstly, they regularly reduce corporate tax level, thus becoming an important region for OFDI by foreign multinationals, which may impact on diversifying their activities even within the EU due to lower labor costs and lower taxes. Secondly, the CEE countries which did not adopt the Euro provide better opportunities to firms operating on their territories to mitigate the negative effects of the global crisis. Both aforementioned factors were of great importance for operation of foreign firms in the CEE region during the global crisis.

Countries from East Asia have taken the advantage provided by the global crisis to intensify the international expansion of their firms in the global marketplace. Due to financial surpluses and lower valuation of the companies in other parts of the world, East Asian countries have increased the level of internationalization of their economies, intensifying purchases of shares in firms abroad during the crisis. This means that East Asian countries and firms have internationalization strategies following identified opportunities. By comparison, the internationalization process of CEE countries has been slowed down during the crisis. There has been a relatively low level of OFDI from that region during the crisis. Undoubtedly, one of the factors that may have impact on the slowdown of the international expansion of firms from CEE countries was the low liquidity of their banking sector and lack of significant financial surpluses in the firms, enabling purchases of foreign companies. During the crisis, some Polish companies successfully financed their plans for international expansion through issuing of new shares on the stock exchange.

Notes

1. In the study, I intentionally do not deal with the question related to the Eurozone concept itself—that is, for example, the fact that the interest rates of the European Central Bank do not match the growth rate and business cycles of particular countries using this currency.
2. It is worth pointing out that the process of reducing direct taxes, in particular corporate tax takes place not only in European countries but also in other OECD countries. In case of most European countries, direct taxes are reduced at the expense of gradual increase in the value of indirect taxes such as VAT or excise tax.
3. 2008 data in the Financial Times report are based on 2007 financials of the companies.

References

Afonso, A., Schuknecht, L., and Tanzi, V. (2010). Public sector efficiency: Evidence for new EU member states and emerging markets, *Applied Economics*, 42(17): 2147–2164.

Andreff, W. (2003). The newly emerging TNCs from economies in transition: A comparison with Third World outward FDI, *Transnational Corporations*, 12(2): 73–118.

Ang, S. and Michailova, S. (2008). Institutional explanations of cross-border alliance modes: The case of emerging economies firms, *Management International Review*, 48(5): 551–576.

Arratibel, O., Furceri, D., Martin, R., and Zdzienicka, A. (2011). The effect of nominal exchange rate volatility on real macroeconomic performance in the CEE countries, *Economic Systems*, 35: 261–277.

Boudier-Bensebaa, F. (2008). FDI assisted development in the light of the investment development path paradigm: Evidence from Central and Eastern European countries, *Transnational Corporations*, 17(1): 37–67.

Buckley, P.J., Cross, A.R., Tan, H., Xin, L., and Voss, H. (2008). Historic and emergent trends in Chinese outward direct investment, *Management International Review*, 48(6): 715–747.

Cuervo-Cazurra, A. and Genc, M. (2008). Transforming disadvantages into advantages: Developing-country MNEs in the least developed countries, *Journal of International Business Studies*, 39: 957–979.

Dunning, J.H. (1981). *International Production and Multinational Enterprise*. London: Palgrave Macmillan.

Dunning, J.H. (1993). *Multinational Enterprise and the Global Economy*. Reading, MA; Wokingham, UK: Addison Wesley.

Dunning, J.H. and Narula, R. (1996). *Foreign Direct Investment and Governments*. London; New York, NY: Routledge.

Fuest, C., Hebous, Sh., and Riedel, N. (2011). International debt shifting and multinational firms in developing economies, *Economics Letters*, 113: 135–138.

Goldstein, A. (2009). *Multinational Companies from Emerging Economies: Composition, Conceptualization and Direction in the Global Economy*. New York, NY: Palgrave Macmillan.

Haidar, J.I. (2012). Currency crisis transmission through international trade, *Economic Modelling*, 29(2): 151–157.

Hill, H. and Jongwanich, J. (2009). Outward foreign direct investment and the financial crisis in developing East Asia, *Asian Development Review*, 26(2): 1–25.

Kalotay, K. (2003). Outward foreign direct investment from economies in transition in the global context, *Journal for East European Management Studies*, 8(1): 6–24.

Lall, S. (1983). *The New Multinationals: The Spread of Third World Enterprises*. Chichester, West Sussex; New York, NY: Wiley.

Lecraw, D. (1977). Direct investment by firms from less developed countries, *Oxford Economic Papers*, 29(3): 442–457.

Lee, B. and Min, B. (2011). Exchange rates and FDI strategies of multinational enterprises, *Pacific-Basin Finance Journal*, 19: 586–603.

Lisitsyn, N.E., Sutyrin, S.F., Trofimenko, O.Y., and Vorobieva, I.V. (2007). Russian telecommunication company MTS goes to the CIS, *Journal of East-West Business*, 11(3/4): 129–147.

Luo, Y. and Tung, R.L. (2007). International expansion of emerging market enterprises: A springboard perspective, *Journal of International Business Studies*, 38: 481–498.

Malo, St. and Norus, J. (2009). Growth dynamics of dedicated biotechnology firms in transition economies. Evidence from the Baltic countries and Poland, *Entrepreneurship and Regional Development*, 21(5/6): 481–502.

Marinov, M. and Marinova, S. (2011). *Internationalization of Emerging Economies and Firms*. London: Palgrave Macmillan.

Narula, R. (2010). *Much Ado About Nothing or Sirens If a Brave New World? MNE Activity from Developing Countries and its Significance for Development*. Paris: OECD Development Centre.

Panibratov, A. (2011). From national leaders to global players: Evidence from Russian MNEs in the high technology sector, in M. Marinov and S. Marinova (Eds.) *Internationalization of Emerging Economies and Firms*, London: Palgrave Macmillan: 169–190.

Ramamurti, R. and Singh, J. (2009). *Emerging Multinationals in Emerging Market*. Cambridge: Cambridge University Press.

Rugman, A.M. and Hoon, Oh Ch. (2011). Regional multinational enterprises and the international financial crisis, in E. Hutson, R.R. Sinkovics, and J. Berrill (Eds.) *Firm-Level Internationalization, Regionalism and Globalization*, London: Palgrave Macmillan: 64–80.

Rugraff, E. (2010). Strengths and weaknesses of the outward FDI paths of the Central European Countries, *Post-Communist Economies*, 22(1): 1–17.

Salidjanova, N. (2011). *Going Out: An Overview of China's Outward Foreign Direct Investment*, U.S. – China Economic and Security Review Commission, USCC Staff Research Report, March.

Samarakoon, L. (2011). Stock market interdependence, contagion, and the U.S. financial crisis: The case of emerging and frontier markets, *Journal of International Financial Markets, Institutions and Money*, 21(5): 724–742.

Sauvant, K. (2008). *The Rise of Transnational Corporations from Emerging Markets*. Northampton: Edward Elgar.

Smith, A. and Swain, A. (2010). The global economic crisis, Eastern Europe, and the former Soviet Union: Models of development and the contradictions of internationalization, *Eurasian Geography and Economics*, 51(1): 1–34.

Svetličič, M. and Rojec, M. (Ed.) (2003). *Facilitating Transition by Internationalization: Outward Direct Investment from Central European Economies in Transition*. Aldershot, UK: Ashgate.

Takagi, S. and Shi, Z. (2011). Exchange rate movements and foreign direct investment (FDI): Japanese, investment in Asia, 1987–2008, *Japan and the World Economy*, 23: 265–272.

Tanzi, V. (2005). The economic role of the state in the 21st century, *Cato Journal*, 25: 617–638.

Tanzi, V. and Schuknecht, L. (1997). Reconsidering the fiscal role of government: The international perspective, *American Economic Review*, 87(2): 164–168.

UNCTAD. (2011). *World Investment Report 2011 Non-Equity Modes of International Production and Development*. New York, NY; Geneva: United Nations.

Wells, L.T. (1983). *Third World Multinationals*. Cambridge, MA: The MIT Press.

Wilinski, W. (2011). Internationalization of companies from former communist countries – OFDI from Central, East and South Europe and CIS countries, in M. Marinov and S. Marinova (Eds.) *Internationalization of Emerging Economies and Firms*. London: Palgrave Macmillan: 40–63.

Wilinski, W. (2012). Internationalization through the Warsaw Stock Exchange – An empirical analysis, *Post-Communist Economies*, 24(1): 145–154.

5

Information and Communication Technologies in the Globalization of Small and Medium-Sized Firms during the Global Crisis: An Empirical Study in China, India, New Zealand, and Singapore

Thomas Borghoff

Literature review

Literature on the influence of information and communication technology (ICT) on the management of firms first focused on its potential to generate competitive advantages. Some authors even promoted the 'magic bullet' theory that the wonder weapon ICT even fires itself. However, this basically proved to be an illusion and empirical studies provided evidence that ICT can contribute to the generation of competitive advantage but only in the context of other organizational resources.

A similar performance-oriented perspective like that of competitive advantage has brought forward the research strand of suggesting that ICT increases the efficiency of organizations. Establishing a direct link between financial performance measures such as profitability soon turned out to be too simplistic. Multidimensional models added more complexity to the link between ICT and efficiency but failed to deliver clear causal links and empirical results. Similar to research on organizational structures in the 1960s (e.g. Woodward, 1965), the impact of ICT can be better observed or measured by establishing more direct causal links, such as improved distribution of information. The latter already points to a third perspective that evolved, linking ICT to strategy.

Majority of studies favored concepts of Porter such as the normative business strategies based on the cost and differentiation dimensions and in the international context, studies built on the global integration vs. local adaptation duality. From a processual perspective, studies focused on the influence of ICT on the strategic decision-making process, particularly from an information processing perspective.

Research on organizational aspects, meanwhile, has provided a larger variety of perspectives, ranging from general influences on organizational structures such as the flattening of hierarchies to more specific influences in functional areas such as computer-integrated manufacturing in production or e-recruitment in human resource management (HRM). General attributes such as firm size or resource endowment proved to be as essential as orientations, experiences, and preferences of management. A further perspective does not represent a distinct research stream but emerged more on the side-lines and reflects on potential downsides and even risks in the use of ICT. Main issues are security, beginning with an increasing dependence on ICT and hence the risk of the unavailability of these technologies.. Security issues also arise due to the misuse of information and even industrial espionage or 'cyber warfare'. Another risk is caused by the reliability of information accessible on the internet and by the difficulty of assessing the reliability of the sources of information. Another difficulty arises from the information overload and the resulting need to select the right information without falling prey to consider mere quantity rather than quality and reliability of information.

Small and medium sized enterprises (SMEs) have limitations such as limited resources and size. A major aspect in the study of ICT in SMEs is the degree of adoption despite these constraints. Most studies suggest that SMEs are rather followers in the adoption of ICT due to these constraints, but on the other hand, studies also suggest a 'levelling of the playing field' in international business (Kazanis, 2004: 18; Shneor, 2009: 9). The extended connectivity of SMEs allows for expanding boundaries of both activities and networks. As suggested by the born global or international entrepreneurship literature, founders and managers of SMEs have a strong impact on the adoption and use of ICT.

A lot of attention has been directed towards the potential of e-commerce as a new and distinct way of internationalization. Despite clear positive examples such as online services, most studies indicate that particularly firms in B2B businesses profit from ICT applications (Nieto and Fernández, 2006). Studies indicate a high correlation of the degree of internationalization and B2B (Luo *et al.*, 2005; Jaw and Chen,

2006). A similar effect is generated by collaborative efforts and network leverage (Samiee, 1998; Morgan-Thomas and Bridgewater, 2004; Luo *et al.*, 2005). There are different views on how ICT can impact the choice of entry modes. While several articles stress the importance of e-commerce and thus B2C, others assume that there is little influence at all (e.g. Hornby *et al.*, 2002; Jaw and Chen, 2006). At least, the literature is basically consistent assuming that ICTs increase the speed of market entry and of internationalization in general (Berry and Brock, 2004).

Another influence of ICT is supposed to be the strengthening of intra- and interorganizational ties. For example, Chen (2002) suggests that ICT promotes cooperation along the international supply chain and enhances international network building (McMahon, 2002). Berry and Brock (2004) even suggest that networks accelerate internationalization. A positive influence on the speed of internationalization is proposed by several authors (e.g. Quelch and Klein, 1996; Moen *et al.*, 2003; Jaw and Chen, 2006). Empirical studies, though with mixed results, are proving on balance simply the accumulation of knowledge about international markets rather than the actual development of international activities. This points to the difference between having knowledge of international options and of doing—the difference between global structures of meaning and action (Borghoff, 2005; Schulz and Borghoff 2008).

Methodology

This study builds on social systems theory (e.g. Luhmann, 1995; Borghoff, 2005) in order to provide a holistic perspective and to allow for the integration of more specific perspectives under this umbrella. From this perspective, globalization is an increasing level of complexity within and across social systems on a geographic and informational level and also on the level of organizations such as SMEs. Globalization thus causes an increase in environmental complexity for the individual organization. The consequence is a necessary increase in its own complexity to provide the 'requisite variety' (Ashby, 1956) in the global context (Figure 5.1).

According to Lübbe (1996: 51), 'With the increasing density of networks, the disadvantages of not being connected to them rise erratically', and according to Castells (1996: 3), 'Our societies are increasingly structured around a bipolar opposition between the Net and the Self.' As the globalization of an individual firm causes a positioning in different markets, this study aims to capture the formation of this globalization process and hence begins at the very beginning—that is,

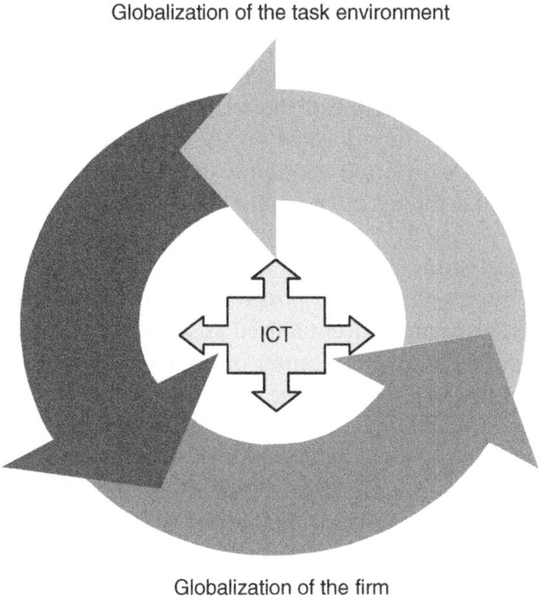

Figure 5.1 ICT in the globalization of the firm

with the foundation of the respective firms. In order to conceptualize the globalization process for the study, it is broken down into four sub-processes (Borghoff, 2005):

1. global foundation;
2. internationalization: changes in the level and dispersion of activities in different national markets;
3. global networking: development and management of internal and external network structures in the global context;
4. evolutionary dynamics: motors of change that drive the differentiation and integration of social systems on global scale. Firms develop in a co-evolutionary process with their environment.

On balance, the rapid development and increasing use of ICT have a significant influence on the development of differentiated organizational profiles in globalization. ICT reduces the communicative distance by facilitating the exchange and use of information on a global scale, enabling the development of global structures and social actors. This study serves to explore the influence of ICT on the globalization of firms.

The focus is on SMEs in order to capture the whole development right from the beginning of this process. A histographic research design covers the whole process from inception to the latest steps in globalization. Due to the gap in research and the resulting newness of the research area, the explorative study focuses on the Asia and Pacific region as it is the most vibrant region in economic development. The case studies serve to develop a theory of the influence of ICT on the globalization of SMEs.

The empirical study aims to be more holistic by going beyond the extremes of interpretation and positivism with their respective 'blind spots'. Rather, firms are conceptualized as social systems. In contrast to traditional approaches, which center on individuals as the elements of social systems, the adaptation of the concept of social evolution requires the definition of meaning (structure) and of social acts such as communication or action as the basic elements of social systems. They do not exist independently from the existence of acting individuals as the social actors. Specific individuals (e.g. the founder or top managers) may have a great influence but in sum are substitutable as the survival of organizations for decades exemplifies. As long as the social system 'finds' individuals who have an interest in contributing to its reproduction (e.g. in order to gain income, or to pursue other interests), the social system 'survives' despite changing structures, practices, products, or even the purpose. Meaning (e.g. purpose, mind-set, experience) and social acts (communications, actions) thus are the central components of the social system. The evolution of social systems thus is a cycle of social acts that are producing a feedback loop, which leads to an adaption of the meaning structure (e.g. through learning). The changes triggered by this feedback process then lead to new action. For example, this seemingly theoretical process is simply reflected in the traditional strategic planning cycle of information gathering and processing, decision-making, implementing, and learning from the results when a new planning cycle begins. Such processes occur on smaller scale every day and drive change in social systems.

The individuals constituting a social system by their social acts may be conceived as stakeholders, catalysts, and 'human resources', driving change of the social system through their communication and action. Such an ontological change has a profound effect on the boundaries of a firm. While traditionally the focus has been on individuals or organizational units, the boundaries are now defined by the (self-reproducing) network of communications and actions, which constitute the firm. Communications in general and social media in particular are playing an increasing role in the globally linked world. The consequences are far reaching. With the new possibilities provided by media such as the internet, triggering and directing communications and actions are becoming more important than just focusing on internal staff or organizational units.

Sampling

The study follows a qualitative sampling strategy (Fletcher and Plakoyiannaki, 2008). The sampling is purposive, which includes the selection of information-rich cases for an in-depth study. Purposive sampling consists of detecting cases within extreme situations as for certain characteristics or cases within a wide range of situations in order to maximize variation (Gobo, 2004). Maximum variation sampling seeks to incorporate as much diversity as possible into the research design (Fletcher and Plakoyiannaki, 2008: 6) and is the most useful strategy for purposeful sampling since it allows investigating the central themes common to a large part of participant variation (Patton, 1990: 172). Purposeful sampling and maximum variation in particular provide a more robust sampling framework (Poulis and Yamin, 2009). In this study, this is assured through the choice of firms from small and large, developed and emerging economies and the choice of firms from different industries, and with different size, age, and globalization patterns. The study is based on case studies of five firms from China, four firms from India, five firms from New Zealand, and four firms from Singapore. Thus, the study included four countries, several industries and internationalization profiles, providing a high variation while still allowing for meaningful pattern-matching (e.g. four firms per country, both service and manufacturing firms, both extensive and limited degree of internationalization). The number of four reflects the lower limit of Eisenhardt's (1989) recommendation in the number of comparable cases. The number of four cases in each country hence allows for pattern-matching both on the within-country level and across the whole sample. The study explores a large variety of firms in order to discover universal patterns and to derive dimensions that might be used to distinguish subsamples and variables. The study includes firms from China, India, New Zealand, and Singapore.

Multiple histographic case studies with a longitudinal perspective serve to explore characteristics of the four sub-processes of globalization and their facilitation by ICT. Interviews with the founders and /or top managers provide an overview on the globalization processes from (pre-)foundation to the current activity profile. The interview design was pretested and adapted with experts from practice and academia. The interviews were taped, transcribed, and analyzed on the basis of open, axial, and selective coding. The reliability of the data was increased by triangulation with other sources of information (e.g. publications or company reports). Particularly the interviewing of founders and managers who have been experiencing the whole globalization process from the start increases the reliability. Research objects are SMEs from big markets (China and India) and small countries (New Zealand, Singapore) based in Asia and Pacific with international activities. All sample firms are local SMEs from the respective countries.

Data collection and analysis

In this study, interviews were used in order to get rich information about the whole globalization process of the firm from respondents who have much retrospective knowledge. This directly points to the founders of the firms as they have the complete histographic knowledge. In cases where the founders were not available, senior managers with vast histographic knowledge and information about the whole globalization process were chosen as respondents. The founders were chosen because they are clearly the most knowledgeable sources of information about venture creation activities (Evangelista, 2005: 182).

The data were coded and analyzed by the use of a software package for qualitative data analysis (QSR NVivo 8). This was used to assist categorization and to render data analysis more systematic (Ghauri, 2004: 119). A major potential advantage of using qualitative data analyzing software is that the approach encourages analytical rigor (Seale, 2002: 656). The emerging data matched the four processual dimensions derived from literature.

Results

Global foundation

The sample firm showed a wide range of motives and prior international experiences of the founders. The scope and speed of globalization among the sample firms was influenced by four key factors:

1. the nature of the products determines the potential market. Firms catering to a niche market seek global markets while firms seeking penetration of markets target global markets later and more passively;

2. the mind-set of the founders and /or top management is decisive to the perception of global markets being a potential target;
3. strongly linked to the mind-set is the global experience of key decision-makers. The founders of the born global firms already had extensive experience and in part also contacts in global markets;
4. incentives and assistance by the government provide both motivation and a lower level of risk. This was a driver particularly for firms from the three Asian countries.

Internationalization

ICT has a strong impact on the internationalization of most sample firms. A major factor is that ICT facilitates the development of international activities very early. Particularly the internet allows for internationalization from the start as the astonishing number of 12 born globals in the sample illustrates. The internet allows for business with foreign markets through exports without the need to set up affiliates abroad in order to serve these markets. The internet allows for both an earlier build-up of international activities and also for a prolongation of the export phase for most sample firms with foreign markets. Among the sample firms, only service firms have own staff and assets in foreign markets for downstream activities. Manufacturing firms have upstream activities due to resource- and efficiency-seeking motives.

Initial internationalization was particularly triggered by important players such as customers, associations, or government agencies. In addition, important events helped initiate early internationalization. More common are key customer projects that serve as a leverage into other markets conferences, and trade fairs. In individual cases even major global events such as the Olympic Games or the Iraq War triggered early internationalization.

All sample firms use ICT to get and to diffuse information. The most common source of information about foreign markets is the internet (e.g. databases, trade portals). Important sources of 'rich' information are particularly government institutions, trade shows, business partners (particularly customers), and personal networks. All sample firms also use ICT for international learning processes. ICTs and particularly the internet are contributing substantially to individual and organizational learning. Several sample firms are already running sophisticated intranets with knowledge repositories, newsletters, databases, and training facilities and begin to connect customers to their intranet facilities.

All active globalizers in the sample generate at least 50 per cent of sales. They all regard ICT as being an important facilitator in building up international knowledge and experience.

Global network development

The influence of ICT on network dimensions is the strongest as expressed by the respondents of the sample firms. The results concerning the influence of ICT on the strength of inter- and intraorganizational links provide evidence for the high importance of ICT in developing and co-ordinating such networks. The findings also support the emerging supply chain perspective on internationalization as well as interorganizational network theories (e.g. Benson, 1977; Thorelli, 1986; Jarillo, 1988). The example of Singapore and the Johor triangle also substantiates the importance of local clusters (Dunning, 2000; Zaheer and Manrakhan, 2001) and industrial districts (Markusen, 1996; Park, 1996) as all sample firms from Singapore have been highly globalized almost 'by default'.

ICT allows all sample firms to find information about customers and makes it easier for them to communicate with each other. Information about customers such as preferences is integrated in databases. This finding shows that all firms have entered at least the first stage of internet adoption of 'information' and the second one of 'mutual communication'. All firms have also reached the third stage of using the internet for transactions though not necessarily through e-commerce. Larger sample firms already integrate their operations completely through enterprise resource planning (ERP) and customer relationship management (CRM). Customer relations are fostered by most firms through CRM and interorganizational ERP. The sample firms thus display a much higher degree of advancement on the four stages continuum in internet commerce development of: (i) presence (ii) use of portals (iii) transaction integration, and (iv) enterprise integration as developed by Jaw and Chen (2006) only a few years earlier. This fact points to a rapid pace and increase in the diffusion and adoption of ICT among SMEs.

Global evolutionary dynamics

The adoption, development, and diffusion of ICT reflects their influence on evolutionary dynamics. On the other hand, ICTs are increasingly important in providing transparency and in controlling the more complex and dynamic environment that they helped to create. Life cycles are getting shorter and ICTs help in keeping pace. Dialectical relations in business are getting more complex and dynamic. The results of this study clearly suggest that ICTs have a strong impact on the recursive interplay of firms and their environment in the process of globalization, fueling a positive feedback loop of accelerating change and increasing complexity.

Discussion

The results of this study support research indicating that ICT and particularly the internet constitute the major engine of the process of globalization (Unni and Rani 2000; Cantwell, 2002; Zhang, 2004). The literature review and the cross-case analysis suggest a distinction of three structural dimensions (environment, system, and ICT) and four processual dimensions (global foundation, internationalization, global networking, and global evolutionary dynamics). The structural dimensions are transformed through the process dimensions but are also providing the basis on which these processes can take place.

The influence of ICT on structural dimensions

The influence of ICT on the global environment

Two main variables in the environment of the sample firms are markets and industries. There is a mutual relationship of these variables with ICT. This finding confirms processual globalization literature, stating that technology is both driven by, and itself a key driver of globalization (e.g. Bradley *et al.*, 1993: 3). ICT in the sample further, has a very strong influence on cooperations and on the integration of supply chains through CRM and ERP, supporting the increasing influence of the network, knowledge, and integrated supply chain (ISC) perspectives in internationalization theory. The most important facilitating organizations in the globalization process of the sample firms are personal contacts, government agencies, and trade organizations. The results confirm former studies indicating that government institutions are more important for the globalization of firms from China, India, and Singapore than from New Zealand. The same applies to the development of ICT infrastructure. The results also confirm institutionalization theory (e.g. Westney, 1993; Kostova, 1999) as the creation of an ICT infrastructure such as that in Singapore, which leads to a deeper and more rapid diffusion of practices that may serve to develop competitive advantages. On the other hand, institutionalization theory also confirmed the opposite influences such as advantages are only temporal due to the dissemination of ICTs. In many key activities ICTs are simply a necessity now. Examples from the sample firms suggest that mechanisms described in population ecology (e.g. McKelvey, 1982; Hannan and Freeman, 1988) apply to the use of ICT as firms that did not adopt ICT in time and therefore went out of business. The same may apply to practices as the results of the life cycle perspective have shown.

The largest influence on the business model among the sample firms is between the service firms, which have had to reinvent themselves in what Rindova and Kotha (2001) call 'continuous morphing' or von Bertalanffy (1950) calls 'dynamics morphing' while the manufacturing firms in the sample are more focused on the design and integration of their supply chain without changing their basic business model very much.

All sample firms observe increasing dynamics and complexity in their environment and some even with an accelerating speed. This finding supports suggestions that dynamics are gaining momentum and have moved to the center stage (Earl and Khan, 2001; Eisenhardt, 2002; Zhu and Kraemer, 2002; Sharma and Gupta, 2004; Zhu, 2004).

The influence of ICT on the social system structure

All firms use ICT in every functional area and in all their operations, supporting the early observation of Picot and Reichwald (1994) that ICT is penetrating all functional activities in the supply chain. More than a half of the sample firms even integrate their whole supply chain through CRM or ERP—pointing to an increasing 'deepening' in the use of ICT and an increasing informational integration of operations both internally and externally. These results indicate a fast adoption rate among internationally active SMEs compared to results of a study by Loane *et al.* in 2006 that still indicated a low and shallow adoption rate of SMEs. This result confirms institutionalization theory as the diffusion of ICT is fast and has reached a considerable level in the sample firms as compared to SMEs in former studies (e.g. Moen *et al.*, 2004; Loane, 2006; Nieto and Fernández, 2006).

For most sample firms, ICT has an influence on organization by flattening structures, increasing the quality of the information flow and decision-making as well as by enhancing the co-ordination capabilities. These results confirm suggestions from existing literature (e.g. Brynjolfsson and Hitt, 2000). Particularly significant is the influence on business and management processes through ICT such as Management information system (MIS) or ERP. More specifically, those firms depending on project management report a shortening of project life cycles and a better multiproject management. On balance, the prediction of Blaine and Bower (2000: 45) that more important than ICTs in themselves is its link to other organizational resources, and ICT exerts its influence through complementary relationships with other firm assets and capabilities (Wade and Hulland, 2004: 109), which is supported by the results of the study. Other studies also support this view (e.g. Powell and Dent-Micallef, 1997; Porter, 2001; Javalgi *et al.*, 2005; Nieto and Fernández, 2006).

ICT has a very different influence on strategy, depending on the industry, mindset of top management, and business model of the sample firms. The contribution of ICT ranges from providing informational input to decision-making to being the backbone of the whole business. The results confirm research stressing the influence of management orientations (e.g. Moen, 2002; Nummela *et al.*, 2004; Mathews *et al.*, 2006) and thus of studies in international entrepreneurship (e.g. Beamish, 1999; Dana *et al.*, 1999). Strategic decision-making within the business is at the very core of the role of key decision-makers so that ICT is seen only as a facilitator in information gathering and processing. This contribution reflects implications of the information processing theory (e.g. Galbraith, 1977; Egelhoff, 1988) and also of the strategic contingency theory (e.g. Hickson *et al.*, 1971; Doz and Prahalad, 1991).

Contrary to early studies connecting ICT to strategy trying to establish a link between norm strategies (e.g. those of Porter, 1986; Bartlett and Ghoshal, 1989) and concepts to IB, the results suggest that the sample firms are not deliberately following any norm strategy. The application of norm strategies to the use and influence of ICT in SMEs thus is not visible in the given sample. The firms follow a rather customized approach catering to their needs though using external sources and to a large extent 'off-the-shelf' ICT without significant internal resources. Studies using norm strategies or concepts in the area of ICT thus appear to be restricted to large MNEs. The sample firms focus on their distinct competitive position, flexibility, reliability, and customer relations. The sample firms use information systems in a very pragmatic rather than normative way.

ICT-based communication is the backbone for all sample firms. While most firms still prefer to establish contacts and trust on a face-to-face basis, once established, communication is overwhelmingly based on ICT. To close the gap between sources of rich and more coded information, the trend goes to more collaborative forms of communication.

While some sample firms (particularly larger and older ones) still basically apply Chandler's (1962) principle of 'structure follows strategy', extended by the principle that ICT then follows structure, other firms observe a recursive interplay of these variables in which ICT may even provide the basis of business models and respective strategy or structure.

Industry or size do not have a major influence on this position among the sample firms so, the strategic mind-set of the management crystallizes as the strongest influence on relating ICT, strategy, and structure. This confirms results from previous studies (e.g. Moen, 2002; Nummela *et al.*, 2004; Mathews *et al.*, 2006).

ICT in the interplay of system and environment

The results suggest that ICT offers the possibility to begin with the development of the international establishment chain earlier, or—in other words—to form born globals. On the other hand, ICT allows exporters to remain in the first stage of the establishment chain, much longer as markets can be served through e-commerce, remote connectivity, ERP, or CRM. The study provided evidence that as predicted by most research (e.g. Berry and Brock, 2004; Jeon *et al.*, 2006; Mathews and Healy, 2008; Rantapusca and Ihanainen, 2008), the mindset of the founder and /or management has a decisive influence on the adoption and use of ICT in the globalization process in general, supporting studies from international entrepreneurship. The results of this study show that contrary to former studies indicating a more operative rather than strategic use of ICT by SMEs in their globalization process (e.g. Giustiniano and Fratocci, 2002; Moen *et al.*, 2004; Nieto and Fernández, 2006; Loane, 2006, Murphy *et al.*, 2007), most sample firms have very sophisticated ISs that perfectly match their needs, even integrating the whole ISC. This result might point to a maduration of SMEs' use of ICT in their globalization process, which is cautious but committed. This finding supports studies from institutionalization theory (e.g. Westney, 1993; Kostova, 1999; Kostova and Roth, 2002).

The sample firms are well aware of risks caused by the use of ICT. Many firms are to a large extent dependent on ICT and thus the failure of ICT is seen as a major risk in itself. The reliability and trustfulness of information and actors in the internet are seen as further obstacles. The problem of sending rich and contextual information is a source of limited exchange of such information. This may also cause misinterpretations and even changes in the communication behavior. Due to these potential risks, the selection of reliable and substantive information is a key practice at the sample firms. All sample firms also choose an active but cautious approach to the use of ICT rather than following every emerging new trend. In addition to the limited resource base of SMEs a learning process in most sample firms led to a preference for reliable and sustainable solutions.

Influence of ICT on the processual dimensions

While the structural dimensions define a firm and reflect its resource endowment, structure, and strategic position at a given point in time, the processual dimensions reflect processes of change along the life span of a firm, beginning with the foundation of a firm, processes of internationalization, network development, and evolutionary drivers.

The influence of ICT on the foundation of global firms

Founders or co-founders of all the born global firms in the sample already had extensive foreign experience and international contacts, showing the high importance of these resources for the globalization of a firm. This finding contradicts the Uppsala model of incremental learning (e.g. Johanson and Vahlne, 1977). The finding rather confirms results from research in international entrepreneurship (e.g. Beamish, 1999) suggesting that international experience and contacts are part of the founding capital (e.g. Oviatt and McDougall, 1994; Knight and Cavusgil, 2004). The finding also supports research that suggests that psychic distance in terms of cultural aspects has a strong influence on the comprehensiveness and the efficacy of internet-based exporting strategies (Bennett, 1997; Samiee, 1998) as all born global firms in the company have founders with intercultural experience. For example, Jaw and Chen (2006: 179) suggest that SMEs doing business through the internet experience accelerated learning about foreign markets and entering them (ibid: 180).

The scope and speed of globalization among the sample firms was influenced by four key factors: (i) the nature of the products, (ii) the mind-set of the founders and/or top management, (iii) the global experience of key decision-makers, and (iv) incentives and assistance by the government. The first key factor reflects particularly the differences between service and manufacturing industries and also the orientation of the strategy (global niche market vs. wider home market penetration first). The second and third factors again confirm theories of international entrepreneurship. The fourth factor is an important finding for governments and regulatory institutions, indicating that 'government intervention' can provide very positive results in helping firms adopt ICT and to globalize. The best example in this sample is Singapore (see also Ein-Dor *et al.*, 1997).

The findings of this study confirm the results of previous research indicating that the mindset of the entrepreneur and/or the management has a dominating influence on both the habit towards globalization and towards the adoption of ICT. For example, Fillis and Wagner (2005: 609) suggested that entrepreneurial owner-managers exhibit a greater likelihood of embracing e-business compared to those who are more risk-averse, which is reflected by the results of this study when comparing active and passive globalizers. The results of this study suggest a correlation but this lacks statistical generalization and might be simplifying too much without considering intervening variables such as firm characteristics or size of the home market. Despite this restriction, the results of this study confirm previous research indicating that international joint ventures (IJVs) form because internationally experienced entrepreneurs are able to link resources from multiple countries (Coviello and Munro, 1992; McDougall and Oviatt, 1991). As a link to the next section, the results of the study suggest that the sample firms become involved in international trade very early but that they do not follow the development of the establishment chain in the same pace as described in the incremental stage models. This finding supports the results of a study by Arenius *et al.* (2006) that although born globals internationalize much faster than traditional stage models would suggest, they may still expand incrementally but at a faster pace.

The influence of ICT on the internationalization of firms

ICTs seem to relieve the sample firms from the necessity to enter foreign markets with more intensive entry modes than exporting. This finding confirms previous research indicating that despite increasing speed in internationalization, exports are still the dominating form in serving international markets (e.g. Aulakh *et al.*, 2000; Child and Rodrigues, 2005; Yiu *et al.*, 2007). This finding supports the observation that firms get into international business earlier but not necessarily skipping stages in the establishment chain or in using more risk- and capital-intensive entry modes (e.g. Meissner and Gerber, 1980). These results contradict studies like that of Hornby *et al.* (2002) who claim that ICT does not relieve firms from the burden of setting up subsidiaries abroad. Similarly, Jaw and Chen (2006: 177) suggest that the internet does not have much influence on SMEs' internationalization process in general. Cases like Bigtree, Endace, Fuyi, Gaurav, Jiayu, Natural Flora, Neto, Newgrand, Sysdoc, WorldUp, and Zeus clearly show that without the internet they would at least need people 'on the ground' in local markets but through remote connectivity they can prolong the export phase indefinitely and this applies to more than half of the sample firms. Of course, this ability depends on the kind of business and other intervening variables such as age or size. However, all these sample firms probably would not have international activities to the extent that they have. It has to be noticed, though, that sample firms with resource-seeking motives or efficiency-seeking motives (Dunning, 1977) build up subsidiaries for upstream activities. On balance, the study confirms results from previous research indicating a positive correlation between the degree of internationalization and the degree of e-business (e.g. Singh and Kundu, 2002; Morgan-Thomas and Bridgewater, 2004; Moini and Tesar, 2005; Jaw and Chen, 2006).

The results of the study suggest that the internationalization process of the sample firms is faster through ICT, confirming results of previous research (e.g. Donovan and Rosson, 2001; Arenius *et al.*, 2005; Luo *et al.*, 2005; Danford, 2008; Mathews and Healy, 2008; Shneor, 2009). Even passive globalizers find international business through unsolicited order or even requests for distributorship through the internet. All sample firms stated that market entries are faster through ICT even if it does not directly influence the choice of which countries to enter and how to do so. The results of this study thus confirm research covering international new ventures (INVs) and born globals in terms of the speed of internationalization due to ICT but not in terms of skipping stages in the establishment chain as argued in the incremental stage models.

Across the whole sample, the decision to enter a market at all is facilitated by ICT but the decision itself is still a strategic one made by the top decision-makers. ICTs are perceived by all respondents to have a positive influence on the speed of market entries for all firms that actively seek international markets and apparently have a moderating effect of the 'lateral rigidity' in decision-making processes as outlined by Luostarinen (1980). The initial internationalization of the sample firms was either influenced actively by the mind-set of the founders or passively when they followed the lead from customers or other organizations. While for passive globalizers, customers or intermediaries alone may be decisive for entering foreign markets, active exporters try to get assistance from a variety of organizations. In most cases, important customer projects were key events in the internationalization of the sample firms, but in other cases trade fairs or conferences were involved too and hence they reflect the 'follow-the-customer' mode in internationalization (e.g. Yip, 1989).

Most sample firms also use a range of different sources in finding information about foreign markets. All firms use information from the internet and most sample firms visit exhibitions or trade fairs to get rich information and to establish contacts. Personal contacts are still an invaluable source of reliable and rich information for most firms. The role of ICT in this process is complementary. Information gathering by ICT or 'richer' sources occurs in iterative processes, matching information from different sources and thus providing a more reliable picture.

Across the sample, ICTs facilitate individual learning particularly through web-based media such as websites, search engines, or trade portals. All sample firms also promote organizational learning on a range from sending e-mails internally to sophisticated knowledge management systems based on intra- and/or extranets. The influence of ICT on global learning has been documented in various studies (e.g. Bennett, 1997; Luo *et al.*, 2005; Nguyen and Barrett, 2006).

ICTs have a strong impact by facilitating the development of international activities early on. Despite early export activities, the incremental establishment chain is still visible with export activities usually beginning much earlier and with the development of more intensive entry modes even later due to e-business. The study also provides evidence for discontinuous models of internationalization (e.g. Kutschker *et al.*, 1997; Macharzina and Engelhard, 1991), as particularly the internet provided several sample firms (e.g. Natural Flora) with a boost in international sales. Other firms depend completely on the Internet. These findings are in line with those of Shneor (2009: 8), who states that internet-enabled internationalization emerges as a significantly different phenomenon with respect to a number of core aspects as it allows for both rapid and gradual international expansion processes; for new methods of knowledge accumulation and development; and for new types of channel relations and governance mechanisms. It accommodates both passive international development and a strategically driven one. The study also confirms findings of research by Mathews *et al.* (2006) indicating that the availability of information, the enhanced interactive capabilities, and heightened international mind-set due to the internet are 'pivotal variable alterations in the internationalization process'. The results are also in line with those of a study by Forsgren and Hagström (2007: 299) indicating that the internationalization process of internet-related firms is fast and discontinuous. On balance, the results of the study provide arguments for the perspective of discontinuous change (e.g. Greiner, 1972; Miller and Friesen, 1984; Tushman and Romanelli, 1985; Malnight, 2000).

The study also shows that the network and resource-based perspectives on internationalization are valuable as all sample firms internationalized on this basis. This finding is also in accordance with the study of Shneor (2009) who suggests that the internet also introduces opportunities for leveraging advantages of network economics on top of economies of scale and scope. Shneor further suggests adding an e-readiness dimension to the concerns of psychic distance and demand levels in market selection decisions (ibid.). The results also confirm outcomes of a study by Mathews *et al.* (2006) that indicate the internet has enhanced more traditional networks and generates new virtual intermediaries for firms to internationalize, both extending traditional mechanisms and creating new pathways for internationalization that would not have been possible previously. In a similar vein, a study by Loane *et al.* (2004: 79, 93) indicates the crucial importance of networks and alliances in internationalization (see also Johannisson (1985) for the importance of personal networks).

The internationalization perspective outlined in the literature review, also the international supply chain perspective (e.g. Overby and Min, 2001), proves to be very valuable in the description and explanation of internationalization processes. This can be seen in the completely integrated supply chains of firms such as Damar, Fuyi, or Natural Flora. ICT such as e-business or ERP are the very basis for such a global integration of supply chains. Indeed, the strategic internet orientation profile of the manager becomes a determinant of internationalization and as noticed in the literature review, post-internet internationalization has been referred to as 'internetalization' as opposed to internationalization (Bell *et al.*, 2001; Buttriss and Wilkinson, 2003). The integrated supply chain management (ISCM) perspective probably has the most practical value and was largely sustained by the results of this study.

In terms of best practices, the sample firms had a clear view of best practices regarding the internationalization process. Particularly international experience and understanding foreign customers and markets are seen as the most important contributors to international success. All active globalizers in the sample had the same view with regard to this. ICTs are seen as important facilitators in building up international knowledge and experience. Importantly, ICT influences strategic thinking and focus particularly in the global context on dynamics and change as well as on network relations.

The influence of ICT on the global networking of firms

The influence of ICT on the strength of internal and external network relationships was particularly strong among the sample firms. This result reflects previous research indicating that ICT is an enabling technology for collaborative commerce amongst firms (e.g. Chen, 2002;

Samii and Karush, 2004) and also on internal co-ordination (e.g. Palvia, 1997; Zaheer and Manrakhan, 2001; McMahon, 2002), particularly in asynchronous co-ordination across time zones and regions (Powell and Dent-Micallef, 1997). The results thus confirm the outcomes of former studies that stress the importance of both inter- and intraorganizational relations in globalization (e.g. Bartlett and Ghoshal, 1989; Malnight, 1996; Dunning, 2000; Mathews, 2002). ICTs are providing not only co-ordination and integration of activities but also learning (Kanjas, 2000) and flexibility within network structures (Cantwell, 2002). Particularly the internet is viewed as an enabler of new collaborative forms of organization (Loane, 2006) and ICT-based network relations may even accelerate internationalization (Earl and Feeny, 1996; Berry and Brock, 2004) as the results of the study have shown. The results also suggest that the influence on the co-ordination of internal and external networks is particularly strong when units are geographically dispersed and when there is a higher ratio of international activities. Most of the sample firms have B2B relations with suppliers or customers and these are to a large extent based on ICT.

The results of the study confirm that network entry is very much a cognitive modeling process as described by Håkansson and Johanson (1993: 43) and a result of history. Entrepreneurial actors who have already established such networks can (potentially) internationalize rapidly as suggested by international entrepreneurship theory (e.g. Knight and Cavusgil, 1996; Beamish, 1999; Oviatt and McDougall, 2005), and ICT can facilitate this process depending on the mind-set of the founder as this study suggests. For example, the internet may help to accelerate the process (Jaw and Chen, 2006: 177).

The results of the study show that network advantages help firms with intensive use of ICT to access network resources and to leverage network externalities (Singh and Kundu, 2002). Network leverage was a major factor in the globalization of most sample firms. Hence, on balance, ICT seems to play a strong complementary role in network building and maintaining, facilitating network relations and structures. Network leverage may be an important driver for early internationalization and for market entry in general. This finding confirms results of a study by Lal (1996: 271) indicating that the networking capability of ICT enhances the international orientation of firms significantly. ICTs do not only facilitate the formation of relationships and networks but are particularly valuable in the ongoing reproduction and co-ordination of both internal and external networks. A central finding further indicates that ICT helps the sample firms to a great extent by adapting to changes in their network environment.

The influence of ICT on the global evolutionary dynamics of firms

The influence of ICT on the evolutionary drivers is throughout positive. This result supports the observation of increasing dynamics in the globalization of firms (e.g. Quelch and Klein, 1996, Moen *et al.*, 2003; Jaw and Chen, 2006). Independent of their business, all sample firms report a strong impact on how they design and develop their business. This finding confirms former studies indicating that particularly the internet has created completely new dynamics in the way SMEs can globalize (Mukherji, 2002: 505) and is expanding boundaries of firms and networks (Samii and Karush, 2004: 15).

Among the five evolutionary motors, strategic decision-making is perceived by the sample firms to be least affected by ICT—an unexpected finding due to the contribution of ICT in gathering, selecting, and integrating information more efficiently. These results are contrary to the position of advocates of the information processing theory such as Galbraith (1977) or Egelhoff (1988). In a similar vein, Karimi and Konsynski (2003: 100) expect that increasing number of global firms' depend on ICT mechanisms for planning, control, and co-ordination. In practice, however, strategic decision-making is the core responsibility of top decision-makers who—as respondents—would not diminish their own critical role in decision-making due to the influence of ICT. ICTs thus are supposed to have a very strong contribution to the reduction of complexity and to provide consistency in preparing but not in guiding the final decision itself. Existing literature suggests an important role of ICT in gathering information and processing as outlined in the literature review, but does not really reflect on the decision-making process as a whole, which is still based on individual reasoning (e.g. Petersen *et al.*, 2002; Mathews and Healy, 2008). A counterexample might be the financial crisis in 2008 when ICT-based systems led to a negative feedback loop in 'floor price' situations, leading almost to a collapse of the global financial system.

The sample firms perceive different influences on the life cycles of products, practices, and organizational units. Life cycles have been addressed by economic theories (e.g. Vernon, 1966), by organizational change literature (e.g. Greiner, 1972; Miller and Friesen, 1984), and by population ecology (e.g. Amburgey and Rao, 1996; Aldrich, 1999). The genuine contribution of this study is to observe not only life cycles of whole organizations or populations of organizations but also on organizational units and on practices, which proved to be particularly valuable in observing and explaining change processes.

Regarding external relations, the focus is naturally on suppliers or customers as the immediate partners in the value chain. Interestingly, while existing literature and practice usually identify an increasing strength of customers' power position due to more available information and thus more alternatives to choose from, most sample firms perceive that ICTs bring these dialectics only to a more complex level rather than changing the fundamental balance of such relations. On the other hand, some examples indicate that even whole industries might be changing their structure and power distribution due to ICT. The major example here is the construction industry in the case of Arrow that expects a complete redistribution of power structures in their industry due to ICT. Another example is the observation of Worldup that ICT already changed the whole fashion and garment industry. This finding might be interesting to be reflected on the level of Chinese and Indian export industries as a whole as both economies profit a lot from sourcing and outsourcing facilitated by ICT. This finding provides questions and input for studies of economic and technological agglomeration or economic geography in general (e.g. Kelley and Helper, 1997; Cantwell and Piscitello, 2000; Cantwell, 2002).

All sample firms perceived an increase of available information and innovative activity through the internet and most of them even observed an acceleration of this process providing evidence for the 'evolutionary theory of globalization' (Borghoff, 2005). The process of variation and retention of social systems seems to be accelerating to drive the evolutionary motor of social differentiation and integration. Particularly the internet is perceived by the sample firms to be a very strong driver of evolutionary change. Simply by providing a huge amount of information and interaction, the internet is a very strong driver of evolutionary change. This finding confirms results of previous studies indicating the increased efficiency of information acquisition, interpretation, evaluation, absorption, and diffusion through ICT (e.g. Berry and Brock, 2004). The results also confirm the significant relationships among internet utilization, information relevance, knowledge internalization, and foreign sales intensity as identified by Nguyen and Barrett (2006).

Main cognitive dimensions for respondents in the sample firms are economic or management dimensions such as efficiency or customer quality. Increasingly, strategic thinking among the sample firms is more focused on network relations, dynamics, and change—with the rate of change itself as the most critical dimension in the globalization processes. These key dimensions are increasingly dominating decision-making and action.

On balance, the results of the study regarding the influence of ICT on the evolutionary dynamics in globalization reflect the observation of researchers such as Eisenhardt (2002: 91) that the economics of disequilibrium and information have moved to the center stage, or of Earl and Khan (2001: 66) that dynamics are gaining momentum and that the new currency is time, not cost. In addition to the increasing importance of dynamics, this study further clearly identified the increasing importance of relationships and network management. The results of this study indicate that all these dimensions are strongly enhanced and even driven by ICT. Given that former studies have identified the strength of ICT in 'levelling the playing field' in internationalization or building up international activities, the results of this study suggest that this process has come to the next stage. As the importance of ICT in internationalization is now perceived as a given or 'necessity' by the sample firms, the focus is now on strengthening relations, network and to build up 'resonance capacity' or robustness in the dynamics of the globalization process.

Management of global evolution

The focus in this section is on managing evolutionary change on the basis of ICT. ICTs provide the potential to better cope with complexity and dynamics per se but most sample firms also actively look for ways to increase their adaptability and to increase their capability for change. The large majority (84 per cent) of the sample firms see a strong or very strong influence of ICT on their adaptability, beginning with the perception of changes in the environment right through to the implementation of measures to address these changes.

ICT in general and particularly the internet increase the 'resonance capacity' of the sample firms to adapt to changes in the environment from the perception of changes to actions driving change (e.g. Berry and Brock, 2004; Nguyen and Barrett, 2006). A main indicator for this capability is the speed with which the firm reacts to changes, which was on average rated as being very strongly influenced by ICT. As the results regarding the foundation of global firms have shown, most sample firms observe that the development and implementation of global business models right from inception is strongly influenced by ICT. Even after inception, the sample firms perceive evolutionary processes to be strongly influenced by ICT both in the external environment and in the firms themselves. ICT have a varying influence on the globalization trajectory of businesses as they can change the underlying technologies, products, and practices ranging from incremental to discontinuous paths. Independent of the mode of trajectory, all firms perceive that ICT is simply very essential to the development of the company and that particularly using the internet is already a necessity to run a company. However, the actual influence of ICT on the business trajectory among the sample firms is very diverse and ranges from smaller or incremental changes in products or practices, to changes of the whole business model. This finding is in line with the study of Loane (2006) that SMEs are too diverse to generalize findings across the whole 'population' of SMEs. The findings have shown that the approach to globalization and the use of ICT in it depend on contextual influences (e.g. infrastructure or government policies of a country) and on firm-specific indicators such as age, FDI, or the mind-set of managers.

The main active driver of adaptation and change is innovation. All sample firms use the internet to gather information and ideas—for example, about markets, customers, products of process technology. Some even use ICT for the integration of whole innovation process. As another active driver, all sample firms use ICT for knowledge management. The intensity ranges from doing research on the internet and then sending e-mails to staff, to the development of integrated intranet-based knowledge management systems including knowledge repositories, newsletters, project management, e-learning, and e-training even on mobile phones. Particularly larger firms (more than 100 employees) built up sophisticated knowledge management systems based on the intranet.

With regard to the development of own ICT capabilities almost all sample firms use customized 'off-the-shelf' products rather than developing such solutions inhouse. Some even completely outsourced ICT management. These results confirm the results of former research that SMEs usually do not build up significant ICT development facilities on their own in terms of having significant ICT staff or even an own department, which does not appear to be efficient with smaller size. However, though not the majority, some sample firms do have such resources for the development of internal ISs and those in ICT-based businesses have such resources anyway. A major finding, which may not contradict but rather 'update' former studies (e.g. Loane, 2006; Abramczuk *et al.*, 2009), is that the majority of firms use ICT not only in operative activities but also in developing very sophisticated solutions, integrating their whole value chain even externally and having intranet-based information and knowledge management systems. The study has also shown that ICTs allowed a large part of the sample firms to globalize instantly from inception and by doing so even generating up to 100 per cent of revenues abroad. The study has also made known that national ICT infrastructure and government policy may provide the respective national companies with potential competitive advantages. The finding that almost half of the firms in the sample generate most and some even almost all revenues abroad from inception raises the question, as to what factors determine the location of a firm. As downstream activities can be increasingly organized through the internet and particularly through remote connectivity, upstream or back office activities appear to become more decisive in location decisions. The most positive example in this regard is Singapore whose sample firms indicated to be able to use such advantages. Also India and China succeeded to promote export-based businesses. This finding may offer insights for policy-makers in order to provide their countries with a competitive infrastructure.

The results of the study contradict those of a study of Apigian *et al.* (2005: 124) that 'many organisations introduce internet technology without a clear understanding of how the internet will enhance their financial and market position'. The results rather support the findings of Powell and Dent-Micallef (1997: 395) that 'high-performers appear to focus on strengthening the organisation's cultural, structural, and systems infrastructures, and not on adding technologies per se.' The study showed that the sample firms have resource restrictions due to their size and that these firms also have learned their lessons and developed very efficient and adaptive systems on the level that is effective for them without introducing ICT as an end in itself—allowing them to globalize more effectively and for a large part to run an almost completely global business. Comparing the results of this study to former studies, the level and pace of ICT diffusion in the globalization of SMEs is very much 'deeper' in 2011 than only a few years before (e.g. Loane, 2006; Nieto and Fernández, 2006) and the sample firms have developed a very professional way to manage the global interplay of ICT, internal processes, and external networks.

Assessment of the study

An important part of any study is a reflection on the validity of results, the contribution of the study to research, the limitations of the study, and implication for future research, which will be discussed in this chapter. Data triangulation was achieved by using information from internal publications and through web-based research—for example, by analyzing the websites of the firms. Triangulation was also achieved through the application of a mixed method design of the study by using both qualitative and quantitative data.

There are limits to data triangulation in this study due to two main reasons. Firstly, reliable information about SMEs in general is difficult to obtain as they often remain 'under the radar' of independent sources. Secondly, getting information about firms in emerging markets is even more difficult (e.g. Shenkar, 1994; Merriam, 1998). A second form of triangulation is theoretical triangulation, which was ensured by using different theoretical lenses such as social systems theory, internationalization theories, network theories, and evolutionary theories. Theoretical triangulation enables a researcher to verify findings by adopting multiple perspectives (Yin, 1994; Gibbert and Ruigrok, 2008: 1466). In order to achieve this, a conceptual model of firm globalization was developed, utilizing multiple cases to provide external and internal validity (Eisenhardt, 1989), as well as enabling replication logic (Yin, 1994). The data analysis was then complemented by comparing identified patterns with those in previous studies and through comparisons of the cases between the four countries. This allowed for the identification of universal patterns across all countries and country- or industry-specific patterns. Internal validity in this study was enhanced by comparing the results across different contexts and different clusters of firms.

On the other hand, analytical generalization is a process that refers to the generalization from empirical observation to theory rather than a population (Kvale, 1996; Yin, 1994) which was provided in this study. The mixed method approach of this study, the triangulation of results, and the application of different theories provide a high level of external validity. This study both derived the conceptual framework from different existing processual theories and projected the gained empirical results back to this framework, confirming the chosen dimensions and proving the overall analytical validity. In addition to confirming the general dimensions of globalization processes, influences of ICT on these dimensions were identified and confirmed. The results show that particularly the influence of ICT on global network relations and on global evolutionary dynamics is perceived to be dominating the globalization process while the influence of ICT on internationalization surprisingly has more a character of 'necessity', which is not in line with many studies stressing the 'levelling of the global playing field' in entering foreign markets (e.g. Kazanis, 2004; Shneor, 2009).

Contribution of the study to the research environment

This study links two basically separate lines of research by developing a conceptual framework to observe and explain the globalization process of social systems in general and by using this framework in studying the influence and use of ICT in these processes. The study is based on a wide range of social systems theories, internationalization theories, network theories, economic and social evolutionary theories, and dynamic organization theories that are outlined in the context of the globalization process and integrated under the umbrella of social systems theory, which provides the structure of the analytical framework.

On a more specific level, the general framework was used to conceptualize the influence of ICT on the globalization of firms. The study provided evidence that ICT has a strong influence on the emergence of firms in the global level from inception. Some sample firms even generate virtually all their revenues abroad through ICT such as ERP or the internet. The study provided evidence that the mindset of the entrepreneur and/or senior manager is decisive for both globalization and the use of ICT, but the processual research also provided evidence that such mindsets can change—even rapidly. Previous international experience and contacts proved to have strong influences particularly on globalization behavior. These results contribute to the study of born global and international entrepreneurship by providing explanations on why and how such phenomena are empirically gaining momentum.

Generally, research suggests that the globalization process is accelerated by ICT (Mathews and Healy, 2008: 179) and this study confirms this observation in some aspects. While active exporters with no FDI see a strong impact of ICT on building up new activities in foreign markets, firms with FDI have the contrary perception, as they are already both 'physically' and socially embedded in foreign markets. Accelerated internationalization due to ICT as predicted by Danford (2008: 390) thus is potentially true for the sample firms of this study but depends still very much on managerial mindsets or objectives and on contingencies such as market size and industry. The study also resonates to the claim of Loane (2006: 275) that underlying dynamics of internationalization are still not well understood and need much further analysis. In addition, the role of ICT during a firm's foreign market expansion has not been investigated on a conceptual level as stated by Danford (2008) and Petersen *et al.* (2002).

Abramczuk *et al.* (2009: 328) stated that there is 'very little academic discussion' about the internet as a factor for the internationalization of SMEs. This study contributes theoretical reasoning and empirical evidence to this discussion. In terms of internationalization processes and theory, the study provides evidence that doing international business for a large part of the sample firms would not even be possible without ICT and thus confirms the positive effect of ICT on internationalization. On the other hand, the results show that despite facilitating earlier internationalization, ICT may also prolong the export stage in the establishment chain even indefinitely through remote connectivity and interorganizational information systems.

On balance, the results of this study may contribute to discussion in a broad range of theoretical streams that may not have looked yet at, for instance, the integration of ICT and international management or globalization in general.

Implications for future research

Research combining ICT and INV from a processual perspective, would be one area of future research. Particularly the link between the global experience and connectedness of founders and their adoption of ICT would be a major area of potential research as the extensive use of ICT by the founders of the eight born global sample firms indicates. ICT as a factor for the internationalization of SMEs could also increasingly focus on more complex structures such as B2B and upstream activities in general. Research might focus in between the born global perspective of instant internationalization and the incremental view, which is surprisingly strengthened by the prolongation of the export stage due to ICT as suggested by the results of this study. Network-based internationalization theories may serve to study the influence of different levels of networks in the internationalization of SMEs ranging from personal to local and business networks. The results of the study suggest that ICT have a major impact on global network development. A further aspect from this perspective is the role that ICTs play in international leaning processes.

The results of the study indicate that the network dimension is central in the globalization of firms and particularly regarding the role of ICT in this process. Studies about the influence of ICT on intra- and interorganizational networks would provide valuable knowledge as the results of this study indicate. The study has shown that local networks such as clusters and industrial districts are facilitated by ICT and vice versa. Business and strategic networks are also facilitated by ICT—for example, by CRM or ERP. The area with the largest need of work is within the evolutionary perspective. The study of the influence of ICT on decision-making is basically only focused on information gathering and processing. Life cycles are only observed on product or organization level, not on practice or organizational unit level. Studies in this field might contribute a lot to the understanding of change processes and the role of ICT within global dynamics. All processual dimensions deserve more attention to better understand change, particularly in globalization. Empirical research itself may also find new venues and methods by using web-based media and applications.

References

Abramczuk, C., Balbinot, S., Macadar, A.N., and Graeml, A.R. (2009). Internet and the internationalization of SMEs in the tourism sector in Brazil, *Revista de Administração e Contabilidade da Unisinos*, 6(4): 328–339.

Aldrich, H.E. (1999). *Organisations Evolving*, London: Sage.

Amburgey, T.L. and Rao, H. (1996). Organizational ecology: Past, present, and future directions, *Academy of Management Journal*, 39(5): 1265–1286.

Apigian, C.H., Nathan, B.S.R., Nathan, T.S.R., and Kunnathur, A. (2005). Internet technology: The strategic imperative, *Journal of Electronic Commerce Research*, 6(2): 124–138.

Arenius, P., Sasi, V., and Gabrielsson, M. (2006). Rapid internationalisation enabled by the Internet: The case of a knowledge intensive company, *Journal of International Enterprise*, 3: 279–290.

Arenius, P., Viveca, S., and Gabrielsson, M. (2005). Rapid internationalisation enabled by the Internet: The case of a knowledge intensive company, *Journal of International Entrepreneurship*, 3(4): 279–290.

Ashby, W.R. (1956). *An Introduction to Cybernetics*, 2nd ed, London: Chapman Hall.

Aulakh, P.S., Kotabe, M., and Teegen, H. (2000). A conceptualization of direct and indirect impact of export promotion programs on export performance of SMEs and entrepreneurial ventures, *International Journal of Entrepreneurship*, 13: 87–106.

Bartlett, C. and Ghoshal, S. (1989). *Managing Across Borders: The Transnational Solution*, Boston, MA: Harvard University Press.

Beamish, P.W. (1999). The role of alliances in international entrepreneurship, in A.M. Rugman and R.W. Wright (Eds.) *International Entrepreneurship: Globalization of Emerging Businesses*, Stanford, CT: JAI Press: 43–62.

Bell, J., McNaughton, R., and Young, S. (2001). Born-again global' firms: An extension to the 'Born Global' phenomenon, *Journal of International Management*, 7(3): 173–189.

Bennett, R. (1997). Export marketing and the internet: Experiences of website use and perceptions, *International Marketing Review*, 14(5): 324–344.

Benson, J.K. (1977). Organizations: A dialectical view, *Administrative Science Quarterly*, 22(1): 1–21.

Berry, M. and Brock, B. (2004). Marketspace and the internationalisation process of the small firm, *Journal of International Entrepreneurship*, 2(3): 187–216.

Blaine, M.J. and Bower, J. (2000). The role of IT in international business research, in E.M. Roche and M.J. Blaine (Eds.) *Information Technology in Multinational Enterprises*, Cheltenham: Edward Elgar: 21–56.

Borghoff, T. (2005). *Evolutionary Theory of the Globalisation of Firms*. Wiesbaden: Gabler.

Bradley, S.P., Jerry, A.H., and Richard, L.N. (1993). *Globalization, Technology, and Competition*, Boston, MA: Harvard Business School Press.

Brynjolfsson, E. and Hitt, L. (2000). Beyond computation: Information technology, organizational transformation and business performance, *Journal of Economic Perspectives*, 14(4): 23–48.

Buttriss, G. and Wilkinson, I. (2003). Towards a process model of internetalisation: Becoming an e-business. *Proceedings of the 19th IMP Conference*, Switzerland.

Cantwell, J.A. (2002). Innovation, profits and growth: Penrose and Schumpeter, in C. Pitelis (Ed.) *The Theory of the Growth of the Firm: The Legacy of Edith Penrose*, Oxford: Oxford University Press: 215–248.

Cantwell, J.A. and Piscitello, L. (2000). Accumulating technological competence: Its changing impact upon corporate diversification and internationalization, *Industrial and Corporate Change*, 9(1): 21–51.

Castells, M. (1996). *The Rise of the Network Society*, Malden, MA: Blackwell.

Chandler, A.D. (1962). *Strategy and Structure*, Cambridge, MA: MIT Press.

Chen, S.-H. (2002). Global production networks and information technology: The case of Taiwan, *Industry and Innovation*, 9(3): 249–265.

Child, J. and Rodrigues, S.B. (2005). The internationalization of Chinese firms: A case for theoretical extension? *Management and Organization Review*, 1(3): 381–410.

Coviello, N.E. and Munro, H., (1992). Internationalizing the entrepreneurial technology intensive firm: Growth through linkage development. *Chapter Presented at the Babson Entrepreneurship Research*, INSEAD, France.

Dana, L.P., Etemad, H., and Wright, R.W. (1999). The impact of globalization on SMEs, *Global Focus*, 11(4): 93–105.

Danford, G.L. (2008). Internet-based of information which can be used to study the internationalization process, *Journal of Teaching in International Business*, 19(4): 389–402.

Donovan, K. and Rosson, P. (2001). The Internet and internationalization: Nova Scotia SMEs. *Proceedings of the 17th IMP Conference*, Oslo.

Doz, Y.L. and Prahalad, C.K. (1991). Managing DMNCs: A search for a new paradigm, *Strategic Management Journal*, 12(Special Issue Summer): 145–164.

Dunning, J.H. (1977). Trade, location of economic activities and the MNE: A search for an eclectic theory, in B. Ohlin, P.O. Hesselborn, and P.M. Wijkman (Eds.) *The International Allocation of Economic Activity*, London: Holmes and Meier: 395–431.

Dunning, J.H. (2000). The eclectic paradigm as an envelope for economic and business theories of MNE activity, *International Business Review*, 9(2): 163–190.

Earl, M.J. and Feeny, D.F. (1996). Information systems in global business: Evidence from European multinationals, in N. Thomas, D. O'Neal, and J. Kelly (Eds.) *Strategic Renaissance and Business Transformation*, Chichester: Wiley: 183–210.

Earl, M. and Khan, B. (2001). E-commerce is changing the face of IT, *MIT Sloan Management Review*, 42(1): 64–78.

Egelhoff, W. (1988). *Organizing the Multinational: An Information Processing Perspective*, New York, NY: Ballinger.

Ein-Dor, P., Myers, M.D., and Raman, K.S. (1997). Information technology in three small development countries, *Journal of Management Information Systems*, 13(4): 61–89.

Eisenhardt, K.M. (1989). Building theories from case study research, *Academy of Management Review*, 14: 532–550.

Eisenhardt, K.M. (2002). Has strategy changed? *MIT Sloan Management Review*, 43(2): 88–91.

Evangelista, F. (2005). Qualitative insights into the international new venture creation process, *Journal International Entrepreneurship*, 3: 179–198.

Fillis, A. and Wagner, B. (2005). E-business development: An explanatory investigation of the small firm, *International Small Business Journal*, 23: 604–618.

Fletcher, M. and Plakoyiannaki, E. (2008). Case study selection: An overview of key issues for International Business Researchers. *Proceedings of the EIBA Annual Conference*, Tallinn, Estonia, 11–13 December.

Forsgren, M. and Hagström, P. (2007). Ignorant and impatient internationalization? The Uppsala model and internalization patterns for Internet-related firms, *Critical Perspectives on International Business*, 3(3): 291–305.

Galbraith, J. (1977). *Organization Design*, Reading, MA: Addison-Wesley.

Ghauri, P. (2004). Designing and conducting case studies in international business, in R. Marschan-Piekkari and C. Welch (Eds.) *Handbook of Qualitative Research Methods for International Business*, Cheltenham: Edward Elgar: 109–124.

Gibbert, M. and Ruigrok, W. (2008). Research notes and commentaries: What passes as a rigorous case study? *Strategic Management Journal*, 29: 1465–1474.

Giustiniano, L. and Fratocci, L. (2002). The virtual internationalization process of Italian SMEs in the food industry, *International Journal of Business Performance Management*, 4(2–4): 231–247.

Gobo, G. (2004). Sampling, representativeness and generalizability, in C. Seale, G. Gobo, J.F. Gubrium, and D. Silverman (Eds.) *Qualitative Research Practice*, London: Sage: 435–456.

Greiner, L.E. (1972). Evolution and revolution in organizations' growth, *Harvard Business Review*, 50(4): 35–46.

Håkansson, H. and Johanson, J. (1993). The network as a governance structure: Interfirm cooperation beyond markets and hierarchies, in G. Grabher (Ed.) *The Embedded Firm*, London and New York, NY: Routledge: 35–51.

Hannan, M.T. and Freeman, J. (1988). Density dependence in the growth of organizational populations, in G.R. Carroll (Ed.) *Ecological Models of Organization*, Cambridge, MA: Ballinger: 7–31.

Hickson, D.J., Hinings, C.R., Lee, C.A., Schneck, R.E., and Pennings, J.M. (1971). A strategic contingencies theory of intraorganizational power, *Administrative Science Quarterly*, 16: 22–43.

Hornby, G., Goulding, P., and Poon, S. (2002). Perceptions of export barriers and cultural issues: The SME e-commerce experience, *Journal of Electronic Commerce Research*, 3(4): 213–226.

Jarillo, J.C. (1988). On strategic networks, *Strategic Management Journal*, 9: 31–41.

Javalgi, R., Radulovich, L., Pendleton, G., and. Scherer, R. (2005). Sustainable competitive advantage of internet firms: A strategic framework and implications for global marketers, *International Marketing Review*, 22(6): 658–672.

Jaw, Y.-L. and Chen, C.-L. (2006). The influence of the Internet in the internationalization of SMEs in Taiwan, *Human Systems Management*, 25(3): 167–183.

Jeon, B.N., Han, K.S., and Lee, M.J. (2006). Determining factors for the adoption of e-business: The case of SMEs in Korea, *Applied Economics*, 38(16): 1905–1916.

Johannisson, B. (1985). Local and international networking as strategy for adaptation to globalizing markets for small- and medium-sized firms, in I. Bamberger (Ed.) *Anpassungsstrategien kleiner und mittlerer Unternehmen an die Globalisierung der Märkte*, Working chapter 7, Faculty of Organisation and Planning, University of Essen and Germany: 35–47.

Johanson, J. and Vahlne, J.-E. (1977). The internationalization process of the firm: A model of knowledge development and increasing foreign market commitments, *Journal of International Business Studies*, 8(1): 23–32.

Kanjas, K. (2000). The role of information technology in building core competencies in MNEs, in E.M. Roche and M.J. Blaine (Eds.) *Information Technology in Multinational Enterprises*, Cheltenham: Edward Elgar: 217–234.

Karimi, J. and Konsynski, B.R. (2003). The information technology and management infrastructure strategy, in R.D Galliers, D.E. Leidner, and B. Baker (Eds.) *Strategic Information Management*, Oxford: Elsevier: 89–112.

Kazanis, P. (2004). *Methodologies and Tools for Transforming Small-to-Medium-Sized Enterprises*. PhD Thesis, Australia: University of Western Sidney.

Kelley, M.R. and Helper, S. (1997). The influences of agglomeration economies and local institutions on the technology adoption decisions of US manufacturing enterprises. *Chapter Presented at the EUNIT International Conference on 'Industry, Innovation and Territory'*, Lisbon, 20–22 March.

Knight, G. and Cavusgil, S.T. (2004). Innovation, organizational capabilities, and the born-global firm, *Journal of International Business Studies*, 35(2): 124–141.

Kostova, T. (1999). Transnational transfer of strategic organizational practices: A contextual perspective, *Academy of Management Review*, 24: 308–324.

Kostova, T. and Roth, K. (2002). Adoption of an organizational practice by subsidiaries of multinational corporations: Institutional and relational effects, *Academy of Management Journal*, 45(1): 215–233.

Kutschker, M., Bäurle, I., and Schmid, S. (1997). International evolution, international episodes and international epochs: Implications for managing internationalization, *Management International Review*, 37(2): 101–124.

Kvale, S. (1996). *An Introduction to Qualitative Research Interviewing*. London: Sage.

Lal, K. (1996). Information technology, international orientation and performance: A case study of electrical and electronic goods manufacturing firms in India, *Information Economics and Policy*, 8(3): 505–517.

Loane, S. (2006). *The Role of the Internet in the Internationalisation of Small and Medium-Sized Companies*, Londonderry: University of Ulster.

Lübbe, H. (1996). Zur Theorie der zivilisatorischen Evolution, in R. Biskup (Ed.) *Globalisierung und Wettbewerb*, Bern: Verlag Paul Haupt: 39–64.

Loane, S., McNaughton, R.B., and Bell, J. (2004). The internationalization of Internet-enabled entrepreneurial firms: Europe and North America, *Canadian Journal of Administrative Science*, 21(1): 79–96.

Luhmann, N. (1995). *Social Systems*, Stanford, CA: Stanford University Press.

Luo, Y., Zhao, J.H., and Du, J. (2005). The internationalization speed of e-commerce companies: An empirical analysis, *International Marketing Review,* 22(6): 709–724.

Luostarinen, R. (1980). *Internationalization of the Firm,* Helsinki: Acta Academicae Oeconomicae Helsingiensis.

Macharzina, K. and Engelhard, J. (1991). Paradigm shift in international business research: From partist and eclectic approaches to the GAINS paradigm, *Management International Review,* 31: 23–43.

Malnight, T.W. (1996). The transition from decentralized to network-based MNC structures: An evolutionary perspective, *Journal of International Business Studies,* 1: 43–65.

Malnight, T.W. (2000). Toward a model of accelerating organizational change: Evidence from the globalization process, in P.C. Earley and H. Singh (Eds.) *Innovations in International and Cross-Cultural Management,* Thousand Oaks, CA: Sage: 267–310.

Markusen, A. (1996). Sticky places in slippery space: A typology of industrial districts, *Economic Geography,* 72(3): 293–313.

Mathews, J.A. (2002). *Dragon Multinational, a New Model for Global Growth,* Oxford: Oxford University Press.

Mathews, S. and Healy, M. (2008). From garage to global and international market growth: An SME perspective, *Journal Internet Marketing and Advertising,* 4(2–3): 179–196.

Mathews, S., Healy, M., and Ali, Y. (2006): The internet and international market growth: A model development, Paper presented at of the *Australian and New Zealand Marketing Academy (ANZMAC) Conference,* Brisbane, Australia.

McDougall, P.P. and Oviatt, B.M. (1991). Global start-ups: New ventures without geographic limits, *The Economic Forum,* Winter: 1–5.

McKelvey, B. (1982). *Organizational Systematics: Taxonomy, Evolution, Classification,* Berkeley, CA: University of California Press.

McMahon, P. (2002). *Global Control.* Cheltenham: Edward Elgar.

Meissner, H.G. and Gerber, S. (1980). Die Auslandsinvestition als Entscheidungsproblem, *Betriebswirtschaftliche Forschung und Praxis,* 32(3): 217–228.

Merriam, S.B. (1998). *Qualitative Research and Case Study Applications in Education.* San Francisco, CA: Jossey-Bass.

Miller, D. and Friesen, P.H. (1984). *Organizations: A Quantum View.* Englewood Cliffs, NJ: Prentice-Hall.

Moen, Ø. (2002). The Born Globals: A new generation small European exporters, *International Marketing Review,* 19(2): 156–175.

Moen, Ø., Endresen, I., and Gavlen, M. (2003). Executive insights: Use of the Internet in international marketing: A case study of small computer software firms, *Journal of International Marketing,* 11(4): 129–149.

Moen, Ø., Gavlen, M., and Endresen, I. (2004). Internationalization of small, computer software firms, *European Journal of Marketing,* 38(9–10): 1236–1251.

Moini, H. and Tesar, G. (2005). The Internet and internationalisation of smaller manufacturing enterprises, *Journal of Global Marketing,* 18(3/4): 79–93.

Morgan-Thomas, A. and Bridgewater, S. (2004). Internet and exporting: Determinants of success in virtual export channels, *International Marketing Review,* 21(4–5): 393–408.

Mukherji, A. (2002). The evolution of information systems: Their impact on organizations and structures, *Management Decision*, 40(5): 497–507.

Murphy, G.B., Celuch, K., and Callaway, S.K. (2007). Small business Internet use and strategic flexibility, *Journal of Small Business Strategy*, 18(1): 57.

Nguyen, T.D. and Barrett, N.J. (2006). The knowledge-creating role of the Internet in international business: Evidence from Vietnam, *Journal of International Marketing*, 14(2): 116–147.

Nieto, M.J. and Fernández, Z. (2006). The role of information technology in corporate strategy of small and medium enterprises, *Journal of International Entrepreneurship*, 3: 251–262.

Nummela, N, Saarenkto, S., and Puumalainen, K. (2004). A global mindset – A prerequisite for successful internationalization? *Canadian Journal of Administrative Sciences*, 1(1): 51–64.

Overby, J.W. and Min, S. (2001). International supply chain management in an internet environment: A network-oriented approach to internationalization, *International Marketing Review*, 18(4): 392–419.

Oviatt, B.M. and McDougall, P.P. (1994). Toward a theory of international new ventures, *Journal of International Business Studies*, 25(1): 45–64.

Oviatt, B.M. and McDougall, P.P. (2005). The internationalization of entrepreneurship, *Journal of International Business Studies*, 36(1): 2–8.

Palvia, P.C. (1997). Developing a model of the global and strategic impact of information technology, *Information & Management*, 32: 229–244.

Park, S.O. (1996). Networks and embeddedness in the dynamic types of new industrial districts, *Progress in Human Geography*, 20(4): 476–493.

Patton, M.Q. (1990). *Qualitative Evaluation and Research Methods*, 2nd ed. Newbury Park, CA: Sage.

Petersen, B., Pederson, T., and Sharma, D.D. (2002). The role of knowledge in firms' internationalization process, in V. Havila, M. Forsgren, and H. Håkansson (Eds.) *Critical Perspectives on Internationalization*, Amsterdam: Pergamon: 36–55.

Picot, A. and Reichwald, R. (1994). Auflösung der Unternehmung? *Zeitschrift für Betriebswirtschaft*, 64(5): 547–570.

Porter, M.E. (1986). *Competition in Global Industries*, Boston, MA: Harvard University Press.

Porter, M.E. (2001). Strategy and the Internet, *Harvard Business Review*, 79(3): 62–77.

Poulis, K. and Yamin, M. (2009). Tourism as a leverage of internationalization for consumer goods firms: A case study approach, *Advances in International Marketing*, 20: 69–85.

Powell, T.C. and Dent-Micallef, A. (1997). Information technology as competitive advantage: The role of human, business and technology resources, *Strategic Management Journal*, 18(5): 375–405.

Quelch, J.A. and Klein, L.R. (1996). The Internet and international marketing, *Sloan Management Review*, 37(3): 60–75.

Rantapusca, T. and Ihanainen, O. (2008). Knowledge use in ICT investment decision making of SMEs, *Journal of Enterprise Information Management*, 21(6): 585–596.

Rindova, V.P. and Kotha, S. (2001). Continuous 'morphing': Competing through dynamic capabilities, form, and function, *Academy of Management Journal*, 44(6): 1263–1280.

Samiee, S. (1998). Exporting and the Internet: A conceptual perspective, *International Marketing Review*, 15(5): 413–426.

Samii, M. and Karush, G. (2004). International business and information technology, in M. Samii and G. Karush (Eds.) *International Business and Information Technology*, New York, NY: Routledge: 1–8.

Schulz, A. and Borghoff, T. (2008): Towards the SME internationalization theory, Paper presented at the *IAMB Conference*, San Diego, USA, May 2008.

Seale, C.F. (2002). Computer-assisted analysis of qualitative interview data, in J.F. Gubrium and J.A. Holstein (Eds.) *Handbook of Interview Research: Context and Method*, London: Sage: 651–667.

Sharma, S.K. and Gupta, J.N.D. (2004). E-strategy model for creating flexible organizations, *Global Journal of Flexible Systems Management*, 4(2–3): 1.

Shenkar, O. (1994). The People's Republic of China: Raising the bamboo screen through international management research, *International Studies of Management and Organisation*, 24(1–2): 9–34.

Shneor, R. (2009). When internet adoption meets the firm's internationalisation process: The emergence of Internet-enabled internationalisation (IEI), Paper presented of the *35th Annual European International Business Academy Conference (EIBA)*, Valencia, Spain, December 2009.

Singh, N. and Kundu, S. (2002). Explaining the growth of e-commerce corporations (ECCs): An extension and application of the eclectic paradigm, *Journal of International Business Studies*, 33(4): 679–697.

Thorelli, H.B. (1986). Networks: Between markets and hierarchies, *Strategic Management Journal*, 7(1): 37–51.

Tushman, M.L. and Romanelli, E. (1985). Organizational evolution: A metamorphosis model, of convergence and reorientation, in L.L Cummings and B.M. Staw (Eds.) *Research in Organizational Behavior*, Greenwich, CT: JAI Press: 171–222.

Unni, J. and Rani, U. (2000). Globalisation, information technology revolution and service sector in India, *The Indian Journal of Labour Economics*, 43(4): 814–819.

Vernon, R. (1966). International investment and international trade in the product cycle, *Quarterly Journal of Economics*, 80(2): 190–207.

von Bertalanffy, L. (1950). The theory of open systems in physics and biology, *Science*, 111: 23–29.

Wade, M. and Hulland, J. (2004). The resource-based view and information systems research: Review, extension and suggestions for future research, *MIS Quarterly*, 28(1): 107–142.

Westney, D.E. (1993). Institutionalization theory and the multinational corporation, in S. Ghoshal and D.E. Westney (Eds.) *Organizational Theory and the Multinational Corporation*, Houndsmill; London: Macmillan: 53–76.

Woodward, J. (1965). *Industrial Organization: Theory and Practice*, Oxford: Oxford University Press.

Yin, R.K. (1994). *Case Study Research: Design and Methods*, Thousand Oaks, CA: Sage.

Yip, G.S. (1989). Global strategy: In a world of nations? *Sloan Management Review*, 31(1): 29–41.

Yiu, D.W., Lau, C.M., and Bruton, G.D. (2007). International venturing by emerging economy firms: The effects of firm capabilities, home country networks, and corporate entrepreneurship, *Journal of International Business Studies*, 38: 519–540.

Zaheer, S. and Manrakhan, S. (2001). Concentration and dispersion in global industries: Remote electronic access and the location of economic activities, *Journal of International Business Studies*, 32(4): 667–686.

Zhang, C.C.Y. (2004). China's leading Internet guru Charles Zhang, Chairman of SOHU.com Inc., on how the Internet has changed the world's most populous nation, *Academy of Management Executive*, 18(4): 145–158.

Zhu, K. (2004). The complementarity of information technology and e-commerce capability: A resource-based assessment of their business value, *Journal of Management Information Systems*, 21(1): 167–202.

Zhu, K. and Kraemer, K.L. (2002). E-commerce metrics for net-enhanced organizations: Assessing the value of e-commerce to firm performance in the manufacturing sector, *Information Systems Research*, 13(3): 275–295.

6

An Analysis of the Macroeconomic Determinants of Indian Outward Foreign Direct Investment

Rakhi Verma and Louis Brennan

Introduction

The growth of international business facilitates foreign direct investment (FDI) and is driven by economic and technological factors. While foreign investors benefit by utilizing their assets and resources efficiently through FDI, the recipients benefit by acquiring technologies and by getting involved in international production and trade networks. It is now widely recognized that economic uncertainties compel a firm to look for markets in other geographical locations. For example, an unstable exchange rate, high interest rate, poor human capital, restrictions on trade and technological backwardness of the country all contribute to the increased cost of production in the home market. Because of the higher production cost, firms may engage in FDI to exploit location advantages of a country. This phenomenon is increasingly being observed in emerging markets, including India.

The internal factors associated with a firm's assets and competencies constitute its major ownership advantages and predominately influence its performance. At the same time, external or environmental factors associated with a firm's country of origin play a crucial role in the development of ownership advantages. The influence of home-country specific factors on the generation of a firm's ownership advantages has been suggested by various researchers and empirically analyzed for several countries (Dunning and Narula, 1996; Buckley *et al.*, 2007). However, the multivariate, country-of-origin approach to studying the influence of these factors on FDI has mostly been applied to the developed nations. Considering the fact that ownership advantages are the building blocks of FDI, it becomes increasingly important in the globalized economy to analyze home-country specific macroeconomic determinants that may influence FDI by a country, particularly an emerging market such as India.

There is a considerable body of literature and empirical studies on ownership advantages of Indian firms and their internationalization process. Nevertheless, there still exists a knowledge gap in the literature on the question of home-country determinants that motivate Indian firms to internationalize. Previous studies have identified various factors that influence outward FDI (OFDI) flows by firms from emerging markets. In terms of the macroeconomic perspective, the main determinant contributing to the OFDI can be associated with the income or economic development of a country (Dunning and Narula, 1996). It is interesting to note that the macro-level characteristics of rapidly developing countries such as India are dynamically changing in all aspects.

A number of factors have been suggested as FDI determinants in previous work. We have recently reported our analysis of the major factors of Indian OFDI including inward FDI (IFDI), gross domestic product (GDP) and exports (Verma and Brennan, 2011a, 2011b). However, there remain some other macroeconomic factors that may play a direct or indirect role in Indian OFDI. The aim of this study is to empirically analyse key macroeconomic factors of Indian OFDI which may have a substantive influence on the decision-making processes of Indian firms to invest abroad. More specifically, we test the relationship between Indian OFDI and six selected macroeconomic determinants: (i) economic development, (ii) effective exchange rate, (iii) interest rate, (iv) human capital, (v) technology, and (vi) openness of the economy. The overall proposed relationship of the explanatory variables to Indian OFDI hypothesized in this study or reported earlier (Verma and Brennan, 2011a, 2011b) is illustrated in Figure 6.1.

This chapter is organized as follows. The literature around the above-mentioned macroeconomic determinants of OFDI is reviewed and hypotheses to explain Indian OFDI patterns are proposed. Following this, the data and methodology to test the hypotheses based on the extant literature are described. The results of our analysis are presented and a discussion and conclusions are provided.

Literature review and hypotheses development

The increasing significance of macroeconomic factors in explaining inward and outward FDI has been highlighted in the international

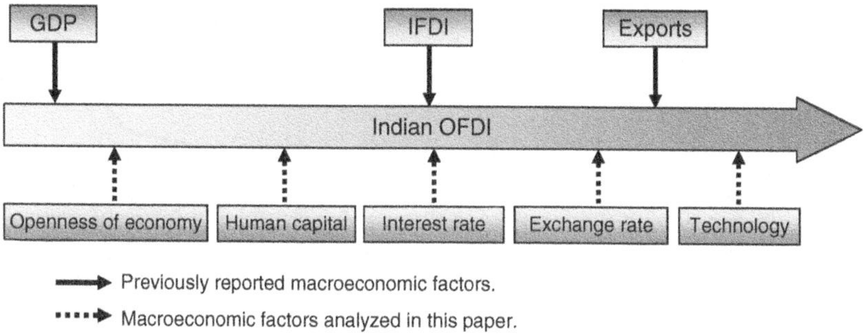

Figure 6.1 A framework of macroeconomic determinants of Indian OFDI

business literature (Dunning, 2009). In this chapter, the OFDI from India is explained in terms of some key macroeconomic variables. Here the FDI stock is used for this purpose. The stock of OFDI used in this study is defined as the amount of cumulative FDI at the end of the year (Figure 6.2a).

Based on the following six selected macroeconomic explanatory variables a few testable hypotheses and a working model to explain Indian OFDI are developed in the following subsections.

Gross domestic product

There is longstanding support for the view of FDI-led growth. Studies such as Borensztein *et al.* (1998) explain how inward FDI plays a crucial role in a country's economic growth. In the case of India also, there is substantial evidence that suggests that the Indian IFDI is central to its growth and affirms that FDI inflows have played an instrumental role in promoting economic growth and development of the Indian economy as a result of the adoption of a series of industrialization initiatives (Chakraborty and Basu, 2002). Also according to the investment development path model (Dunning, 1988; Dunning and Narula, 1996), a steady high economic growth in the home economy could foster a higher level of economic development, in which domestic firms would have established ownership advantages before they expand their operations abroad. Thus, sustainable economic growth is a prerequisite for OFDI. Studies such as Desai *et al.* (2005) also suggest that OFDI allows firms to enter new markets, to import intermediate goods from foreign affiliates at lower prices, to produce a greater volume of final goods abroad at lower cost, and to access foreign technology. Outward investing firms combine home production with foreign production to reduce

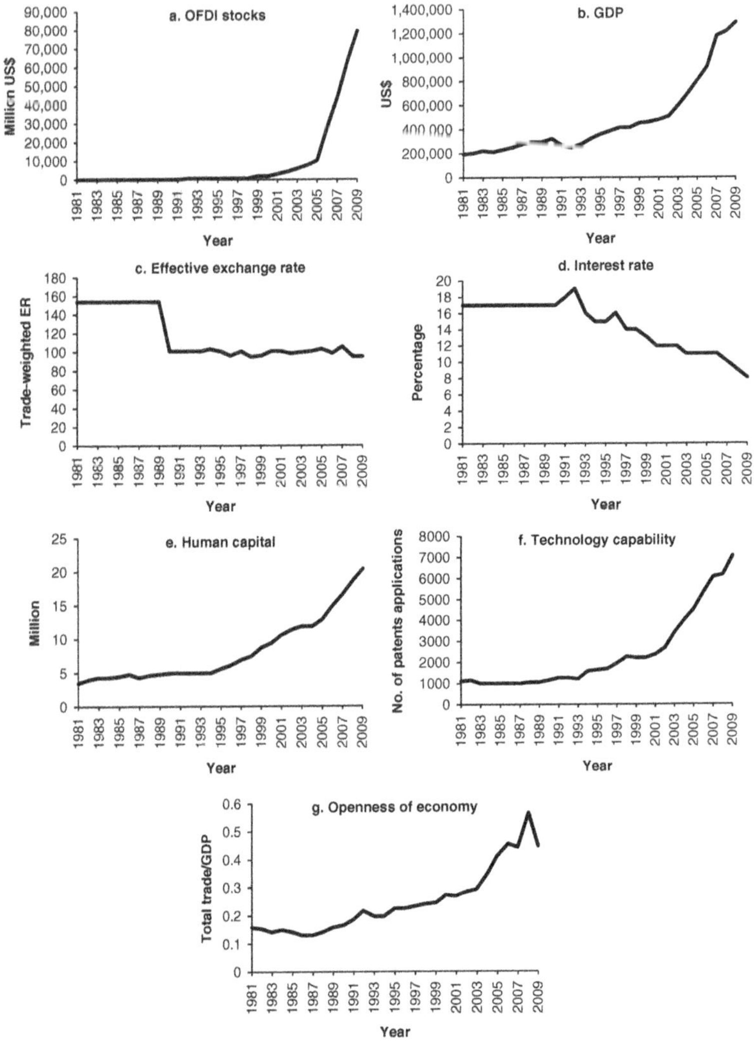

Figure 6.2 Time series data on macroeconomic determinants of Indian OFDI, 1981–2009

Note: (a) Indian OFDI stocks, (b) GDP, (c) effective exchange rate, (d) interest rate, (e) human capital (based on number of students in millions enrolled in tertiary education), (f) technology capability (based on number of patent applications), and (g) openness of Indian economy (calculated as the ratio of total trade (exports + imports) to GDP).

Source: UNCTAD (2010), UN Statistical Division (2008), and Ministry of Commerce and Industry (2010).

costs and to increase their competitiveness both internationally and domestically, stimulating domestic factor demand and domestic output. However, the evidence for the domestic output effects of OFDI is limited (Herzer, 2008). Figure 6.2b depicts the GDP of India over the period 1981–2009. We observe an upward trend of Indian GDP. Based on the above studies, it is proposed that:

Hypothesis 1. *Indian OFDI is influenced by the home country gross domestic product.*

Exchange rate

The currency area hypothesis postulated by Aliber (1970) states that the pattern of FDI can be best explained in terms of the relative strengths of the various currencies. The stronger the currency of a certain country, the more likely it is that firms from that country will engage in foreign investment, and the less likely that foreign firms will invest in the domestic country. This argument is based on capital market relationships, exchange rate risks and the preferences of the market for holding assets in selected currencies. By lowering the capital requirements of OFDI in domestic currency units and reducing the nominal competitiveness of exports, the appreciation of the home country's currency encourages OFDI. Kohlhagen (1977) and Stevens (1993) suggest that a low exchange rate encourages exports but discourages OFDI. As the home country exchange rate appreciates, more profitable opportunities for OFDI occur as foreign currency denominated assets become cheaper (Buckley *et al.*, 2007). In other words, a depreciation of the host country currency raises the relative wealth of home country agents and can raise multinational acquisitions of certain host country assets.

The literature suggests that scholars have different views on the OFDI–exchange rate relationship. Froot and Stein (1991) showed that the depreciation of the US dollar increased the propensity of foreign firms to invest in the US by lowering their capital costs for FDI, and encouraging the aggressive acquisition of US dollar-denominated foreign assets. Blonigen (1997) also found a strong correlation between a weaker US dollar and a higher level of Japanese acquisitions in the US, but no effect was found in the case of greenfield investments. Baek and Kwok (2002) demonstrate that firms with a stronger home currency have a higher propensity to establish a subsidiary in a foreign market. Based on five European Union members and four non-European Union countries, Kyrkilis and Pantelidis (2003) showed mixed support for a link between exchange rates and OFDI. They suggest that the exchange rate is an influential factor in determining OFDI for some countries, such as the UK, Germany, Brazil, and Singapore, whereas it is insignificant in the case of OFDI for Italy, the Netherlands, and Korea. In a recent study, Russ (2007) shows that a multinational enterprise's (MNE's) response to exchange rate volatility vary depending on whether the volatility arises from shocks in the firm's home or host country. Based on the above studies it is proposed that a depreciated currency of a country will increase its inward FDI and decrease the OFDI of a country.

The use of trade-weighted exchange rate has been advocated in international business (Blonigen, 1997). Trade-weighted exchange rate index evaluates the strength of a country's currency by weighting its value according to the relative amount of trade carried out with each of its trading partners. Therefore trade-weighted exchange rate indices were used in this study (Figure 6.2c). In the light of above discussion, it is hypothesized that:

> ***Hypothesis 2.*** *Indian OFDI is influenced by the home country effective exchange rate.*

Interest rate

Foreign operations require significant commitment in capital, especially if they are undertaken in capital-intensive sectors where production is characterized by extensive economies of scale. The capital abundance of the home country may provide the necessary background for establishing a firm with adequate financial means and relatively easy access to capital markets. Capital abundance is associated with relatively low interest rates—that is, the level of interest rate is a proxy for the capital abundance or scarcity of a country. Relatively low interest rate associated with a home country's capital abundance decreases the opportunity cost of capital and enhances the profitability of investments abroad.

Previous studies suggest that a relatively low interest rate in the home country leads to a greater tendency for OFDI (Lall, 1980; Hong and Kim, 2003). Moreover, the interest rate is one of the significant determinants of the choice of FDI location (Billington, 1999; Jeon and Rhee, 2008). In the case of India, we observe that the interest rate has decreased over the period 1981–2006 and that may explain Indian OFDI (Figure 6.2d). Therefore, we hypothesize that:

> ***Hypothesis 3.*** *Indian OFDI is influenced by the home country interest rate.*

Human capital

It is now widely recognized that the presence of sophisticated human capital is one of the most important factors of FDI attractiveness in emerging markets (Dunning and Narula, 1996; Zhang and Markusen, 1999). It is also one of the major foundations of firms' capability to invest abroad. The more the human capital of a country advances, the more a country's firms are able to retain qualified staff, absorb the latest technologies, and thus enhance their productivity in home and foreign countries (Meyer and Sinani, 2009). Firm-level analyses also confirm the crucial role of human capital in OFDI motivations (Lall and Siddarthan, 1982).

A high level of education is regarded as the most important element in human capital development (World Investment Report, 1994; OECD, 1998). Following previous studies, we used the number of students in the tertiary level education in India to approximate Indian human capital in this study (Paloni and Youssef, 2001; Kyrkilis and Pantelidis, 2003; Meyer and Sinani, 2009). Thus this variable captures high-level technical and managerial skills available in the country (Paloni and Youssef, 2001). Data shows an upward trend in human capital during the period 1981–2009 (Figure 6.2e). Here, we hypothesize that:

> ***Hypothesis 4.*** *Indian OFDI is influenced by the home country human capital.*

Technology

Firms may exploit their technological superiority in the world market. Depending upon relative technological benefits and costs, firms may decide to manufacture the products in their home country and export to overseas markets, license out their technology to host country players in the foreign market, or produce the product in the overseas host location by themselves (Pradhan, 2007). Firms embedded in technological efforts have a stronger chance to succeed, locally or internationally (Barnard, 2008).

There is also evidence that Asian firms with higher levels of technological advantage are more likely to undertake OFDI especially in the developed countries (Chen and Chen, 1998; Makino *et al.*, 2004). Accumulated technological capabilities is considered as an important competitive advantage of Indian firms to invest in more advanced countries particularly in the pharmaceutical and information technology sector (Pradhan, 2005, 2006, 2007). An upward trend in the technological advances by Indian firms approximated by the number of patent applications from India can be seen during the period 1981–2009 (Figure 6.2f). Therefore, it is appropriate to hypothesize that:

> ***Hypothesis 5.*** *Indian OFDI is influenced by the home country technological capability.*

Openness of economy

The influence of trade liberalization of a country's economy on FDI is another subject in the international business empirical literature, given that the concentration of most FDI is in the trade sector. The liberalization of a country's foreign economic transactions is expected to positively influence the OFDI activities of its firms. In other words, a higher degree of openness of a country is expected to be associated with a higher level of FDI activity (Lall, 1996; Chakrabarti, 2001). The trade openness of a country is considered to improve its capacity to respond to the opportunities offered by global economic integration (OECD, 1998) and is, thus, the main determinant of economic growth in developing countries (Cuadros *et al.*, 2004). An export-oriented economy permits firms to acquire information about foreign markets and organize foreign operations (Kogut, 1983). The OFDI of US and Japanese MNEs was found to be positively associated with their market openness during the period 1982–1994 (Kumar, 2001). We observed the openness of Indian economy gradually increased during the years 1981–2009 as approximated by its exports plus imports level relative to the GDP (Figure 6.2g). The observed data and the above-cited evidence from the literature that a country's openness is more likely to be correlated with FDI lead us to hypothesize that:

> ***Hypothesis 6.*** *Indian OFDI is influenced by the degree of openness of the home country.*

Methodology and data

Model

Based on the above-mentioned hypotheses, we propose a model for Indian OFDI as follows:

$$\text{OFDI} = \beta_0 + \beta_1\text{GDP} + \beta_2\text{ER} - \beta_3\text{IR} + \beta_4\text{HC} + \beta_5\text{TECH} + \beta_6\text{OPEN} \quad (6.1)$$

where

OFDI = Indian Outward Foreign Direct Investment stocks
GDP = Gross domestic product
ER = Home country effective exchange rate per US dollar
IR = Home country interest rate
HC = Human capital (approximated by the number of enrollments of students in tertiary education)
TECH = Technology capability of home country (approximated by the number of patent applications in the home country)
OPEN = Openness of the economy (approximated by the ratio of exports plus imports to GDP of that year)

The signs (negative or positive) before the variables indicate the expected type of correlation between the independent variables and the OFDI.

Data

The year-wide time series data on the selected macroeconomic determinants of Indian OFDI for the period 1981–2009 were obtained and compiled from the UNCTAD Handbook of Statistics, the UNESCO official website, and Intellectual Property division, Ministry of Commerce and Industry, 2010. The reason for using the data from 1981 was mainly because it was only around that time the Indian government introduced an outward oriented industrialization policy and India started liberalizing the economy and opening up to the rest of the world. The potentially important influence of government intervention on OFDI is necessarily omitted as the Indian government has consistently encouraged FDI and trade particularly exports during the sample period of 1981–2009.

It is also important to note that the earlier published data on investment projects abroad and home understates the true magnitude of Indian FDI for several reasons. Some existing foreign investment projects have not been properly registered, subsidiaries were generally left out, and the measurement of the size of the investment has been inadequate (Morris, 1987). As a consequence of these shortcomings, the Government of India revised (starting November 2002) its computation of FDI figures in line with the best international practices and based on the recommendations of a committee set up to examine this issue. This has led to a substantial improvement in FDI figures, which is rectified in UNCTAD's database (Jha, 2003).

Statistical analysis

In order to include the proliferative effect of time, all the variables were expressed in logarithms. A correlation coefficient matrix of the variables was determined using a simple regression model. The multi-collinearity of the time series variables was analyzed following the Augmented Dickey Fuller (ADF) test. ADF tests are applied to detect the integration order of the variables and co-integration is tested using the Johansen and Juselius (1990) procedure in which two tests are conducted based on the maximal eigenvalue and trace test, and the maximum likelihood method is used to test for the presence of co-integration relationship between the economic variables. A simple linear regression method, ordinary least squares (OLS) was used to estimate the relationship between dependent and explanatory variables.

Results

The results of correlation coefficient matrix are presented in Table 6.1. The analysis indicates that there exists a high-order serial correlation between the dependent and the independent variables. There exist negative correlations between Indian OFDI and the effective exchange rate and the interest rate, while GDP, human capital, technology, and openness of Indian economy are positively correlated with OFDI. Since these variables are highly correlated, they do not contribute independently toward explaining the variations in Indian OFDI.

To examine the stationary property of the time series variables selected in this study, we carried out unit-root tests for the dependent and explanatory variables. The results of the ADF statistic unit-root test are presented in Table 6.2. In this test, the more negative a value, the stronger the rejection of the hypothesis that there is a unit root at some level of confidence. Our estimations show that all the economic

Table 6.1 Correlation coefficient matrix of the variables

Variables	L_OFDI	L_GDP	L-EER	L_IR	L_HC	L_TECH	L_OPEN
L_OFDI	1	0.9790	−0.6789	−0.9650	0.9853	0.9896	0.9769
L_GDP		1	−0.6542	−0.9530	0.9755	0.9776	0.9509
L_EER			1	0.5871	−0.6673	−0.6699	−0.7417
L_IR				1	−0.9692	−0.9634	−0.9194
L_HC					1	0.9773	0.9532
L_TECH						1	0.9763
L_OPEN							1

Table 6.2 Unit-root test (ADF test)

Variables	Level 0	First Difference
L_OFDI	−4.59003***	−5.65141***
L_GDP	0.819636	−2.88199**
L_EER	−1.40697	−3.72043***
L_IR	1.39774	−3.45421***
L_HC	−4.39088***	−3.75013***
L_TECH	−3.62622*	−3.29659*
L_OPEN	−3.82014**	−0.153778

*, **, and *** Denote significance at 10%, 5% and 1%, respectively.

variables except GDP, effective exchange rate and interest rate are non-stationary at zero-level. However, it is rejected after first differencing for all the variables at 1 per cent, 5 per cent, or 10 per cent significance levels as indicated in Table 6.2 confirming that they are integrated in order one. Thus, the robustness of the result allows this study to treat the variables as $I(1)$ to proceed with further analysis.

The results of the estimation of the linear equation (6.1) using OLS are given in Table 6.3. Considering the general statistics of the estimation, the adjusted R^2-statistic indicates that over 99 per cent of the variance of the dependent variable is explained by the variables. Looking at the coefficients of the variables, the results show expected signs with significant values for the variable 'human capital' and 'openness of economy' at the 1 per cent acceptance level. 'GDP' is also a significant factor (at 5 per cent significance) for Indian OFDI.

Other variables 'exchange rate', 'interest rate', and 'technology' are statistically insignificant for Indian OFDI. Thus, we accept hypotheses

Table 6.3 OLS estimates of Indian OFDI, 1981–2009

Variables	Coefficient	Standard Error	*t*-stat	*p*-value
Constant	2.10406	3.96972	0.5300	0.6017
L_GDP	1.81007	0.675564	2.679	0.0140**
L_EER	0.457455	0.507859	0.9008	0.3779
L_IR	−0.315171	0.840231	−0.3751	0.7113
L_HC	2.11857	0.430691	4.919	7.26e-05***
L_TECH	0.421556	0.518792	0.8126	0.4256
L_OPEN	1.90611	0.510300	3.735	0.0012***
$R^2 = 0.992456$				

*, **, and *** Denote significance at 10%, 5% and 1%, respectively.

1, 4, and 6 that Indian OFDI is associated positively with its economic development, the degree of openness, and the human capital accumulated in the home economy. The analysis rejects hypotheses 2, 3, and 5 that Indian OFDI is associated positively with the home country's currency (effective exchange rate), interest rate, and technology

Discussion

This study empirically analyzes potential macroeconomic determinants of FDI in order to understand their relationship with Indian OFDI. The study employed time series data for the selected macroeconomic factors for the period 1981–2009. The major contribution of this analysis is testing the previously theorized relationships between a selected set of macroeconomic variables and OFDI from an emerging market economy, viz. India. The results show that not all the theorized relationships that are thought to influence the FDI of emerging markets hold in the case of India.

The findings of our analysis indicate that the economic development is a significant variable and has a positive relationship with its OFDI. For the case of India, Verma and Brennan (2011a) underscore the importance of its economic development for the inward and outward FDI of India. Chakraborty and Basu (2002) have also showed that economic development of India has significantly contributed to its inward FDI. This finding supports several studies which affirm that the economic development is the engine of inward as well as outward FDI (Dunning, 1988; Dunning and Narula, 1996).

Apart from the economic development, the openness of the Indian economy shows a positive and significant relationship to its OFDI (Table 6.3). This may be due to the economic policy adopted by the Indian government particularly export-oriented approach during the 1980s and the 1990s. The expansion of Indian export activities as a result of robust trade liberalization momentum in the 1990s enabled Indian firms to obtain information regarding foreign markets and knowledge as well as skills in establishing operations abroad. It has been argued that the uptrend in overseas investments during the 1990s by Indian firms was motivated by the goal of supporting and assisting export markets with local presence, developing marketing networks, and providing after-sales services among others (Kumar, 1998). However, we find at least one study by Chiou Wei and Zhu (2007) that does not support the hypothesis that openness of economy is a significant determinant of FDI.

It is generally assumed that human capital accumulation of a country leads to growth of the economy, followed by IFDI and finally OFDI. The presence of sophisticated and improved human resources elevate the volume and also the quality of the FDI that a country can attract (Paloni and Youssef, 2001). Lall (1998) argues that high level of human capital skills attract high-technology activities and thus may achieve faster economic growth and vice versa. According to the Investment Development Path (IDP) theory, a sound economic condition of a country is a prerequisite for it to start overseas investment. Human capital as a determinant of developing country FDI has been embodied in the previous theoretical literature (Dunning, 1988; Zhang and Markusen, 1999). However, the role of human capital in FDI outflows from emerging markets has not been verified as yet, except in a few studies such as Liu *et al.* (2005). Therefore, we considered it imperative to analyze the relationship between Indian OFDI and its human capital. The influence of human capital on the growing OFDI from India in recent years was adequately captured in the reasonable number of time series annual data used in this study. The results of this study suggest that human capital has a positive impact and is highly significant to Indian OFDI. It is essential to note here that there has been a tremendous increase in service OFDI from India in recent years particularly after 2000s. Thus the human capital forms an essential base for such overseas investments.

We find exchange rate as positive but an insignificant factor of Indian OFDI. A previous study by Blonigen (1997) suggests that the effect of exchange rate movement is more visible in the OFDI made in the form of acquisition than greenfield. Since the data used in this study does not differentiate between different forms of OFDI, further investigation is warranted to comprehensively understand the influence of exchange rate on Indian OFDI.

Among several researchers, Lall (1980), Prugel (1981), and Grubaugh (1987) suggest that low interest rates in the home country may encourage OFDI. However, a few studies including a recent one by Kueh *et al.* (2009) failed to demonstrate any direct causal relationship between OFDI and the interest rate. The impact of interest rates on FDI may vary across host countries. The influence of long-term interest rates explains FDI in Canada but not in Japan, the UK, or the US (Chowdhury and Wheeler, 2008). In this study, although we find that the interest rate has a positive sign it is insignificant in explaining OFDI from India, supporting the finding of Kueh *et al.* (2009). There have been a considerable number of studies which have attempted to explain the financing arrangements of Indian MNEs from different perspectives (Khanna and

Palepu, 2000; Ghosh, 2006). Ghosh (2006) particularly highlights that the liberalization of financial market in India has no effect on the investment by the domestic firms. Thus, further studies are required to explore the financing capability of the Indian MNEs in order to understand the role of interest rate in Indian OFDI.

In this study, we did not find any relationship between the technology capability of India and its OFDI. India has significantly improved from its initial status of mere adaptor of foreign technologies to continuously move nearer to the global frontier of technology in many of the knowledge-based industries like information technology, telecommunications, transport, and pharmaceuticals. In this regard, Indian Government's strategic interventions in the form of large-scale public investment in skill formation through general, technical and management education, public funded research and development (R &D) establishments, and fiscal incentives for innovating firms like duty-free imports of inputs had contributed greatly in strengthening indigenous technological capabilities leading to increasing number of patents. However, the result does not necessarily suggest that the technological capabilities of Indian MNEs do not lead to its increased OFDI. One possible explanation to this could be the motivation of firms investing overseas. A firm that does not possess any technological ownership advantage can invest overseas to acquire such strategic assets. Thus technology capability and its relationship with OFDI can be better explained at a firm level than on a macro level.

Conclusion

In conclusion, our analysis confirms the role of some characteristics of the home country on Indian OFDI. We analyzed the time series data of various macroeconomic determinants for their influence on Indian OFDI. The time series data was checked for stationary properties using the ADF test. The OLS estimation was employed to find out the relationship between these factors and Indian OFDI. We observed that GDP, openness of the economy, and the human capital of India to be significant determining factors of Indian OFDI. In sum, macroeconomic variables such as economic development, openness, and human capital of the Indian economy play an important role in India's FDI outflows. The implication here is that in seeking to accumulate ownership advantages for Indian MNEs at home, Indian government needs to pay more attention to the policies on domestic growth, trade, and human resources. Future research should focus on these three variables to get a more comprehensive picture of Indian OFDI.

References

Aliber, R.Z. (1970). A theory of direct foreign investment, in C.P. Kindleberger (Ed.) *The International Corporation*, Cambridge, MA: MIT Press: 17–34.

Baek, H.Y. and Kwok, C.C.Y. (2002). Foreign exchange rates and the corporate choice of foreign entry mode, *International Review of Economics and Finance*, 11: 207–227.

Barnard, H. (2008). Capability development and the geographic destination of outbound FDI by developing country firms, *International Journal of Technology and Globalisation*, 4: 39–55.

Billington, N. (1999). The location of foreign direct investment: An empirical analysis, *Applied Economics*, 31: 65–76.

Blonigen, B.A. (1997). Firm-specific assets and the link between exchange rates and foreign direct investment, *American Economic Review*, 87: 447–465.

Borensztein, E., De Gregorio, J., and Lee, J.W. (1998). How does foreign direct investment affect economic growth? *Journal of International Economics*, 45: 115–135.

Buckley, P.J., Clegg, J.L., Cross, A.R., Liu, X., Voss, H., and Zheng, P. (2007). The determinants of Chinese outward foreign direct investment, *Journal of International Business Studies*, 38: 499–518.

Chakrabarti, A. (2001). The determinants of foreign direct investment: Sensitivity analysis of cross-country regressions, *Kyklos*, 54: 89–113.

Chakraborty, C. and Basu, P. (2002). Foreign direct investment and growth in India: A cointegration approach, *Applied Economics*, 34: 1061–1073.

Chen, H. and Chen, T.J. (1998). Network linkages and location choice in foreign direct investment, *Journal of International Business Studies*, 29: 445–468.

Chiou Wei, S.Z. and Zhu, Z. (2007). A revisit to the outward FDI determinants: Further evidence from count panel data models with fixed effects, *Applied Economics Letters*, 4: 809–812.

Chowdhury, A. and Wheeler, M. (2008). Does real exchange rate volatility affect foreign direct investment? Evidence from four developed economies, *International Trade Journal*, 22: 218–245.

Cuadros, A., Orts, V., and Alguacil, M. (2004). Openness and growth: Re-examining foreign direct investment, trade and output linkages in Latin America, *Journal of Development Studies*, 40: 167–192.

Desai, M.A., Foley, F., and James, R.H. Jr. (2005). Foreign direct investment and domestic capital stock, *American Economic Review Chapters and Proceedings*, 95: 33–38.

Dunning, J.H. (1988). The eclectic paradigm of international production: A restatement and some possible extensions, *Journal of International Business Studies*, 19: 1–31.

Dunning, J.H. (2009). Location and the multinational enterprise, a neglected factor? *Journal of International Business*, 40: 5–19.

Dunning, J.H. and Narula, R. (1996). *Foreign Direct Investment and Governments: Catalysts for Economic Restructuring*, London; New York, NY: Routledge.

Froot, K.A. and Stein, J.C. (1991). Exchange rates and foreign direct investment, an imperfect capital markets approach, *Quarterly Journal of Economics*, 106: 1191–1217.

Ghosh, S. (2006). Did financial liberalisation ease financing constraint? Evidence from Indian firm-level data, *Emerging Markets Review*, 7: 176–190.

Grubaugh, S. (1987). Determinants of direct foreign investment, *Review of Economics and Statistics*, 69: 149–151.

Herzer, D. (2008). The long-run relationship between outward FDI and domestic output: Evidence from panel data, *Economics Letters*, 100: 146–149.

Hong, S. and Kim, S. (2003). Locational determinants of Korean manufacturing investments in the European Union, *Hitotsubashi Journal of Economics*, 44: 91–103.

Jeon, B.N. and Rhee, S.S. (2008). The determinants of Korea's foreign direct investment from the United States, 1980–2001: An empirical investigation of firm-level data, *Contemporary Economic Policy*, 26: 118–131.

Jha, R. (2003). *Recent Trends in FDI Flows and Prospects for India*. Working chapter, Australia: Australian National University, August 18.

Johansen, S. and Juselius, K. (1990). Maximum likelihood estimation and inference on cointegration with applications to the demand for money, *Oxford Bulletin of Economics and Statistics*, 52: 169–210.

Khanna, T. and Palepu, K. (2000). The future of business groups in emerging markets: Long-run evidence from Chile, *Academy of Management Journal*, 43: 268–285.

Kogut, B. (1983). Foreign direct investment as a sequential process, in C. Kindleberger and D. Audretsch (Eds.) *The Multinational Corporation in the 1980s*, Cambridge: MIT Press: 38–56.

Kohlhagen, S.W. (1977). The effects of exchange-rate adjustments on international investment: Comment, in P.B. Clark, D.E. Logue, and R. Sweeney (Eds.) *The Effects of Exchange Rate Adjustments*, Washington, DC: US Government Printing Office: 194–197.

Kueh, S.H., Puah, C.H., and Mansor, S.A. (2009). Empirical analysis on emerging issues of Malaysia outward FDI from macroeconomic perspective, *International Review of Business Research Chapters*, 5: 124–134.

Kumar, N. (1998). Emerging outward foreign direct investment from Asian developing countries: Prospects and implications, in N. Kumar (Ed.) *Globalisation, Foreign Direct Investment and Technology Transfers*, London; New York, NY: Routledge: 177–194.

Kumar, N. (2001). WTO regime, host country policies and global patterns of MNE activity: Implication of recent quantitative studies for India, *Economic and Political Weekly*, 36: 39–50.

Kyrkilis, D. and Pantelidis, P. (2003). Macroeconomic determinants of outward foreign direct investment, *International Journal of Social Economics*, 30: 827–836.

Lall, S. (1980). Monopolistic advantages and foreign involvement by US manufacturing industry, *Oxford Economic Chapters*, 32: 102–122.

Lall, S. (1996). The investment development path: Some conclusions, in J.H. Dunning and R. Narula (Eds.) *Foreign Direct Investment and Governments, Catalysts for Economic Restructuring*, London: Routledge: 422–441.

Lall, S. (1998). Exports of manufactures by developing countries: Emerging patterns of trade and location, *Oxford Review of Economic Policy*, 11: 54–73.

Lall, S. and Siddarthan, N.S. (1982). The monopolistic advantages of multinationals: Lessons from foreign investment in the U.S., *The Economic Journal*, 92: 668–683.

Liu, X., Buck, T., and Shu, C. (2005). Chinese economic development, the next stage: outward FDI? *International Business Review*, 14(1), 97–115.

Makino, S., Isobe, T., and Chan, C.M. (2004). Does country matter? *Strategic Management Journal*, 25: 1027–1043.

Meyer, K.E. and Sinani, E. (2009). When and where does foreign direct investment generate positive spillovers? A meta-analysis, *Journal of International Business Studies*, 40: 1075–1094.

Morris, S. (1987). Trends in foreign direct investment from India (1950–1982), *Economic and Political Weekly*, 22(45): 1909–1918.

OECD. (1998). *Foreign Direct Investment and Economic Development: Lessons from Six Emerging Economies*, Paris: OECD.

Paloni, N.F. and Youssef, A. (2001). Human capital and FDI inflows to developing countries: New empirical evidence, *World Development*, 29: 1593–1610.

Pradhan, J.P. (2005). *Outward Foreign Direct Investment from India: Recent Trends and Patterns*. Working chapter 153, Ahmedabad: Gujarat Institute of Development Research.

Pradhan, J.P. (2006). *Global Competitiveness of Indian Pharmaceutical Industry: Trends and Strategies*. Working chapter 605, New Delhi: Institute for Studies in Industrial Development.

Pradhan, J.P. (2007). *National Innovation System and the Emergence of Indian Information and Software Technology Multinationals*. Working chapter 09, New Delhi: Institute for Studies in Industrial Development.

Prugel, T.A. (1981). The determinants of foreign direct investments: An analysis of US manufacturing industries, *Managerial and Decisions Economics*, 2: 220–228.

Russ, K.N. (2007). The endogeneity of the exchange rate as a determinant of FDI, *Journal of International Economics*, 71: 344–372.

Stevens, G.V.G. (1993). *Exchange Rates and Foreign Direct Investment: A Note*. International finance discussion chapters, April, no. 444, Washington, DC: Board of Governors of the Federal Reserve System.

Verma, R. and Brennan, L. (2011a). The investment development path theory: Evidence from India, *International Journal of Emerging Markets*, 6: 74–89.

Verma, R. and Brennan, L. (2011b). The influence of exports on outward foreign direct investment: The case of India, in E. Huston, R.R. Sinkovics, and J. Berrill (Eds.) *Firm-Level Internationalisation Regionalism and Globalisation*, London: Palgrave Macmillan: 113–125.

World Investment Report. (1994). *Transnational Corporations, Employment and the Workplace*, Geneva: UNCTAD.

Zhang, K. and Markusen, J. (1999). Vertical multinationals and host country characteristics, *Journal of Development Economics*, 59: 233–252.

7
Influence of Cultural Distance on Chinese Outward Foreign Direct Investment

Rian Drogendijk and Katarina Blomkvist

Introduction

Since 2005, Chinese outward foreign direct investment (OFDI) has shown a striking positive trend, and today China is the main foreign investor in countries like Australia and South Africa (Evenett, 2009). This has triggered an increased interest among scholars and others to understand this development, and several studies have been performed to describe the trend and explain Chinese OFDI (Deng, 2004; Sauvant, 2005; Buckley *et al.*, 2007, 2008; Morck *et al.*, 2008; Voss, 2011). Although previous works indicate the potential role of culture and cultural differences for the internationalization of Chinese firms (e.g. Voss, 2011), a proper test of this explanatory factor has not been done. In this chapter, we test whether cultural distance (cf. Kogut and Singh, 1988; Hofstede, 2001; Drogendijk and Slangen, 2006) explains the investment behavior of Chinese companies.

Following Deng Xiaoping's tour of South China in 1992 and the introduction of the 'Go Global' policy in 1999, Chinese OFDI has experienced a significant increase, reaching a staggering US$55.9 billion in 2008. Previous research points out that the main drivers of Chinese OFDI are natural resources and sovereign wealth funds (Morck *et al.*, 2008; Evenett, 2009). Specific patterns of investments have also been found, indicating that Chinese multinational companies (MNCs) follow a regionalization strategy rather than a global one (Rugman and Doh, 2008). The main part of Chinese OFDIs is located in the neighboring countries of Asia, and China's Special Administrative Region Hong Kong is the foremost receiver of Chinese OFDI (Gugler and Fetscherin, 2010). It is also suggested that Chinese OFDI is heavily influenced by the Chinese state and that Chinese trends in OFDI cannot be understood without reference to the Chinese government and its policies (Gugler and Fetscherin, 2010). However, even though 'China's distinctive cultural and institutional legacy (...) may be expected to increase the liability of foreignness faced by its firms as they seek to internationalize' (Child and Rodrigues, 2005: 385), there is a lack of research investigating cultural differences as an explanatory factor of Chinese OFDI.

The relative lack of research on how cultural differences influence the direction of Chinese OFDI stands in contrast with public and policy debates in many countries around the world trying to attract Chinese OFDI and seeking factors to foster it. In the current study we draw upon previous research, suggesting that the cultural distance between countries affects investment decisions by firms (Johanson and Wiedersheim-Paul, 1975; Kogut and Singh, 1988; Barkema *et al.*, 1996). Large cultural differences may lead to uncertainty and misunderstanding, and may increase costs associated with adapting to the local context or control of local subsidiaries. Differences in culture are widely acknowledged as an explanatory factor for the internationalization of Western MNCs (Johanson and Vahlne, 1977; Barkema *et al.*, 1996; Dow and Larimo, 2009), yet the value of this factor for understanding OFDI from developing countries still remains unknown. Until now, studies on Chinese OFDI have controlled for culture by inserting a variable, capturing Chinese minority groups in host countries. This chapter contributes by empirically testing the influence of cultural distance on Chinese OFDI and in doing so adds to the current research discussion on the value of established theoretical models and concepts, developed to explain the internationalization of Western MNCs, for understanding the internationalization of MNCs from developing countries.

The chapter is organized as follows. First, Chinese OFDI is discussed, emphasizing its development and determinants as discussed and investigated in previous literature. Thereafter, the concept of cultural distance and its established influence on OFDI flows are highlighted and we develop hypotheses on the effect of cultural distance on Chinese OFDI patterns. Our results indicate that Chinese OFDI indeed is influenced by cultural distance. We further find that particular differences in the cultural dimensions of power distance and uncertainty avoidance affect the direction of Chinese OFDI.

Chinese OFDI

Since China introduced its 'Go Global' policy promoting overseas investment, its OFDI has amplified significantly. OFDI became permitted in 1979 during the 'Open Door' policies and it has increased thereafter (Buckley *et al.*, 2008). The literature distinguishes several stages in the development of Chinese OFDI (see Table 7.1 for an overview). Initially, OFDI was permitted on a very limited scale. Foreign investment was, for example, restricted to some appointed champions within certain industries, all of which were state-owned enterprises (SOEs). This changed first around 1992, after Deng Xiaoping's journey to the south, and subsequently in 1999, when the government instigated the 'Go Global' policy (Child and Rodrigues, 2005; Buckley *et al.*, 2007, 2008; Voss, 2011). One of the main aims of the 'Go Global' initiative in 1999, officially announced in the Tenth Five-Year Plan in 2001, was to make Chinese firms competitive globally. Today, administrative controls are reduced to a large extent and also the numbers of non state-owned enterprises actively investing abroad have gone up (Buckley *et al.*, 2007, 2008; Voss, 2011).

Chinese OFDI has been studied from various perspectives since the mid-1990s. A number of researchers have focused on the regulatory framework and the influence of the Chinese government as well as the investment motives of Chinese firms (Zhan, 1995; Wang, 2002; Hong and Sun, 2006). It is argued that Chinese OFDI is heavily influenced by the Chinese state and cannot be understood without reference to the Chinese government and its policies (Gugler and Fetscherin, 2010). The institutional setting of a country is likely to have a profound effect on a country's FDI, both inward and outward (Buckley and Casson, 1976). Although China's policies regarding FDI have changed over the years, the institutional frame is still very much regulated by the state, and thus governments at various levels have been and still are the main operational decision-takers concerning the approval of investment projects (Buckley *et al.*, 2008).

Other studies have emphasized the role of natural resources as a main driver for Chinese OFDI leading to recent upsurges of investments in resource-rich areas, such as Africa (Morck *et al.*, 2008; Evenett, 2009). Since China is comparably poor in most natural resources, the strategic need of securing supply of natural resources is essential; hence a large part of China's OFDI is directed toward countries and regions rich in natural resources, such as Africa, Central Asia, Australia, the Russian Federation, and Canada. Further, several researchers have suggested that firms from China and other developing countries invest in developed markets to make up for resource and knowledge deficiencies (Peng and Wang, 2000; Rui and Yip, 2008). In other words, Chinese OFDI in Europe and North America can be explained from a resource-exploration

Table 7.1 Key stages in Chinese OFDI policy development

1979–1985 *Stage One: Cautious internationalization*
With the 'open-door' policy, Chinese ODI was identified by government as one means of opening and integrating China into the world economy. Chinese state-owned firms start to set up their first international operations. Only state-owned trading corporations under MOFERT (later MOFCOM or the Ministry of Commerce) and provincial and municipal 'economic and technological cooperation enterprises' under the State Economic and Trade Commission (now part of the National Development and Reform Commission [NDRC]) are allowed to invest abroad. Some 189 projects were approved, amounting to about US$197 million in value.

1986–1991 *Stage Two: Government encouragement*
The government liberalized restrictive policies and allowed more enterprises to establish foreign affiliates, provided they had sufficient capital, technical and operational know-how, and a suitable joint venture partner. Approval was granted to 891 projects, totaling some US$1.2 billion.

1992–1998 *Stage Three: Expansion and regulation*
Encouraged by domestic liberalization, initiated by Deng Xiaoping's journey to the South and the incorporation of enterprise internationalization into the national economic development policy, sub-national level authorities actively promote the international business activities of enterprises under their supervision, especially in Hong Kong to engage in real estate and stock market speculation. The Asian crisis in 1997 and the subsequent collapse of some enterprises slow down this development. Latterly, concerns about loss of control over state assets, capital flight and 'leakage' of foreign exchange lead to a tightening of approval procedures, notably for projects of US$1 million or more. Individual ODI project activity declines, despite an increase of total ODI of US$1.2 billion in value terms.

1999–2001 *Stage Four: Implementation of the 'Go Global' policy*
Contradictory policies characterize this period. Further measures to control illicit capital transfers and to regularize ODI toward genuinely productive purposes are introduced. By contrast, ODI in specific industries is actively encouraged with export tax rebates, foreign exchange assistance, and direct financial support, notably in trade-related activities that promoted Chinese exports of raw materials, parts and machinery and in light industry sectors like textiles, machinery, and electrical equipment. In 2001 this encouragement is formalized within the 10th Five-Year plan which outlined the *'Going Global'* or *'zou chu qu'* directive. Total approved ODI rises by US$1.8 billion, with an average project value of US$ 2.6 million.

Since 2001 *Stage Five: Post WTO period (included here for completeness)*
Heightened domestic competitive pressures, due to the opening of once-protected industries and markets to foreign and domestic competitors, forces some Chinese firms to seek new markets abroad. In the 11th Five-Year Plan the Chinese government stressed again the importance of *'zou chu qu'* for Chinese firms and the Chinese economy. Although the approval system is decentralized and streamlined to become less burdensome, contradictory regulations still prevail. Direct, proactive support of ODI continues to be limited, mainly aimed at preventing illegal capital outflows and loss of control of state assets.

Source: Based on Buckley *et al.* (2007).

rationale (Al-Laham and Amburgey, 2005). Accordingly, Chinese firms behave as late comers performing strategic asset-seeking FDI, trying to close the gap between them and leading companies in their respective industries to become globally competitive. By acquiring European firms, Chinese firms get access to potential capabilities and sources of new knowledge (Gugler and Brunner, 2007). On the other hand, research has also shown that firms from developing countries build on their experiences with underdeveloped institutional environments when investing in the least developed countries of the world (Cuervo-Cazurra and Genc, 2008). In this light, the institutional challenges that Chinese firms experience at home may provide them with an advantage over firms from developed countries when investing in regions like Africa.

In relation to the cultural aspect of foreign investments, previous research has emphasized the role of Chinese minorities in host countries when studying the internationalization of Chinese firms (see, e.g. Chen and Chen, 2004; Tong, 2005). It is suggested that strong economic connections abroad and the significance of guanxi[1] affect Chinese OFDI (Luo, 1997; Standifird and Marshall, 2000). Ethnic and family guanxi provide firm-specific advantages to Chinese firms reducing business risks abroad (Braeutigam, 2003). Guanxi relations can also help to identify new business opportunities in the host country (Zhan, 1995). Hence, Chinese minority groups are argued to serve as a bridge between China and the host country and are mentioned to help reduce psychic distance and the liability of foreignness, and thus to form an important base for Chinese firms internationalization.

Cultural distance and FDI

It is generally accepted that the international expansion of firms is negatively affected by differences among countries in terms of their economic, political, social, cultural, linguistic, and other characteristics, and that these continue to affect international expansion (Johanson and Vahlne, 1977; Barkema *et al.*, 1996; Ghemawat, 2001; Flores and Aguilera, 2007). Researchers have tried to capture these country differences in many ways, most notably by means of measures of cultural (Kogut and Singh, 1988; Barkema *et al.*, 1996; Drogendijk and Slangen, 2006) and psychic distance (Johanson and Wiedersheim-Paul, 1975; Stöttinger and Schlegelmilch, 1998; Dow and Larimo, 2009). In particular the influence of national cultural differences and its most popular measure, the Kogut–Singh index based on Hofstede's (1980) four dimensions of national culture,[2] have become standard variables in studies of international business (Shenkar, 2001; Harzing, 2003; Kirkman *et al.*, 2006).

Cultural distance is defined as the extent to which the shared norms and values in one country differ from those in another (Kogut and Singh, 1988; Hofstede, 2001). The general argument in the international business literature is that the larger the cultural distance between two countries, the more difficult it is to understand and interpret information, to manage inter-cultural relations, and to organize and operate in the foreign context. It therefore affects many aspects of international management, including foreign investment. Cultural distance has in relation to this field of study for example been found to affect decisions on entry mode (Kogut and Singh, 1988) and establishment mode (Drogendijk and Slangen, 2006), internationalization patterns (Johanson and Vahlne, 1977; Barkema *et al.*, 1996), and location choices (Li and Guisinger, 1992; Benito and Gripsrud, 1992; Flores and Aguilera, 2007). Though the concept of cultural distance has been under critique recently (Shenkar, 2001; Shenkar *et al.*, 2008), several scholars plea for its value, in particular for explaining issues like location decisions (Zaheer *et al.*, 2012) and entry decisions of firms from one specific country (Tung and Verbeke, 2010). Location decisions are driven by the perception of cultural distance and the expected potential problems related to it rather than actual frictions or miscommunications that may influence acquisition integration processes or knowledge transfer (Zaheer *et al.*, 2012). We therefore judge cultural distance to be a valuable concept to investigate, in the context of Chinese outward FDI decisions.

Hypotheses

Johanson and Wiedersheim-Paul (1975) observed that firms often started with exporting to foreign countries, and only after learning about the local culture invested through FDI in these countries. They also found that firms preferred to start investing in countries that were relatively similar to their own in terms of culture. Several studies support that firms prefer to do business in markets at smaller cultural and psychic distance and are less likely to select markets at larger distance for exporting (Dow, 2000; Brewer, 2007; Martín Martín and Drogendijk, forthcoming). These patterns were further confirmed by research on FDI. Barkema *et al.* (1996) find that Dutch firms were more successful in foreign investments by building up experiences in nearby markets first, before entering markets at a larger psychic distance from the home market. In another study, Dutch firms were further found to benefit from following a step-wise investment pattern in new cultural settings, in particular when lacking international experience (Barkema and Drogendijk, 2007). Also studies on the location choices of firms confirmed the negative relation between that cultural distance and investment decisions of firms (Li and Guisinger, 1992; Flores and Aguilera, 2007). Furthermore, Flores and Aguilera (2007) compared US location choices in 1980 and 2000 and conclude that the role of cultural distance continues to explain location choices of US firms in today's globalized world. In the case of Chinese companies, which are in the starting stage of internationalization and generally lack foreign investment experience, we expect that cultural differences between China and respective host countries negatively relate to the level of Chinese OFDI to these countries. Accordingly, our hypothesis is:

> ***Hypothesis 1.*** *The larger the cultural differences between China and a host market, the less Chinese firms invest into that market.*

Data and method

In order to best test the value of cultural distance as explanatory factor for Chinese OFDI, we designed our study partly as a replication of previous studies, in particular the work by Buckley and co-authors (Buckley *et al.*, 2007, 2008; Voss, 2011). We analyzed outward FDI by Chinese firms into 174 host countries[3] between 2003–2009.[4] In accordance with earlier studies on Chinese OFDI and to obtain a more robust variable we calculated the mean OFDI of 2003–2009 from China to each country (Buckley *et al.*, 2007). Similarly, we accessed several publicly available secondary data sources published, for example, by the World Bank and the United Nations, and Hofstede (1980, 2001) in our analyses.

Variables

Dependent variable

Our dependent variable is the mean amount of Chinese OFDI[5] over the years 2003–2009. We used official data from the 2009 statistical bulletin of Chinese OFDI 2003–2009, published by China's Ministry of Commerce (MOFCOM), the National Bureau of Statistics of the People's Republic of China, and the State Administration for Foreign Exchange (SAFE, one of the main agencies concerned with the investment approval process in China), which is in line with how previous research has measured Chinese OFDI (Buckley *et al.*, 2007). The data includes pre-approved reinvested earnings and intra-company loans, plus in-kind investment up to the total authorized value of a given project, in addition to equity capital. Following previous studies we used the natural logarithm of the mean Chinese OFDI 2003–2009 in our models.

Independent variables: Cultural distance

We measured aggregated cultural distance between China and other countries through the index developed by Kogut and Singh (1988). Like the original Kogut and Singh index we measured countries' scores on the four original dimensions of national culture (Hofstede, 1980, 2001): power distance, uncertainty avoidance, individualism, and masculinity. The scores on the four dimensions were available for 78 of the 174 countries in our dataset. We retrieved the scores for a further number of 43 countries through extending the area scores of 'East Africa', 'West Africa', and 'Arab world' to more countries than those originally included in Hofstede's study and added another 14 countries by building on earlier empirical studies publishing scores on countries not included in his work.[6] In our models on the full sample of 174 host countries we inserted means for missing values on the cultural distance index. We also tested our hypotheses based on more restrictive samples of countries for which we retrieved Hofstede data, and for countries included in the original Hofstede (1980, 2001) study only, and the study is indicating similar results.

Using the Kogut and Singh index has advantages and disadvantages as has been discussed extensively in the literature (Shenkar, 2001, 2012; Drogendijk and Slangen, 2006; Kirkman *et al.*, 2006; Zaheer *et al.*, 2012). In a recent exchange in the Journal of International Business Studies (in January 2012) Zaheer *et al.* (2012) argued that distance measures that capture an aggregate concept of ex-ante perceived distance between markets with respect to relevant issues are relevant in studies aiming to explain location choice. Tung and Verbeke (2010) further argued that the illusion of symmetry that is associated with distance measures (see Shenkar, 2001) is less problematic when one studies the behavior or business choices of firms from one country into many others. These arguments justify the use of a distance measure in the context under investigation here: the direction of Chinese investments to other countries globally. Finally, Drogendijk and Slangen compared different measures of cultural distance, based on the studies on culture dimensions by Hofstede (1980) as well as Schwartz (1994) and found no major improvements when using indices based on the latter, more recent data. Based on their conclusion 'that it may thus be premature to dismiss Hofstede's work as outdated or as inaccurately reflecting national cultures' (Drogendijk and Slangen, 2006: 362) and because it provides scores on cultural dimensions for more countries, we decided that employing the Kogut and Singh index was accurate.

Control variables

Following the work by Buckley *et al.* (2007) and Voss (2011), we included control variables representing different motivations or different types of Chinese OFDI: strategic asset-seeking, market-seeking, and resource-seeking. To measure strategic asset-seeking FDI we used the total (resident plus non-resident) annual patent registration in the host country (cf. Buckley *et al.*, 2007). The data was collected from the World Intellectual Property Organisation, for the year 2007. We used GDP of the host country to control for market-seeking Chinese OFDI (cf. Buckley *et al.*, 2007). We retrieved this data from the World Bank Development Indicator for the years 2003–2009, using the mean of these years. In order to control for resource-seeking Chinese FDI we used the ratio of ore and metal exports between 2003 and 2009, calculating the mean (cf. Buckley *et al.*, 2007). Also this data were obtained from the World Bank Development Indicator statistics. For all three variables, we used the natural logarithm in line with how previous research has operationalized the different types of Chinese OFDI (Buckley *et al.*, 2007).

We also controlled for the effects of inflation and exchange rate. Data for inflation was collected from IMF's World Economic Outlook, and data for exchange rates were collected from the World Bank Development Indicator. Again data were collected for the years 2003–2009, and the mean was calculated to give a more robust value controlling for fluctuations. We also followed previous work (Buckley *et al.*, 2007; Voss 2011) and controlled for import and export flows between China and respective host countries. Data were retrieved from the China Statistical Yearbook (National Bureau of Statistics, 2009). We calculated the mean over the years 2003–2009, and used the natural logarithm in our models (cf. Buckley *et al.*, 2007). To include the potential influence of Chinese minorities in host countries, a variable capturing the numbers of ethnic Chinese in host countries was included. This variable is in line with previous studies predicting Chinese OFDI, such as, Kent (2003), Buckley *et al.* (2007) and Voss (2011), and the data were acquired from the Ohio University (Distribution of the Ethnic Chinese Population Around the World, 2006). Among the countries with the largest ethnic Chinese minorities are neighboring Asian countries like Indonesia, Thailand, and Malaysia, but we also find large groups of ethnic Chinese in the USA,

Canada, and the Russian Federation. Finally, we followed Voss (2011) to include a variable controlling for World Trade Organization (WTO) membership of host countries.

Analyses, findings, and discussion

We test our hypotheses with ordinary least squares regression analyses, in accordance with previous literature (e.g. Buckley *et al.*, 2007; Voss, 2011).

Descriptive findings OFDI

Over the years 2003–2009, trade between China and other countries increased. We illustrate this in Figures 7.1 and 7.2, presenting the exports and imports from and to China in this period. The figures show that there is a striking overall positive trend. In line with the financial crisis it shows the decline in economic activity in 2009. Though import figures show a steady increase, export figures rise sharply after 2006.[7] From 2006, the exports to and imports from Africa show a striking increase relative to imports from and exports to other parts of the world. This corresponds to the introduction in 2006 of China's official

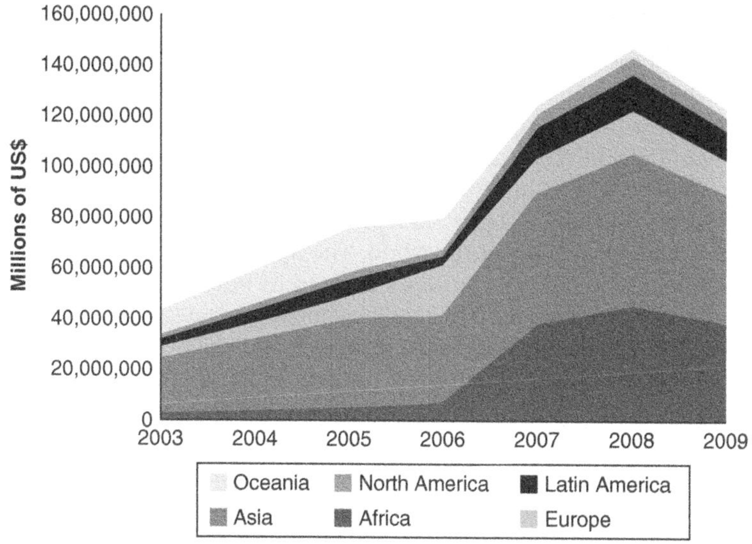

Figure 7.1 Exports from China, 2003–2009
Source: Based on China Statistical Yearbook.

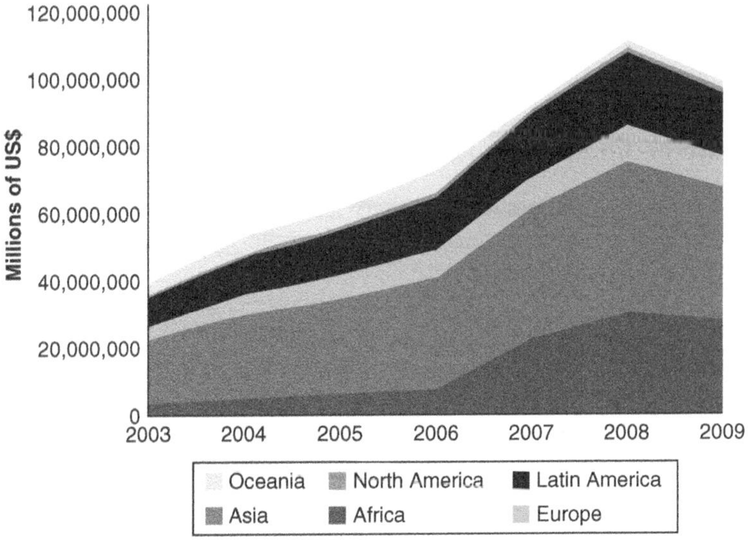

Figure 7.2 Imports to China, 2003–2009
Source: Based on China Statistical Yearbook.

Africa policy by the Chinese government (China Ministry of Foreign Affairs, 2006).

Total Chinese OFDI stock increased from US$33.2 billion to US$ 645.7 billion in 2009, with an average of US$625.74 million per country per year. According to our data, averages of Chinese OFDI stocks per world region (2003–2009) are US$77,871 million in Asia, 18,798 in Latin America, 3,871 in Africa, 3,272 in Europe, 2,342 in North America, and 2,095 in Oceania. Figure 7.3 represents the increasing FDI outflows to the different regions of the world. The figure clearly shows that the majority of Chinese FDI continues to go to its home region: Asia. This suggests that Chinese investors follow a regional strategy for FDI rather than a global strategy as has been suggested previously by Rugman and Doh (2008).

According to the data reported in the 2009 Statistical Bulletin of China's Outward FDI, the top ten destination countries for Chinese OFDI between 2003–2009 are neighboring countries and regions like Hong Kong, Singapore, and Macau, tax havens (the Cayman Islands, the British Virgin Islands, and Luxembourg), and further Australia, the US, Russia, and South Africa (Table 7.2 shows the top ten destinations per year).

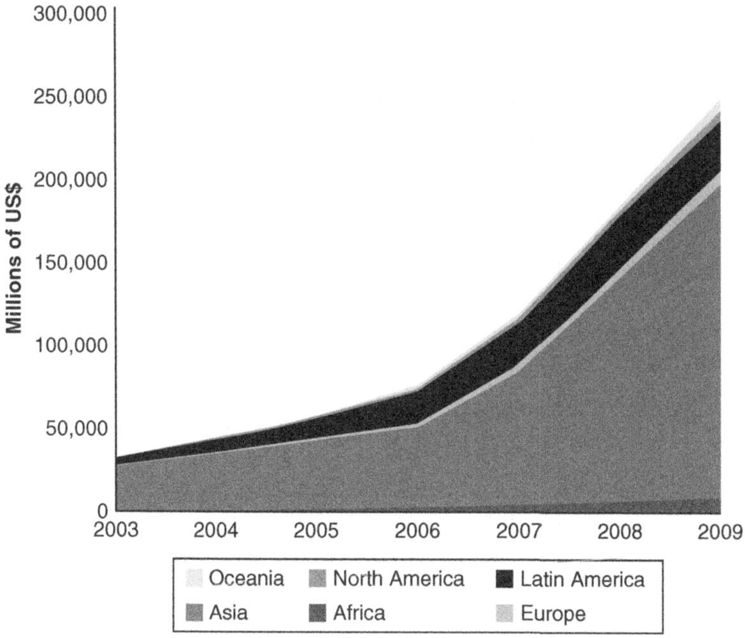

Figure 7.3 Chinese OFDI per region
Source: Own calculations based on data from the 2009 Statistical Bulletin of China's Outward FDI.

Descriptive findings of cultural differences

We calculated the cultural distance from China to the host countries in our sample and find that the countries ranked farthest from China are countries in Scandinavia, Baltic countries, and the Netherlands (see the last column in Table 7.3). Not surprisingly, the countries ranking closest to China are Asian countries and regions like Hong Kong, the Philippines, Indonesia, Malaysia, Singapore, and India. When looking at the individual national culture dimensions, however, we find that the patterns are more varied. When we look at absolute differences in power distance (column 1 in Table 7.3) we find that Arab countries are closest to China, as are Central American countries like Mexico and Venezuela. Next to neighboring Asian countries Vietnam and Hong Kong, also Sweden, the UK, and Ireland show similar scores to China on the next dimension, uncertainty avoidance. On the dimension of individualism, Western African countries complement Asian neighbors as nearest to China, and another set of countries is close to China in

Table 7.2 Top ten destinations for Chinese OFDI

	2003	2004	2005	2006	2007	2008	2009
Top Ten Receivers of Chinese OFDI	Hong Kong	Hong Kong	Hong Kong	Hong Kong	Hong Kong	Hong Kong	Hong Kong
	Cayman Islands	Cayman Islands	Cayman Islands	Cayman Islands	Cayman Islands	Cayman Islands	British Virgin Islands
	British Virgin Islands	British Virgin Islands	British Virgin Islands	British Virgin Islands	British Virgin Islands	British Virgin Islands	Cayman Islands
	US	US	Rep. Korea	US	US	Australia	Australia
	Macau	Macau	US	Rep. Korea	Australia	Singapore	Singapore
	Iraq	Rep. Korea	Macau	Russia	Singapore	South Africa	US
	Australia	Australia	Australia	Australia	Russia	US	Luxembourg
	Rep. Korea	Iraq	Russia	Macau	Canada	Russia	South Africa
	Singapore	Singapore	Iraq	Sudan	Rep. Korea	Macau	Russia
	Thailand	Bermuda	Sudan	Germany	Pakistan	Kazakhstan	Macau

Sources: 2009 Statistical Bulletin of China's Outward FDI (MOFCOM, National Bureau of Statistics of the People's Republic of China, and SAFE).

Table 7.3 Cultural distance to China, per factor

	Power Distance	**Uncertainty Avoidance**	**Individualism**	**Masculinity**	**K&S Index**
China's score (Hofstede, 2001)	80 (high)	30 (low)	20 (low)	66 (high)	–
Countries, Regions nearest to China	Arab countries (incl. e.g. Egypt, Iraq, Kuwait, Lebanon), Mexico and Venezuela	Vietnam, Hong Kong, Sweden, UK, Ireland	Vietnam, Singapore, West Africa (incl. e.g. Ghana, Nigeria, Sierra Leone), Bangladesh, Thailand	Germany, UK, Colombia, Philippines, Jamaica	Hong Kong, Philippines, Indonesia, Malaysia, Singapore, India
Countries, Regions at largest distance from China	Ireland, New Zealand, Denmark, Israel, Austria	Russia, Malta, Uruguay, Portugal, Greece	Netherlands, Hungary, UK, Australia, US	Denmark, Netherlands, Latvia, Norway, Sweden	Israel, Netherlands, Norway, Denmark, Sweden

Source: Own calculations and interpretations based on Hofstede (1980, 2001).

terms of masculinity scores: Here we find for example Germany, the UK, Colombia, and the Philippines. We find similar variation when we look at the countries furthest, or most different from China with regard to the four national culture dimensions (see Table 7.3).

Descriptive statistics

The correlation matrix of the dependent and independent variables is shown in Table 7.4, showing modest correlations between the dependent variable and some of the control variables, the highest being a Spearman r of 0.506 between OFDI and import, and of 0.476 between OFDI and export. The explanatory variable cultural distance shows moderate correlations with political risk ($r = 0.580$), inflation rates (-0.430), and GDP (0.322). Higher correlations are logically found between import, export, and GDP (0.700 and higher). These results make intuitive sense, but show that we will need to check whether multi-collinearity affects the interpretation of the results in our regression analyses.

In order to control for potential multi-collinearity, we calculated the variance inflation factors (VIF) for all independent and control variables included in the models. Multi-collinearity is an indicator of correlation between two or more independent variables and, if present, may make the independent variables skewed to the data used. Common cut-off points for VIF values are generally set to around 5 (Studenmund, 1992) or as high as 10 (Hair *et al.*, 2006; Marquardt, 1970). With no VIF values over 5, we conclude that the risk of miss-interpretation of the results due to multi-collinearity is limited.

Test of hypothesis

In order to test our hypothesis on the effect of culture distance on Chinese OFDI, an ordinary least square (OLS) regression analysis was performed. Table 7.5 presents the results of these tests, including a controls-only model (Model 1) and a model including cultural distance (Model 2). The adjusted explanatory value for Model 2 is 33 per cent, with an F-value of 9.018 ($p < 0.001$).

In our first model we included our control variables based on previous research in the field and concluded that the variables that most significantly relate with Chinese OFDI are the import and export to the respective host markets. In contrast to previous studies, we do not find that market size (in terms of GDP), natural resources (measured as export of ore and metals), and strategic assets (the number of patents registered in the host country) significantly explain Chinese OFDI, suggesting that Chinese firms are less inclined to invest abroad with market

Table 7.4 Spearman's correlations between dependent and independent variables

		1	2	3	4	5	6	7	8	9	10	11
1	LOFDI	1.000	–	–	–	–	–	–	–	–	–	–
2	LGDP	.400	1.000	–	–	–	–	–	–	–	–	–
3	LORE	.025	–.074	1.000	–	–	–	–	–	–	–	–
4	LPatents	.117	.152	.006	1.000	–	–	–	–	–	–	–
5	LRATE	.056	–.273	.119	–.065	1.000	–	–	–	–	–	–
6	LINFL	.055	–.204	.169	–.089	.208	1.000	–	–	–	–	–
7	Minority	.240	.129	–.049	.094	–.091	–.073	1.000	–	–	–	–
8	Limport	.506	.700	.022	.096	–.125	–.209	.131	1.000	–	–	–
9	Lexport	.476	.723	.002	.111	–.141	–.190	.128	.743	1.000	–	–
10	WTO	–.042	.166	.012	–.033	–.095	–.242	.011	.134	.140	1.000	–
11	CultDist	–.090	.322	.040	.213	–.430	–.106	.069	.148	.157	–.058	1.000

Table 7.5 Regression analysis: Determinants of Chinese OFDI, 2003–2009

	Model 1	Model 2	Model 3
LGDP	0.076 (0.114)	0.155 (0.114)	0.212 (0.158)
LORE	–.010 (0.092)	0.010 (0.091)	0.023 (0.093)
LPatents	0.090 (0.048)	0.129 (0.049)†	0.035 (0.052)
LExchange rate	0.115 (0.052)	0.043 (0.054)	0.051 (0.057)
LInflation	0.098 (0.292)	0.100 (0.284)	0.220 (0.297)**
LImport	0.245 (0.085)*	0.237 (0.083)*	0.183 (0.100)
LExport	0.237 (0.124)*	0.216 (0.121)*	0.258 (0.131)*
Minority	0.149 (0.129)*	0.150 (0.213)*	0.127 (0.250)†
WTO	–0.121 (0.168)†	–0.128 (0.163)†	–0.024 (0.192)
Cultural distance	–	–0.234 (0.058)***	–
Power distance (ABS)	–	–	–0.154 (0.006)†
Uncertainty avoidance (ABS)	–	–	–0.254 (0.004)**
Individualism (ABS)	–	–	–0.057 (0.006)
Masculinity (ABS)	–	–	–0.002 (0.006)
F	8.452***	9.018***	6.645***
Observations	164	164	133
Adjusted *R*-square	0.292	0.330	0.357

Dependent variable: Chinese OFDI; standard errors in parentheses.
† = < 0.10, * = < 0.05, ** = < 0.01, *** = < 0.001.

and resource seeking motivations than in studies based on OFDI data from earlier periods (see e.g. Buckley *et al.*, 2007). Potential explanations for these results may be the different time period analyzed in our study, as well as other factors suggested by previous research, like the role of the Chinese state and its impact on Chinese OFDI (Morck *et al.*, 2008). The controls-only model shows significant relations between Chinese OFDI and the levels of import and export to and from the host markets. We also find that countries with more than 1 per cent ethnic Chinese among their population are more likely to receive Chinese investments than countries with smaller ethnic Chinese minorities. Finally, countries that are members of the WTO are less likely to receive Chinese OFDI according to our analyses, in accordance with previous studies (e.g. Voss, 2011).

We continue with the tests of our hypothesis on the effect of culture distance on Chinese OFDI. We find that the larger the cultural distance between China and a host country, the less Chinese firms invested in this country, in accordance with hypothesis 1. This result is in accordance with behavior shown by Western firms reported in the literature, like the location choices of US firms (Li and Guisinger, 1992; Flores and Aguilera, 2007).

The last column of Table 7.5 presents additional analyses on the explanatory power of the individual national culture dimensions on

Table 7.6 Collinearity statistics for OLS regressions models

	VIF Model 1	VIF Model 2	VIF Model 3
LGDP	2.824	2.981	4.807
LORE	1.048	1.066	1.069
LPatents	1.084	1.122	1.250
LExchange rate	1.118	1.248	1.470
LInflation	1.092	1.092	1.139
LImport	2.929	2.930	3.570
LExport	2.896	2.907	3.022
Minority	1.042	1.042	1.173
WTO	1.072	1.073	1.293
Cultural distance	–	1.363	–
Power distance (ABS)	–	–	2.272
Uncertainty avoidance (ABS)	–	–	1.304
Individualism (ABS)	–	–	2.845
Masculinity (ABS)	–	–	1.194

Chinese OFDI. We calculated the absolute difference between China's score and host countries' scores on the respective dimensions: power distance, uncertainty avoidance, individualism, and masculinity.[8] As we have seen in the descriptive results presented above (see Table 7.3), different countries are similar and dissimilar to China, depending on the respective dimension studied. Our analysis shows that distance on all culture dimensions is negatively related to Chinese OFDI, although this relation is only significant for the dimensions power distance (at $p < 0.1$) and uncertainty avoidance (at $p < 0.01$). The results of this exploration suggest that in particular differences with respect to uncertainty avoidance negatively affect investment decisions of Chinese firms (Table 7.6).

Discussion

In our analyses we find that the cultural distance between China and host countries negatively influences FDI. This is in correspondence with established literature, all based on empirical observation of Western firms, which emphasizes the negative effect of cultural differences on international business (Johanson and Wiedersheim-Paul, 1975; Li and Guisinger, 1992; Barkema *et al.*, 1996; Flores and Aguilera, 2007). Hence, our results suggest that the effect of cultural distance based on Hofstede's four dimensions has not disappeared over time and the effect remains valid for the specific context of Chinese FDI in the new millennium.

With regard to the effects of the individual culture dimensions of Hofstede and in accordance with earlier observations (e.g. Barkema and Vermeulen, 1997), we find that there is a variety in their explanatory power. More specifically, our results show that differences in power distance and uncertainty avoidance have a higher negative impact on the direction of Chinese OFDI than those in individualism and masculinity.

Indeed, this opens up the discussion regarding how culture and cultural distance should be operationalized and adapted to specific contexts. Earlier studies on China have included a variable capturing Chinese minority groups to control for cultural proximity (Buckley *et al.*, 2007). Our results confirm the significant impact of Chinese minority groups in host countries on Chinese OFDI. But our analyses also show that cultural distance has a separate and significant influence on Chinese OFDI on top of the impact of ethnic minorities. Taken together this suggests that the variable controlling for Chinese minority groups in host countries does not capture the same effect as cultural distance. We propose that the variable of Chinese minority groups captures the importance of established network relationships and guanxi, both mentioned as important factors influencing internationalization by Chinese firms, whereas cultural distance measures the aggregated differences in values between countries.

Our study cannot answer questions on how cultural differences disrupt or affect business contacts and operations of Chinese firms abroad. More research studying individual firms' investment behavior and success in order is needed to understand how culture affects relationships and success in international business. Such work could draw upon the contributions of Brannen and Salk (2000), Clausen (2007), McSweeney (2009), and Fischer (2009), who suggest dynamic and multi-level approaches to studying how culture can be negotiated and given meaning in business interaction (for an overview of alternative approaches to cultural distance see Drogendijk and Zander (2010)).

Taken together this suggests that the internationalization process of Chinese firms is not significantly different from that of other countries with respect to the effects of cultural differences. We also support Rugman and Doh (2008) who argue that Chinese firms follow a regional rather than a global strategy. This stands in contrast to the suggestion that China has a global strategy decided by the Chinese state (see e.g. Gugler and Fetscherin, 2010). More research is needed to single out and understand into more depth the role of the Chinese state for Chinese OFDI.

Conclusions

The aim of this chapter was to empirically investigate the role of culture on Chinese OFDI. In doing so, this chapter adds to the current literature explaining OFDI from developing countries. Our findings suggest that cultural differences indeed influence investment decisions by Chinese firms. More specifically, we find that cultural distance negatively influences Chinese OFDI: Chinese firms invest less in countries at a larger cultural distance to China. In particular, differences on the cultural dimensions of power distance and uncertainty avoidance affect the direction of Chinese OFDI. Indeed, culture has long been acknowledged as a key explanatory factor for the internationalization path of firms from developed countries in terms of entry mode choice, FDI, trade flows, and market selection (Kogut and Singh, 1988; Li and Guisinger, 1992; Benito and Gripsrud, 1992; Barkema *et al.*, 1996; Drogendijk and Slangen, 2006; Flores and Aguilera, 2007). However, culture has been neglected as an explanatory variable for determining the internationalization path of MNCs from developing countries. When looking at Chinese OFDI the existence of large Chinese minorities has been used as a proxy capturing the effect of cultural differences; yet we show in this study that both Chinese minorities and cultural distance significantly influence Chinese OFDI and should be treated as two separate explanatory variables. This chapter contributes by highlighting the significant impact of cultural distance on Chinese OFDI, and thereby supports the continued explanatory power of this established construct for explaining internationalization paths of MNCs.

Notes

1. Guanxi can be defined as the ancient system of personal relationships and social connections based on mutual interest and benefit (Buckley *et al.*, 2007).
2. Power distance is the extent to which people believe and accept that power and status are distributed unequally in society. Uncertainty avoidance expresses the extent to which people are threatened by uncertain, unknown, or unstructured situations. Individualism (and collectivism) refers to the degree to which a society emphasizes the role of the individual as opposed to the group. Finally, masculinity (and femininity) refers to the extent to which a society holds traditional masculine values such as competitiveness, assertiveness, and achievement, as opposed to feminine ones such as nurturing, helping others, and minding the quality of life (Hofstede, 1980).
3. In the current chapter both the terms China and Mainland China refer to the People's Republic of China (PRC). In this study the PRC excludes the

special autonomous regions of Hong Kong and Macau as the Republic of China Taiwan is referred to as a separate economy.

4. Due to varying statistical methodologies and data collection problems statistics on China's inward and outward FDI do not have the same quality as international standards (UNCTAD, 2007), something that causes limitations when trying to explain Chinese OFDI. Previous researches on Chinese OFDI have explained the specific problems of different data bases (Buckley *et al.*, 2008; Voss, 2011), and have suggested that one should be aware of this and preferably triangulate data from the different sources. In this chapter we use data for several years, which are obtained from the three most commonly used sources regarding statistics on Chinese OFDI; China's Ministry of Commerce (MOFCOM), the National Bureau of Statistics of the People's Republic of China, and the State Administration for Foreign Exchange (SAFE, one of the main agencies concerned with the investment approval process in China) to increase validity.
5. The definition of FDI in this chapter draws upon UNCTAD hence FDI is an investment involving a long-term relationship and reflecting a lasting interest and control by a firm in an enterprise resident in a foreign country (UNCTAD, 2005). Moreover, it includes three factors; equity capital, reinvested earnings, and intra-company loans or debt transactions (UNCTAD, 2005).
6. We followed Suanet and Van de Vijver (2009) and estimated the scores for Paraguay and Bolivia by using the average scores for Uruguay and Colombia. Suanet and Van de Vijver (2009) further propose to use Russia's scores for Ukraine and Uzbekistan. We have extended this and use scores for Russia also for Byelorus, Kirghizia, Tadzhikistan, and Turkmenistan. Scores for Myanmar were retrieved from Rarick and Nickerson (2008), whereas scores for Latvia and Lithuania are from Huettinger (2008). Sri Lanka received the same scores as India, as was proposed by a working chapter retrieved from the World Bank (Hazarika *et al.*, 2009, retrieved from http://siteresources.worldbank.org/INTFR/Resources/Hazarika_Nahata_Tandon0709.pdf, September 23, 2011). We further entered the average scores of Switzerland and Austria for Liechtenstein, the average scores of Turkey and Greece for Cyprus, and employed Hofstede's original scores for Hong Kong also for Macau, South Africa's scores for Lesotho, and India's scores for Nepal.
7. In January 2007, the Chinese government regulated the statistical system of direct overseas investment (Voss, 2011); changes in calculating and reporting investment data can therefore be the cause of this increase.
8. In these analyses, we did not include the countries for which we inserted the sample mean for cultural distance, resulting in a smaller number of observations ($n = 133$).

References

Al-Laham, A. and Amburgey, T.L. (2005). Knowledge sourcing in foreign direct investments: An empirical examination of target profiles, *Management International Review*, 45(3): 247–275.

Barkema, H.G., Bell, J.H., and Pennings, J.M. (1996). Foreign entry, cultural barriers, and learning, *Strategic Management Journal*, 17(2): 151–166.

Barkema, H. and Drogendijk, R. (2007). Internationalising in small, incremental or in larger steps, *Journal of International Business Studies*, 38(7): 1132–1148.

Barkema, H.G. and Vermeulen, F. (1997). What differences in the cultural background of partners are detrimental for international joint ventures? *Journal of International Business Studies*, 28(4): 845–864.

Benito, G.R.G. and Gripsrud, G. (1992). The expansion of foreign direct investments: Discrete rational location choices or a cultural learning process? *Journal of International Business Studies*, 23: 461–476.

Braeutigam, D. (2003). Close encounters: Chinese business networks as industrial catalysts in Sub-Saharan Africa, *African Affairs*, 102(408): 447–467.

Brannen, M.Y. and Salk, J.E. (2000). Partnering across borders: Negotiating organisational culture in a German-Japanese joint venture, *Human Relations*, 52(4): 451–487.

Brewer, P.A. (2007). Psychic distance and Australian export market selection, *Australian Journal of Management*, 32(1): 73–94.

Buckley, P.J. and Casson, M.C. (1976). *The Future of the Multinational Enterprise*, London: Homes and Meier.

Buckley, P.J., Clegg, L.J., Cross, A.R., Liu, X., Voss, H., and Zheng, P. (2007). The determinants of Chinese outward foreign direct investment, *Journal of International Business Studies*, 38: 499–518.

Buckley, P.J., Cross, A.R., Tan, H., Xin, L., and Zheng, P. (2008). Historic and emergent trends in Chinese outward direct investment, *Management International Review*, 48(6): 715–748.

Chen, X.-P. and Chen, C.C. (2004). On the intricacies of the Chinese *guanxi*: A process model of *Guanxi* development, *Asia Pacific Journal of Management*, 21: 305–324.

Child, J. and Rodrigues, S. (2005). The internationalisation of Chinese firms: A case for theoretical extension? *Management and Organ*isation *Review*, 1: 381–410.

China Ministry of Foreign Affairs. (2006). *China's Africa Policy*, Beijing: Ministry of Foreign Affairs.

Clausen, L. (2007). Corporate communication challenges: A 'negotiated' culture perspective, *International Journal of Cross Cultural Management*, 7(3): 317–332.

Cuervo-Cazurra, A. and Genc, M. (2008). Transforming disadvantages into advantages: Developing-country MNEs in the least developed countries, *Journal of International Business Studies*, 39(6): 957–979.

Deng, P. (2004). Outward investment by Chinese MNCs: Motivations and implications, *Business Horizons*, 50(1): 71–81.

Dow, D. (2000). A note on psychic distance and export market selection, *Journal of International Marketing*, 8(1): 51–64.

Dow, D. and Larimo, J. (2009). Challenging the conceptualisation and measurement of distance and international experience in entry mode research, *Journal of International Marketing*, 17(2): 74–98.

Drogendijk, R. and Slangen, A. (2006). Hofstede, Schwartz, or managerial perceptions: The effects of various cultural distance measures on establishment mode choices by multinational enterprises, *International Business Review*, 15(4): 361–380.

Drogendijk, R. and Zander, L. (2010). Walking the cultural distance – In search of direction beyond friction, in T. Devinney, T. Pedersen, and L. Tihanyi, L. (Eds.)

The Past, Present and Future of International Business and Management, *Advances of International Management*, 23: 189–212.

Evenett, S.J. (2009). *Broken Promises: A G-20 Summit Report by Global Trade Alert*, London: CEPR.

Fischer, R. (2009). Where is culture in cross-cultural research? An outline of a multi-level research process for measuring culture as a shared meaning system, *International Journal of Cross Cultural Management*, 9(1): 25–49.

Flores, R.G. and Aguilera, R.V. (2007). Globalisation and location choice: An analysis of US multinational firms in 1980 and 2000, *Journal of International Business Studies*, 38(7): 1187–1210.

Ghemawat, P. (2001). Distance still matters: The hard reality of global expansion, *Harvard Business Review*, 79(8): 137–146.

Gugler, P. and Brunner, S. (2007). FDI effects on national competitiveness – A cluster approach, *International Advances in Economic Research*, 13/3: 268–284.

Gugler, P. and Fetscherin, M. (2010). The role and importance of the Chinese government for Chinese outward foreign direct investments, *AIB Insights*, 10(4): 12–15.

Hair, J.F. Jr., Black, W.C., Babin, B.J. Anderson, R.E., and Tatham, R.L. (2006). *Multivariate Data Analysis*. 6th ed., Upper Saddle River, NJ: Prentice Hall.

Harzing, A.W.K. (2003). The role of culture in entry mode studies: From negligence to myopia? *Advances in International Management*, 15: 75–127.

Hazarika, S., Nahata, R., and Tandon, K. (2009). *Success in Global Venture Capital Investing: Do Institutional and Cultural Differences Matter?* Working chapter published in the World Bank's Resource Center, http://siteresources.worldbank.org/INTFR/Resources/Hazarika_Nahata_Tandon0709.pdf, Accessed September 23, 2011.

Hofstede, G. (1980). *Cultural Consequences: International Differences in Work Related Values*, Beverly Hills, CA: Sage.

Hofstede, G. (2001). *Cultures Consequences: Comparing Values, Behaviors, Institutions and Organisations Across Nations*, 2nd ed. Thousand Oaks, CA: Sage.

Hong, E. and Sun, L. (2006). Dynamics of internationalisation and outward investment: Chinese corporations' strategies, *China Quarterly*, 187(September): 610–634.

Huettinger, M. (2008). Cultural dimensions in business life: Hofstede's indices for Latvia and Lithuania, *Baltic Journal of Management*, 3(3): 359–376.

Johanson, J. and Vahlne, J.-E. (1977). The internationalisation process of the firm: A model of knowledge development and increasing foreign market commitments, *Journal of International Business Studies*, 8(1): 23–32.

Johanson, J. and Wiedersheim-Paul, F. (1975). The internationalisation of the firm: Four Swedish cases, *Journal of Management Studies*, 12(October): 305–322.

Kent, R.B. (2003). A diaspora of Chinese settlement in Latin America and the Caribbean, in L.J.C. Ma and C. Cartier (Eds.) *The Chinese Diaspora: Space, Place, Mobility, and Identity*, Lanham: Rowman & Littlefield: 117–138.

Kirkman, B.L., Lowe, K.B., and Gibson, C.B. (2006). A Quarter century of cultures consequences: A review of empirical research incorporating Hofstede's cultural values framework, *Journal of International Business Studies*, 37: 285–320.

Kogut, B. and Singh, H. (1988). The effect of national culture on the choice of entry mode, *Journal of International Business Studies*, 19(3): 411–432.

Li, J. and Guisinger, S. (1992). The globalisation of service multinationals in the 'Triad' regions: Japan, Western Europe and North America, *Journal of International Business Studies*, 23(4): 675–696.
Luo, Y. (1997). Guanxi: Principles, philosophies, and implications, *Human Systems Management*, 16(1): 43–51.
Marquardt, D.W. (1970). Generalised inverses, ridge regression and biased linear estimation, *Technometrics*, 12(3): 591–612.
Martín Martín, O. and Drogendijk, R. (forthcoming). Objective country distance and the internationalisation of SMEs, *Journal of Small Business Management*, Accepted for publication, November 15, 2011.
McSweeney, B. (2009). Dynamic diversity: Variety and variation within countries, *Organisation Studies*, 31(9): 933–957.
MOFCOM. (2009). *2009 Statistical Bulletin of China's Outward FDI*. Beijing: MOFCOM, National Bureau of Statistics of the People's Republic of China, SAFE.
Morck, R., Yeung, B., and Zhao, M. (2008). Perspectives on China's outward foreign direct investment, *Journal of International Business Studies*, 39: 337–350.
National Bureau of Statistics. (2009). *China Statistical Yearbook 2009*, Beijing: China Statistics Press.
Ohio University. (2006). *Distribution of the Ethnic Chinese Population Around the World*, University Libraries, Ohio University, http://cicdatabank.library.ohiou.edu/opac/population.php, Accessed on March 16, 2011.
Peng, M.W. and Wang, D.Y. (2000). Innovation capability and foreign direct investment: Toward a learning option perspective, *Management International Review*, 40(special issue): 79–93.
Rarick, C. and Nickerson, I. (2008). Combining classification models for a comprehensive understanding of national culture: Metaphorical analysis and value judgements applied to Burmese cultural assessment, *Journal of Organisational Culture, Communications and Conflict*, 12(2): 9–19.
Rugman, A.M. and Doh, J.P. (2008). *Multinationals and Development*. New Heaven, CT; London: Yale University Press.
Rui, H. and Yip, G.S. (2008). Foreign acquisitions by Chinese firms: A strategic intent perspective, *Journal of World Business*, 43(2): 213–226.
Sauvant, K. (2005). New sources of FDI: The BRICs. Outward FDI from Brazil, Russia, India and China, *Journal of World Investment and Trade*, 6 (October): 639–709.
Schwartz, S.H. (1994). Beyond individualism/collectivism: New cultural dimensions of values, in U. Kim, H.C. Triandis, C. Kagitcibasi, S.C. Choi, and G. Yoon (Eds.) *Individualism and Collectivism: Theory, Methods, and Applications*, Thousand Oaks, CA: Sage: 85–119.
Shenkar, O. (2001). Cultural distance revisited: Towards a more rigorous conceptualisation and measurement of cultural differences, *Journal of International Business Studies*, 32: 519–536.
Shenkar, O. (2012). Beyond cultural distance: Switching to a friction lens in the study of cultural differences, *Journal of International Business Studies*, 43(1): 12–17.
Shenkar, O., Luo, Y., and Yeheskel, O. (2008). From 'distance' to 'friction' substituting metaphors and re-directing intercultural research, *Academy of Management Review*, 33(4): 905–923.

Standifird, S.S. and Marshall, R.S. (2000). The transaction cost advantage of guanxi-based business practices, *Journal of World Business*, 35(1): 21–42.

Stöttinger, B. and Schlegelmilch, B.B. (1998). Explaining export development through psychic distance: Enlightening or elusive? *International Marketing Review*, 15(5): 357–372.

Studenmund, A. (1992). *Using Econometrics: A Practical Guide*, New York, NY: Harper Collins.

Suanet, I. and Van de Vijver, F.J.R. (2009). Perceived cultural distance and acculturation among exchange students in Russia, *Journal of Community and Applied Social Psychology*, 19: 182–197.

Tong, S.Y. (2005). Ethnic networks in FDI and the impact of institutional development, *Review of Development Economics*, 9(4): 563–580.

Tung, R.L. and Verbeke, A. (2010). Beyond Hofstede and GLOBE: Improving the quality of cross-cultural research, *Journal of International Business Studies*, 41(8): 1259–1274.

UNCTAD. (2005). *World Investment Report 2005: Transnational Corporations and the Internationalisation of R&D*, New York, NY; Geneva: United Nations.

UNCTAD. (2007). *Rising FDI into China: The Facts Behind the Numbers*. www.unctad.org/en/docs/iteiiamisc20075_en.pdf, Accessed on March 15, 2011.

Voss, H. (2011). *The Determinants of Chinese Outward Direct Investment*, Cheltenham: Edward Elgar.

Wang, M.Y. (2002). The motivations behind China's government-initiate industrial investments overseas, *Pacific Affairs*, 75(2): 187–206.

World Bank, http://data.worldbank.org/indicator/NY.GDP.MKTP.CD, Accessed on April 5, 2011.

World Bank. (2009). http://siteresources.worldbank.org/INTFR/Resources/Hazarika_Nahata_Tandon0709.pdf, Accessed on September 23, 2011.

World Intellectual Property Organisation (WIPO). (2007). http://www.wipo.int/ipstats/en/statistics/patents/wipo_pub_931.html#a13, Accessed on March 19, 2011.

Zaheer, S., Spring Schomaker, M., and Nachum, L. (2012). Distance without direction: Restoring credibility to a much-loved construct, *Journal of International Business Studies*, 43(1): 18–27.

Zhan, J. (1995). Transnationalisation and outward investment: The case of Chinese firms, *Transnational Corporations*, 4(3): 67–100.

8
Russia's Emerging Multinationals in the Global Crisis

Sergey Filippov

Introduction

The financial crisis of 2007–2010 that was triggered by a liquidity shortfall in the US banking system resulted in the collapse of large financial institutions, the bailout of banks by national governments, and downturns in stock markets around the world. The crisis is considered by many to be the worst economic downturn since the Great Depression of the 1930s. It has led to the failure of multinational companies and key businesses, decline in consumer wealth, and a significant drop in economic activity worldwide.

As the crisis unfolded globally, its impact became pronounced for both developed and emerging economies. Consequently, the global downturn has impacted both Western multinational companies and 'emerging multinationals'—multinational companies originating from emerging economies. Many multinationals have had to deal with falling demand and tightening access to loans. In the same fashion, the crisis has negatively impacted the internationalization plans of emerging multinationals lacking finances for further expansion.

In spite of the negative effect of the crisis on emerging economies and emerging multinationals, it is often argued that the main drivers of global economic growth will be the emerging economies. *The Economist*'s, 'The World in 2012' predicts gross domestic product (GDP) growth of 3.5 per cent in Brazil, 3.7 per cent in Russia, 7.8 per cent in India, and 8.2 per cent in China. In contrast, GDP of the Eurozone countries is expected to contract by 0.3 per cent (*The Economist*, 2011). Likewise, the world might see an accelerated growth of emerging multinationals. Specifically in times of crisis, distressed assets from Western companies, or whole business units, became attractive targets for acquisition. Volvo's acquisition by Chinese automaker Geely provides an illustrative example. In 2009, amidst the economic downturn,

Geely Holding Group announced it was close to an agreement to acquire Volvo Cars from Ford Motor Company; and a US$1.8 billion deal was signed on March 28, 2010. At the end of 2011, Chinese companies Youngman and Pang Da announced their intention to buy the distressed Swedish car manufacturer Saab.

Many scholarly studies, policy reports, and practitioner-oriented publications have sought to examine various facets of the global crisis, from both macro- and micro-economic perspectives. Several studies have examined the impact of the economic crisis on emerging multinationals. Yet, this subject remains an under-researched area, and this chapter aims to contribute to it by focusing on emerging Russian multinationals. Prior to the global downturn, these companies, many of whom operate in the natural resources sector, had benefited greatly from staggering natural-resource commodity prices and had extended their foreign presence from the neighboring republics to advanced Western economies. Their responses to the global economic crisis, however, have been mixed, from contraction to further expansion. The objective of the chapter is to trace internationalization strategies of emerging Russian multinationals and to analyze the impact of the global financial crisis on these strategies.

The study combines quantitative and qualitative methods. Available data from international financial and business databases is used. To broaden the insight gained through these quantitative analyses, the chapter also presents qualitative data—several practical examples of Russian multinationals' responses to the crisis. We specifically focus on the period 2008–2010 at the peak of the global crisis as experienced by the Russian economy.

The chapter is structured as follows. The second section reviews the relevant literature on the topics of emerging multinationals and effects of crisis on internationalization paths of these companies. This is followed by a background of the study that portrays the effect of the crisis on the Russian economy and the policy responses of the Russian government. Subsequently, the chapter presents the effects of the crisis on Russian multinationals and the reaction of these companies to the crisis. Finally, the main conclusions of the study are drawn with relevant managerial and policy implications, and directions for further research.

Theoretical background

This section provides a brief overview of the concept of the emerging multinationals, and it studies the responses of multinational companies to the economic crisis.

Emerging multinationals

The academic literature on multinational companies originating from emerging markets has grown explosively in recent years. Child and Rodrigues (2005) were among the first authors who examined internationalization of Chinese firms and raised a question whether the existing theory of the multinational company should be revised. Likewise, Buckley *et al.* (2007) studied the determinants of Chinese outward FDI. Gammeltoft (2008) provided a comparative analysis of outward FDI from BRIC (Brazil, Russia, India, and China) countries. Andreff (2003) focussed on the emerging economies from economies in transition. The study of Mathews (2006) covered emerging Asian multinationals. Mathews (2006) argues that 'new', emerging multinationals adopt a different perspective to the resources accessed through internationalization, relying on 'linkage, leverage and learning' of international resources (LLL paradigm) rather than adopting the eclectic OLI (Ownership, Locational, Internalization) paradigm by Dunning (1988).

Dunning (2006) acknowledges deficiencies of the ownership advantages of emerging multinationals. Dunning (2006) argues that emerging multinationals will internationalize via a two-stage model: first, by investing in more advanced economies 'to access or to augment, rather than exploit their ownership advantages', and the nature of the second stage of internationalization would follow the logic of OLI paradigm. Narula (2010) argues that firms engaging in strategic asset-seeking are primarily seeking learning opportunities rather than seeking to invest for strategic purposes in specific assets. This is in line with the claim that emerging multinational companies internationalize in order to enhance their ownership advantages.

Furthermore, several edited volumes have been published on the topic of outward FDI from emerging economies and emerging multinationals (e.g. Benito and Narula, 2007; Goldstein and Shaw, 2007; Ramamurti and Singh, 2008; Sauvant *et al.*, 2010). International organizations have also paid considerable attention to the internationalization of firms from emerging economies. In 2006, both OECD and UNCTAD published reports dedicated to emerging multinationals (UNCTAD, 2006; OECD, 2006).

In the context of emerging economies and multinational companies from these countries, the main focus has been on China, India, and Brazil. Russian companies have received less attention. Yet, a stream of literature focusing on emerging Russian multinationals can be identified (e.g. Bulatov, 2001; Crane *et al.*, 2005; Heinrich, 2003, 2006; Kalotay, 2002, 2004, 2005, 2007, 2008; Kets de Vries *et al.*, 2004; Vahtra and Liuhto, 2006; Filippov, 2010). These papers have examined various facets of Russian companies' internationalization trajectories, such as first attempts to reconnect with former Soviet trade and production networks, to expand into the 'near-abroad' of the Commonwealth of Independent States (CIS), and to search out resources or assets to enhance or complement domestic production. Several studies addressed the export strategies of Russian multinationals, taking into account the impact of foreign partners' presence, turnover of senior management, product development strategies on export intensity and so on.

The studies on the internationalization paths and strategies of Russian companies suggest that the motivation of their internationalization does not always fall into the traditional four categories outlined by Dunning (1988)—market-seeking, resource-seeking, efficiency-seeking and strategic assets-seeking. Among other factors of internationalization are 'push' factors, such as unstable economic situation at the home base—that is, 'system escape' motivation (Bulatov, 1998). This proposition is corroborated by the Index of Economic Freedom, annually compiled by The Wall Street Journal and The Heritage Foundation. It has consistently placed Russia at the bottom of its list; and in the 2011 edition, Russia was ranked 143th (out of 179 countries), below other key emerging economies—Brazil (113), India (124), China (135).

Political considerations are often cited as drivers of the internationalization of (state-owned) Russian companies. Liuhto and Vahtra (2007) propose a typology of Russian multinationals on the basis of their ownership structures and the level of state involvement in their operations. The focus on ownership structure and the state involvement provide a strong indication about the important role of the Russian state in the internationalization strategies of many Russian companies.

Multinational companies and the economic crisis

The current global economic crisis became an object of scholarly analysis. Several studies adopted a macroeconomic perspective. For example, Dejuan *et al.* (2011) studied the impact of the crisis on the global economy on a macro-level; Forrest and Yip (2011) investigated the impact of the crisis on households. Other publications sought to study the financial side of the crisis (Allen, 2009; Gup, 2010). Gray (2009) investigated the financial contagion in the EU—mechanisms of spill over of the crisis to the national currencies of eight EU member states, not part of the Eurozone. Shabri Abd Majid and Hj Kassim (2009) studied the impact of the crisis on the emerging equity markets, with particular reference to Asia. Several studies were devoted to the regulatory responses of national governments to the crisis (Goodhart, 2009; Green *et al.*, 2011). Desai (2010) offered a macro-economic overview of the financial crisis' dynamics in Russia and policy responses.

The analysis by Varum and Rocha (2011) of prior studies on the behavior of multinational companies in economic crises (specifically, the Asian crisis) shows that the empirical results on this question are not unanimous. Potentially, these studies can be classified in one of three categories—(i) multinational companies as a stabilizing agents, (ii) multinational companies as a destabilizing agents, and (iii) foreign ownership as a neutral characteristic.

Several studies (Athukorala, 2003; Narjoko and Hill, 2007) have found multinational companies to exhibit a better reaction to crises and to recover faster after crises than domestic firms. Such behavior can be explained by ownership advantages of multinational companies (financial, knowledge, and technological advantages). Subsidiaries may be less reliant on local markets and hence less exposed to a negative shock.

Multinational companies make substantial commitment when entering foreign markets as they need to overcome 'the liability of foreignness'. It involves financial investments (sunk costs) as well as investments in long-term relationship and local embeddedness. Therefore, the decision to leave a host market is not an easy one.

Several studies perceive multinational companies as a destabilizing agents. Because multinational companies possess a global network of subsidiaries, it is easier for them to transfer production facilities internationally (Gorg and Strobl, 2003; Lee and Makhija, 2009), to cut operational costs (Gao and Eshaghoff, 2004), to switch their sales from host countries to export markets (Lipsey, 2001), and even to exit the local economy (Alvarez and Gorg, 2009). Such reactions accelerate job losses, output contractions and result in the decline in business activities.

A number of studies do not find any significant differences between multinational companies and domestic firms in their reaction to crises (Wang *et al.*, 2005; Alvarez and Gorg, 2007). They claim that both groups display identical patterns of reaction when accounting for various firm and industry-level specificities.

It is important to note that the description above (in line with Varum and Rocha, 2011) analyzes distinctions between subsidiaries of multinational companies and domestic firms responding to a crisis within the limits of a host country. For example, the empirical examination of Varum and Rocha (2011) looks at differences between foreign subsidiaries and domestic companies in the times of crisis, within Portugal.

Likewise, Filippov and Kalotay (2011) investigate responses of multinational companies to the crisis in the context of new EU member states, both in terms of new FDI inflows and response strategies of already established foreign subsidiaries.

Looking from a broader perspective of responses of multinational companies to the crisis, several studies emerged. Enderwick (2009) studied how exposure to the dynamic conditions of emerging markets can contribute to strategic adaptation and international competitiveness of Western multinationals. Six differentiated strategies are identified, and illustrations are drawn primarily from the global automobile industry. Pradhan (2009) provided an overview of the dynamics of Indian outward FDI in the period of the economic recession, showing a decline in the investment and expansionary activity.

Sauvant *et al.* (2010) present an analysis of outward FDI by four BRIC economies and the impact of the financial crisis and recession. The crisis affects the ability of emerging multinationals to invest abroad. This difficulty is further accentuated by declining earnings, weakening balance sheets, and the need for deleveraging. As a consequence, a number of emerging multinationals already had to divest themselves of foreign affiliates or repatriate a larger share of their foreign earnings. However, state-owned multinationals in countries with high foreign currency reserves remain in a position to expand abroad. Crisis provides a good moment for them, as asset prices in a number of potential host counties are low or in distress. In terms of policy responses, Sauvant *et al.* (2010) warn about the rise of FDI protectionism that may make it more difficult for emerging multinational to expand their international production networks. A deepening crisis may well lead to more FDI protectionism and discourage investments from emerging markets.

The impact of the crisis on emerging multinationals is also regarded within the framework of the Emerging Market Global Players project, a collaborative effort led by the Vale Columbia Centre bringing together researchers on FDI to produce annual reports identifying the top multinationals from each of a number of emerging markets. Presently it includes reports on ten countries (Argentina, Brazil, China, India, Israel, Korea, Mexico, Russia, Slovenia, and Turkey) covering some 200 emerging multinationals.

Specifically in the case of Russia, the interplay between the global economic crisis and the internationalization of Russian companies was raised by Skolkovo Research (2009). An analytical report published in May 2009 presented an analysis of the crisis adjustment of Russian multinationals in comparison with their Chinese counterparts. The report noted a decrease in investment activity as the expansion of Russian multinationals had been stifled by the lack of external financing. Most severely affected were companies engaged in scale-seeking expansion (in metals/mining sector); in contrast companies involved in downstream integration (in oil and gas sector) were not hit hard. Expansion of Russian companies into the emerging markets was slowing but had not stopped. Amidst the crisis, in early 2009, the prospects looked mixed. Access to financing and the protectionism (of host governments) seemed as the two most evident challenges.

Due to the novelty of the research topic, currently the stream of literature on the interplay of the international expansion of emerging multinationals and their (post-)crisis adjustments is only being shaped. The extant body of literature remains inconclusive regarding specific responses and strategic choices of emerging multinationals, and particularly, Russian companies.

The impact of the global financial crisis on Russia

This section provides an overview of the effects of the global economic crisis on the Russian economy as well as policy responses by the Russian government.

Crisis in Russia

The decade between the 1998 Russian economic crisis and the current global economic crisis was characterized by Russia's growing economy and improvement in living standards. The country enjoyed rapid increase in its GDP and growth of foreign exchanges reserves. The Russian government paid off its sovereign debt (including the inherited Soviet debt). One of the reasons for this economic performance was the national currency devaluation carried out in the course of the 1998 crisis. The further growth of the economy was facilitated by political stability. Among the external factors, high world prices on commodities, specifically, on oil and gas, were key to the economic growth. In the 2000s, domestic Russian companies began pursuing internationalization strategies.

The financial downfall in the US and the following global chain reaction has had strong impact on Russia's economy. Russia's export-oriented commodities faced a situation where demand and prices fell; oil prices fell sharply from nearly US$100 to US$62 per barrel in 2008 and 2009, respectively. Russian stock market plummeted and the value of Russian companies was wiped off. Similarly, Russia's foreign reserves fell sharply as the Central Bank of Russia adopted a policy of gradual devaluation of the national currency.

The crisis exposed internal weaknesses of the Russian economy such as the weak banking system that was causing a liquidity crisis in the country. Banks raised interest rates for loans, and as a result, the access of Russian companies both to domestic and foreign credit became reduced and complicated. Not to say that many banks even went bankrupt. The decline in the economic activity has inevitably adversely affected Russia's economic growth. In the first half of 2009, when Russia was hit hardest by the crisis, its GDP fell by 10.4 per cent compared to the same period in the previous year, and industrial production dropped by nearly 15 per cent. This economic performance affected the federal budget as the deficit was recorded for the first time in ten years.

Foreign investors pulled billions of dollars out of Russia and the inflow of FDI decreased as a consequence of the suppressed investing activity of the global business. Table 8.1 presents an overview of Russia's FDI and cross-border mergers and acquisitions (M&A) statistics for the years 2007–2010, as reported by UNCTAD. In the pre-crisis year of 2007,

Table 8.1 Russia's FDI and cross-border M&A statistics, 2007–2010

Indicator	2007	2008	2009	2010
FDI Flows				
Inward FDI flows, US$ mln	55,073	75,002	36,500	41,194
Inward FDI flows, percentage of GFCF	20.2	20.3	13.8	13.6
Outward FDI flows, US$ mln	45,916	55,594	43,665	51,697
Outward FDI flows, percentage of GFCF	16.8	15.0	16.5	17.1
FDI Stocks				
Inward FDI stocks, US$ mln	491,232	213,734	252,456	423,150[a]
Inward FDI stocks, percentage of GDP	38.2	12.9	31.0	28.7
Outward FDI stocks, US$ mln	370,161	202,837	248,894	433,655[a]
Outward FDI stocks, percentage of GDP	28.8	12.3	24.9	29.4
Cross-Border M&A				
Cross-border M&A, sales (net), US$ mln	22,529	13,507	5,079	2,907
Cross-border M&A, purchases (net), US$ mln	18,598	16,634	7,599	9,082

Note: [a]Expected.
Source: Based on UNCTAD (2010, 2011).

the annual inward FDI inflow in Russia constituted US$55 billion, or 20.2 per cent of the gross fixed capital formation (GFCF). In 2009, this amount decreased to US$36.5 billion, or 13.8 per cent of GFCF. The year 2009 witnessed global decline in FDI activity and as many other countries Russia was hit by the global liquidity crisis. Inward FDI flows showed an increasing trend in 2010. Regarding the outward FDI from Russia, the amount has remained relatively stable—around US$50 billion annually. The static outward FDI should be considered with caution. It represents only approximation to the real activity of Russian multinational companies. It might be argued that a certain part of these investments relate to 'capital flight' rather than genuine investment projects abroad.

Russian companies became less engaged in cross-border M&As, both sales and purchases. In 2009, cross-border M&A, purchases—that is, acquisitions of foreign assets by Russian residents constituted US$7.6 billion, in contrast to US$18.5 billion in 2007. The number shows a slight increase in 2010—up to US$19 billion. Likewise, the value of sales dropped to US$5 billion in 2009 from US$22.5 billion in 2007, and even further—to US$2.9 billion in 2010.

Policy responses

The Russian government reacted vigorously to the crisis. The principal objectives of the government's anti-crisis program were to maintain the banking sector's financial liquidity, stimulate internal demand, alleviate the negative impact on society and support the key domestic enterprises. More specifically, the anti-recessionary measures of the Russian government could be provisionally divided into the following categories:

- expansion of access to financial resources for business companies;
- provision of incentives to expand domestic demand;
- reduction in tax and administrative burdens on businesses;
- support of small and medium-sized enterprises; and
- development of the labor market (Gurvich *et al.*, 2010).

At the end of 2008, the Russian government resolutely carried out a number of measures. Firstly, urgent financial help was provided to the largest Russian companies. This help was offered through the state corporation 'Bank for Development and Foreign Economic Affairs', known in Russian as Vneshekonombank (VEB), an institution used by the Russian government to support and develop the Russian economy, to manage Russian state debts and pension funds. VEB granted loans to Russian borrowers for refinancing their foreign loans, with their assets based on the Russian territory as collateral. Between 27 October and December 1, 2008 nine large companies were supported by VEB, for a total amount of US$9.78 trillion.

Secondly, the tax burden on businesses was reduced. The corporate profit tax was lowered from 24 per cent to 20 per cent; depreciation premiums for certain types of fixed assets were increased from 10 per cent to 30 per cent; and the maximum level of interest rates was increased on liabilities recognized as costs. Besides, procedural changes were made in the calculation of certain taxes to alleviate a shortage of funds—for example, companies were given the right to deduct VAT from advances. Thirdly, policy measures were taken to protect domestic markets, such as increases in customs duties on imports, and introduction of preferential prices for Russian suppliers of goods to state and municipal entities (Gurvich *et al.*, 2010).

Wiśniewska *et al.* (2010) enlist several main characteristics of the anti-crisis policy conducted by the Russian government. The policy was characterized by the arbitrary selection of beneficiary sectors and enterprises, often based on political decisions and unclear criteria. A related point is the lack of transparency. Initially, the terms of foreign debt refinancing were defined quite precisely—that is, state aid was to be offered only to those Russian companies or their foreign subsidiaries whose activities are of significant importance for the economies of the respective regions or strategic branches of industry. However, subsequently the procedure was made secret, and no official information was disclosed. As mentioned, strategic branches of industry were supported, meaning that the aid was extended to the traditional sectors of the economy, including the raw materials sector; the machine-building industry, especially the automotive industry; as well as agriculture, construction, and air and rail transport. The aid was directed toward big businesses (that received more than 60 per cent of the total assistance offered), while small businesses received only around 5 per cent of the total public aid.

The policy was of compensatory nature—that is, the measures undertaken were aimed at mitigating losses. The current situation was conserved and no instruments were implemented to motivate companies to pursue more active policies, diversify production or seek new markets. That was the non-conditionality principle of the policy—the government set practically no requirements for the aid beneficiaries. Overall, the design of the policy was rushed by the pressure of time and powerful lobbying by various interest groups. And last but not least, typically

Russian characteristics can be applied to this specific policy too—ineffective implementation of approved normative acts (Wiśniewska *et al.*, 2010).

Despite all possible inefficiencies of the anti-crisis policy measures, they managed to largely contain and neutralize the most adverse manifestations of the crisis.

Impact of the global financial crisis on emerging Russian multinationals

In this section, we examine various facets of Russian companies' response to the crisis. I start with an exploration of Russian companies' financial performance. This statistics will provide background to the analysis of foreign acquisitions and foreign divestments. This quantitative analysis is further supported by qualitative analysis of several cases across various industries. Analysis of Russian initial public offerings (IPO) abroad will follow.

Financial performance

In order to provide context to the analysis of foreign acquisitions and divestments, this section gives insights into financial performance of major Russian companies, relying on a study by the German agency Handelsblatt Research (Table 8.2). The study reports financial performance of the 500 largest European companies. The global economic slowdown is shown evidently, as in 2009 the revenues of these 500 companies fell by 9.6 per cent on average; and their net profit declined by 26 per cent, in comparison to 2008.

This rating of 500 largest European companies includes some 30 Russian companies. Virtually all of these companies are multinationals as they have distinctive presence abroad, with the minor exception of power generating company Mosenergo and retail chain Magnit. Therefore, the list is a good indication of the financial performance of Russian multinationals in 2009. Similar to their Western counterparts, most resource-based companies (in the oil and gas, steel and minerals sectors) sustained decline in revenue in 2009. However, they managed to maintain a high, double-digit, level of profitability. While Russia's largest company Gazprom suffered a decline of 18.2 per cent in its revenue in 2009, its profitability stood at the 26.1 per cent. Overall, the profitability of Russian companies on average constituted 13.7 per cent (Handelsblatt Research, 2010). Most German companies in the rating even before the crisis reached only half of this amount. Gazprom, Surgutneftegaz, Transneft, Norilsk Nickel, and Roshydro reported profitability of over 25

Table 8.2 Russian companies in the rating of the top 500 largest European companies, 2009

Rating	Company	Sector	Revenue		Net Profit		Profitability (%)
			€ mln	Change to 2008 (%)	€ mln	Change to 2008 (%)	
12	Gazprom	Oil and gas	67,806	−18.2	17,673	1.0	26.1
23	Lukoil	Oil and gas	49,654	−2.4	5,118	−5.0	10.3
57	Rosneft Oil	Oil and gas	25,325	−8.5	4,755	−27.4	18.8
61	TNK-BP	Oil and gas	24,124	−9.3	3,452	−8.2	14.3
106	Gazpromneft	Oil and gas	14,758	−33.9	2,199	−31.8	14.9
114	Surgutneftegaz	Oil and gas	13,584	−21.1	3,451	48.8	25.4
118	Sistema	Telecom	13,015	12.8	1,141	>100	8.8
164	Severstal	Steel	9,529	−27.8	−757	–	−7.9
168	IDGC	Supplier	9,299	3.7	260	22.8	2.8
177	Tatneft	Oil and gas	8,629	−17.5	1,233	>100	14.3
197	MMC Norilsk Nickel	Minerals	7,302	−23.6	1,906	–	26.1
203	MTS	Telecom	7,064	17.0	722	−36.5	10.2
210	Evraz	Steel	6,783	−43.5	−868	–	−12.8
224	Transneft	Oil and gas	6,478	4.7	1,661	−0.9	25.6

227	X 5 Retail	Retail	6,363	29.3	121	–	1.9
228	Vimpelcom	Telecom	6,353	6.6	803	>100	12.6
245	Rusal	Minerals	5,871	−36.5	590	–	10.1
284	AvtoVAZ	Automotive	4,525	−13.4	−574	–	−12.7
288	Novolipetsk Steel (NLMK)	Steel	4,482	−35.0	157	−88.3	3.5
306	Mechel	Steel	4,138	−29.4	53	−92.1	1.3
312	GAZ Auto	Automotive	4,015	−5.7	−225	–	−5.6
317	Magnit	Retail	3,908	24.1	201	81.7	5.1
327	Magnitogorsk Iron & Steel	Steel	3,709	−40.3	169	−73.3	4.6
394	Bashneft	Oil and gas	2,872	1.9	256	−30.0	8.9
416	Aeroflot	Airlines	2,718	0.6	33	−84.7	1.2
431	Rushydro	Power generation	2,621	3.3	695	–	26.5
441	Mosenergo	Power generation	2,590	15.9	38	−21.3	1.5
457	Salavatnefteorgsintez	Chemicals	2,471	−8.6	135	22.0	5.4
461	Slavneft	Oil and gas	2,460	−8.6	219	−43.1	8.9
474	TMK	Steel	2,402	−28.3	−225	–	−9.4

Sources: Own interpretations based on Handelsblatt Research (2010).

per cent, the highest among other companies in the rating. At the same time, companies in steel industry (Severstal, Evraz, TMK) and automotive sector (AvtoVAZ and GAZ Auto) have been adversely hit by the crisis and posted negative net profit and negative profitability.

Competitive advantages allowing Russian companies to occupy positions in ratings of the leading European companies are multifaceted. On the domestic market they include, inter alia, natural resource base, low energy prices, dominant (quasi-monopolistic) market positions, low labor costs, and last but not least, strong governmental support and aid. These factors suggest that major Russian multinational companies were able to advance their expansion into foreign markets in the crisis period.

Foreign acquisitions

The section uses the data provided by Zephyr database (managed by Bureau van Dijk), one of the most comprehensive and authoritative databases on deal information, containing data on IPO, private equity, and venture capital deals. The period between January 1, 2000 and January 1, 2011 is defined for analysis, to show a more long-term trend of internationalization, with particular attention to the crisis stage of 2008–2010. In total, 18, 026 completed M&A and joint venture deals are recorded for the whole period. Apart from international acquisitions, they include intra-Russian deals, management buyout deals, deals where bidders are undisclosed, an acquirer is a governmental entity or a physical person. A prime example of such deal would be the acquisition of the UK-based Chelsea Football Club Ltd. by the Russian national Mr Roman Abramovich in 2003. More recently, in April 2010, an unnamed Russian individual acquired the 100 per cent stake in the Spanish manufacturer of jewellery Carrera y Carrera S.A. for an unidentified amount.

After removing these entries, as well as 146 joint venture deals, we obtain 770 deals. These are acquisitions by Russian companies of stakes in foreign companies (minority stakes, increases in stakes, majority stakes and 100 per cent acquisitions). 'A Russian company' is defined as a legal entity registered/incorporated on the Russian territory under the Russian jurisdiction; it ranges from SMEs to well-established Russian multinationals. On the side of acquisition targets, it should be noted that although technically these deals involve acquisition of foreign (non-Russian) companies, these entities are not always 'foreign' per se. These can be firms established according to the host country's regulations and jurisdiction but either partially-owned or controlled by Russian firms or individuals.

Cyprus is very popular among Russian businesses thanks to its highly developed financial infrastructure and legislation facilitating tax optimization and offshore business operations. In Cyprus, for example, affiliates of the shareholders of the oil and gas company Itera, Norilsk Nickel, Rostelekom, the railway operator Globaltrans, automaker KamAZ, electric company TGK-4, investment company Troika Dialog and others are registered. Many Russian brokers carry out operations on the Russian stock market through their Cypriote offices. The Russian Federal Financial Markets Service, the Russian financial regulator, had always intended to stop or at least minimize this practice. The global economic crisis acted as a trigger and in November 2008 the Russian regulator signed a memorandum of mutual understanding with the Commission on Securities and Stock Operations of Cyprus. The agreement created a base to ensure transparent regulation of financial institutes as the Russian Federal Financial Markets Service seeks to obtain information on real ownership of Russian companies registered in Cyprus (Kommersant, 2008).

In the following analysis, the number of deals is used, not their amounts, as the values are not readily available for all deals; hence using value would hinder comparative analysis. As the data shows (Table 8.3), since 2000, Russian companies have been increasingly

Table 8.3 Number of acquisition deals by Russian companies, 2000–2010

	2000	2001	2002	2003	2004	2005	2006	2007	2008	2009	2010
Total	16	28	35	53	60	70	103	114	119	102	70
CIS	6	10	16	25	34	30	35	29	32	35	28
EU	8	12	17	18	17	28	41	50	56	44	31
Non-EU Europe	–	3	–	4	–	2	7	3	5	6	1
Northern America	2	3	–	1	2	2	5	10	11	9	5
Africa	–	–	1	1	4	1	–	1	4	–	–
Latin America	–	–	–	–	1	–	1	–	–	4	1
Asia and Australia	–	–	1	3	1	5	3	5	8	–	2
Offshores	–	–	–	1	1	2	10	9	3	2	1
Unidentified	–	–	–	–	1	–	1	7	–	2	1

Source: Based on Zephyr database.

involved in foreign acquisitions. The amount of these deals had been steadily rising—from just 16 in 2000 to 119 in 2008. In fact, the year 2008 became a turning point. The amount decreased slightly in 2009, and even further fell in 2010, to 70 deals, the level of 2005.

The geography of Russian corporate expansion is diverse. Russian companies feel at ease in their traditional markets—former Soviet republics, now the members of the CIS. Within this grouping, the major share belongs to Ukraine, followed by Kazakhstan and Belarus, traditional Russia's trading partners. In parallel, Russian companies expand their presence in the European Union. Within the EU, the lion's share is taken by Cyprus due to the aforementioned reasons. Other leaders in the EU are the Netherlands, the UK, Italy, Germany, and France in Western Europe, and Romania, Latvia, and Czech Republic in Eastern Europe. Among non-EU European countries, Switzerland is the prime target for Russian acquisitions.

The North American market, consisting of the US and Canada, represents another attractive destination for Russian companies for a variety of motives and reasons. It is also notable that Russian companies acquire legal entities in a number of offshore locations, such as Bermuda, British Virgin Islands, Cayman Islands, etc. Companies acquired in offshore locations and Cyprus may serve as subsidiaries of Russian multinationals, and assets elsewhere might be bought through them later on.

According to the data, the number of acquisition deals decreased in the crisis years 2008–2010, from 119 in 2008 to 70 in 2010. Yet, the expansion did not stop. In total, 291 deals are recorded in 2008–2010 (Table 8.4). The analysis shows a great variety of deals. Companies, operating in various industries, from mining, oil, and gas to telecommunications, biotechnologies, and banking, were involved in the deals. Likewise, acquirers themselves represent a very heterogeneous group. They range from medium-sized regional enterprises with limited foreign presence, to 'real' multinationals like Gazprom, TNK-BP, VTB Bank, etc. Besides, various holding companies and investment funds are active in foreign acquisitions. Such diversity though, is not an inherent characteristic of the crisis period alone. Similarly, it was present during the entire 2000s period.

It can be seen that despite the crisis, Russian companies continued their foreign expansion, driven by a number of motives, such as resource-, market-, efficiency-, and asset-seeking. Russian companies have been acquiring infrastructural assets (gas distribution networks, electricity transmission, and energy generation) in the CIS and Eastern Europe. Manufacturing assets have been purchased on almost all

Table 8.4 Summary of acquisition deals by Russian companies, 2008–2010

Country/Region	No	Main Industries	Acquirers – Russian Multinationals
CIS	**95**		
Armenia	6	Electricity transmission, gas distribution, banking	Gazprom, Rosneftegaz, Gazprombank, Russian Railways
Azerbaijan	2	Banking, brewery	VTB Bank, Baltika
Belarus	18	Banking, insurance, oil and gas, telecommunications	Gazprom, Svyaznoy, VEB Bank, Sberbank, RESO group
Georgia	4	Banking	VTB Bank
Kazakhstan	21	Banking and finances, uranium mining telecommunications, electric manufacturing, pipe manufacturing, food and beverages	RTS Stock exchange, VTB Bank, Severstal, TMK, PIK Group, Beeline, Sibirskii Bereg
Moldova	1	Energy (hydroelectric power plant)	InterRAO EES
Ukraine	42	Banking, insurance and investments, oil and gas, food and beverages, steel/metal manufacturing, R&D, aircraft/spacecraft, pharmaceuticals	Bank of Moscow, Alfa-Bank, VEB, Bank Petrokommerts, MICEX and RTS, Troika Investment, TNK-BP, Gazprom, VSMPO, Sibirskii Bereg
Uzbekistan	1	Pump-power equipment manufacturing	Uralelektrotyazhmash-Uralgidromash
EU	**131**		
Austria	6	Hotels, machinery, oil and gas, Avionics, agricultural, chemical, and motor vehicle parts manufacturing	Azimut Hotels, Sibur Holding, Lukoil, Traktornye Zavody

Table 8.4 (Continued)

Country/Region	No	Main Industries	Acquirers – Russian Multinationals
Belgium	4	Iron and steel manufacturing, retail	Boston NV, Severstal, Magnitogorsk Metallurgy Combinat
Cyprus	41	Asset management, investment services, auditing, mobile telecommunications, pharmaceuticals, coal and iron ore mining, construction management	KAMAZ, Sberbank, mechel, MTS, UFG Asset Management, Gazprombank, PIK Group, MMK, InterRAO EES, Farmstandart, Uralsib
Czech Republic	6	Aircraft manufacturing, water turbines manufacturing, engineering	OMZ, UGMK, Tyazhmash
Denmark	4	Car and machinery manufacturing	AvtoVAZ, Agromashholding
Estonia	3	Banking, chemical manufacturing	Bank of Moscow, Acron
Finland	4	Banking, machinery manufacturing	Onexim Group, VTB Bank
France	4	Locomotive part manufacturing, chemical manufacturing, alcoholic beverages	SVL group, Uralvagonzavod, Uralkhim
Germany	8	Chemical and nuclear technology, chemical manufacturing, timber products manufacturing, gas distribution, biotechnology	Gazprom, Ilim Timber Industry, Atomstroieksport, Concern Traktornye Zavody
Hungary	2	Oil and gas production, airlines	Surgutneftegaz, VEB Bank
Ireland	1	Oil and gas exploration and production	Centrofervel Ltd
Italy	8	Steel manufacturing, machinery manufacturing, oil and gas refining	Severstal, Gazprom Neft, Sibirskii Agrarnyi Holding, Kosmos Association
Latvia	3	Pharmaceuticals, steel manufacturing, ceramic tile manufacturing	Severstal, Farmstandart, SU-155 Group

Netherlands	18	Engine manufacturing, mobile telecommunications, petroleum refining, investment holding, investment services	MTZ Transmash, Mechel, Lukoil, Baring Vostok Capital, MTS, St. Petersburg Sea Port
Portugal	1	Banking and investment	VTB Bank
Romania	4	Steel and metal manufacturing, software	Lyuksoft, Mechel, Severstal
Slovakia	2	Freight transportation, refractory materials manufacturing	Transkonteiner, Combinat Magnezit
Spain	2	Ventilation equipment, hotels	Interskol, North-Western Oil Group
UK	10	Mineral, oil and gas exploration and production, telecommunications, financials, ISP, gold mining	Gazprom Neft, Mechel, Millhouse, Renaissance Capital, Comstar
Non-EU Europe	**12**		
Montenegro	2	Oil and gas, hotels	Lukoil, Korston Group
Norway	1	Banking	Turris
Serbia	3	Banking, bus manufacturing	Gazprom Neft, Tehnika Servis
Switzerland	6	Logistics, locomotive manufacturing, pumps and compressors manufacturing, banking services	Mechel, Gazprombank, Renova
Northern America	**25**		
US	22	Oil and gas, steel manufacturing, computer and software, land and sea launch services	Energia Overseas, Onexim Group, Severstal, Gazprom Neft, Investment company Troika, Mechel, Almaz Capital, Severstal, TMK
Canada	3	Potassium mining services, gold exploration, residential building construction	Severstal, Akron, Growth Technologies

Table 8.4 (Continued)

Country/Region	No	Main Industries	Acquirers – Russian Multinationals
Asia	**10**		
Israel	2	Engineering, internet technologies	Yandex, IST Group
Cambodia, China, Hong Kong, India, Mongolia, Taiwan	8	Mobile telecommunication services, railways operator, computer manufacturing, cathode blocks manufacturing, turbine manufacturing	United Company Russian Aluminium, Novorossiysk Sea Trade Port, Sistema, Silovye Machiny, Vympel (Beeline), Russian Railways, Rover Computers
Latin America	**5**		
Brazil, Colombia, Panama, Peru	5	Helicopter transport services, mechanical engineering, electric machinery, equipment for power stations	Airline YutAir, Tyazhmash, Silovye Mashiny
Africa	**4**		
Ghana, Seychelles, South Africa, Zambia	4	Building materials, securities brokerage	Renaissance Capital, Brikor Ltd
Offshores	**6**		
Bermuda, British Virgin Islands, Marshall Islands	6	Investment banking services, offshore lifeboat vessels construction services	Onexim Group, Bashneft, Vympel (Beeline)
Other	**3**		
Country unknown	3	Investment services, telecommunications	Nafta Moskva, Megafon, Investment Company Finam

Source: Based on Zephyr database.

continents. Moreover, Russian financial institutions have strengthened their positions; banks acquired stakes in foreign financial institutions and Russian stock exchanges RTS and MICEX extended their control over the financial infrastructure in Ukraine and Kazakhstan.

Russian companies continue seeking advanced technology in the west, particularly in Western Europe. In many cases, they acquire a 100 per cent ownership of medium-sized technology-intensive manufacturing companies. In certain instances, complete acquisition is not seen as necessary; as even a minority stake may provide access to superior know-how. An example is the Human Stem Cell Institute, a Russian biotechnology company; amidst the crisis, in August 2009, it acquired a minority stake of 25.01 per cent in Germany's developer of treatments for cancer Symbiotec GmbH for €1 million. The intention is to learn from Symbiotec's expertise and knowledge.

Some Russian companies used the opportunities offered by the crisis to increase their stake in their foreign assets. In November 2010, the Russian railway equipment manufacturer MTZ Transmash increased its stake in the engine manufacturer Wartsila TMH Diesel Engine, based in the Netherlands, from 50 per cent to 100 per cent. In July 2008, the Russian mobile telecommunication provider MTS increased its minority stake of 10 per cent in the Dutch holding company Cezanne BV to 75 per cent.

The crisis should have led to decreased liquidity and forced companies to be cautious regarding their foreign investments. Nonetheless, some companies continued foreign expansion, and even acquired non-core assets. For example, in December 2008, Russia's North West Oil Group Inc. acquired a 100 per cent stake in Spain's Hotel Los Monteros sl. for €115 million. Similarly, in May 2010, the Russian private equity investment company services Onexim Group bought an 80 per cent stake in the US professional basketball team operator New Jersey Nets, for €158.3 million.

Last but not least, the influence of the Russian government has strengthened. The state-owned investment vehicle VEB bank has become a distinctive actor on foreign markets in the crisis years, specifically in the CIS markets, both directly and indirectly.

Foreign divestments

It is expected that the global crisis might have a moderating effect on expansion abroad. In addition to putting their expansion plans on halt, companies may even divest, to dispose of their assets abroad. While a company may divest its assets at home, I intentionally analyze only divestments abroad in order to analyze the effect of the crisis on foreign activities of Russian multinationals. The Zephyr database is used to track all deals in which a Russian company (not an individual or a governmental body) acted as a vendor, and a target was located elsewhere than Russia. For the period 2008–2010 only 27 entries meeting these criteria are retrieved—6 deals in 2008, 13 in 2009 and 8 in 2010 (Table 8.5).

Two main regions of these deals are the CIS and the EU. In the CIS, Ukraine and Kazakhstan were the countries of most targets; and in fact it reflects the geography of acquisitions by Russian companies. In the EU, Latvia, Estonia, and Austria can be highlighted. Deals with offshore companies were recorded too. Two prime examples are here. Firstly, in January 2009, Roman Abramovich's asset management fund Millhouse LLC sold the 31.25 per cent stake in Primerod International Ltd based in British Virgin Islands to another entity registered in the same country. In December 2010, Gazprom sold its investment holding ZGG Cayman Holding registered in Cayman Islands for €2 billion, by doing so, it effectively sold its 9.4 per cent stake in the Russian gas producer Novatek. Novatek is the largest independent natural gas producer, and second-largest in Russia overall after Gazprom.

Regarding the sectoral composition, there was a great variety—oil and gas, uranium mining, perfumes and cosmetics retail, food and beverages production, banking and insurance services, etc.

As data show, several Russian companies sold minority stakes, stakes in non-core assets—for example, Mirax Group, one of the leading Russian construction services companies, involved in the construction of the business district Moscow-City, faced liquidity problems and had to sell a 100 per cent stake in a hotel in Turkey for €190 million in February 2010. Another company, the cosmetics retailer Arbat Prestizh had to sell its foreign assets as it had gone bankrupt, on grounds unrelated to the global economic crisis. Its top management faced tax fraud charges in 2008 and the company ceased to exist in 2010.

Some deals seeming pure divestments represented corporate consolidation. In August 2010, the Russian beer manufacturer Baltika Breweries sold 100 per cent of its wholly owned Kazakhstani subsidiary Baltika-Almata for an undisclosed amount. This deal in fact represented integration of companies within the Carlsberg Group (the owner of Baltika). This deal completed the process of the integration of Baltika Breweries and Derbes Breweries within the Carlsberg Group on the territory of Kazakhstan. Likewise, the sale of a stake in Kazakhstan's Karatau

Table 8.5 Divestment deals by Russian companies, 2008–2010

Date	Vendor	Industry	Target	Country of Target	Country of Acquirer	Stake (%)	Value, € 000
2008							
17-10-2008	Arbat Prestizh	Perfumes and cosmetics retailer	Arbat Prestizh's 31 perfume and cosmetics stores in Ukraine	Ukraine	Ukraine	100	n.a.
31-07-2008	N-Trans	Sea port operator	Vopak EOS AS	Estonia	The Netherlands	15	n.a.
30-06-2008	Paterson-Invest	Land and supermarket estate operation services	Paterson's 3 Kiev-based supermarkets	Ukraine	Ukraine	100	n.a.
21-05-2008	Lukoil	Oil and gas	Lukoil' 54 gas stations in Poland	Poland	Poland	100	n.a.
05-05-2008	Gazprom Media	Media services	Mediatopprim Ltd	Moldova	US	100	n.a.
15-04-2008	Nakhodka Re	Reinsurance services	Pasifik Oushen SK	Ukraine	US	100	634.20
2009							
28-12-2009	TMK	Metallurgy	NS Group Inc.	US	US	51	n.a.
15-12-2009	Atomredmetzoloto	Uranium mining services	The Karatau Uranium Mine	Kazakhstan	the Netherlands	50	301,050.03
11-12-2009	Stock Exchange RTS	Stock exchange	Ukrainian Stock Exchange	Ukraine	Ukraine	9	n.a.

Table 8.5 (Continued)

Date	Vendor	Industry	Target	Country of Target	Country of Acquirer	Stake (%)	Value, € 000
06-11-2009	Rolf GK	Car dealer	FF Sheffe BV	The Netherlands	Japan	40	48,408.31
06-11-2009	Bryansk Machine-building factory	Machinery manufacturer	Luganskteplovoz Holding Company	Ukraine	Ukraine	76	n.a.
28-10-2009	AvtoVAZ	Car manufacturer	Delta Motor Group OY	Finland	UK	n.a.	n.a.
12-08-2009	Managing company Estar	Steel manufacturer holding company	Donetsk electrometallurgy factory	Ukraine	Ukraine	100	706,800.00
11-08-2009	Gidromashservis	Electric engine manufacturer	NPO Gidromash	Ukraine	Ukraine	99.53	n.a.
07-05-2009	Antanta PIO Global Investment Group	Investment holding company	PIO Hlobal Ukrayina, Asset Management Company	Ukraine	Ukraine	100	n.a.
30-04-2009	Basic Element	Asset investment management holding	Strabag SE	Austria	Austria	25	493,620.00
20-03-2009	Nutritek	Baby food, diary food producer	Agro PIIM AS	Estonia	Estonia	100	n.a.
29-01-2009	Veritas SPA	Multi-utility services	Veritas Energia SRL	Italy	Italy	51	1,300.00

13-01-2009	Millhouse LLC	Asset management	Primerod International Ltd	British Virgin Islands	British Virgin Islands	31.25	n.a.
2010							
20-12-2010	Gazprom	Oil and gas	ZGG Cayman Holding	Cayman Islands	Ireland	100	2,146,080.65
29-10-2010	Farmstandart	Medical manufactur-ing/pharmaceuticals	Grindeks AS	Latvia	Latvia	11.381	9,840 64
06-08-2010	Baltika	Beer manufacturer	Baltika-Almata	Kazakhstan	Kazakhstan	100	n.a.
08-07-2010	Petrovsky Bank	Banking services	IEFK Banka AD	Bosnia-Herzegovina	Bosnia-Herzegovina	99	6,544.54
12-05-2010	Ingosstrakh	Insurance services	Garant Versicherungs-AG	Austria	Belgium	33	n.a.
18-03-2010	Russian Alcohol Group	Alcohol manufacturer	Ushba Distillery	Georgia	Georgia	100	3,640.28
24-02-2010	Mirax Group	Construction services	Sungate Port Royal De Luxe Resort Hotel	Turkey	Turkey	100	190,000.00
19-02-2010	Kavitatsionnye Tekhnologii	Financial leasing services	Dnepropetrovsk factory for repair and building of passenger rail wagons 'Dneprovagonremstroy'	Ukraine	Ukraine	96.12	n.a.

Source: Based on Zephyr database.

uranium mine by Atomredmetzoloto in December 2009 represented an organizational and corporate restructuring.

Overall, no general trend can be recorded and also no overall conclusion can be derived. It might well be that many of these deals would have occurred in any case, even in a non-crisis period.

Sectoral analysis and cases

Previous subsections outlined the overall picture of Russian companies' foreign acquisitions and divestments. While there are generic responses of the emerging Russian multinationals to the global crisis, sectoral idiosyncrasies are strongly pronounced too. I further analyze sectoral differences more in-depth, using relevant examples, with a focus on their expansion or contraction abroad. Table 8.6 briefly summarizes key deals discussed in this section.

Oil and gas companies

Initially, the oil and gas sector was hardest hit by the crisis (leading to the substantial fall of energy prices). However, the policy measures initiated by the Russian government helped mitigate the adverse effect of the crisis. Firstly, Russian oil companies earned considerable amounts as a result of the national currency devaluation (since most contracts were nominated in foreign currencies). Additionally, anti-crisis policy measures in the form of tax breaks added billions of profit. It can be said that the negative effects of the crisis for the Russian oil and gas companies ceased to exist at the beginning of 2009, and it is mainly due to

Table 8.6 Overview of deals concluded in the crisis period, 2008–2010

Industry	Russian company	Expansion	Contraction
Oil and gas	Lukoil	TRN (Netherlands)	
Steel	Severstal	Lucchini (Italy) & Crew Gold (UK)	
Metallurgy	Mechel	Bluestone (US)	
Automotive	Basic Element		Magna Int. (Canada)
Construction	Basic Element		Hochtief (Germany)
Construction	Basic Element	Strabag (Austria)	Strabag (Austria)
Engineering	Renova	Oerlikon (Switzerland) & Sulzer (Switzerland)	
Financials	VEB	Prominvestbank (Ukraine) & Belvnesheconombank (Belarus)	
Internet	DST	ICQ & Facebook (US)	

the rise of oil prices. A recent report by Moody's Investor Services confirms that the financial robustness of the Russian oil and gas companies during the economic downturn was sustained by the policy measures such as the devaluation of the Russian national currency and changes in the tax system. Moreover, cost cutting actions and access to funding boosted the companies' resilience to the problems (Moody's, 2010). The agency's forecast for the Russian oil and gas companies is positive; and Moody's overall outlook for the sector is stable due to the rising demand for oil and gas globally.

Russian oil and gas multinationals have continued their foreign expansion supported by the rising revenues. On September 1, 2009, the Russian private oil company Lukoil completed the purchase of Dow Chemicals' 45 per cent stake in the Dutch refinery Total Raffinaderij Nederland (TRN). The value of the deal, excluding crude oil and products inventory was US$600 million in line with an agreement reached between Lukoil and Total in June 2008. TRN is located in the Vlissingen Oost harbor area in the south-western part of the Netherlands. This is one of world's largest oil and oil-product trading hubs (Amsterdam–Rotterdam–Antwerp) benefiting from access to the well-established infrastructure, including Maasvlakte Olie Terminal, in which TRN owns a 22 per cent share. Prior to the acquisition, Lukoil was already a major supplier to TRN from its Timan-Pechora fields. Lukoil's press release emphasizes that 'these advantages enable Lukoil to strengthen its positions in North Western Europe and increase efficiency of its trading operations. The company will also be able to use TRN to supply and further develop its retail presence in Western Europe. The acquisition of a share in TRN represents another milestone in Lukoil's strategy to acquire world-class refining assets located in direct proximity to end-user markets' (Lukoil, 2009).

The stake became available for purchase because Dow Chemicals was acting under pressure to sell assets quickly and cut costs and manpower in order to repay debts in the US. Lukoil reported a net cash reserve of US$3.2 billion at that time as resource available to finance acquisitions abroad. The price paid by Lukoil for the 45 per cent stake is a deeply discounted valuation, due to the global economic downturn; therefore Lukoil acquired this asset on the cheap, an opportunity created by the crisis (Socor, 2009). In fact, this is not the first Lukoil's acquisition in Europe. Several years ago, Lukoil had embarked on a strategy to acquire stakes in refineries and retail marketing networks in the European Union. It acquired refineries in Bulgaria and Romania prior to the accession of these countries into the European Union.

However attempts to buy assets in other countries (UK, Germany, Spain, Lithuania, and the Czech Republic) were unsuccessful. The assets were too expensive to acquire. As the global oil prices started to fall in the second half of 2008, assets lost in value too. At this moment Lukoil realized its first major acquisition in Western Europe. It bought a 49 per cent stake, with an option to expand it later, in the Italian ERG group's ISAB refinery in Sicily.

Steel industry

Russian steel industry is dependent both on foreign markets and domestic construction and automobile industries. The first sign of the crisis in the sector were reported at the end of September 2008. Magnitogorsk Iron and Steel Works dismissed many of its workers and reduced output. Likewise, drop in production (both at home and overseas) and layoffs (or decreases in wages) were reported for Severstal and Evraz Group. Overall, substantial decline in production and output in raw material industries; automobile and tool-making industries was recorded in Russia; and hence prices of aluminum and nickel plummeted to a break-even point.

The industry appealed to the state for aid and relied on the government funds through VTB loans in the framework of the anti-crisis policy measures. VTB issued a 10 billion roubles emergency loan to Evraz to finance its current tax payments. A 5 billion roubles loan was issued to TMK. In its investment report, Moody's Investor Services forecasts slow recovery of domestic demand in Russia, which will continue to limit the growth prospects of the Russian steel industry. While some signs of prospects are seen as the demand for steel increases globally, domestic demand is important for steel producers' long-term stability and growth prospects (Moody's, 2010).

Despite this industry's downfall, companies did not stop their international expansion. Severstal, a Russian steel manufacturer, has also been hit by the crisis, but returned to profit in the third quarter of 2009, thanks to a strong performance at its domestic mills. Even before that, it continued corporate consolidation. In November 2008, it acquired a 100 per cent stake in Severstal Belgium Holding and increased its stake from 49.23 per cent to 51.25 per cent in Severstal US Holdings in December 2009. In March 2010, the company increased its stake in the Italian steel manufacturer Lucchini SpA, from 79.8 per cent to 100 per cent, paying some €100 million. And in May 2010, it increased its stake in another foreign affiliate—Canada's High River Gold Mines Ltd, from 50.1 per cent to 68.86 per cent having paid €92.5 million.

Severstal first acquired a stake in Lucchini back in 2005. Lucchini has a network of domestic and international facilities, possesses a wide product range and the integral cycle technology. Following this original deal, Severstal acquired 79.8 per cent and the Lucchini family retained a minority stake of 20.2 per cent. As the crisis unfolded, Lucchini started posting negative earning. On one hand, the situation offered the Lucchini family to sell its remaining stake in the loss-making company. On the other hand, Severstal acquired the stake for a lower prices (as it is speculated, Severstal paid €100 million instead of €160 million). Following the transaction, Severstal now owns 100 per cent of Lucchini SpA. However, as the company continues to make loss and the prospects for Severstal on the European steel market are bleak, the Russian multinational is looking for a strategic buyer.

Financial problems in another foreign company allowed Severstal to expand to West Africa. In February 2010, Severstal acquired, through its subsidiary Bluecone Ltd, ownership and control of 15.71 per cent of shares in Crew Gold, a London-based gold mining company, holding major assets in Guinea, West Africa. This transaction effectively raised Severstal's ownership to 19.79 per cent (Severstal, 2010). This acquisition followed a corporate restructuring at Crew Gold in response to financial difficulties. In June 2010, Severstal became a control shareholder and, after acquiring a 43.21 per cent stake from another shareholder, Endeavour Financial Corporation, Severstal became a 93.38 per cent shareholder. The final step was done on January 10, 2011, when Nord Gold N.V., a Dutch subsidiary of Severstal acquired a remaining 6.62 per cent stake in Crew Gold. Following this transaction Severstal has become a 100 per cent shareholder (Severstal, 2011).

Metallurgy

The metallurgy sector faced problems similar to the steel industry as aforementioned. The Russian extraction and metallurgic concern Mechel represents a relevant case in point. At the beginning of the crisis, the majority of the company's debt was current/short-term. To enable the company to continue operations, Mechel started restructuring its debt into payable in the long-term. Several financing deals were concluded—15 billion roubles (approximately US$560 million) in December 2008 by VTB Bank, US$1 billion in February 2009 by Gazprombank, refinancing of US$2.6 billion in July 2009, and an agreement with VTB Bank to prolong its 15 billion roubles loan for another 3 years.

It is at this adverse period, Mechel signed and closed an agreement and acquired a foreign company. On April 22, 2009, Mechel's press release reported an acquisition of 100 per cent shares and interests of a number of US entities, including 'Bluestone', privately-held West Virginia-based coal businesses engaged in the mining, processing and sale of premium quality hard coking coal. The deal amount of US$ 436 million was paid in cash, approximately 83.3 million preferred shares, and it is assumed that approximately US$132 million was the net debt (Mechel, 2009).

Commenting on the deal, Mechel's CEO emphasized the strategic nature of this acquisition, 'The addition of Bluestone's production assets and large, high-quality coking coal reserves and resources establishes Mechel as one of the largest producers of coking coal in the world... Following the closing, we expect... a more diversified asset base, including a strong foothold in North America and enhanced European, American and Asian sales channels' (Mechel, 2009). In other words, Mechel expects to continue serving Bluestone's existing customer base, primarily in Northern America and Europe.

Automotive industry

At the beginning of the crisis, the Russian automotive sector faced declining demand due to general uncertainty among consumers and a collapse in auto loan programs. The sector had always enjoyed favorable conditions due to Russia's high tariffs on car imports. The government further increased these tariffs as part of the anti-crisis measures.

Gaz and Kamaz were the first auto makers to declare production cuts in September–October 2008. The financial difficulties forced Kamaz to request a state-backed loan and a private loan from Citigroup. Kamaz was the target of acquisition by Daimler AG; and in December 2008 the deal was realized, as Daimler AG acquired the first 10 per cent in Kamaz stock. Avtovaz disclosed emergency measures on October 16, 2008. The company requested a government-backed interest-free loan of US$1 billion through VTB.

The Russian automotive industry can hardly boast the presence of Russian emerging multinationals. Russian automotive companies have only limited presence abroad. Therefore the crisis did not have a sizeable effect on foreign operations. However, some Russian multinationals had to sell shares in foreign automotive companies. The example of 'Russkie Mashiny'/Russian Machines, part of the Basic Element conglomerate, is illustrative. In May 2007, Basic Element acquired 20 per cent of shares in Canada's Magna International, the second largest auto parts maker in North America, for US$1.54 billion. The Russian company aimed to get access to the advanced Western technologies, and Magna International, in its turn, secured local partner in the fast-growing auto markets. Success, however, did not last long. The shares were used as collateral for a loan, and as stock prices of Basic Element plummeted in autumn 2008, Magna's shares were sold to the loan providers.

Yet, the crisis offered an opportunity to buy foreign assets in the sector. The end of 2009 was marked by negotiations between GM, the parent company of German car manufacturer Opel and a consortium of the very same Magna International and Russian lender Sberbank. The intention of the consortium was to acquire a 55 per cent stake in Opel (Sberbank—35 per cent, Magna—20 per cent). The offer contemplated a total equity investment by the consortium of €500 million over time. The primary intention of the Russian side was access to technology and know-how rather than market. German Gref, Sberbank's chief executive stated, 'If the import of technologies does not take place, it will mean that (the deal) was just a waste of time' (Reuters, 2009). On November 4, 2009, after months of painstaking negotiations, the Board of GM, the parent company of Opel, announced its intention to reject the deal and to implement a restructuring plan, keeping Opel within its corporate structure. It is speculated that the negative perception of the Russian government's involvement in the deal was one of the reasons behind its failure.

Construction

In May 2007, Basic Element Holding acquired a 10 per cent stake in the German construction company Hochtief Aktiengesellschaft. On October 9, 2008, Oleg Deripaska, the Russian billionaire and Basic Element's owner announced his decision to exit Hochtief due to the steep drop in its value following the decline in construction industry amidst the global crisis. The shares were transferred to Commerzbank that provided a loan for the original deal. In fact, this transaction took place less than a week after Deripaska's decision to divest a big stake from the Canadian car parts maker Magna Int.

Right before the crisis, in April 2007, Basic Element acquired a 25 per cent stake in the Austrian construction company Strabag SE, through a subsidiary company Rasperia Trading Ltd, for €1.05 billion. As the global crisis struck and the Basic Element Holding started facing pressure in its construction projects and a lack of liquidity, it surrendered its 25 per cent stake to the other two core shareholders in May 2009 to repay the loan taken for its original acquisition and to be able to fund other activities in the wake of the global financial crisis.

However, as the Russian company began to re-emerge from the crisis, it considered re-purchasing Strabag. On November 8, 2010, Basic Element's Rasperia Trading Ltd. announced an agreement with Strabag's two core shareholders to repurchase a 17 per cent stake in the company for €373 million; and the transaction was completed on November 30, 2010. Furthermore, the members of the syndicate agreed to provide Rasperia with an extension of the call option for the remaining 8 per cent until July 15, 2014. The initial option covered 25 per cent, exactly as the stake acquired initially in 2007 (Strabag, 2010).

Engineering and high-tech

A good example in relation to engineering is the acquisition of two Swiss engineering companies by the Renova Group, a large Russian conglomerate. Both investments are particularly important as they offer Russian multinational companies access to new technologies that may be used on the Russian market.

By the crisis, the Renova Group had held 27.10 per cent in shares and 4.10 per cent in purchase positions of Swiss engineering company Sulzer AG. Sulzer's activities include machinery, equipment, surface technology, and thermal turbo machinery. Amidst the crisis, on March 27, 2009, the Renova Group announced that it had increased its shareholding to 31.20 per cent.

Renova had already had a stake in the Swiss company OC Oerlikon, the leader in the market of semiconductor and vacuum technologies, manufacturing of textile machinery, and data storage technologies. In addition, the company develops innovative technologies in outer space exploration, solar energy, laser, and nanotechnologies. In May 2008, Renova increased its stake to 39 per cent, and in June 2010 it further tightened the grip by increasing its ownership up to 46.11 per cent stake following Oerlikon's capital increase and acquisition of further shares in the Swiss company (Renova, 2010).

Financial services

The Russian financial sector was one of the first to suffer from the crisis. However, timely intervention by the Russian government prevented the escalation of the crisis in the financial sector and consequently, in other sectors of the national economy. The state-owned development bank Vnesheconombank (VEB) is one the main vehicles of the government's policy. VEB itself can be regarded not only as a government-owned corporation (100 per cent of its shares are owned by the Russian government), but also as a multinational company. VEB possesses a network of representation offices in the UK, Germany, Italy, France, US, China, India, and the Republic of South Africa.

In January 2009, VEB purchased additional shares issued by Ukraine's Prominvestbank. In September 2009, VEB paid a total of US$500 million to increase its share in the bank's charter capital to 93.84 per cent. Prominvestbank is one of Ukraine's leading financial institutions, with an extensive branch network across Ukraine; it plays a leading role in supporting the industrial sector of Ukraine and in the development of the national economy. As the crisis began to unfold, the Ukrainian bank found itself on the verge of a default and the acquisition deal offered a chance to successfully resolve its most acute problems and to conduct a structural reorganization (VEB, 2009). VEB is also the owner of the majority stake of Belvnesheconombank, based in the Republic of Belarus. In 2009, VEB increased Belvnesheconombank's capitalization, which enabled it to build up the volumes of financing to ensure the exports of the Russian equipment and technologies to the Belarusian market (VEB, 2009).

IT and media

Russian IT, software, and media companies have been expanding over the recent years. Digital Sky Technologies (DST), an investment firm based in Moscow, is one of the main players in this sector. The company is a major investor in the Russian, CIS, and Eastern European internet markets. It owns stakes in various internet companies. In May 2009, DST bought a 1.96 per cent stake in Facebook, the social media website for US$200 million. On April 28, 2010, AOL and DST reached an agreement for DST to acquire ICQ instant messaging service for US$187.5 million. At the beginning of January 2011, DST announced its decision to further increase its stake in Facebook, up to 10 per cent. In this deal Facebook raised US$50 million from DST and US$450 million from Goldman Sachs.

Going public: Foreign IPO

The Moscow Interbank Currency Exchange (MICEX), which was set up in 1992 at the start of the economic transition, is one of the largest universal stock exchanges in the Russian Federation and Eastern Europe. Next to it, the Russian Trading System (RTS) is a stock market established in 1995 in Moscow, consolidating various regional trading floors into one exchange. In addition to floating on national stock exchanges, in the mid-1990s, the first Russian companies began to issue stocks and bonds in IPO, and raise money through global depositary receipt (GDR) in the west; that could also be seen as a sign of internationalization. The reasons can be different—some smaller companies seek capital to expand, other companies (particularly privately-owned) look to become publicly traded to facilitate acquisitions, diversify their equity base and enhance prestige and exposure.

The London Stock Exchange (LSE) is one of the favorite global stock exchanges among Russian companies. As of November 30, 2011, some 32 Russian companies with a total market value GBP 311 billion are listed on LSE. Russian companies account only for around 1 per cent of all companies listed on LSE; however, it represents a first, important step on the way to high standards of corporate governance.

Gazprom was the first to be listed on LSE on October 28, 1996. It was shortly followed by other large oil and gas producers—Tatneft (December 13, 1996) and Lukoil (May 7, 1997). The next Russian company (OMZ JSC) was listed on LSE at the end of 2003. Since then, IPOs by Russian companies on LSE became a clear rising trend—three in 2005, six in 2006, and the last pre-crisis year (2007) witnessed nine IPOs. All these companies operate in various sectors—from oil and gas, and mining, to banks and biotechnology.

As the crisis hit, the number of IPOs by Russian companies plummeted. Only two Russian (private) companies became listed on LSE in 2008—the food and drug retailer Magnit in April and the chemicals producer Acron in August. In 2009, at the peak of the crisis, only one Russian company proceeded with IPO. It is Rushydro, the world's second-largest hydroelectric power producer and Russia's largest power-generating company that is the largest successor to RAO UES, a former Russian electricity monopoly. Rushydro is partly government-owned (the Russian government has a stake of 58 per cent). Likewise, only one Russian company—TransContainer—became listed on LSE in 2010. TransContainer is an intermodal transport company based in Russia, a subsidiary of the Russian state-owned railway company. The year 2011 may be regarded a turning point. Six Russian companies emerged on LSE (Table 8.7).

Although LSE remains the most attractive foreign stock exchange, Russian companies have also explored other exchanges. The mobile telecommunications providers Mobile TeleSystems and Vimpel-Communications (BeeLine), the iron and steel producer Mechel, and

Table 8.7 Russian companies listed on LSE, as of November 30, 2011

London Stock Exchange			
List Date	**Company**	**Sector**	**Market Capitalization £m**
2011			
28-11-2011	Inter RAO UES JSC	Gas, Water, & Multiutilities	0
16-08-2011	Hals-Development JSC	Real Estate Investment & Services	11
18-07-2011	PhosAgro OJSC	Chemicals	519
01-07-2011	Sberbank of Russia	Banks	0
27-04-2011	Nomos Bank OJSC	Banks	309
28-03-2011	Federal Grid Co Uni Energy Sys OJSC	Company Bonds	0
2010			
12-11-2010	Transcontainer OJSC	Industrial Transportation	157
2009			
06-07-2009	Rushydro OJSC	Electricity	6,910
2008			
12-08-2008	Acron JSC	Chemicals	1
22-04-2008	Magnit OJSC	Food & Drug Retailers	6,279
2007			
16-11-2007	LSR Group OJSC	Construction & Materials	122
08-11-2007	Novorossiysk Commercial Sea Port	Industrial Transportation	156
19-10-2007	Uralkali JSC	Banks	15,929
06-06-2007	PIK Group OJSC	Real Estate Investment & Services	61
17-05-2007	VTB Bank JSC	Banks	15,984
11-05-2007	Pharmastandard OJSC	Pharmaceuticals & Biotechnology	546

Table 8.7 (Continued)

London Stock Exchange			
List Date	**Company**	**Sector**	**Market Capitalization £m**
30-04-2007	Magnitogorsk Iron & Steel Works	Industrial Metals	3,410
13-02-2007	Sitronics JSC	Technology Hardware & Equipment	12
12-02-2007	Polymetal OJSC	Mining	705
2006			
18-12-2006	Polyus Zoloto OAO	Mining	2006
14-11-2006	Severstal OAO	Industrial Metals	8,675
13-11-2006	Chelyabinsk Elektrolit Zink Plant	Industrial Metals	19
03-11-2006	TMK OAO	Industrial Metals	259
19-07-2006	Rosneft OJSC	Oil & Gas Producers	49,228
15-05-2006	Cherkizovo Group (OJSC)	Food Producers	196
2005			
15-12-2005	Novolipetsk Iron and Steel Corp	Industrial Metals	9,219
27-07-2005	Novatek OAO	Oil & Gas Producers	29,486
14-02-2005	Sistema JSFC	Mobile Telecommunications	6,143
2003			
30-09-2003	OMZ JSC	Industrial Engineering	0
1990s			
07-05-1997	Lukoil OAO	Oil & Gas Producers	60,808
13-12-1996	Tatneft AO	Oil & Gas Producers	7,460
28-10-1996	Gazprom OAO	Oil & Gas Producers	86,739

Source: Based on London Stock Exchange, www.londonstockexchange.com.

food and beverages producer Wimm-Bill-Dann Foods float on the New York Stock Exchange (NYSE). Vimpel started floating in May 2010.

In the same year (January 2010), United Company Rusal, the world's second largest aluminum producer, became listed on the Hong Kong Stock Exchange (HKEx). The company chose Hong Kong as it expected to attract Chinese investors and China is the world's largest aluminum consumer. Although headquartered in Moscow, Rusal is incorporated at Jersey, Crown dependency, from where its financial Centre operates. Therefore the company is listed on HKEx as a company incorporated in Jersey, with a principal office in Hong Kong, without any reference to Russia.

Overall, regarding floating on (foreign) stock exchanges, despite improvements in the economic climate, risks are still too high for many companies. It is possible to expect some growth but only in comparison to 2008–2010. Companies may be listed in order to repay debts and to realize investment programs because it is very hard to finance them by means of credits since banks issue credits only for short time and under high interest rates. Moreover, certain companies do not have a chance to take out a loan at all and such opportunity will hardy be available for them soon.

Conclusions

The early and mid-2000s were marked by bold behavior of Russian multinationals on foreign markets characterized by acquisition of assets in the former Soviet and socialist republics, as well as in Western Europe and elsewhere. The global economic crisis that erupted in late 2007 has affected growth of Russian companies and their foreign operations of emerging Russian multinationals. The largest companies have reduced their investment programs. Certain Russian companies have had to withdraw their investments from various projects in order to repay their debts. The paper has discussed the interplay between two parallel developments, both critically important for the global economy—the global economic crisis and the internationalization of Russian multinational companies. Various data sources are used in order to explore the effect of the global crisis on international expansion of Russian multinationals. It is important to note that the focus of the paper lies in the international operations (internationalization) of emerging Russian multinationals and not in their responses to the crisis on the domestic Russian market (where responses were much harsher than abroad). Several main conclusions can be formulated.

General outlook

The crisis has had a moderating effect on the Russian expansion abroad. Empirics described in the paper show that Russia sustained decline in its outward FDI, the amount of foreign acquisition diminished and the number of Russian companies going public on Western stock exchanges decreased. This contraction, however, was not radical. In many instances, indicators returned back to the mid-2000s level.

Overall, it can be concluded that on one side some companies sustained financial losses and re-thought their expansion strategy, on the other hand, the crisis offered an opportunity for acquisition of assets abroad going down in market value. After all, Russian companies have been born and grown in unstable institutional and challenging business environment; many of them have gone through the 1998 Russian financial crisis, enabling them to develop resilience to adverse economic conditions that helps them overcome the consequences of the global economic crisis.

The 1998 Russian crisis has led to reconfiguration of the Russian national economy, impacting market shares of the largest companies (banks in the first instance). In contrast, the global economic crisis has not led to dramatic changes in the structure of the Russian economy and market shares. The current positions have been largely preserved, mainly due to the decisive intervention of the Russian government.

Russian government and state aid

The Russian government has played a pro-active role to mitigate the negative effect of the crisis. State aid granted to (a select number of) Russian large and multinational companies has sustained and enhanced their competitive position. Given that oil and gas are of strategic importance to Russia, the policy-makers continue to advance the state's influence in the energy sector. Specifically, Russian oil and gas multinationals benefited greatly from these policy measures, and re-emerged from the crisis even more financially sound. In many instances, the crisis enabled the Russian government to strengthen its grip over the national economy. This can be even referred to as 'soft re-nationalization'.

While the economic crisis has halted the foreign expansion of Russian private capital, state-owned capital strengthened its position as an investor. Companies with a controlling stake held by the Russian government (e.g. Gazprom, VTB Bank, Sberbank) continued their expansion; the state-owned entity 'Russian Development Bank' (VEB) has started playing a much more pronounced role in Russia's foreign expansion, directly and indirectly.

Sectoral differences

Russia's raw materials companies continue to be the main category of foreign investors. These companies have benefited from the state support and are presently enjoying rising commodity prices. These factors allow them to continue their expansion abroad. Likewise, financial institutions who benefited from the state aid continue internationalizing. Companies in steel manufacturing sector are visible international players too.

However, new technologies are gaining prominence as the other main direction of Russian investments. Mobile telecommunications companies actively explore foreign markets, particularly, the CIS. Similarly, Russian companies in software, IT, internet technologies, and media markets expand abroad. Acquisition of a stake in the social network Facebook by a Russian company is illustrative.

Divestments

The crisis has had a moderating effect on the foreign expansion of Russian multinationals too. Some companies had to divest their foreign assets. Basic Element, a diversified investment company, is a case in point. Mounting financial pressure forced Basic Element to sell the investment in the Canada-based auto-parts maker Magna, a year after the acquisition deal to the bank that financed the deal. Similarly, even if Basic Element had to divest its assets (Strabag) in the wake of the crisis, it effectively restored its ownership and control in the late 2010.

As the analysis shows, several Russian companies sold minority stakes, or stakes in non-core assets, others compensated foreign divestments by acquisition elsewhere abroad (e.g. Lukoil's sale of its gas stations network in Poland and purchase of a network in Montenegro). In total, it can be concluded that the global economic crisis has not led to massive divestments of foreign assets by Russian multinationals.

To sum up, the emergent class of Russian multinational companies has been touched by the global economic crisis. However, facilitated by the Russian government, emerging Russian multinationals have managed to withstand the blow and improve their competitive positions and financial performance. Further recovery of the Russian economy and Russian multinationals will depend on the performance of the world's leading economies and the recovery in the emerging markets, particularly the other BRIC countries.

The literature stream on emerging multinationals has been dynamically evolving in the recent years. Nevertheless, it has not reached its maturity and has not provided definite and sharp conclusions. Responses of emerging multinationals to the global economic crisis are one of the aspects of this research area. This is a new and key issue to address on which the extant literature remains scant. This paper makes one of the first steps on this promising avenue of academic research by putting together empirical evidence on this topic and providing descriptive analysis of these current developments. The findings of the study broadly correspond to the propositions of Sauvant *et al.* (2010) regarding strategic responses of emerging multinationals to the crisis. There is still a large potential for academic elaboration and theory-building, as a better understanding of this issue is a concern of scholars as well as policy-makers. More specifically, Russian multinationals have become and will remain important players in the world FDI market, and the topic provides an avenue for further research.

References

Allen, R. (2009). *Financial Crises and Recession in the Global Economy*, 3rd ed. Cheltenham: Edward Elgar.

Alvarez, R. and Gorg, H. (2007). *Multinationals as Stabilizers? Economic Crisis and Plant Employment Growth*. Working Paper No. 412, Central Bank of Chile.

Alvarez, R. and Gorg, H. (2009). Multinationals and plant exit: Evidence from Chile, *International Review of Economics and Finance*, 18(1): 45–51.

Andreff, V. (2003). The newly emerging TNCs from economies in transition: A comparison with the Third World outward FDI, *Transnational Corporations*, 12(2): 73–118.

Athukorala, P. (2003). FDI in crisis and recovery: Lessons from the 1997–1998 Asian crisis, *Australian Economic Review*, 43: 197–213.

Benito, G. and Narula, R. (2007). *Multinationals on the Periphery*. London: Palgrave Macmillan.

Buckley, P., Clegg, J., Cross, A., Liu, X., Voss, H., and Zheng, P. (2007). The determinants of Chinese outward foreign direct investment, *Journal of International Business Studies*, 38(4): 499–518.

Bulatov, A. (1998). Russian direct investment abroad: Main motivations in the post-Soviet period, *Transnational Corporations*, 7(1): 69–82.

Bulatov, A. (2001). Russian direct investment abroad: History, motives, finance, control and planning, *Economics of Planning*, 34(3): 179–194.

Child, J. and Rodrigues, S. (2005). The internationalisation of Chinese firms: A case for theoretical revision? *Management and Organization Review*, 1(3): 381–410.

Crane, K., Peterson, D.J., and Oliker, O. (2005). Russian investment in the Commonwealth of Independent States, *Eurasian Geography and Economics*, 46(6): 405–444.

Dejuan, O., Febrero, E., and Marcuzzo, M.C. (2011). *The First Great Recession of the 21st Century*. Cheltenham: Edward Elgar.

Desai, P. (2010). Rethinking Russia: Russia's financial crisis: Economic setbacks and policy responses, *Journal of International Affairs*, 63(2): 141–151.

Dunning, J.H. (1988). The eclectic paradigm of international production: A restatement and some possible extensions, *Journal of International Business Studies*, 19(1): 1–31.

Dunning, J.H. (2006). Comment on Dragon multinationals: New players in 21st century globalization, *Asia Pacific Journal of Management*, 23(2): 139–141.

Enderwick, P. (2009). Responding to global crisis: The contribution of emerging markets to strategic adaptation, *International Journal of Emerging Markets*, 4(4): 358–374.

Filippov, S. (2010). Russian companies: The rise of new multinationals, *International Journal of Emerging Markets*, 5(3/4): 307–332.

Filippov, S. and Kalotay, K. (2011). Global crisis and activities of multinational enterprises in new EU member states, *International Journal of Emerging Markets*, 6(4): 304–328.

Forrest, R. and Yip, N. (2011). *Housing Markets and the Global Financial Crisis. The Uneven Impact on Households*. Cheltenham: Edward Elgar.

Gammeltoft, P. (2008). Emerging multinationals: Outward FDI from BRICS countries, *International Journal of Technology and Globalisation*, 4(1): 5–22.

Gao, T. and Eshaghoff, T. (2004). MNCs' preferred responses to the Argentine financial crisis: A classification and empirical investigation, *Latin American Business Review*, 5(1): 23–44.

Goldstein, A. and Shaw, T.M. (2007). *Multinational Companies from Emerging Economies: Composition, Conceptualisation and Direction in the Global Economy*. London: Palgrave Macmillan.

Goodhart, Ch. (2009). *The Regulatory Response to the Financial Crisis*. Cheltenham: Edward Elgar.

Gorg, H. and Strobl, E. (2003). 'Footloose' multinationals? *The Manchester School*, 71(1): 1–19.

Gray, D. (2009). Financial contagion among members of the EU-8: A cointegration and Granger causality approach, *International Journal of Emerging Markets*, 4(4): 299–314.

Green, C., Pentecost, E., and Weyman-Jones, T. (Eds.) (2011). *The Financial Crisis and the Regulation of Finance*. Cheltenham: Edward Elgar.

Gup, B. (2010). *The Financial and Economic Crises. An International Perspective*. Cheltenham: Edward Elgar.

Gurvich, E., Lebedinskaya, E., Simachev, Y., and Yakovlev, A. (2010). Russia Country Report, in B. Stiftung (Ed.) *Managing the Crisis. A Comparative Assessment of Economic Governance in 14 Economies*, Gütersloh: Bertelsmann Stiftung: 97–136.

Heinrich, A. (2003). Internationalisation of Russia's Gazprom, *Journal of East European Management Studies*, 8(1): 46–66.

Heinrich, A. (2006). Russian companies in old EU member states: The case of Germany, *Journal of East-West Business*, 11(3–4): 41–59.

Kalotay, K. (2002). Outward foreign direct investment and governments in Central and Eastern Europe: The cases of the Russian Federation, Hungary and Slovenia, *The Journal of World Investment*, 3(2): 267–287.

Kalotay, K. (2004). Will foreign direct investment take off in the Russian Federation? *The Journal of World Investment and Trade*, 5(1): 119–138.

Kalotay, K. (2005). Outward foreign direct investment from Russia in a global context, *Journal of East-West Business*, 11(3–4): 9–22.

Kalotay, K. (2007). The rise of Russian transnational corporations, *The Journal of World Investment and Trade*, 8(1): 125–148.

Kalotay, K. (2008). Russian transnationals and international investment paradigms, *Research in International Business and Finance*, 22(2): 85–107.

Kets de Vries, M., Shekshnia, S., Korotov, K., and Florent-Treacy, E. (2004). The new global Russian business leaders: Lessons from a decade of transition, *European Management Journal*, 22(6): 637–648.

Lee, S. and Makhija, M. (2009). Flexibility in internationalization: Is it valuable during an economic crisis? *Strategic Management Journal*, 30(5): 537–555.

Lipsey, R. (2001). *Foreign Investment in Three Financial Crisis*. NBER Working Papers 8084, Cambridge, MA: National Bureau of Economic Research.

Liuhto, K. and Vahtra, P. (2007). Foreign operations of Russia's largest industrial corporations – Building a typology, *Transnational Corporations*, 16(1): 117–144.

Mathews, J. (2006). Dragon multinationals: New players in the 21st century globalisation, *Asia Pacific Journal of Management*, 23(1): 139–141.

Narjoko, D. and Hill, H. (2007). Winners and losers during a deep economic crisis: Firm-level evidence from Indonesian manufacturing, *Asian Economic Journal*, 21(4): 343–368.

Narula, R. (2010). *Keeping the Eclectic Paradigm Simple: A Brief Commentary and Implications for Ownership Advantages*. MERIT-UNU Working Paper 2010–031, Maastricht: UNU-MERIT.

OECD. (2006). *Emerging Multinationals: Who Are They? What Do They Do? What Is at Stake?* Paris: OECD.

Pradhan, J.P. (2009). Indian FDI falls amid global economic crisis: Indian multinationals tread cautiously, *Columbia FDI Perspectives*, No. 11, August 17.

Ramamurti, R. and Singh, J.V. (2008). *Emerging Multinationals from Emerging Markets*. Cambridge, UK: Cambridge University Press.

Sauvant, K.P., McAllister, G., and Maschek, W.A. (2010). *Foreign Direct Investments from Emerging Markets. The Challenges Ahead*. London: Palgrave Macmillan.

Shabri Abd Majid, M. and Hj Kassim, S. (2009). Impact of the 2007 US financial crisis on the emerging equity markets, *International Journal of Emerging Markets*, 4(4): 341–357.

Skolkovo Research. (2009). Global expansion of emerging multinationals: Post-crisis adjustment. *SIEMS Monthly Briefings*, Skolkovo Institute of Emerging Market Studies, May 2009.

The Economist. (2011). *The World in 2012*. London: The Economist.

UNCTAD. (2006). *World Investment Report 2006. FDI from Developing and Transition Economies: Implications for Development*. New York, NY; Geneva: United Nations.

UNCTAD. (2010). *World Investment Report 2010*. New York, NY; Geneva: United Nations.

UNCTAD. (2011). *World Investment Report 2011*. New York, NY; Geneva: United Nations.

Vahtra, P. and Liuhto, K. (2006). An overview of Russia's largest corporations abroad, in K. Liuhto (Ed.) *Expansion or Exodus – Why Do Russian Corporations Invest Abroad?* New York, NY: International Business Press: 23–40

Varum, C.A. and Rocha, V.C.B. (2011). Do foreign and domestic firms behave any different during economic slowdowns? *International Business Review*, 20(1): 48–59.
Wang, H., Huang, H., and Bansal, P. (2005). What determined success during the Asian economic crisis? The importance of experiential knowledge and group affiliation, *Asia Pacific Journal of Management*, 22(1): 89–106.
Wiśniewska, I., Dubas, A., and Rogoża, J. (2010). *Russia in Crisis: Year One*. OSW Report, Warsaw: Centre for Eastern Studies (OSW), WAW.

Press releases and media reports

Handelsblatt Research. (2010). Europas Top 500. http://script01.vhb.de/tabellen/html/500unternehmen.php, Accessed on September 19, 2009.
Kommersant. (2008). Capital Discypriotization. http://www.kommersant.com/p1075465/r_529/offshore_taxation_financial_regulation/, Accessed on November 20, 2008.
Lukoil. (2009). Lukoil Completes Acquisition of 45 per cent in Oil Refinery in Holland (Press Release September 1, 2009). http://www.lukoil.com/press.asp?div_id=1&id=3121, Accessed on September 19, 2009.
Mechel. (2009). Mechel Announces Definitive Agreement to Acquire Coking Coal Assets of Bluestone Coal Corp (Press Release 22 April 2009). http://www.mechel.com/news/article.wbp?article-id=C66E4582-3E40-4864-A994-24597A8A2314, Accessed on September 19, 2009.
Moody's. (2010). Moody's Says Russian Integrated Oil and Gas Company Performance Remains Robust (Announcement October 21, 2010). http://www.moodys.com, Accessed on September 19, 2009.
Renova. (2010). About Renova. http://www.renova.ru, Accessed on September 19, 2009.
Reuters. (2009). Sberbank-Opel Deal Meaningless Without Tech Transfer. http://www.reuters.com/article/idUSLJ39897220090919, Accessed on September 19, 2009.
Severstal. (2010). Severstal Acquires a Stake in Crew Gold. http://www.severstal.com/eng/media/news/document3109.phtml, Accessed on September 19, 2009.
Severstal. (2011). Severstal Acquires 100 per cent of Crew Gold Corporation. http://www.severstal.com/eng/media/news/document4196.phtml, Accessed on September 19, 2009.
Socor, V. (2009). Lukoil goes Dutch. http://www.atimes.com/atimes/Central_Asia/KG01Ag02.html, Accessed on September 19, 2009.
Strabag. (2010). Basic Element Group Exercises the Call Option for 17 per cent Stake in STRABAG. http://www.strabag.com, Accessed on September 19, 2009.
VEB (Vnesheconombank). (2009). Annual Report 2009. http://veb.ru/common/img/uploaded/files_list/VEB_Annual_2009_e.pdf, Accessed on September 19, 2009.

9
Internationalization of Chinese Car Manufacturers

Françoise Hay, Christian Milelli, and Yunnan Shi

Introduction

While 2009 was a very bad year for most national economies and industries, it proved a prominent milestone for the Chinese automotive industry, which ranked first in the worldwide league both as a car manufacturing base and a final market.

In the Maoist period, private passenger car owners were severely reprimanded as selfish symbols of private property and, until 15 years ago, there were hardly any private cars around in China. So, the recent change is striking and to some extent it mirrors the Chinese rapid economic growth in which the car industry plays an important role.

Furthermore, it is well known that because of its intrinsic nature as a quintessential assembly industry, car manufacturing is the locus of many upward and backward linkage effects. As such, it is a powerful manufacturing driver in any country, yet more particularly in the developing economies willing to set and shore up their manufacturing. Moreover, the entry barriers in this industry are particularly high due to its global consolidation and capital intensity. As the car industry is both capital and technology intensive, any firm attempting an entry should have a large amount of financial resources and substantive technical expertise. So far, China has had no problem with access to financial resources and Chinese firms have gained capabilities by ramping up their manufacturing activities. Technology and cumulative experience was the element that the Chinese newcomers were lacking. The Chinese authorities circumvented this drawback thanks to their 'open-door policy'. Consequently, to date, the automotive industry in China holds the importance it had gained in the US, Europe and Japan after World War II.

Until 2000, the development of the Chinese automotive industry was driven primarily by joint ventures. In the last few years there has been a new trend in which a handful of somewhat 'independent' Chinese car manufacturers have emerged, the domestic markets have expanded and Chinese firms have rushed to acquire specific assets owned by ailing automobile manufacturers in Europe and the US. These new trends are quite challenging for China's statecraft, not to mention World Trade Organization (WTO) requirements, but to date the Chinese government is still pursuing the same policy as before—that is, it is continuously supporting its 'national champions'.

This chapter is structured as follows. In the next section, we characterize the emergence of the Chinese automotive industry with the central role played by the Chinese state. Following this, we identify the models of development followed by the Chinese car manufacturers. Finally, we explore the perspectives to be drawn from the current trends.

The take-off of the Chinese automotive industry

Historical perspective

During the whole Maoist period (1949–1976), the Chinese automotive industry remained embryonic. The priority was to satisfy the requirements and the needs of agriculture and the army—the backbone of the Chinese Communist Party—through the production of commercial vehicles.

In the post-Mao period, the development of a national automotive industry was hampered by the fiscal decentralization which aimed to put local governments on a self-financing basis and resulted in the fragmentation of the fledgling industry. Automotive manufacturers were unable to reap the economies of scale that the potential Chinese domestic market offered and which could be a crucial driver in the development of this industry. In 1978, Chinese automotive industry output totaled 150,000 units from over 50 different plants. Moreover, as Chinese manufacturers were allowed to develop only very limited relations with foreign automobile makers up to the 1960s—with the exception of some USSR *kombinats*—they were trapped in low-quality standards.

The onset of the 'Open-Door' policy in 1978 was a turning point for the whole Chinese economy since the country then embarked on the road of modernization and openness. The central government decided to sustain the Chinese automotive industry's development through a mixed policy, allowing the development of national companies and attracting foreign companies to set up manufacturing facilities for the Chinese domestic market.

China's entry into the WTO in 2001 represents a second turning point. Decreased trade tariffs and the removal of quotas intensified competition and therefore accelerated the restructuring of the Chinese automotive industry. Increased competition reinforced incumbent foreign manufacturers, attracted new ones and encouraged the emergence of new Chinese enterprises from outside the joint venture framework. As a consequence, these new companies are often regarded as independent even though they are, in the large majority, supported by public authorities—more particularly provincial or even municipal governments—and therefore expected to acquire specific technologies from foreign companies.

The dramatic growth spurt of the Chinese automotive output

From 2001 to 2010 the Chinese automotive output grew more than 16 times (increase of 36.7 per cent per year). As a result, with its 18.3 million units manufactured and 18.1 million sold in 2010, China was, for the second consecutive year, the number one single production base and national market in the world. It superseded Japanese and US car output by 9.6 and 7.8 million units, respectively.

The surge of the Chinese automotive output has been driven by passenger cars. In 2001 their share was 30 per cent of total output and in 2010 it was 76 per cent.

The impetus behind this growth can be explained by the very low initial level of motorization of the Chinese market—indeed, China has a ratio of 46 cars for 1,000 inhabitants whereas the US has a ratio of 820/1,000 and France, Germany, and Japan have around 500–600/1,000—and above all by the large increase in domestic consumption driven by the rise in disposable income. In 2004–2009 the average annual disposable income per inhabitant increased by 80 per cent. This growth concerned urban and rural incomes although the huge gap between them was not reduced. For example, in this period, average annual urban income grew from RMB9,422 (€942) in 2004 to RMB17,175 in 2009, whereas the corresponding rural income grew from RMB2,936 to RMB5,153.

If the predictions of the Chinese authorities for the next ten years are fulfilled—that is, an average annual domestic market growth of 9 per cent—the number of cars bought by Chinese customers will rise from 30 million to date to 140 million in 2020 (Figure 9.1).

Contrary to the views or the majority of car manufacturers in developed countries, the Chinese authorities and car manufacturers perceive

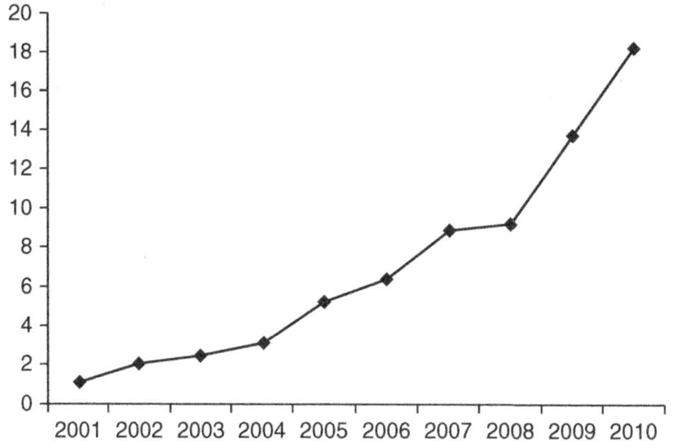

Figure 9.1 Evolution of the Chinese automotive output, 2001–2010 (millions of units)
Source: Data obtained from Chinese Association of Automobile Manufacturers (2011).

the global economic crisis as an opportunity to accelerate the catching-up process and thus become more autonomous vis-à-vis their foreign partners in joint ventures.

The cars 'made in China' for export

China generally exports only a few cars: Only 3 per cent of cars manufactured in 2010 were exported (566,000 units) as the Chinese automobile groups mainly aim to satisfy their vibrant domestic market.

Developing markets are preferred by Chinese firms for their forays abroad because they are an opportunity to develop a presence in growing markets. Indeed, most Chinese automotive enterprises are young and have little experience of the international arena. These 'good enough' markets are very attractive to them. Certainly, their inhabitants are poor, but they aspire to buy cars and, preferably, low-cost ones. Their needs tally with the capabilities of Chinese firms used to satisfying customers with limited purchasing powers whereas such markets are often neglected by the large automotive manufacturers from developed countries. Obviously, Chinese manufacturers see these markets as a means to acquire more experience and as a springboard to expand their presence abroad in selling small and cheap cars. As the second-hand car markets are more and more regulated in the developing countries and ecological standards are becoming largely endorsed, Chinese firms have to offer good products at a low price to savvy consumers in these markets.

Table 9.1 The first ten destinations of Chinese automobile exports, 2010

Destination	Number of Vehicles Exported
Algeria	47,200
Syria	32,800
Vietnam	31,300
Russia	31,200
Chile	30,600
Iran	30,000
Egypt	28,900
Brazil	25,300
Bangladesh	24,200
Iraq	22,900
Total of top ten	304,400 (54% of overall Chinese export)

Source: Data obtained from China Customs Statistics (2011).

Africa and South America are the preferred destinations for cars 'made in China' (Table 9.1) with Great Wall, GAIC, Chery, and BAIC being the main Chinese automotive exporters.

A new trend is emerging with Chinese trailblazers testing the acceptance of their products by sophisticated customers in developed markets. As a matter of fact, Great Wall Motor Co., which has already started selling its Hover sport utility vehicles in Italy, aims to expand into other west European markets in the next few years. The automobile and battery manufacturer BYD, for its part, has opened its US headquarters in Los Angeles. Launched in December 2008 in China, the model F3DM of BYD (a family sedan with hybrid gasoline) has been marketed in the US since 2011.

The developed markets are more challenging for Chinese car manufacturers to penetrate than the markets of developing countries. This is because the requirements in terms of technology (performance, comfort, safety, and energy consumption) are significantly greater in these countries. Thus, Brilliance Auto, BMW's partner in China, suspended its car exports to Europe after the BS6 and BS4 had a cold reception after the crash safety test.

The role of the central government

Since 1978, the central government has adopted an opportunistic and incremental policy, which has so far been highly efficient in leveraging the skills and capabilities of the Chinese automotive industry. It was another illustration of the 'developmental state' philosophy and policy that originated in Japan after World War II, but did not include the openness of the national economy to potential foreign companies (Johnson, 1982). Indeed, the Chinese authorities selected a handful of 'national champions', which were all state-owned enterprises (SOEs), to work in association with foreign automotive manufacturers willing to set up plants in China. Setting up a joint venture was the only mode of entry allowed to foreign companies and their financial commitment was capped to 50 per cent. In doing this, the government was aiming to secure transfer of up-to-date technology, management capabilities and subsequently their absorption by the Chinese enterprises in the joint ventures.

At the very beginning, the process raised questions and was even met by reluctance from both sides. On the Chinese side, the reluctance came from having to open up to multinational corporations which were held responsible for numerous evils. To put it simply, was it not tantamount to 'setting the fox to mind the geese?' (*lang lai le,* in Chinese). Was an infant industry policy not more appropriate to deal with this type of issue?

On the side of foreign companies, several questions were also raised concerning the following points. Had the official authorities been honest in their intentions? Had the risk of nationalization been totally discarded despite the very nature of the Chinese political regime? What were the prospects for the development of the Chinese domestic marker since the foreign firms did not have any prior experience in China? What were the manufacturing capabilities and the technical level of their Chinese partners in the joint ventures? What were the general qualifications of their workforce?

Due to fierce opposition within the ranks of the Communist Party, the initiative had to be progressive and experimental. Thus, a handful of Special Economic Zones were selected in some coastal provinces such as Guangdong—with the Chinese authorities keeping control on the industry through the affiliates of foreign companies which were requested to share their Chinese inroads with local SOEs.

Since the Ninth Five-Year Plan (1996–2000), the automotive industry has been considered a strategic sector. It is monitored by the National Development and Reform Commission (NDRC) and all the decisions taken by the related enterprises—the standardization of components and pieces, the coordination of the innovation processes, and so on—have to be consistent with the general framework. NDRC is also in charge of the restructuring aspects for the national economy, and as

Table 9.2 The ten biggest Chinese car manufacturers and their sales, 2010

Firm Names	**Sales (1,000 units)**	**% of Total**
SAIC[a]	3,558	19
Dongfeng	2,725	15
FAW[b]	2,558	14
Chang'An	2,379	13
BAIC[c]	1,490	8
GAIC[d]	724	4
Chery	682	4
BYD[e]	520	3
Brilliance	501	3
JAC[f]	459	3
Total of top ten	15,596	86

[a]Shanghai Automotive Industry Corporation.
[b]First Automobile Works.
[c]Beijing Automotive Industry Corporation.
[d]Guangzhou Automotive Industry Corporation.
[e]Build Your Dreams.
[f]Jianghuai Automobile Corporation.
Source: Data obtained from Chinese Association of Automobile Manufacturers (2011).

a consequence it promoted the consolidation of the whole industry because it comprised too many manufacturers: indeed, more than 100 firms produce vehicles in China—some of which are very small in size—even though ten firms produce 86 per cent of the whole automobile output (Table 9.2). This has resulted in a fierce price competition that has reduced the profit margins in the industry. However, the constraints on Chinese companies were compensated for by direct and indirect support incentives, such as financial and technical support, exports subsidies and accelerated construction of roads across the country. For example, while China had no highways 20 years ago, it now has 52,000 km of highways crisscrossing the country and the figure will double over the next five years.

State support for national car makers

Consistent with the 'developmental state' philosophy, the Chinese authorities do not hesitate to support their champions—for example, to help them to innovate, increase their size and their market share, assert their own brands, increase their exports and join forces to deal more effectively with increasing competition.

All Chinese car makers are supported in different ways despite their status, be they SOEs or not. The makers of small-engine cars and environmentally friendly vehicles have been specially favored. Specific public aid was granted to the firms which innovate in hybrid engines, fuel cells, natural gas, or hydrogen engines. According to the Chinese authorities, electric motors and hybrid cars are expected to represent 15 per cent of the Chinese market by 2020, and between 7 per cent and 12 per cent of the world market. Since April 2010 the first electric taxis have started to drive around China: Taxi contractors in Shenzhen began taking delivery of the BYD (e6) electric car and in Beijing from Beiqi Foton (a BAIC subsidiary), while some Zotye electric cars are for rent in Beijing.

State support of Chinese consumers

Several measures have been adopted by the central government both to support the acquisition of cars by Chinese customers and to modify the preferences toward the acquisition of new types of vehicles.

First, special subsidies have been granted to consumers buying small vehicles priced between RMB3,000 and RMB6,000. Second, the buyers of cars with low CO_2 emissions enjoy a 50 per cent tax rebate.

Third, farmers in the countryside have also been targeted. They were already eligible for grants provided by the 'Go West Policy' implemented in 2000 and reactivated at the beginning of 2009 in the aftermath of the global economic crisis. Since then, they have also been benefiting from the new program entitled 'Car to the Countryside' with resources of RMB5 billion to purchase new vehicles.

All these measures have obviously contributed to upholding and increasing car sales in China in 2009, more specifically the sale of private cars.

In 2010 the government extended all of these measures, initially planned for one year only. If the subsidies granted for the purchase of new cars have been increased, the purchase taxes have also increased to 7.5 per cent from 5 per cent in 2009.

The models of development of Chinese car manufacturers

Theoretical considerations

The academic literature cannot properly explain the dynamics of the Chinese automotive industry because of the combination of old-fashioned practices rooted in state interventionism—that is, industrial policy—with a strong 'pick the winners' approach, including the promotion of mergers and consolidation at industry level, the allocation of subsidies for technological upgrading and more up-to-date practices based on the firm's ability and resource allocation—for example, in-house learning and innovation capabilities, international expansion through exports, *de novo* investments or acquisitions. It would certainly be quite challenging but one does need to forge a new theory to grasp and unfold the intricacies of China's politics and economics in general, and their manifestations in the Chinese automotive industry in particular. The 'developmental state' approach provides enlightening insights which remind us of the importance of the state as an architect and also of its pivotal role in setting up and expanding national industries. As Bardhan (2010) argued, the Chinese way of 'developmental state' is genuinely 'a state-led capitalism from above and network (*guanxi*) capitalism from below'. Yet, the international environment that prevailed when the Chinese economy emerged is not similar to that of the 1960s and 1970s when the Japanese economy started to grow at a fast pace. The cautious but real transition towards a market economy went hand in hand with the emergence of Chinese multinationals and the opening up to foreign companies. As far as Chinese multinationals are concerned, recent research by some scholars has been particularly apt to address their rationale and drivers. The 'Linkage, Leverage, and Learning' framework stressed by Mathews (2006) is particularly clear as far as the role played by the outflows of Chinese foreign direct investment. It also emphasizes that a country or a firm arriving late on the industrial scene has a potential advantage, insofar as it is able to directly access advanced technologies and use them, sometimes faster and at a lower cost than the very firms that first developed them. Thanks to 'Linkage' (through FDI or partnership), the latecomer firms can acquire knowledge and market access, and so compensate for their own limited resources: Leverage is this capacity for a firm to derive more from a relationship than it had originally invested in it. When repeated over and over again, these sequences of linkage and leverage enhance the capabilities of the latecomers, and can be described as a form of industrial learning. Mathews also notes that the 'special institutions' (administration, finance, R&D) of their governments generally allowed the emerging countries' firms to rapidly catch up with the advanced firms and, possibly, move up from imitation to innovation.

To date, not only many Chinese firms have consolidated their operations (and they can now compete with Western companies), but also some of them have become world leaders in their niches or even have purchased their former European partners or contractors. Somehow, for the most dynamic firms, the Matthews framework could be completed and re-formatted, with the addition of a fourth L for 'Leadership'.

Two models of international development: 'Bringing' and 'go out'

Some authors have conducted research on the mode of development of the Chinese automobile industry and the models of internationalization of Chinese car manufacturers (Wang, 2002; Kang and Ke, 2004; Liu, 2009). Chinese auto manufacturers have adopted two modes of development: 'Bringing' and 'go out'. 'Bringing' is a mode of development adopted in the 1980s and 1990s. Based on the fact that China's auto industry started late with small-scale and backward technology, China decided to establish many joint ventures with foreign car firms in order to bring advanced technologies. The objective was, using the comparative advantage of low labor costs, to become a major producer of automobiles. By the end of the 1990s, the Chinese government encouraged the car firms to adopt the strategy of going abroad.

The 'bringing' approach

At the onset of the 'Open-Door' policy, the central government was well aware that the national auto industry was lagging behind, especially when compared to similar foreign industries, in particular to the successful development and achievement of the Japanese and South-Korean national automotive industries which enjoyed strong brand recognition and quality standards.

In China, the technology transfers through joint ventures between Chinese and foreign companies took off quickly. Foreign firms brought mature and, in some cases, even outdated technologies in an effort to preserve their latest technologies in their respective countries, whereas their Chinese partners were entrusted with developing auto part activities either on their own or through relationships with independent firms. This latter strategic choice by some foreign companies brought setbacks, as in the Peugeot SA/PSA case, which took place in Guangzhou (in the province of Guangdong) in 1984. The French firm had transferred to China a plant with obsolete technologies—a manufacturing line and models no longer used in France—which profoundly humiliated their Chinese partners in the joint venture. However, other European manufacturers have done quite well during the same period. Volkswagen AG (VW) is a case in point. The German company expanded its market share by offering a specific model (the Santana), which took account of the very needs and preferences of Chinese consumers.

In parallel, VW's brand recognition has soared across China from its Shanghai customer base where it has been selected by the local government as sole provider of the taxi cars needed in the rapidly expanding and prosperous city.

Much empirical research provided convincing evidence of the fruitful learning process that was at play to the advantage of the Chinese partners during the 1980s and beyond, essentially SOEs, in joint ventures with foreign firms (e.g. Zhao *et al.*, 2004). They received extensive know-how, technical capabilities, and field-level training for technicians and engineers. Chinese companies were taught how to act rationally, deal with security constraints and better cope with the preferences and the demanding nature of overseas markets. The usual bottleneck—how to absorb so many different ideas, practices, and conducts—has been overcome in basically all of the 40 joint ventures set in the Chinese automotive industry and the learning process has progressively evolved into a catch-up race. It has resulted in an industrial upgrading through extensive learning processes and building greater absorptive capacities.

To date, most large foreign automotive manufacturers have a sizeable presence in China where they conduct manufacturing, design, or development tasks. Interestingly, if some foreign companies have set up join ventures with several Chinese companies, the reverse is also true. The general picture shows a great variety of relationships. On the foreign side, for example, Toyota has six joint ventures with two Chinese enterprises, General Motors has four joint ventures with one Chinese company and Volkswagen has three joint ventures with three Chinese companies. On the Chinese side, the same distribution more or less applies: First Automobile Works has three joint ventures with three different foreign companies and Dongfeng also has three joint ventures with three different foreign companies (see Figure 9.2).

In three decades, this model of development had made China a major producer of cars, the largest producer in the world. However, as core technology was still controlled by the foreign partners in the joint ventures, China's attempts to master modern automotive technology was not very successful.

The 'go out' approach

At the end of the 1990s, the Chinese auto industry has entered the stage of 'go out' in order to advance. Since the beginning of 2009, the Chinese state has specifically encouraged its firms to take advantage of the global financial crisis and search for 'good bargains' abroad. The automobile firms have welcomed this move.

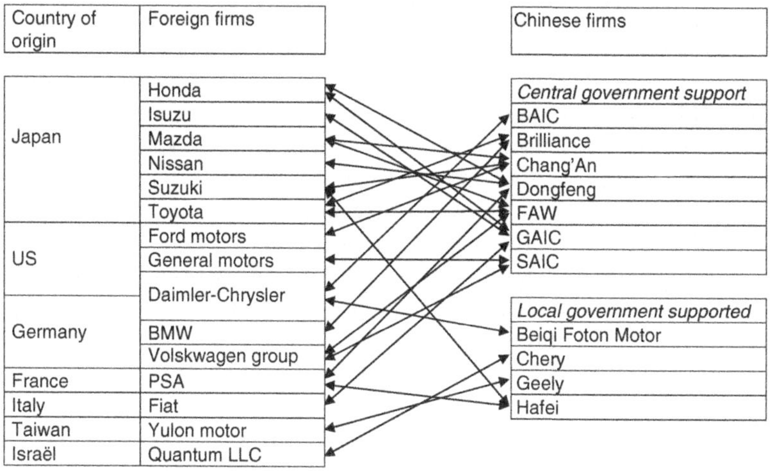

Figure 9.2 Major joint ventures between Chinese enterprises and foreign automotive manufacturers
Source: Chinese Association of Automobile Manufacturers.

The acquisitions are primarily made in developed countries. Several Chinese firms entered the list to buyout Western automobile companies that were totally or partially for sale in 2009. Although all this positioning did not become a reality due to some protectionist reactions or lack of Chinese state support, it clearly shows the Chinese firms' willingness 'to climb the ladder' and to assert themselves internationally.

Two cases which hit the headlines are particularly illustrative of this new trend. First, three Chinese automobile manufacturers, Geely, Chery, and Chang'An, were short listed for the acquisition of Volvo by US company Ford Motors. Finally, Geely was Ford's choice: The deal was clinched in March 2010 at the relatively low price of US$1.8 billion compared with the US$6.5 billion paid by Ford in 1999.

However, the amount to be paid by Geely was still huge in comparison with its size. Indeed, it was a really big challenge for Geely to take up for several reasons. First, Geely is a very young firm in the automotive sector: It was created in 1986 to make refrigerators and only started to make cars in 1998. Second, it is still small in absolute terms not to mention in relative terms. Indeed, in 2009 its turnover represented only 16 per cent of Volvo's turnover, whereas its profits were ten times a tenth of the losses registered by Volvo (US$1.69 billion). Third, Geely bought out a company encountering deep financial problems that Ford, a highly experienced company, was not able to address.

Nevertheless, Geely has had ambitions to get to the top of the ladder and acquire know-how abroad. For example, it produced its first 'sports coupé' in 2003 (the Beauty Leopard equipped with a karaoke) and its first Formula 1 car in 2006. It had previously acquired 20 per cent of the London taxi maker Manganese Bronze and intended to take a majority stake in it as well as in Drivetrain, an Australian maker of gear boxes. Geely's managers suggest that the purchase of Volvo can help them to improve their brand image, to integrate rigorous quality and safety tests into their assembly lines, and, finally, to be more consistent with world market standards. The company also longs to gain greater market share in the Chinese rapidly expanding market. Indeed, if Volvo's production lines and R&D activities are maintained in Sweden, a new factory will be set up in China (Beijing) where a niche market for luxury cars is flourishing.

Beijing Automotive Industry (BAIC) is another interesting case of a Chinese firm trying to acquire competences overseas even though its different moves have not always been successful because of protectionism and strategic reasons, due to technology transfer issues.

In 2009, BAIC entered the lists to acquire Opel (Germany) from General Motors, before being quickly eliminated from the deal. The same year it took part in a project to acquire a minority stake in Saab with a Swedish partner, Koenigsegg, specializing in the production of luxury cars. But the European Investment Bank refused to provide the financing and Saab was eventually sold to Spyker (Netherlands), a maker of luxury cars which obtained the required financial support. It seems that its European nationality finally proved a determining factor. However, in December 2009, BAIC acquired some patents to produce new 'middle-range' cars in China under the Saab brand.

In October 2009, BAIC succeeded in acquiring LDV, a British van producer, via its subsidiary Dr Qu Li Eco Concept, which specializes in automobile engineering. The production has been transfered to Shanghai but BAIC maintained a commercial presence in the UK (Longbridge) following the purchase of its Chinese counterpart, Nanjing Automobile, which had formerly bought out MG Rover.

The inroads made by Chinese automotive manufacturer in developing countries are not limited to exports only and they set up of production lines also. There, they test their capacity to invest abroad and fine tune their world strategy for the coming years. They have a preference for joint ventures with local partners. Table 9.3 shows the variety of these

Table 9.3 Main investments made by Chinese automotive manufacturers in developing countries

Chinese Firm	Foreign Firm	Nationality	Year	Host Country	Vehicles
Brilliance	BMW	Germany	2004	Vietnam	Small vans
Chery			nd	Argentina Egypt Indonesia Iran Malaysia Ukraine Uruguay Thailand	Assembling plants
Geely			nd	Indonesia Malaysia Mexico Ukraine Russia	Assembling plants
JAC	Local manufacturer	Vietnam	2009	Vietnam	
Beiqi Foton Motor	Two local manufacturers Daimler Chrysler	Indonesia Germany	nd	Indonesia India (Pune) South Africa Thailand	Cars, commercial vehicles, trucks, and buses
Zoyte	Premier	India	2010	India	Assembling plant

Source: Chinese Association of Automobile Manufacturers.

operations with the majority of them dating back over the last two or three years.

The push at home

The main driving force of this dynamism is the attempt by Chinese manufacturers to become less dependent on their foreign partners in joint ventures. The share taken by foreign companies in the sales of private cars is still large: According to the China Association of Automobile Manufacturers it amounted to more than 50 per cent in 2010. Actually, the vast majority of Chinese car manufacturers are still dependent on their foreign partners after years of effort to leave them despite the support of the public authorities. Obviously it is not an easy road to walk.

To become more independent, Chinese car manufacturers have selected and experimented with several strategies since they have limited experience and no clear idea of what lies ahead. An early first strategy was for both the SOEs and the 'independent' firms to diversify their foreign relationships. SOEs have diversified the relations and exchanges with foreign companies through joint ventures and specifically targeted production facilities. For example, Shanghai Automobile (SAIC) has partnerships with General Motors (US) and Volkswagen (Germany); Dongfeng with PSA (France), Nissan (Japan), and Honda (Japan); and First Automobile Works (FAW) with Toyota (Japan), Mazda (Japan), and Volkswagen (Germany). The 'independent' firms have diversified overseas by taking advantage of the presence of numerous independent auto parts companies and clinching deals to get specific know-how and expertise.

A second strategy is to improve the recognition of their own brand names in parallel with the brands shared with their foreign partners. Chinese firms have the capability to sustain such a move by mimicking their foreign partners and through the acquisition of foreign companies or patents, particularly in Europe. For example, SAIC has produced it own model, Roewe, whose name is deliberately reminiscent of the Rover trademark from the UK whose remaining assets it acquired two years ago and whose brand was particularly praised by Chinese consumers. Furthermore, SAIC announced in November 2009 that it would set up its own plant based on the blueprint and technologies acquired from Rover.

A third strategy is aimed at acquiring technologies, technical expertise, and other specific assets overseas. In 2009, some Chinese automobile manufacturers received specific grants to acquire overseas firms or patents. For example, the Bank of China opened an RMB20 billion credit line to BAIC to help with the purchase of the Swedish car maker Saab—a deal which did not go through in the end. Geely, for its part, benefited from a loan of RMB10 billion to support its purchase of the other Swedish car maker, Volvo, and several signs are converging to show that the Chinese state is going to take a 49 per cent stake in Beijing Geely Kaixuan International Investment, a subsidiary, in order to consolidate the acquisition of Volvo (*China Daily*, March 30, 2010).

Clearly, all these strategies were designed to reinforce the confidence and the ability of the Chinese automotive manufacturers. The impact of the global economic crisis on Western car manufacturers has been seen as a blessing, to some extent, and not a curse, particularly due to the swift reaction by the Chinese authorities to contain the economic impact of the crisis.

The US$500 billion government stimulus package adopted in early 2009, which aimed to boost economic growth, investments, and household consumption, has benefited the automotive sector directly through the implementation of the Automotive Industry Readjustment and Revitalization Programme, which supports the whole industry and indirectly through reflationary measures stimulates private consumption.

What does the future hold?

The automotive sector has really become a global industry that includes newcomers from emerging countries, with Chinese firms at the forefront. These newcomers learn quickly, innovate and will have more influence on tomorrow's car design and functionality, such as small, clean, and low-emission vehicle. This ongoing trend has been accelerated by the global economic crisis, which has adversely affected developed countries and their industrial bases. Even huge incumbent automotive firms, such as Ford Motors and General Motors, have been severely struck.

In some regards, the dominance of large automotive firms from developed countries over the world automobile industry is under threat and many experts are questioning if a new balance of power is not taking place between newcomers from emerging economies, such as China and India, and incumbent enterprises from developed economies. However, the Chinese firms do not yet have the capability to replace them.

The surge of the Chinese automotive firms has benefited from the strong benevolence of the state, relatively low labor costs, and a potential big domestic market, which can be viewed as transitory advantages. Five reasons have been put forward to sustain this argument:

1. Chinese labor costs are increasing, particularly in the coastal regions where the minimum wage has nearly doubled in the last five years, not to mention rising demands for better conditions at work by employees.
2. The share of the labor costs in most manufacturing processes, including the automotive industry, is declining while mechanization and automation are becoming commonplace.
3. Information technology enabled equipment and components have a more causal influence on prices.
4. Automobile production is more and more standardized and many manufacturers use the same basic parts and gears.

5. The role of subcontractors is gaining importance due to technological evolution, the complexity of tasks, and increasingly scattered intermediate activities.

In 1975, passenger car assemblers received approximately 75 per cent of the final prices against 25 per cent for their subcontractors. Now the figure is totally reversed with subcontractors taking the lion's share (Maxton and Wormald, 2004).

Furthermore, in recent years, many leading players in the world automotive sector have transfered technologies to China to expand their market share in the promising domestic Chinese market. They have been successful so far. Indeed, in 2009, General Motors claimed a 13.5 per cent market share; so its sales are henceforth superior in China than in the US. Since 2009, China has also been Volkswagen's first market. PSA is building a third Chinese plant in Wuhan, and Daimler AG is increasing its Chinese production capacities (*China Daily*, October 14, 2010).

Similarly, their success is not guaranteed for the near future because numerous Chinese firms are willing to corner a market share at home. The central government encourages Chinese manufacturers, whether SOEs have established joint ventures or private 'independent' companies, to develop and promote their own brands (Chery, Geely, JAC, BYD, Great Wall). It is expected that by the end of the 12th Five-Year Plan (2015), sales of Chinese brands will exceed 50 per cent of total sales of passenger cars in the Chinese market (against 30 per cent in 2010 and less than 15 per cent in 2001).

References

Bardhan, P. (2010). *Awakening Giants, Feet of Clay: Assessing the Economic Rise of China and India*. Princeton, NJ: Princeton University Press.

Johnson, C. (1982). *MITI and the Japanese Miracle: The Growth of Industrial Policy, 1925–1975*. Stanford, CA: Stanford University Press.

Kang, R. and Ke, Y. (2004). *Theoretical Exploration of Chinese Multinational Corporations (in Chinese)*. Beijing: Chinese Business Press.

Liu, L. (2009). *Factors Influencing Chinese Auto Companies' Internationalization Strategy (in Chinese)*, MBA thesis, University of Shenzhen.

Mathews, J.A. (2006). Dragon multinationals: New players in the 21st century globalization, *Asia Pacific Journal of Management*, 23: 93–113.

Maxton, G. and Wormald, J. (2004). *Time for a Model Change: Re-engineering the Global Automotive Industry*. Cambridge, MA: Cambridge University Press.

Richet, X. (2008). The Chinese automobile industry: Cooperation and growth, in J.-F. Huchet and W. Wang (Eds.) *Chinese Firms in the Era of Globalisation*. Beijing: Development Press: 276–298.

Wang, H. (2002). *Restructuration de l'industrie automobile chinoise. Quelle trajectoire dans la mondialisation?* thèse de Doctorat en sciences économiques, Université de Grenoble II.

Zhao, Z., Anand, J., and Mitchell, W. (2004). Transferring collective knowledge: Teaching and learning in the Chinese auto industry, *Strategic Organization*, 2(2): 133–167.

Articles on Websites

Chinese Independent Brand Car to Increase the Pace of Expansion of Overseas Markets. www.caam.org.cn/hangye/20110722/1105058801.html, Accessed on July 22, 2011.

Development Trend of China's Auto Industry Policy. http://news.bitauto.com/others/20110106/1505274381.html, Accessed on January 6, 2011.

Geely, BAIC Target Foreign Brands. www.ce.cn, Accessed on September 14, 2009.

The Internationalization Path of China's Auto Enterprises. www.nbweekly.com/news/business/200803/7780.aspx, Accessed on March 25, 2008.

Report of Chinese Automobile Industry Under International Financial Crisis. www.shcri.com, http://www.prlog.org/10199939-report-of-chinese-automobile-industry-under-international-financial-crisis-2009.pdf, Accessed on March 17, 2009.

When Can China's Auto Industry Be 'Independent'? http://business.sohu.com/20110704/n312274100.shtml, Accessed on July 4, 2011.

10

Location Determinants of Polish Outward Foreign Direct Investment and the Impact of the Global Crisis

Aleksandra Wąsowska and Krzysztof Obłój

Introduction

This chapter focuses on the patterns of Polish outward foreign direct investment (FDI). In particular, it explores the host-country-specific determinants of Polish outward FDI. The research is motivated by the need to test the extent to which the mainstream theoretical explanations of FDI from developed countries are useful also in addressing and explaining the FDI motives from Poland, one of the emerging economies of Central Europe. Given that the most important determinants of FDI are economic factors (Buckley *et al.*, 2007; Sauvant *et al.*, 2010), we decided to test whether the crisis that hit the global economy in 2008 and the worsening economic situation that followed have had any significant impact on the strategic decisions of Polish investors.

Poland started to build an institutional framework appropriate to a market economy and a political democracy immediately following the introduction of drastic austerity and institution development programs in 1989, in order to transform the economy (Kolverid and Obloj, 1994). The immediate results of the implementation of these programs received high praise from the World Bank, the International Monetary Fund (IMF), and Western economists, who treated it as an exemplary, fast and holistic transformation from planned to market economy (Slay, 1994). One of the important features of this process was the systematic opening of the Polish economy, which resulted in the rapid growth of FDI inflows (Gorynia, 2009). The large size of the Polish economy and its rapid growth in the 1990s provided major incentives, but other factors, such as highly skilled, low-cost labor, and stable institutional regime, also played an important role. The initial performance in outward FDI (OFDI), however, was very weak due to several factors. Successive governments did not offer Polish firms any clear support in their internationalization strategies in the form of guidance, financing, insurance, or promotional efforts. On the other hand, firms did not have the ownership advantages necessary to overcome the liability of foreignness. They lacked capital, modern plants and machinery, and intangible assets, such as managerial skills, brands, or reputation (Obloj and Obloj, 2006; Obloj and Capron, 2011). The relatively limited size of domestic firms combined with the fast growth of the Polish economy and the abundance of domestic opportunities made entrepreneurs and managers more focused on the local market (Gorynia, 2009). Only after the accession to the EU in 2004 did we observe a slow increase in the outward investment position of Poland. The thorough and rapid transformation of Poland, combined with its initial stage of investment development path, makes Poland an interesting setting to test the explanatory power of existing theories of motives and patterns of OFDI. This will address the recurring question of whether the motives and strategies of internationalization of the firms from emerging economies demand new frameworks or if they can be explained by amending existing theories (Barney and Zhang, 2009; Sauvant *et al.*, 2010).

Our study of the motives and patterns of Polish OFDI makes three specific contributions to the literature. Firstly, it provides insight into the seldom examined patterns of outward FDI from an emerging economy in Central Europe, where OFDI is a very recent phenomenon. Secondly, it provides empirical support for Dunning's typology of internationalization motives, thus supporting the notion that existing theoretical frameworks explaining the patterns of FDI, even if they need refinement when applied to the specific business context, are pretty robust, and we do not need a special theory for emerging economies (Barney and Zhang, 2009). Third, it shows that the global economic crisis had an immediate impact on strategic decisions related to internationalization—the outward FDI flows declined, and their character has changed.

The chapter is structured as follows. We first discuss the theoretical framework of outward FDI. Then we provide basic information about Polish OFDI. In the next section we detail model specification and hypotheses on the Polish FDI pattern. The data selection procedure and the set of variables are similar to Buckley *et al.* (2007), but a simpler research design is followed. We then provide the results of the analysis and conclude with a discussion of the implications and limitation

(Dunning and Lundan, 2008) and inspired by the work of North (1990). Institutions may be defined as formal regulations and informal constraints that set the rules of the game for the companies. These are, for instance, transparency and accountability of the government, property and contract rights enforcement policies, oversight of financial institutions, and informal norms and values that enforce social trust.

Another popular theoretical approach to internationalization, the Uppsala model (Johanson and Vahlne, 2009), focuses not on the motive, but on the feasibility of the internationalization process itself. We draw on this model to include in our analysis of location determinants of Polish OFDI the 'boundary conditions' in which the internationalization of Polish companies takes place. In the Uppsala model, the internationalization process is defined as overcoming, through incremental steps, the distance (geographic, cultural, psychic), between the home and host countries (Johanson and Vahlne, 1977). Thus, according to the Uppsala model, the choice of a host country is dependent upon the geographic, cultural, and psychic distance. By beginning an international operation in countries with low psychic distance, located close to the home base, firms minimize potential surprises and costs, leveraging their accumulated knowledge and experience.

The extensive research on the determinants of location of FDI has included the following factors: Market size, economic growth, labor costs, trade barriers, openness of the economy to foreign capital, trade deficit, foreign exchange rates, and taxes. A detailed review of the empirical literature, performed by Chakrabarti (2001), identified numerous limitations and areas for future research. First, the results of the current research are inconsistent, which can be explained by both methodological differences (samples, statistical techniques) and theoretical limitations. Many of the studies reviewed by Chakrabarti (2001) do not refer to any specific theory of internationalization; instead they identify factors determining the location of FDI, among a wide spectrum of variables. The second limitation of current studies is that they tend to focus on macroeconomic factors, neglecting the cultural and institutional environment. Finally, there is a scarcity of research on internationalization of emerging economies from Central Europe. There is also a growing number of studies of Chinese OFDI (Buckley *et al.*, 2007), and there are OECD-led studies of FDI from some emerging economies (Sauvant *et al.*, 2010), but Central European countries are mostly represented by research of FDI from the smallest economy in the region—that is, Slovenia (Jaklic and Svetlicic, 2003).

Polish outward FDI

Polish companies invest mostly in Europe. In 2007, 61 per cent of the stock of Polish outward FDI was located in the EU—25 countries, 23 per cent in EFTA countries (Switzerland, Norway, Iceland, and Liechtenstein) and 9 per cent in CIS countries. The remaining percentage was divided among North and South America, Africa, and Asia. In 2007, the main recipients of Polish investments (in terms of FDI stock) were Luxembourg, Switzerland, the Netherlands, Czech Republic, Lithuania, and the UK (see Figure 10.1).[1]

One of the principal destinations of the Polish FDI is the Czech Republic, due to easy access to information, low transportation costs, and cultural proximity (Ministerstwo Gospodarki, 2008). In 2007 the total Polish FDI stock in the Czech Republic amounted to €880 million, the main investor being PKN Orlen, the largest Polish petrochemical company, which in 2005 invested €530 million in the Czech Unipetrol, becoming its principal shareholder. A significant part of the FDI stock in Lithuania (€782 million in 2007) is related to one transaction—the acquisition of a Lithuanian refinery in Mozejki by PKN Orlen, completed in 2006. It was the biggest foreign investment ever undertaken by a Polish company, and the acquisition of Mozejki made Poland the biggest foreign investor in Lithuania.[2] In recent years, one of the most popular destinations among Polish investors has become Ukraine. In 2007, 1,123

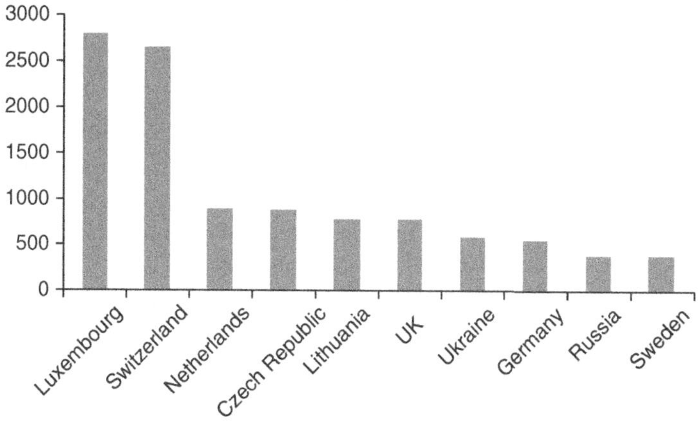

Figure 10.1 Stock of Polish FDI in 2007 (€ millions), main destinations
Source: Data obtained from the National Bank of Poland (2008).

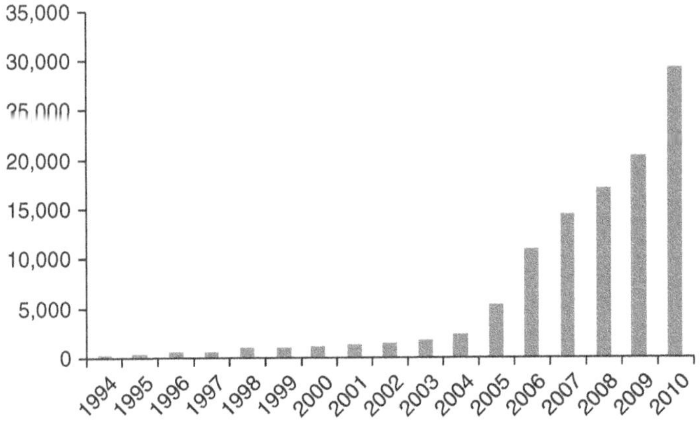

Figure 10.2 Polish outward FDI (€ millions)
Source: Data obtained from the National Bank of Poland (2011).

companies had Polish capital registered in Ukraine. Some 43 per cent of the Polish FDI stock in Ukraine is located in financial sector companies (Ministerstwo Gospodarki, 2008). This fact is related to the activities of three Polish banks operating in Ukraine—that is, Getin Bank (investment in Prikarpattya Bank), Pekao S.A. (UniCredit Bank Ukraina), and PKO BP (Kredobank). The total stock of Polish OFDI has been steadily increasing since 2004, but the pace of growth declined during the global crisis (see Figure 10.2).

Research model and hypotheses

The objective of the present study is to identify determinants of Polish OFDI, taking into account companies' motives and host-countries' characteristics. Drawing on the broad typology of motives of internationalization from Dunning and Lundan (2008), we propose the following research model of Polish OFDI (see Figure 10.3). The model focuses on two types of MNE activity—resource seeking and market seeking—that are primarily motives of MNCs from emerging economies. We do not study efficiency-seeking motives because Polish MNCs are at the early stages of their internationalization strategies, and we do not expect them to invest heavily in rationalizing the management system of many local subsidiaries.

Market-seeking companies should invest in countries with big and fast-growing domestic markets. Previous research (Chakrabarti, 2001)

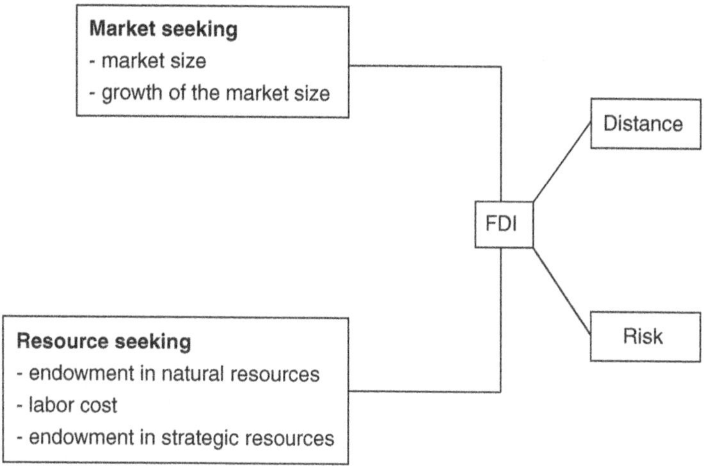

Figure 10.3 Hypothetical relations between host-country characteristics and Polish outward FDI

confirms the relation between the market size of a host country and the outflow of FDI from both developed (Chakrabarti, 2001) and developing countries (Buckley *et al.*, 2007). At the same time, fast market growth is regarded as an indicator of future market potential (Billington, 1999). On this basis, we pose the following hypotheses:

> ***Hypothesis 1a.*** *Polish outward FDI is positively related to the host market size.*
> ***Hypothesis 1b.*** *Polish outward FDI is positively related to the host market growth.*

Resource seekers should invest in the countries endowed in particular resources. Dunning and Lundan (2008) describe three types of resource seekers. First, there are companies that are mainly primary producers and seek access to physical resources, such as fuels, metals, and agricultural products. During recent years, such investments have been made by many Indian and Chinese companies, especially in developing countries. Second, there are companies searching for supplies of cheap and skilled or semi-skilled labor. This kind of FDI is prompted by MNCs that face increasing labor costs in their home market. We expect that, with a systematic increase in minimum wage and rising costs of semi-skilled labor in Poland, we will observe some labor-seeking investments among Polish companies. The third type of FDI is triggered primarily by a search for technological knowledge or capabilities. We can expect that Polish companies, which have a limited resource base and innovativeness (Jasiński and Okoń-Horodyńska, 2002), to be induced to invest in developed economies, especially through M&As, in order to upgrade their knowledge and technological resource base. Thus, taken together, we propose the following:

> ***Hypothesis 2.*** *Polish outward FDI is positively related to the endowment of the host country in natural resources.*
> ***Hypothesis 3.*** *Polish outward FDI is negatively related to the host country's labor costs.*
> ***Hypothesis 4.*** *Polish outward FDI is positively related to the endowment of the host country in technological resources.*

Hypotheses 1–4 refer to Dunning's typology of the motives of internationalization. Additionally, on the basis of neoinstitutional interpretations of the OLI model that point out the importance of a stable and developed institutional environment as a factor influencing OFDI decisions (Buckley *et al.*, 2007), we hypothesize the following:

> ***Hypothesis 5.*** *Polish outward FDI is positively related to the level of political stability of the host country.*

Polish companies have only recently started to invest abroad (see Figure 10.2). Therefore, in accordance with incremental models of internationalization, they will probably invest in the countries of a relatively low geographic and psychic distance (Hakanson and Ambos, 2010). On this basis, we hypothesise the following:

> ***Hypothesis 6.*** *Polish outward FDI is negatively related to geographic distance between the home and host countries.*
> ***Hypothesis 7.*** *Polish outward FDI is negatively related to the psychic distance between the home and host countries.*

Methods

To test hypotheses 1 through 7, developed in the previous section, we built multiple regression models describing the level of the stock value of Polish OFDI in 2007. We used cross-sectional data instead of panel data, because Polish OFDI almost did not exist until 2004, and only since then have we observed a rapid increase in outflows of FDI—in 2005 (€2.7 billion), in 2006 (€7 billion), and in 2007 (€3.9 billion). The stock of Polish OFDI reached €14.4 billion in 2007 (NBP, 2009), which is insignificant compared with the level of FDI from mature economies. What we observe is an initial stage of development of Polish outward FDI, and therefore panel data are no more informative than a cross-sectional view.

Detailed data on Polish outward FDI are available for 60 host countries. Countries with a negative stock value[3] of Polish outward FDI were excluded from the analysis. Our data set comprises 53 host countries. Table 10.1 summarizes the variables included in the study and their operationalization. All of the variables (except for psychic distance indicators) have been transformed into natural logarithms. This procedure, recommended for variables that increase by multiplication (in geometric proportion), such as GDP (Doane and Seward, 2007), was used in previous studies of the determinants of FDI in emerging economies for a similar set of variables (Buckley *et al.*, 2007).

Results

Below we present the results of regression analysis for Polish outward FDI. It was not possible to include all of the variables in one model because of the limited number of degrees of freedom and collinearities between some of the variables (see Table 10.2). For this reason we did not estimate models simultaneously including labor cost and GDP per capita (correlation between these variables amounting to 0.97), strategic resources and GDP (correlation amounting to 0.75), and political stability and GDP per capita or labor cost (correlations amounting to 0.85 and 0.82 respectively). Table 10.2 presents descriptive statistics and a correlation matrix of the data employed in the present study.

The redundancy of variables, resulting from interdependencies between independent variables, not observable in the correlation matrix, was also an issue. This was the case for the level of export, initially included as a control variable (Model 1). However, having performed tests for redundancy, we decided to exclude this variable from models 2 and 4, since 89 per cent of its variation could be explained by the variations in GDP and geographic distance (see Table 10.3), which were both included in these models as independent variables.

Table 10.1 Operationalization of variables

Variable	Proxy	Source	Function in the Model
FDI (**FDI**)	Stock of Polish outward FDI in 2007	National Bank of Poland (2009)	Dependent variable
Market size (**GDP; GDP_pc; GDP_g**)	Two proxies: (a) host country GDP; (b) host country GDP per capita	UNCTAD Handbook of Statistics (2008)	Main variable
Market growth (GDP_g)	Annual percentage increase in host country GDP	UNCTAD Handbook of Statistics (2008)	Main variable
Natural resource endowment (res_nat)	The ratio of ore and metal exports to merchandise exports of host country in 2006	Calculated on the basis of UNCTAD Handbook of Statistics (2008)	Main variable
Strategic asset availability (pat)	The number of patents registered in 2005	WIPO Statistics Database (2009)	Main variable
Labor cost (wage)	Average wage per hour in manufacturing sector in 2006	Calculated on the basis of Labour Statistics Database, ILO (2010)	Main variable
Political stability (stability)	Political risk index (higher value corresponds to lower risk)	International Country Risk Guide (2008)	Main variable
Geographic distance (geo)	Geographic distance between the capitals of host and home country	Calculated using www.geobytes.com	Main variable
Psychic distance (lang; rel; edu; ideo; demo; dev)	Five indicators, relating to differences in: language, religion, education, political systems (ideology and democracy), and economic development level	Psychic distance stimuli indicators, calculated by Dow and Karunaratna (2006), available at: http://www.mbs.edu/home/dow/research/	Main variable
Exports (exp)	Polish exports to the host country in 2007	GUS, Yearbook of foreign trade statistics (2008)	Control variable
Openness to FDI (IFDI)	Ratio of inward stock of FDI to host country GDP in 2007	Calculated on the basis of UNCTAD FDI Stat (2009) and UNCTAD Handbook of Statistics (2008)	Control variable

Notes: All monetary values are in current USD prices. We do not account for inflation, since we perform a cross-sectional analysis. For countries for which the average number of hours worked was not provided by the ILO database, we applied 40-hour week for our calculations. We used the following exchange rates into USD: https://www.cia.gov/library/publications/the-world-factbook/fields/2076.html, Accessed February 17, 2010.

Table 10.2 Descriptive statistics and correlation matrix

	Mean	Std. dev.	FDI	GDP	GDP_pc	GDP_g	res_nat	Pat	Risk	Lang	Rel	Dev	Edu	Demo	ideo	Exp	IFDI	geo	wage
FDI	1.40	1.31	1.00																
GDP	12.41	1.62	0.20	1.00															
GDP_pc	9.65	1.14	0.28	0.14	1.00														
GDP_g	1.52	0.52	−0.02	−0.35**	−0.55**	1.00													
res_nat	−2.78	1.15	−0.25	0.03	−0.06	0.09	1.00												
Pat	7.64	2.44	0.12	0.75**	0.08	−0.20	−0.06	1.00											
Risk	4.32	0.14	0.31**	0.04	0.85**	−0.49**	−0.11	0.12	1.00										
Lang	0.19	0.29	−0.28	0.16	−0.08	−0.30**	−0.04	0.18	−0.02	1.00									
Rel	−0.49	0.87	−0.22	0.03	−0.61**	0.32**	0.01	0.02	−0.64	0.29**	1.00								
Dev	0.62	0.41	0.22	0.42**	0.57**	−0.46**	0.10	0.37**	0.52	0.23	−0.06	1.00							
Edu	0.50	0.30	−0.12	0.52**	−0.01	−0.22	0.18	0.35**	0.07	0.27	0.20	0.33**	1.00						
Demo	0.40	0.47	−0.16	0.03	−0.61**	0.36**	0.20	−0.13	−0.56	0.22	0.56**	−0.15	0.13	1.00					
Ideo	0.46	0.35	−0.05	−0.13	0.14	0.02	−0.08	0.07	0.04	−0.06	−0.11	−0.11	−0.39**	−0.31**	1.00				
Exp	13.36	1.87	0.65**	0.47**	0.32**	−0.28	−0.14	0.24	0.24	−0.35**	−0.29**	0.15	0.13	−0.27	−0.02	1.00			
IFDI	−0.92	0.74	0.27	−0.44**	0.47**	−0.17	−0.10	−0.31**	0.52	−0.03	−0.33**	0.07	−0.41**	−0.32**	0.34**	−0.01	1.00		
Geo	7.61	1.11	−0.55**	0.27	−0.22	0.04	0.20	0.42**	−0.19	0.46**	0.32**	0.09	0.23	0.23	0.04	−0.67**	−0.25	1.00	
Wage	1.85	1.29	0.19	0.15	0.97	−0.62**	−0.04	0.08	0.82**	0.03	−0.57**	0.54**	0.10	−0.53**	0.13	0.27	0.43**	−0.16	1.00

**$p < 0.05$.

Table 10.3 Regression analysis for Polish export

	Beta	Std error
GDP	0.69***	0.05
Geo	−0.85***	0.00
R^2	0.89**	–
Adj R^2	0.89**	–
F	213.39*	–

*$p<0.1$; **$p<0.05$; ***$p<0.01$.

Table 10.4 Regression analysis for Polish FDI, 2007

Variable	Model 1		Model 2		Model 3		Model 4	
	Beta	Std Error	Beta	Std Error	Beta	Std Error	Beta	Std Error
GDP			0.56***	0.12			0.63***	0.13
GDP_g					0.28***	0.12		
Zas_n			−0.10	0.10	−0.13	0.10		
Pat					0.07	0.11		
Wage			−0.27*	0.15	−0.08	0.16		
Risk			0.17	0.16	0.17	0.16		
Geo			−0.59***	0.10			−0.55***	0.12
Lang							−0.10	0.12
Rel							0.11	0.13
Edu							−0.20	0.13
Demo							0.02	0.13
Ideo							−0.15	0.12
Exp	0.65***	0.10			0.68**	0.10		
IFDI	0.27***	0.10	0.37***	0.14	0.27**	0.12	0.41***	0.13
R^2	0.50		0.56		0.59		0.57	
Adj R^2	0.48		0.51		0.52		0.49	
F	25.10		9.95		9.22		7.31	

*$p<0.1$; **$p<0.05$; ***$p<0.01$.

Four basic empirical models are estimated to test for hypotheses referring to the value of Polish outward FDI (Table 10.4). All models are statistically significant below the 1 per cent level.

Model 1 included only control variables: Export and openness to foreign capital, which, as expected, prove to be statistically significant and positively related to Polish outward FDI. Model 2 included variables relating to the motives of FDI—market size (absolute value of GDP), endowment in natural resources, labor cost and geographic distance, and openness to FDI. Endowment in strategic resources was not included in the model because of the collinearity problems described above. In Model 3 the absolute value of GDP was replaced by another variable related to 'market seeking'—growth of GDP. As collinearity was not an issue, strategic resources were included in the model but they proved to be statistically insignificant. Model 4 includes variables described in incremental approaches to internationalization (Uppsala model)—psychic and geographic distance. Variance inflation factor tests for models 2–4 proved that collinearity was not an issue in the final specification of the models (VIF below 10) (Doane and Seward, 2007).

Discussion and conclusions

As expected, the market size, measured by the absolute value of GDP and the growth of GDP, proved to be statistically significant; thus provide evidence to support hypotheses 1a and 1b. We do not observe statistically significant relations between Polish outward FDI and endowment of a host country in natural or strategic resources. Thus we find no evidence to support hypotheses 2 and 4 referring to asset-seeking motives. One possible explanation is that Hypothesis 3 was supported, as labor cost proved to be statistically significant ($p < 0.1$) in one of the estimated models. Thus we may conclude that Polish investors seem to search for efficiency, but not for strategic assets, which indicates that they are in the early stages of the internationalization process and follow a simple incentive structure looking for immediate gains from their efforts. Our analysis partially confirms the hypotheses based on incremental models. Geographic distance is a statistically significant variable, thus confirming Hypothesis 6, but cultural proximity (Hypothesis 7) is not relevant for Polish investors. Finally, the levels of host country political risk (Hypothesis 5) are not significant for Polish investors. This result may be explained by the fact that much of the Polish FDI is concentrated in the countries of Western and Central Europe, which are perceived by the managers as institutionally stable. This may mitigate the political risk. The fact that Polish managers seem to be neither afraid of risk nor worried about geographic distance may also result from path dependence. They developed and grew their firms in a risky and turbulent environment; therefore, those that survived and prosper are very optimistic, proactive and not afraid of political risks (Obloj *et al.*, 2010). The different mix of support for the significance of cultural and geographical proximity and levels of risk is an interesting find, and it demands further research. The concept of international entrepreneurial dynamics (Mathews and Zander, 2007), present at the intersection of internationalization and entrepreneurial perspectives, may offer an explanation for the apparent contradiction between searching for cultural proximity and, at the same time, accepting high political risk.

Impact of the global crisis

Since the accession of Poland to the EU in 2004, we have observed a dynamic increase in Polish OFDI (see Figure 10.4). A record high value of Polish OFDI was reached in 2006 and was partly a result of one big transaction—that is, the acquisition of Mozejki by the Polish petroleum giant, PKN Orlen. In 2007 the outflow of FDI amounted to almost €4 billion and consisted of many individual transactions, reflecting the rising importance of internationalization in the strategies of both big and small players.

In 2008 we observed a decline in Polish OFDI, which may be attributed to the global crisis. The impact of the economic meltdown of 2008 on Polish FDI flows was negative, for reasons related to both supply and demand (Sauvant *et al.*, 2010). First, the main destinations of Polish OFDI are EU countries that were severely impacted by the global economic slowdown. Declining demand and growing competition discouraged foreign investors. Second, the capacity of Polish companies to finance international expansion deteriorated. Banks across the world

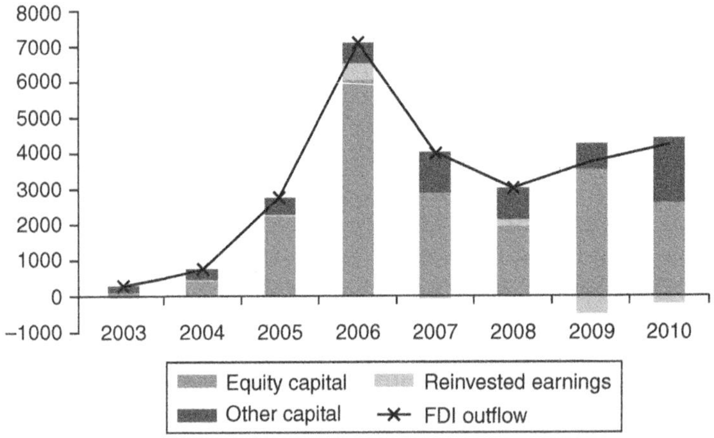

Figure 10.4 Structure of Polish FDI outflow, 2003–2010

Table 10.5 Regression analysis for Polish FDI, 2010

Variable	Model 1		Model 2		Model 3		Model 4	
	Beta	**Std Error**	**Beta**	**Std Error**	**Beta**	**Std Error**	**Beta**	**Std Error**
GDP			0.75***	0.14			0.66***	0.11
GDP_g					0.15			
Zas_n			−0.08	0.11	−0.06	0.14		
Pat					0.22	0.17		
Wage			−0.22*	0.19	−0.24	0.24		
Risk			0.08	0.19	0.27	−0.22		
Geo			−0.68***	0.12			−0.69***	0.10
Lang							−0.16	0.10
Rel							0.10	0.10
Edu							−0.08	0.10
Demo							0.03	0.10
Ideo							−0.05	0.09
Exp	0.63***	0.10			0.64***	0.14		
IFDI	0.24**	0.10	0.54***	0.15	0.41**	0.18	0.42***	0.11
R^2	0.48		0.61		0.48			
Adj R^2	0.46		0.54		0.38			
F	23.68		9.50		4.82			

*$p < 0.1$; **$p < 0.05$; ***$p < 0.01$.

became more risk averse and limited credit expansion in order to secure liquidity.

Surprisingly, during the culmination of the global crisis in 2009, the outflow of Polish FDI increased by 24 per cent, compared with the previous year, amounting to €3,745 million. This was achieved despite the high negative value of reinvested earnings, decreasing the total outflow of FDI (Figure 10.4). The estimated outflow of Polish FDI in 2010 reached €4,142 million, exceeding the pre-crisis value.

The analysis of the location determinants of FDI, based on the stock value in 2010 (Table 10.5), has proved that the host country market size and the geographic proximity continue to be the most important factors attracting Polish investors. The growth of GDP is no longer significant, which may be explained by the overall decline in the economic growth rates among the countries hosting Polish FDI.

There are at least two possible explanations for the limited impact of the global crisis on Polish FDI. First, this phenomenon can reflect the inertia of the strategic decisions to undertake foreign direct investment.

Second, it may result from the specificity of the Polish market. The Polish economy seems to be relatively immune to the global crisis, with the GDP growth rate reaching 1.9 per cent in 2009 and 3.8 per cent in 2010. This may give Polish investors a privileged position, as compared with the investors from economies more severely impacted by the global crisis. We may also hypothesize that the international entrepreneurial dynamics (Mathews and Zander, 2007) of Polish investors could be a factor stimulating the search for opportunities for growth during the economic slowdown. Acquisitions of under-priced assets or undervalued companies located in the foreign markets, undertaken by some Polish investors, could be an example of such practices.

Limitations

The results reported in this study are subject to several limitations. First, following Beugelsdijk *et al.* (2010), we admit that FDI stocks are an imperfect measure of the activity of multinational companies.[4] Second, the sample used to estimate models of Polish outward FDI was relatively small due to the limited scope of the phenomenon itself. Third, the cross-sectional nature of this study limits our interpretation of causality between the variables. Therefore future research, based on larger samples and panel data, may extend our initial understanding of the patterns of Polish OFDI and allow for comparison with the pattern of other countries, thus aiding theory development and refinement.

Notes

1. The analysis conducted by the Polish Ministry of Economy (2008) suggests that part of the Polish investments in Luxembourg and Switzerland is for tax optimization purposes. We tested our models both including and excluding those countries from our analysis, and this does not influence the final results.
2. The ensuing conflicts between Polish companies and Lithuanian railroads and other local companies also illustrate the complexity of such deals and demonstrate the lack of experience in managing large-scale acquisitions by Polish companies.
3. A negative value in FDI position may occur when the loans granted by the direct investment enterprise to the parent company exceed the loans—or even the original capital—given by the parent to the direct investment enterprise (OECD, 2012).
4. FDI stocks tend to overestimate the level of MNCs' activity in tax-haven countries and undervalue it in most other countries, particularly in the countries with well-developed financial markets and productive labor force—that is, developed countries.

References

Barney, J.B. and Zhang, S. (2009). The future of Chinese management research: A theory of Chinese management versus a Chinese theory of management, *Management and Organisation Review*, 5(1): 15–28.

Beugelsdijk, S., Hennart, J.-F., Smeets, R., and Slangen, A. (2010). Why and how FDI stocks are a biased measure of MNE affiliate activity, *Journal of International Business Studies*, 41(9): 1444–1459.

Billington, N. (1999). The location of foreign direct investment: An empirical analysis, *Applied Economics*, 31(1): 65–76.

Buckley, P.J., Clegg, L.J., Cross, A.R., Liu, X., Voss, H., and Zheng, P. (2007). The determinants of Chinese outward foreign direct investment, *Journal of International Business Studies*, 38(4): 499–518.

Chakrabarti, A. (2001). The determinants of foreign direct investment: Sensitivity analysis of cross-country regressions, *Kyklos*, 54(1): 89–114.

Doane, D.P. and Seward, L.E. (2007). *Applied Statistics in Business and Economics*. Boston, MA: McGraw-Hill/Irwin.

Dow, D. and Karunaratna, A.R. (2006). Developing a multidimensional instrument to measure psychic distance stimuli, *Journal of International Business Studies*, 37(5): 578–602.

Dunning, J.H. (1988). The eclectic paradigm of international production: A restatement and possible extensions, *Journal of International Business Studies*, 19(1): 1–31.

Dunning, J.H. (2001). The eclectic (OLI) paradigm of international production: Past, present and future, *International Journal of the Economics of Business*, 8(2): 173–190.

Dunning, J.H. and Lundan, S. (2008). *Multinational Enterprises and the Global Economy*. Cheltenham: Edward Elgar.

Gorynia, M. (2009). *International Business in Transition*. Warsaw: Difin.

Hakanson, L. and Ambos B. (2010). The ancedents of psychic distance, *Journal of International Management*, 16(3): 195–210.

International Country Risk Guide (2008) http://lsedatalibrary.blogspot.com/2009/01/international-country-risk-guide-icrg.html, Accessed September 20, 2011.

Jaklic, A. and Svetlicic, M. (2003). *Enhanced Transition through Outward Internationalisation*. Basingstoke: Ashgate.

Jasiński, A.H. and Okoń-Horodyńska, E. (2002). *Innovation in Transition. The Case of Poland*. Warszawa: Wydawnictwo Naukowe Wydzialu Zarządzania Uniwersytetu Warszawskiego.

Johanson, J. and Vahlne, J.-E. (1977). The internationalisation process of the firm: A model of knowledge development and increasing foreign market commitments, *Journal of International Business Studies*, 8(1): 23–32.

Johanson, J. and Vahlne, J. (2009). The Uppsala model revisited: From liability of foreignness to liability of outsidership, *Journal of International Business Studies*, 40(9): 1411–1431.

Knickerbocker, F.T. (1973). *Oligopolistic Reaction and the Multinational Enterprise*. Cambridge, MA: Harvard University Press.

Kolverid, L. and Obloj K. (1994). Entrepreneurship in transitional versus mature economies—an exploratory study, *International Small Business Journal*, 12(4): 12–28.

Labour Statistics Database, ILO (2010) http://www.ilo.org/stat/lang–en/index.htm, Accessed Sepetmber 15, 2011.

Mathews, J.A. and Zander, I. (2007). The international entrepreneurial dynamics of accelerated internationalisation, *Journal of International Business Studies*, 38(3): 387–403.

Ministerstwo Gospodarki. (2008). *Polskie inwestycje bezpośrednie 2006/2007*, Warszawa.

NBP. (2009). *Polskie bezpośrednie inwestycje za granicą w 2008 roku*, Warszawa.

North, D.C. (1990). *Institutions, Institutional Change and Economic Performance*. Cambridge: Cambridge Economic Press.

Obloj, T. and Capron, L. (2011). Role of resource gap and value appropriation: Effect of reputation gap on price premium in online auctions, *Strategic Management Journal*, 32(4): 447.

Obloj, T. and Obloj, K., (2006). Diminishing returns from reputation: Do followers have a competitive advantage? *Corporate Reputation Review*, 9(4): 213–224.

Obloj, T., Obloj, K., and Pratt, M. (2010). Dominant logic and entrepreneurial firms' performance in a transitional economy, *Entrepreneurship: Theory and Practice*, 34(1): 151–170.

OECD. (2012) FDI Statistics and Data. http://www.oecd.org/document/32/0,3746,en_2649_33763_45922144_1_1_1_1,00.html#Q2, Accessed January 19, 2012.

Polish Ministry of Economy. (2008). *Poland Economy Report*. Warsaw: Polish Ministry of Economy.

Sauvant, K.P., Maschek, G., and McAllister, W. (Eds.) (2010). *Foreign Direct Investment from Emerging Markets: The Challenges Ahead*. New York, NY: Palgrave Macmillan.

Slay, B. (1994). *The Polish Economy*. Princeton, NJ: Princeton University Press.

UNCTAD Handbook of Statistics. (2008). Geneva and New York: UNCTAD.

UNCTAD Manual on Statistics of FDI and the operations of TNCs, Vol. I, UN Symbol: UNCTAD/DIAE/IA/2009/1, Accessed October 20, 2010.

UNCTAD. (2010). *World Investment Report*. New York, NY; Geneva: United Nations.

WIPO Statistics Database (2009) http://www.wipo.int/freepublications/en/intproperty/941/wipo_pub_941.pdf, Accessed January 10, 2012.

11

Reactions of Slovene Multinational Firms to the Global Crisis*

Marjan Svetličič and Andreja Jaklič

Introduction

The objective of this chapter is to study the impact of the global economic and financial crisis on the most prominent Slovene multinational enterprises (MNEs). It is based on the study of top Slovene MNEs during the period 2006–2010. The basic research questions were:

- What was the impact of the crisis on Slovene MNEs?
- Has the crisis affected Slovene MNEs differently than other firms and what were their strategic responses?
- How have the institutional factors and the firms' embeddedness in a specific environment affected their crisis position?

After the short introduction stating the objectives, we elaborate on the theoretical framework and methodology applied. We discuss the historical context and the general impact of the crisis on the Slovene economy and its firms. Following this, we analyze the response of MNEs to the crisis, including trends in outward FDI, general reaction to the crisis, specific reaction by Slovene MNEs, changes in the list of top MNEs and their reaction to the crisis. In the end we conclude and raise some policy implications.

Theoretical framework

S. Hymer (1960) established that foreign firms experience liability of foreignness when internationalizing. Foreign firms have many advantages

*The content of this chapter is based on the findings from the research project PS-177 financed by the Slovenian Research Agency.

over domestic ones due to their international spread, stronger ownership, and the fact that they are more footloose. This applies to MNEs irrespective of the observation angle: from host or from home countries' point of view. Nevertheless, most of the empirical studies looking at the impact of the crisis on MNEs have been based on the comparison between operations of affiliations of MNEs and domestic firms from host countries' point of view. Their conclusions have not demonstrated totally unanimous results. Firms with foreign operations can behave differently during the crisis from domestic firms, meaning that multinationality matters. Multinationals can either help to alleviate the effects of the crisis because of their ownership advantages and their subsequent superior performance or they could add to macroeconomic instability due to the ease with which they can transfer production facilities from one country to another. Thus they can be stabilizers or destabilizes during the crisis. In essence, they can react differently; they may be able to resist or exacerbate the crisis better. The effects can also be neutral, suggesting that there is no difference between foreign and domestic firms' reaction to the crisis (see Varum and Rocha, 2011: 48, 49).[1]

The major impact of the crisis on outward foreign direct investment (FDI) was their slowdown and more careful investment behavior. Outward FDI declines because it is primarily financed from retained earnings, which contract in downturns. At the same time, as banks, markets and investors have become more risk averse, firms face difficulties in tapping into external sources of funding to support their investments. Paradoxically, FDI inflows may occasionally also increase during the crisis. Net increase may occur due to asset-cheapening effects of a crisis[2] and may outweigh short-term capital flight. Such a response was documented at the time of the Asian financial crisis in 1997–1998 (see Hill and Jongwanich, 2009: 2, 24). In the current crisis the liquidity constraints make such a 'fire-sale' of FDI less widespread (Calderon and Didier, 2009). The question whether fire sale FDI is a general characteristic of the economic crisis (Skovgaard and Hufbauer, 2011: 8) therefore remains open.

Theoretically there are three major responses to crises. Firstly, firms can try to improve their current operations, and reduce costs and employment. Secondly, firms can adjust/change their strategies to increase sales, look at new markets and redefine the implementation of their strategies. Thirdly, they can permanently try to develop new capabilities (products, services, and business models) that could improve their performance in the future. Of course, firms can combine all three strategies. The first option is most frequently applied since firms traditionally reduce operations in recessions and mount transformational initiatives only in good times (see Lowell and Hulme, 2003). The course taken depends much on the perception of the seriousness of the crisis by CEOs, how they actually see the crisis: As a long-term phenomenon or more a short-term problem. Surviving a crisis is determined less by the severity of the crisis than by the timeliness and effectiveness of the management response. Usually the first reaction is 'wait and see' and reaction comes only after a certain time. It means that managers are by definition initially more defensive. More proactive or combined approaches are more of an exception and could take place later on with the escalation of the crisis. In more proactive approaches, firms take crisis as an opportunity to change their strategies (second strategy), introduce new products to new markets, and further internationalize their operations (third strategy).

The effects of the recession can be short, medium and long term. Short-term effects reflect in falling investments due to falling profits and worsened access to external financing (credit crunch). Managers become more reluctant toward long-term investment due to unpredictable economic development prospects and increased risks. These imply medium-term changes in their strategies and can be considered as a medium-term crisis effect on FDI as well. In contrast, medium-term effects can also be positive by inducing investments due to asset depreciation as a result of crisis. Long-term crisis implications are reflected in larger changes in strategies because a crisis may have triggered more energetic moves to change the strategies of firms, to restructure their activities considering the tectonic changes in the global economic environment.

In transition economies, the crisis has affected firms' strategies, and inward and outward FDI flows more than in industrial countries. During the period 2007–2009, there were a sixth of the FDI inflows in the Eastern European new EU Member States (NMSs), while the respective amount for the European Union was a third (UNCTAD, www.unctad.org/fdistatistics). The decrease in outward FDI flows by NMSs was even larger—that is, as much as 198 times less outward FDI was recorded by NMSs. Developing countries' outward investment also declined by 28 per cent in 2008. Despite its severity, that decline was significantly below the 45 per cent drop in FDI flows from developed countries (see Aykut, 2011). It is also expected that the bouncing back will be slower this time (Skovgaard and Hufbauer, 2011: 1). Normally, FDI is relatively resilient (as explained by the sunk costs 'theory'), but this sharp decline in outward FDI reflects the parent companies' reliance on international debt markets to finance their overseas expansion. Drying up financing from local bank sources (credit crunch) and depleted own funds weakened the ability of firms to invest abroad. Put differently, even if MNEs were not deterred by the deteriorating economic situation in foreign markets, the supply side for FDI deteriorated sharply. A number of emerging markets' MNEs already had to divest from foreign affiliates or repatriated a larger share of their foreign earnings (see Sauvant *et al.*, 2010: 13). A natural response is therefore to concentrate more on domestic opportunities at the expense of cross-border projects.

The impact of the crisis thus differs substantially regarding host countries' performance during the crisis including government anti-crisis programs (see also Kalotay and Filippov, 2009: 32). Countries which weathered the crisis better still attracted FDI (BRICSs for instance). The impacts of the crisis also differ substantially regarding the industries in which MNEs operate and the types of outward FDI, MNE motivation, and/or type of firm-specific advantages. Strategic asset-seeking and resource-seeking FDI can be the least vulnerable. They are more immune to crisis since higher value added activities are less affected by slowing demand. Market-seeking investments are on the other hand much more affected by declining purchasing power of local population. It means that the geography matters. If MNE operations are concentrated in hard hit countries they would suffer more. Efficiency-seeking investment varies by activity/industries. Those in manufacturing (like automotive, electronics, and garments) are likely to be more affected than those in export-oriented services. In turn, crisis can provide new opportunities for cost efficient locations. Finally, the impact also depends on the strategy applied by the management of MNEs and lastly on the size of MNEs. Although large ones are in a better position to be assisted by governments (too big to fail argument) many smaller MNEs have proved to survive better through crisis due to their flexibility, niche orientation, and more proactive strategies, as 'hidden champions' have demonstrated (see Simon, 2010).

Methodology

We base our analysis on the survey of top Slovene multinationals conducted each year among the largest Slovene firms. This survey, amended by generally available data on the firms, each year serves for selection of top Slovene MNEs. Methodology and definition of MNEs is coordinated by the Vale Columbia Center on sustainable international investment (Columbia University) project on emerging multinationals which includes only non-financial MNEs and excludes those owned by foreigners.[3] Indirect investors abroad (outward investment by foreign owned firms; see Altzinger *et al.*, 2003) are thus not included. Top MNEs are ranked by assets, number of employees, and revenues abroad.

Survey analysis was amended by the case study method for most of the firms from the list.[4] The case studies presented offer a broad overview of how the top Slovene MNCs have been performing during the crisis and how they survive the crisis. In particular, we have amended such case studies with media reports and other available sources (credit ratings, financial reports, national data bases, etc.) and empirical studies on Slovenian enterprises in the period 2007–2011 (which include also Slovene MNCs among many other firms[5]). In addition we have also made a special crisis-related survey in June 2009 (later named Survey 2009). Unfortunately only 11 enterprises out of the top 25 MNEs responded in detail, while some information about the rest was taken from press clippings and interviews.

Impact of the crisis on the Slovene economy and firm-level response

General impact

The region of Central and Eastern Europe had been hard hit during the economic crisis. Slovenia was hit with some delay[6] but more than other new EU member states. Although, otherwise considered as a good case of transition, Slovenia recorded the second deepest decline in GDP in the Organization for Economic Cooperation and Development (OECD) in 2009,[7] but is poised to grow modestly in 2010 before growth picks up to 2 per cent in 2011–2012 (OECD, 2011: 2). The drop of growth rates (that were above average before the crisis) was deeper than in the Eurozone.

The delayed impact of the crisis was partly due to the low contamination of the banking sector with US bonds. Crisis seemed far away from Slovenia, and the politicians and managers underestimated the interdependency of contemporary markets, the effects of financial crisis on the real sector, the changes in the global business environment and, basically, missed the signs of the coming crisis. Good experiences with many crises in the past (with the disintegration of the Yugoslav market and the permanent crisis in socialist times…) 'blinded' them, made most CEOs quite optimistic; not perceiving immediate danger, they resisted major strategy changes. The conviction of firms that they were better equipped to deal with the crisis, thanks to previous experiences while being part of Yugoslavia, led to underestimated risks. Many of existing

Slovenian firms went through the crisis of disintegration of Yugoslavia, the collapse of the Eastern block, and the Russian crisis in 1998. Nevertheless, they survived quite successfully. In the current crisis, Slovenian export fell more than in other NMSs. With the escalation of the crisis a big concern about the safety of deposits in banks surfaced. It was soon reduced by the fast reaction of the Central Bank and the Ministry of Finance who provided guarantees for savings in local and foreign banks. By the beginning of 2009, demand started to decrease substantially on the local market as well as abroad. The crisis was moving from the financial to the real sector. Reduced orders translated the banking crisis into a crisis of the real/tradable sector. Since the Slovene economy depends heavily on export, reduced demand on international markets had dramatic consequences, for which the very small domestic market could not compensate. Consequently a first 'wait and see' approach was substituted by strategic, although mostly defensive, response.

Out of the sample of 113 exporters, accounting for approximately 50 per cent of Slovenian GDP and exports, 93 per cent claim to have been affected negatively by the crisis, while only 5.3 per cent have been affected positively (with 1.8 per cent being neutral). Among the factors why the current crisis has affected them so heavily were: decreased international demand followed by domestic demand, exchange rates, payment delays and protectionist measures on foreign markets, payment delays on the domestic market, and high costs of domestic financing (see, Cirman *et al.*, 2009: 275, 282). Financial debt, which substantially increased during the crisis, has to be added to these factors. The share of non-financial Slovene companies in GDP is much higher than in most OECD countries.[8] An essential part of the increase in financial debt during the period 2006–2008, is attributed to the increase in non-core activities.[9] Groups of companies with cap ownership,[10] big owners and foreign concentrated ownership behaved normally and therefore had better chances of increased core business investment activities (Bole *et al.*, 2010: 117, 129). The fact that foreign controlled companies are much less in debt and stable, points to bad management of Slovene firms operating under the same circumstances.

At the beginning of the crisis, two major reactions were identified at corporate level: Those that were the first to face the crisis reacted mainly defensively by cutting operational and investment costs and/or by opting for more active sales promotion, still (modestly) investing[11] or freezing their expansion plans and adjusting market portfolio. Few of them followed a strategy of combined approaches and simultaneous development of new product/services/models. Delayed restructuring, delayed privatization with leverage management buyouts (MBO) and political interference in management that stimulated risk aversion and slowed down decision-making process and operation were among the major reasons for the poor performance, or even collapse of some privatized firms. The credit crunch coupled with extremely high payment indiscipline severely inhibited firms' activities.[12]

The more difficult access to financial resources till 2010 did not (yet) dramatically influence R&D activity. According to a survey of 61 manufacturing companies, R&D expenditures in 2009 reached 87 per cent of the 2006–2008 level (Redek *et al.*, 2010: 155). Most of the companies spent at least 3 per cent of revenues on R&D.[13] Companies claimed to introduce a significant number of new products (88 per cent on domestic and 27.9 per cent on global markets). The most important types of innovation were (ranked in order of importance): improving existing products, introducing new product lines, expanding existing product lines, and repositioning products. About half of the companies were believed to be among the leading companies in product innovation in their industries and relevant markets. Nevertheless the majority of sales (77.5 per cent) were derived from existing (old) products. One major problem was the long time needed to develop completely new products since the majority of firms were believed to be worse than competitors, and similar percentage were convinced that they could contribute little to setting new trends in the market (Redek *et al.*, 2010: 150–151).

According to the survey carried out by Filipović (2009: 4),[14] the short-term reaction demonstrated that the majority of firms viewed formulation of priorities as 'highly regular', including strategic review, rather than 'spontaneous' or aiming at fast response to external pressures. The initial reaction was seen as a normal response, nothing special, initiating first internal changes and adjustments, aiming at the company survival. Firms focused on 'bread and butter' issues such as cost cutting, operational efficiencies, downsizing, and cash flow. Only 10 per cent of CEOs indicated this as their top priority. It was done only if not jeopardizing other priorities—for example, critical competences (Filipović, 2009: 4). Business or longer-term challenges/strategies were predominantly not changed although many of the interviewed managers represented the best-performing firms in Slovenia.

In the medium term, firms placed more emphasis on the implementation of their strategies but still within the existing business model rather than rethinking the fundamentals of the way they do business. Firms started to concentrate on penetrating new markets (initially by using their old products), with modest adjustment of strategies. 'Firms still put the strongest emphasis on launching new products to existing markets, followed by launching existing products to new markets. Much less effort is devoted to launching new products to new markets' (see Cirman *et al.*, 2009: 285). Boosting investments into learning and innovations was more of an exception. This implicitly means that strategic exit strategy was primarily in existing production programs and not focused on enhancing innovation and launching new products. With the escalation of the crisis, more long-term reactions such as, enhancing firm competitiveness by innovations and new product development gradually penetrated firms' strategies. According to Filipović's survey 'fight for the top line' including strengthening sales efforts, investment of time and resources into improved customer relationships, as well as adjustment of the offering in pursuit of new market opportunities was the most common reaction (Filipović, 2009: 4). This was applied by more proactively oriented managers having positive attitude to the needed changes: They started to focus on increasing competitiveness through innovations of the business model, investments in new competencies and in particular in training with more decentralized decision-making in order to motivate employees to enhance productivity. More ambitious firms focused on innovation and people-related issues seen as a key source of competitive advantage in the future. This was the reason they were not willing to stop investing their time and company resources in this area[15] (see Filipović, 2009: 4). Such short-, medium- and long-term reactions have been frequently intertwined. Filipović reported that reaction was multilevel, meaning that some reacted to the first signs of the crisis even before 2008, others did so only after internal strategic discussions. Such an approach balanced the much-needed short-term response with long-term company objectives (Filipović, 2009: 2–4). With the exception of the initial 'wait and see' period or 'we are not going to be really affected' period, Slovenian companies reacted generally in a similar way as the CEOs of firms in other European countries.[16] Some significant differences were nevertheless found. The first difference is related to the importance given to the BRIC countries. While the research of Barrington *et al.* (2008) detected the reduced focus on promising markets as a consequence of giving priority to internal necessities, managers of many Slovene MNEs really started to think more about new markets outside the traditional European and Balkan markets. They were regarded as risky but opportunities outweighed risks, while in other European firms risks outweighed opportunities (see Filipović, 2009: 2–4). Entering new markets was also recorded as a successful survival strategy in the previous crisis. When Yugoslavia collapsed, several Slovene enterprises successfully compensated for the loss of Yugoslav markets in less than 2 years.

The different ('more easy') approach to crisis management can be explained by the different perception of the crisis and the better 'improvisation in implementation' competence since for many Slovene managers (used to the unpredictable environment of the socialist system) long-term strategic planning was not yet mastered to the level applied at other European firms. This was particularly true for most of the largest firms (and also largest MNEs) since their managers were still mainly from the older generation that was used to improvising and being very 'innovative' in the unpredictable environment of the socialist economic system.

The next difference was in the more centralized management practices. Slovene managers concentrated decisions on strategic changes much more in the top management echelons, while underestimating its leadership role in inspiring changes at all levels of decision-making and hence involving middle management and especially other employees. Concentration of decisions in top management to a much greater extent than in firms from market economies is a transition-specific phenomenon. It may be a result of lack of decision-making power and negative selection in socialist times. Top management has frequently underestimated the role of leadership and human capital as well as the role of communication with other employees. Consequently, we are witnessing strikes which are in many cases inspired by comments such as 'we did not know the situation'. Slovene firms and employees are also less flexible than European competitors. As one executive commented: 'we have more of those employees who get divorced than those changing their job position even within the company'.

The capacity for coping with crisis arises from several other firm-level characteristics. Comparison of domestically owned firms with some foreign owned firms has shown that the latter are more resistant to crisis and reacted more proactively. According to a survey among foreign investors, several foreign investors in Slovenia performed better during the crisis. Some increased sales and hired new workers, while the large majority retained similar sales and production levels (Burger *et al.*, 2011). Some of them (less than 23 per cent in domestic market and less than 15 per cent in international markets) performed worse than before, and some even worse than Slovene competitors.[17]

Quite resistant to crisis is also the segment of smaller and dynamic firms[18] (identified as hidden champions). The survey on the performance of SMEs showed that as much as 29 per cent of SMEs claimed that their revenues did not change substantially in the first half of 2009 compared to the first half of 2008. More than half of the respondents claimed that they had not cut jobs. Twenty-six percent reduced investment in technology, 23 per cent lowered the spending on materials and services, 14 per cent reduced the number of employees, 15 per cent reduced inventories and only 4 per cent sold some property (Chamber of Craft and Small Business of Slovenia, 2009; Stergar, 2009: 11).

Most of the hidden champions increased sales and profits, expanding to new markets. Although this was done on a more limited scale[19] it still reflects that only the most dynamic Slovene MNEs[20] could match the performance of selected largest foreign firms[21] and hidden champions. Most of the hidden champions increased sales, employment, training, and R&D even more. Many of these firms speeded up or started internationalization.[22] Contrary to the hidden champions who enhanced innovation or using the crisis as opportunity hasn't been the main approach of Slovene SMEs, which are less innovation-led than European SMEs in general.[23]

Apart from the above-stated differences in coping with the crisis one of the reasons for the harsh blow of the crisis on Slovene enterprises was the low level of international production and outsourcing since studies (Kasahara and Rodrigue, 2008) showed that 'intermediate inputs allow firms to adapt to partners, competitors, and technology from abroad and, as a result, benefit from foreign research and development'. This may partly explain the clouded perception and slower reaction of Slovene firms. Recent studies (Burger *et al.*, 2011; Zupan *et al.*, 2010) found that only 16–18 per cent of Slovene enterprises use international sourcing, although growth during 2001–2003 and 2004–2006 had increased. MNEs are the most involved in international sourcing (Burger *et al.*, 2011) and most of international sourcing (also offshore outsourcing) takes place in MNEs. More than 36 per cent of the largest Slovene MNEs source internationally (see Jaklič and Svetličič, 2011: 138). However, even many MNEs could not cope with the challenges of the crisis efficiently.

Historical context

Operations of Slovene MNEs during the crisis are deeply embedded in the specific context and characteristics of the Slovene economy and its transition might have important implications. Among them we can single out:

- social ownership and self-management system of governance (introduced in the 1950s) which gave companies higher level of autonomy than in other socialist countries already in socialist times;
- decentralized development pattern on the Yugoslav level and particularly of the Slovene economy;
- more open economy following a kind of market-oriented reform in 1965, which led to more international economic cooperation with market economies;
- more developed forms of international economic cooperation in general and particularly with Western economies (after the split with Stalin in 1948) including contract manufacturing and specific joint ventures with foreign partners starting already in 1967 and investments abroad in the late 1960s;[24]
- gradual type of transition and privatization (see Mrak *et al.*, 2004) which led to a very late initiation of the privatization process, which is still not ongoing.[25] The gradual approach to transition and privatization is consequently present in corporate ownership and management, resulting frequently in a (too) slow decision-making process coupled with risk and responsibility aversion.

Such general background can offer relevant insights into the implications of the crisis for other post-communist and developing countries as well. Just before the crisis started, late privatization brought about MBOs and excessive financial leveraging, which coincided with the crisis and brought some firms to insolvency, others to bankruptcy. A sample of 203 Slovene firms in the period 2006–2009 demonstrated that the crisis highly impacted the performance of all Slovene firms although some differences related to the ownership structure were found (firms with dispersed ownership, firms with management buyouts and cap firms).[26] Using regression analysis Kneževič *et al.* reported negative but insignificant relationship between performance and MBO ownership as well as ownership of holding companies in concentrated/disclosed ownership. The authors found out that firms with dispersed ownership (mostly larger and so called 'blue chips' firms) were addressing the challenges posed by the crisis better than others (positively and significantly related to productivity in 2009). Conversely, MBO firms were the most affected by the economic crisis. The debt in MBO firms was growing faster than in other groups of companies. In most cases managers privatized these companies with high bank loans (Kneževič *et al.*, 2010: 100). The high debts that the managers took were pressuring the firms' business operations already in 2008 (Bole *et al.*, 2010, cited in Kneževič *et al.*,

2010: 101). However firms with cap had high productivity growth in the observed period although they were controled by managers, and mainly the manufacturing firms were affected the most by the crisis. The main difference between cap firms and MBOs is that the slow process of taking over the control of the cap companies (among which 39 per cent are top Slovene MNEs, op. SM) did not harm the business operations during the process. They have also not significantly increased their debt.

Slovene MNEs' response to the global economic crisis

Macro trends in Slovene outward FDI

The growth of Slovene outward FDI before the crisis was relatively dynamic. From 1994 to 2000 the stock of outward FDI increased 2.9 times, while the period 2001–2009 recorded a 4.6 times increase, which amounted to €5,484 million in 2009. Outward investments were growing at an average of 24.2 per cent per annum from 1993 to 2008, but then they fell by 3.4 per cent year-on-year change in 2009. This drop was much smaller when compared to some other countries (Table 11.1).

Although companies with FDI abroad represent only about 2 per cent of the Slovene corporate sector, they are vital players in export, employment, innovation, and value-added activities and account for a very important share in GDP formation.[27] According to the number of firms, the small and medium sized represent over three-quarters of the Slovene outward investors, yet they are less important in terms of volume of capital invested abroad, as most of the value is invested by a handful of large enterprises.

The geographical concentration of outward FDI is completely different from the export structure. While the EU is a major export destination, former Yugoslavia is major outward FDI destination (69 per cent of total FDI stock). Slovenia has obviously benefited from first mover advantages and small psychic distance since those markets were

Table 11.1 Outward FDI flows, 2006–2009 (US$ millions)

Country	2006	2007	2008	2009
Slovenia	863	1,802	1,366	868
Austria	13,670	39,025	29,399	3,766
Czech Republic	1,468	1,620	4,323	1,340
Hungary	18,616	66,787	59,815	−6,886

Source: Bank of Slovenia, Direct investment 2009, Available at: www.bsi.si and UNCTAD, FDI/TNI database.

Table 11.2 Slovene investments and representative offices in BRIC countries

	China	Russia	India	Brazil	Total
Affiliations Number	13 (7 Slo MNEs)	8 (5 Slo MNEs)	4 (2 Slo MNEs)	5 (4 Slo MNEs)	30 (14 Slo MNEs)
Slovene OFDI stock 2009, € million	8.7	314.4	3.5	7.5	334.1 (6%)
Representative offices	11 (3 Slo MNEs)	80	5 (1 Slo MNE)		96
Representative offices of JAPTI (established)	Shanghai (2007)	Kazan (2008)		Sao Paulo (2008)	

Source: Bank of Slovenia and Chamber of Economy.

home market previously. Gradually these advantages started to evaporate and the relative share of Slovene investors' in these host markets decreased. Firms tried to diversify markets as the impact of the crisis became severe. BRICs' and other emerging economies' markets, which are still experiencing dynamic growth, have become more attractive. A number of new ventures have been initiated in Russia and some in China and India (Table 11.2).[28]

Such affiliations and representative offices have been established in the last three years (and may be identified as the third type of strategy; developing new markets, models, and products/services). Facilitating business cooperation and entry to more distant markets, has been identified as the strategic need at the level of national economic policy. Having recognized that the share of Slovene trade with China is the lowest among all EU member countries, the economic policy-makers and particularly the Chamber of Commerce started to promote cooperation with the BRIC countries. Several activities have been undertaken for the promotion of bilateral cooperation.[29] 'The neglect of cooperation outside the EU, which dominated in the first years of transition, also as a reaction to, perhaps too much political attention being given to cooperation with non-aligned and developing countries during socialism, has changed into active promotion of economic ties with BRICs and other developing countries' (Jaklič and Svetličič, 2011: 140) in order to grasp major new demand coming from this part of the world.[30]

Slovene MNEs' response to the global economic crisis

Slovene top MNEs[31] faced the global economic and financial crisis earlier than other Slovene firms, yet the consequences of the crisis can hardly be generalized. A survey on the effects of the global economic crisis among top 25 Slovenian MNEs in 2009 revealed that the consequences of the crisis vary considerably among the MNEs.[32] The most significant consequence of the crisis for the largest MNEs has been substantial decrease in sales (80 per cent of surveyed firms reported sales decrease, most frequently between 20 per cent and 49 per cent) and lower profits. Conversely, none of the surveyed MNEs experienced a decrease in market share and none of them had lost suppliers or key personnel. Even laying off was not universal: 40 per cent reduced the number of employees by less than 20 per cent or used the instrument of shortened working week (partly subsidized by the government); the majority of MNEs did not reduce the number of employees (see Jaklič and Svetličič, 2011: 139).

One explanation as to why Slovene MNEs were the first to be hit is also in the type of their activities performed abroad, the markets in which they operate and the severity of the recession there, including local government rescue plans.[33] Because most of Slovene affiliates abroad are located in the hard hit Western Balkan countries, they were also hit hard due to absence of effective national rescue plans. The prevailing market and efficiency seeking investors[34] (automotive, electronics, and garments), which suffered substantially from falling demand experienced a harsh blow. Rescue plans in the automotive industry on the major European markets such as Germany and France, and in China, improved their operations. Strategic investments (in R&D or high value added activities) suffered the least, but very few Slovene investments abroad fall in this category.

Most Slovene MNEs have not divested or substantially curtailed their internationalization process. Financial constraints and aggravated liquidity slowed down or postponed some investment decisions, yet MNEs in general face above-average access to capital markets at home or abroad and can draw on their own sources. In spite of decreasing demand in target markets, Slovene parent firms have not tried to disinvest such investments, but rather they have tried to use their affiliates strategically to enhance sales locally and on neighboring markets. Affiliates abroad got additional functions, sometimes also to expand into new production lines tapping new customers. Others started to keep or increase market share by offering higher value products and services in order to keep return on investment. The strategic importance of such affiliates in fact increased, although sales dropped.

Generally, lower sales were accompanied by cost cutting, reduced investment and employment, but by much less than those in domestic firms. Frequently, the pool of unemployed people included those who should have been dismissed already before the crisis, but management had postponed the implementation of this decision. Long-term investment has been postponed, investment in R&D and marketing was reduced, but sales promotion activities focusing on retention of key customers, maintaining good relationship with main business partners, and rationalizing product portfolio were enhanced. Few companies tried to upgrade their products and services to address richer customers.

Strategic alliances, international R&D cooperation, outsourcing, and captive offshoring have been identified as the most promising escape routes from the crisis and are expected to be used to a greater extent in the future, but only by the most proactive oriented MNEs. Forty percent of surveyed enterprises in June 2009 plan to increase or have recently invested in new markets.[35]

Changes in the list of top Slovene MNEs in the period 2006–2010

The list of largest MNEs from Slovenia between 2006 and 2009 was relatively stable, but in 2009 several changes in rankings were seen (see Jaklič and Svetličič, EMGP 2009). As many as 11 companies disappeared from the list in 2009. Five of them were not included in the 2008 list. There are several different reasons:

- Top Slovene MNEs are attractive targets for larger European enterprises that are looking for better market position in Central and Eastern Europe. Some companies disappeared because they were overtaken by foreign firms: Among the top 25 listed MNEs were Kompas (by a Croatian firm), Droga Kolinska (by a Serbian firm), SIJ (by a Russian firm) and Lesnina (after the MBO, sold to Austrian XXXLutz).
- Some disappeared due to lack of dynamics in their development, which could not keep them among the largest Slovene MNEs (ACH, Valkarton, ERA, Alpina, Elan). Unrealized growth potential was also a result of delayed reactions and lagging behind the main competitors.
- Pre-crisis inefficient performance and governance problems that resulted in frequent management changes and slower response to market changes. ELAN lost its position because of the pre-crisis stagnation, ownership changes, and hard recuperation after a bankruptcy.
- The most abundant group is composed by firms which disappeared due to the crisis, who neglected the changes in the environment and had internal managerial problems (Merkur, Prevent, Interevropa

and Viator, and Vektor). Governance problems can be divided in two subgroups:

i. Manipulated[36] management buyouts (MBO) and crisis-related problem group. Merkur is the most obvious case. Before the crisis managers hired huge loans to buy out the firm, while not paying enough attention to cost cutting and process efficiency (compared to main competitors). Crisis made it incapable of repaying such huge loans which brought the firm close to bankruptcy. Similar is the story with Viator and Vektor, which is faced with problems alike.
ii. Internal managerial reasons and lack of strategy (that would consider steps taken by major competitors and changes in the external environment and demand), such as lack of attention to cost cutting and efficiency, lack of effort for sales increase and the absence of new products/services/market development for further growth. These reasons mostly explain the exit of Prevent and Intereuropa. Low demand for their products (car seat covers) during the crisis contributed a lot to Prevent's decline, being already in bankruptcy procedure and strong disagreements between the two major owners about future development. In spite of the domestic crisis, the affiliate in Brazil performed well. Intereuropa is facing difficulties due to the wrong internationalization decision at the wrong time (large investment in Russia just before the escalation of the crisis) and management crisis (politically appointed management that made this internationalization decision, is now facing damage suits).

Types of MNEs' reaction to the crisis

Firm-level responses to the crisis have been different in terms of timing (rapid/delayed response), type of response (defensive/proactive), content (employment and innovation/training policies), and implementation (strategies, management changes[37]). We can distinguish four approaches[38] illustrated figuratively: (i) dinosaurs, (ii) endangered koalas, (iii) hedge hogs, and (iv) cheetahs (Table 11.3). Most of the firms in fact combined elements of all four approaches as the crisis was developing. Defensive reactions prevailed at the beginning to a certain extent in cheetahs as well. This resulted in some cases in disinvestment but in the majority of cases, in consolidation of the firm's international network. Later on, such a strategy was transformed into a more proactive approach, in technological upgrading in a minority of cases and

Table 11.3 Strategic response to the global crisis

	Dinosaurus	**Endangered Koalas**	**Hedgehogs**	**Cheetahs**
Time of response	No or delayed	Delayed	Temperate	Rapid
Type of response	Defensive	Defensive	Defensive, with active following the competitors	Offensive, proactive
Content/strategic focus	No focus	Late cost cutting, also in training and R&D, waiting for governmental support	Cost cutting & reduction of employees, efficiency seeking consolidation, Sales increase, particularly in new markets,	←+innovation Simultaneous development of new markets/product/services/business model, diversification
Implementation process	Poor implementation	Centralized management, vulnerable to external pressures (MBO + cap), lack of leadership, no adaptation to external environment incomplete and non-implemented restructuring	'Stable' management of existing models, modest adaptation, postponed investment	Change management, strategic acquisitions Integrative management, implementation of new business models

in an increased degree of internationalization by new investments and acquisitions abroad.

The major characteristics of the 'dinosaurs group' (Prevent, Merkur and recently Viator and Vektor) is that these firms collapsed during the crisis due to poor pre-crisis governance and management problems.[39] MBO firms, like Merkur, were affected most severely by the economic crisis. Although the crisis had a severe negative effect, it played only the role of a catalyst. Absence of structural reforms, lack of timely restructuring and delayed internationalization as well as internal reasons such as too high debt levels linked to late MBO privatization methods[40] are the main explanations for problems.[41] Many of these large, originally state-owned companies, started privatization by MBOs just before the onset of the crisis. Financial debt was based on a very high level of financial leveraging. The financial leverage coefficient increased from just bellow 0.8 to 1.5 in the period 1995–2009 (Kovač, 2011: 14). An additional problem arose from the fact that such credits for MBOs (by definition long-term obligations) were financed by short-term credits. It was a problem since empirical studies demonstrated that type of financing influenced company performance. 'The companies with the highest internal funds to fixed capital ratios have the highest total sales to fixed capital ratios' (see Domadenik *et al.*, 2010b: 110, 111).

Management buyouts put ownership and control issues along with rent seeking higher on the agenda than improving performance or adjusting strategy (see Valentinčič *et al.*, 2010: 132). Top management became politically vulnerable, as demonstrated by frequent changes in top management positions parallel to changes in the government. Political parties were trying to get hold of firms to get economic backing for their political activities. Consequently MBOs were also an instrument of running away from political influence. Apart from managers' greed,[42] politics obviously also played a role in such excessive financial leveraging. Banks, particularly the largest state owned also contributed by giving loans without in-depth evaluation of the firms' business plans. As one manager said in an interview for Finance in 2007: 'collateral was my good (manager) name' (Sovdat, 2010: 4). Managers were not in a position to repay high credits because they were counting to repay them from the cash flow of the acquired firms. General (political) climate also contributed to MBOs to be seen as a better solution compared to foreign acquisitions based on the 'national interest' argument. As J. Šušteršič said recently, 'firms were a prey of national interest and managers'.

The second group consists of 'endangered koalas'—that is, MNEs under severe threats of insolvency or facing major restructuring and management problems (Interevropa, Hit, Iskra Avtoelektrika, Telekom).[43] They have been facing similar problems as dinosaurs (manipulated MBOs resulting in frequent management changes, too high debt levels, wrong management decisions), but at a lower level and/or with some delay. Revenues dropped substantially, firms faced severe losses and started to disinvest both abroad and at home, cut on R&D spending and training and some even stopped paying the workers. Iskra Avtoelekrika is a typical example of this group; after a loss in 2009, they realized very good results in the first half of 2010. Intereuropa performed below the plan but better than in 2009 (Špacapan, 2010: 20–21). Telekom invested in FYR of Macedonia nearly €215 million, in Kosovo about €200 million with no positive results. Now they want to consolidate these operations there but divest from Albania and BiH (Smrekar and Weiss, 2011: 4; Smrekar and Urbas, 2011: 9).

The third group consists of 'hedge hogs', which are firms with prevailingly defensive strategies, trying to consolidate or divest from existing operations in response to the crisis[44] (Trimo,[45] Telekom,[46] Petrol, Unior, Kovintrade, Hidria), some with the potential to speed up internationalization after the initial defensive reaction. No substantial changes in strategic planning, no new design in scenario planning in coping with predicted discontinuities or greater vulnerabilities have been undertaken. Management was operating within existing models adapting them to the crisis. The very first strategic reaction was reduction of all costs, facing substantial decrease of sales (20–49 per cent as claimed by 80 per cent of surveyed firms; Survey 2009), investment reduction, reduced working hours and lastly also reducing (temporarily) employment, trying to keep key personnel (also emphasized by Filipović, 2009). Most of the firms from this group have not been searching for crisis exit by investing in new products, services, or markets, but concentrated mainly on the consolidation of their activities.

Although MNEs have been forced to slow down their investment, the strategic orientation that was adopted was to do it first on the Slovene market and not abroad. Like SMEs, major Slovene MNEs cut investments substantially already in January 2009 (Gorenje and Mercator nearly halved them; Poslovni Dnevnik, January 12, 2009: 17). They also started to cut costs (production, logistics, inventories), reduced working hours, slowed down recruitment, and dismissed some personnel. Divesting abroad and selling foreign affiliates were a last resort. Elan, who used to be among the top 25 Slovene MNCs, is planning to sell its subsidiary in Austria. Consolidation of existing affiliates network has been a predominant strategic approach of this group of MNCs. Ambitious internationalization plans have not been abandoned, instead they were put on hold. Reinvesting of profits was also limited. Hidria was operating at a loss in 2009 (revenue dropped by 10 per cent but performed better in 2010 (Bertoncelj, 2011: 4) due to a friendly merger with the German company Dr. Karl Bausch, a leading European development suppliers of top technological solutions for the automotive industry with 392 employees and generating €50 million in revenues per year).

A major characteristic of the more proactive response of the 'cheetahs' (Krka, Kolektor, Mercator, Helios, Gorenje,[47] Perutnina) was a rather fast transition from defending to offensive strategy. Initially, firms also reacted by rationalizing operations and adapting them to the new circumstances, but mostly kept their original internationalization plans. Kolektor for instance, as supplier to the automotive industry, reduced working hours because of reduced orders, but later acquired a company in Germany and in Slovenia as part of its diversification strategic plans. At the same time, they sold two firms, one in Brazil and one in China.[48] After a period of rapid expansion abroad, Helios temporarily put internationalization by acquisitions on hold and concentrated on consolidation of the existing international network. Some of the firms reduced working hours and expenditures on salaries by 20 per cent being subsidized by the government program. Reduction of wages was done in agreement with the trade unions. The policy was to keep employment in expectation of the end of the crisis. Quite a number of firms reduced first managers' salaries and then those of other workers.

However, the major emphasis of these firms was on upgrading of activities abroad toward higher value activities and broadening of their sales base by expanding on new (industrial) customers. Many have invested and acquired new firms abroad in spite of contractions of revenues in 2008. They revisited the firms' long-term strategies. The emphasis shifted as the crisis developed. Initial reduction of costs strategy, reducing working hours (laying off workers only as a last resort) and keeping international networks untouched was gradually substituted by a strategy of diversification (products and markets) and developing new products and services or at least adapting products to new markets/customers. In spite of the crisis, Krka increased sales in the first half of 2009 in international markets (Russia and Croatia). They plan to build another factory for €135 million in Russia in 2011 (Bertoncelj and Pikon, 2010: 2). But in Eastern Europe sales revenues decreased substantially due to the devaluation of currencies in Ukraine (90 per cent) and in Russia although the sales levels remained the same. Nevertheless, they had to revise their original ambitious investment plans, from €161 million to €104 million. Employment has increased, more overseas than in Slovenia (Finance, November 6, 2009; 7). Perutnina Ptuj increased sales in all countries where they had affiliates (first half of 2009 (Finance July 20, 2009: 2–3). Mercator opened the largest supermarket in Westgate near Zagreb in November 2009 and is contemplating to buy what Tuš is selling on the Balkans (Hren and Vuković, 2009). Most of these firms intensified innovation activities (in terms of product/services/technologies, and process and organizational innovation) to gain new market share. This is in line with historical experience, when many new technologies and models emerged during or after a crisis. Crises are a curse and a blessing. Many innovations have been born during recessions.[49] It means that successful firms try to exit the crisis by stimulating and not decreasing investments[50] (in general, but also those in R&D[51]) although many other firms put their R&D costs on hold in their costs-cutting effort during the first stages of the recession.[52]

In spite of the crisis Slovene MNEs remain among the most respected firms in Slovenia[53] (though not supported by operational results) more respected than, for instance, foreign owned firms. Among the first 50 most respected firms in 2011, including public utilities, banks, holdings, and foreign owned firms, 12 are Slovene top MNEs (in 2010 they were 14), while only five are foreign owned firms. Top 10 include four largest MNEs (three in 2010) (Kline, 2011: 19). The crisis contributed to improved reputation of six Slovene MNCs,[54] two remained unchanged and four worsened their position. The long-term view also reveals that multinationals are among those who are the permanent stars in terms of reputation (like Krka, Gorenje, and Mercator[55]). Some MNEs are among pulsing stars, sometimes enhancing and sometimes dropping their reputation from year to year (Kompas but also Mercator, Gorenje, and Perutnina; Kline, 2011: 19) and some are dying stars (mostly banks and holdings) (Kline, 2009: 27).

Conclusions

Reactions of Slovene MNEs to the crisis have been strongly contingent to

- past historical context (protectionist environment, absence of or late restructuring, underdeveloped managerial capabilities);
- conditions in the home economy (late reaction and deep recession);
- type and timing of privatization (gradualism);

- industry (traditional industries still prevail) with poor diversification,
- motives for internationalization (mostly market, less efficiency seeking),
- too narrow a strategy, particularly internationalization strategy (existing products in new markets, too gradual approach); and
- management competences and strategies.

The most important immediate factors contributing to the intensity with which the crisis has impacted their operations were the following:

- slow reaction and neglected changes in international markets (government and firms),
- delayed restructuring (traditional economic structure),
- weak competitiveness (ignoring changes in competitors and customers)
- a rather high level of debt (mostly due to leveraged MBOs),
- lack of geographical diversification of their international economic relations (weak ties with fast growing emerging economies),
- too narrow development strategies,
- weak innovativeness compared to global multinationals but much better than that of other Slovene firms.

All these factors contributed to the late reaction to the crisis based on the assumption that Slovenia would not be hurt and that firms had good capabilities to deal with crises based on past experience and improvization capabilities. However, the financial crisis soon moved to the real sector and Slovene firms started to feel its detrimental effects. Thus the economy of Slovenia and its firms were hit later but much more severely.

The Slovene MNCs were among the first to feel the impact of the crisis due to their international exposure but were, with some exceptions, able to cope with its effects better and faster. Although their reaction to the crisis has been diverse in terms of markets and sector of activity, it has changed over time from being defensive to becoming more proactive.

We distinguish four approaches to dealing with the effects of the crisis—that is, those of (i) cheetahs, (ii) hedge hogs, (iii) endangered koalas, and (iv) dinosaurs. Firms have often combined elements of all four approaches as the crisis developed. Defensive reactions prevailed at the beginning. In some cases, they led to divestment, but mainly as a consolidation of a firm's international networks of affiliates. Later, such a strategy was transformed into a more proactive approach focused on new investments and acquisitions abroad and enhancing/introducing offshore outsourcing. Cheetahs first concentrated on cost reduction strategies, but subsequently engaged in more intensive internationalization. They were moving from market-driven to market-driving marketing strategies. Hedge hogs were less offensive and kept their prevailingly defensive old strategies for a longer period of time sticking to their traditional strategy with not much change. They have not divested, but concentrated on consolidating existing international networks. The last two groups are those MNCs that have been hit severely. Some collapsed (dinosaurs) partly due to wrong managerial decisions (particularly MBOs), and partly due to late restructuring. Others are still in serious difficulties (endangered koalas) largely also due to bad management, rent-seeking strategies abandoning their main goals, but engaging in financial speculations outside their core business and too ambitious and greedy MBOs, sometimes influenced also by politicians. Government support for endangered koalas dried up and little income is expected even if these enterprises are sold out. While the latest group of enterprises is less attractive for foreign investors and distress selling, both cheetahs and hedge hogs remain potential targets of competitors. 'Dinosaurs' may gain attention only as 'numismatic' acquisition if possessing some specific assets.

There are at least four major lessons that Slovene MNEs draw out of this crisis. Firstly, timeliness determines the effectiveness of the response, and experience (only) matters when used quickly. Slovene MNEs who had started to invest abroad earlier and diversified their operations geographically before the crisis, fared much better during the crisis. Secondly, those who had invested more in R&D and training before the crisis proved to be more crisis resistant and were able to exit the crisis sooner. Thirdly, management with more long-term and international orientation (and less short-term orientation), who started internationalization early, performed better as they were more aware of the changes in international markets and had better ability to evaluate risks. For them, slicing down international operations was a last resort.

Although Slovene MNEs felt the crisis earlier than most local market-oriented large firms, they on average performed better during the crisis also thanks to their early internationalization start, stronger export orientation, greater diversification of markets (and in some cases also products/services), and innovativeness. Consolidation of international networks was the first cost reduction strategic reaction to the crisis in most of them, but many soon realized that enhancing selective but intense outward internationalization is an appropriate long-term response to the crisis. Shifting global development nuclei of large MNEs (potential partners of Slovenian MNEs) to Asia forced Slovene MNEs to begin strengthening their economic ties with the BRIC countries. Apart from the top MNEs, SMEs and entrepreneurs in general also plan to enhance internationalization. The crisis contributed to the realization that smallness can be only outweighed by internationalization, by global mindset.

Slovene MNEs appear to become an important development instrument for the national economy, which was not the case some 15 years ago, when many attitudinal barriers and managerial mindset actually restricted outward internationalization. Over time, even the most skeptical policy-makers and managers have realized that in the era of globalization outward internationalization has became a precondition for growth and enhanced global competitiveness. Due to the small size and openness of the Slovene economy, it is expected that it will become dominated by highly internationalized firms, domestic and foreign-owned.[56]

Managing human resources is one of the most important challenges to existing MNEs. Several MNEs, even among those at the top, still lack systematic internal HRM and replace it by ad hoc activity. Lack of skilled and internationally mobile managers, has turned out to be a major barrier to internationalization in the past (see Jaklič and Svetličič, 2007) and this sets demands to existing education and training programs. These shortages highlight the need for holistic education that provides interdisciplinary knowledge of international business, innovation, HRM, including soft skills (negotiations, communications, rhetoric, strategy, and leadership) and knowledge about diplomacy, cross-cultural management[57] and ethics accompanying 'traditionally' needed and emphasized financial skills. Opportunities for existing Slovene MNEs also lie in improved corporate governance, international integration of activities, international sourcing, organization, and management. Especially the largest publicly owned MNEs face difficulties with managing higher international risk and needs for swift response and strategy adaptation. Case studies and surveys illustrate that MNEs employ better labor policies, have higher than the average salaries and work in sectors which can enhance demand.

Major challenges faced by MNEs include geographical diversification of international economic cooperation, particularly to fast-growing emerging economies, becoming more flexible and adaptable to changes coming from the global economy, and adopting a long-term orientation. The too high reaction gap[58] has to be narrowed, ideally closed. Consequently they have to strengthen their cross cultural competencies, modernize and adapt strategies, and improve leadership competences. A lot can be learned in this regard from hidden champions. Since crises are inbuilt in the capitalist system, management has to improve risk management[59] including undertaking pre-mortem analysis[60]—that is, before final decisions are taken. Pre-mortem analysis should become a permanent activity or firms' 'stress testing' similar to what banks are doing.

The crucial tasks for the future are firstly to enhance organizational flexibility and improve the agility of firms, and preserving their major capabilities and social capital. The crisis has to be seen as a kind of a 'cleaning service' for firms' strategies and organizations that can strengthen firms' core competencies. It can be done either by 'fitness-ing', by permanently restructuring firms' activities and strategies, enhancing competencies for facing new challenges, stimulating innovations and value added, learning quickly and avoiding too high risk exposure. It could also be achieved by installing appropriate 'circuit breakers to prevent the contagion of failure of one part of the system' in order to incorporate policies and structures to prevent contagion before a crisis occurs (see Stiglitz, 2010: 4, 28). As crises cannot be avoided completely, one has to have an alarm system for early reaction and prevention. Stiglitz therefore suggests 'economic architecture of risk sharing relationships among countries by creating circuit breakers. Without circuit breakers, no liberalization may be preferable to liberalization; but with circuit breakers, a higher degree of integration may be desirable' (2010: 39).

Notes

1. Although they have evaluated foreign owned firms' effects on host economies, the same basically apply also to domestic MNEs particularly since there have been few studies on the behavior of outward FDI (see Hill and Jongwanich, 2009: 17).
2. So called 'fire-sale' FDI, meaning that lower prices of firms in domestic currency and a depreciating exchange rate as well as a more liberal FDI regime, frequent by-product of a crisis attract foreign investors. Crises deflate asset prices, companies in severe problems are forced to sell ('distress selling' as auditors call it) and therefore create buying opportunities for resource-flush investors.
3. Since firms are free to respond or not to our survey it means that in some cases firms are not included due to non-response to our questionnaire. Particularly recently some firms, if in financial difficulties (insolvency), or involved in some scandals regarding changes in the management, don't want to respond to such surveys.

4. Apart from some 2009 list's newcomers (MK Založba, Tab d. d.,) and some of the top MNEs included in the 2006 list which later disappeared from the list (ELAN, Lesnina, Kompas, Prevent, Viator and Vector, Era, ETI) for different reasons, most of the top MNEs have been included in our case studies.
5. About one-third of the sample was Slovene MNCs.
6. Majority of largest Slovene MNEs performed still positively in 2008. Out of 18 company groups (many of them are MNCs) only four realized losses, others realized profits in 2009 (Delo FT, October 12, 2009; 20–21). But some firms realized less sales already in 2008 (Merkur, Trimo, Gorenje and Prevent; all of them among top Slovene MNEs op. SM; Bertoncelj and Matejčič, 2009; 3). The crisis is yet to hit consumers. Marketing monitor showed their highest (almost 75 per cent) perception of crisis and drop of purchasing power in the last five years only in 2011.
7. Estonia was the only country in the whole OECD where growth rate decreased more than 8.1 per cent as in Slovenia.
8. In Slovenia 80 per cent in 2008 (in 2004, 52 per cent), Austria 71 (in 2004, 68 per cent), Germany 64 per cent (in 2004, 63 per cent) (see, Bole *et al.*, 2010: 117).
9. Instead of concentrating on strategic challenges, firms (their owners) opted more for short-term rent-seeking strategy buying other companies.
10. For cap ownership definition see footnote 33.
11. Investments represented in the period 2006–2008 more than 20 per cent of fixed capital assets (drop from 23 per cent in 2007). In 2009 they dropped to 16 per cent (see Domadenik *et al.*, 2010b; 109). The drop was the highest in case of Holdings and firms with cap, while MBO firms actually slightly increased share of investment. But was actually less than on average in OECD countries where global investment decreased by 50 per cent in 2007 (Domadenik *et al.*, 2010b: 110,112).
12. More than 70 per cent of firms claim that they are paid only after 31 days while payments longer than 120 days are not at all exceptions. This is much higher as compared to Scandinavian countries with about 20 days payment terms and only 7 days payment delays. These countries are above the average of European countries, which is still better than in Slovenia (Svenšek, 2011, citing Swedish firm Intrum Justitia: 5).
13. 48.2 per cent out of 61 manufacturing companies in the sample, while MNCs on average spend more than 3 per cent.
14. Filipović interviewed 20 CEOs or members of managing boards in March/April 2009. Among the 20 firms six are also top Slovene MNEs, while others are smaller but much internationalized firms (2009: 4).
15. We should not get the impression that such pro-active response is a general characteristic of most of Slovene firms' reaction to the crises. Filipovič interviewed some of the best, very dynamic, larger, and smaller Slovene firms.
16. See research of Barrington *et al.* (2008) based on the survey of 190 CEOs around the world.
17. Lek (Sandoz) however, performed worse compared to Slovene pharmaceutical firm Krka.
18. Pipistrel (leading producer of small ultralight planes), Instrumentation technologies (laboratory equipment), and Dewesoft (supplier of program equipment to NASA) for instance.

19. Thirteen cases were evaluated.
20. Which we call cheetahs (see later); on average the performance of hidden champions was better than most of the cheetahs.
21. Foreign firms like Revoz (Renault) and Hella Saturnus basically increased employment and sales in spite of the crises. They also strengthened training, and R&D.
22. Out of evaluated 13 hidden champions seven increased revenues (two no changes), but only three profits, seven increased employment (two no changes), five invested more in R&D and training (two remain the same). Export was increased in five cases, while three of them boosted internationalization. Only three firms invested during the crises less than before.
23. Only 18 per cent of Slovene SMEs are innovative compared to 32 per cent of European counterparts (EU-25). Slovenia has also poor record in patenting activity and the commercialization of research activity. Large firms are much more innovative (see Barlet and Bukvič, 2006: 341). There are also significant differences in terms of marketing. SMEs reduced costs of marketing substantially while large firms did much less.
24. Outward internationalization actually started before the inward one. Therefore we call this reversed internationalization (see Svetličič *et al.*, 1994 and Svetličič, 2008).
25. Domadenik *et al.* (2010a) established that out of 157 large and medium sized privatized firms analyzed in the period 1996–2000, 51 per cent of firms opted for internal privatization. In large firms that were forced into external privatization method, managers tried to consolidate ownership by buying shares from small shareholders or establishing a separate firms ('družba pooblaščenka') owned by insiders (managers and/or employees) that control the main firms (Domadenik *et al.*, 2010a: 85).
26. Out of our list of 25 top MNEs, 13 were included in the sample but they accounted for 39 per cent of the assets. Their distribution by type is rather even—that is, 39 per cent with dispersed ownership, 39 per cent were firms with a cap and 23 per cent MBOs. Cap firms are those having as the main owner a firm controlled by a wider management group and, in many cases, even workers—for example, Kolektor.
27. Outward investors provide over 40 per cent of employment and 50 per cent of exports of total Slovenian corporate sector (Jaklič and Svetličič, 2011).
28. Entering more distant markets is also part of a national internationalization promotion strategy, which has been launched a few years ago by the government. However many firms entered these markets before the crisis and the launch of the state-driven 'official' strategy.
29. In November 2007 bilateral Slovenia–China Business council was established and in August 2009 bilateral business conference took place in Ljubljana (79 Chinese and 60 Slovene firms) with the participation of Slovene prime minister and vice president of the Chinese government (Repovž, 2009: 3).
30. Also by indirect export to China through Germany, because many Slovene firms are producing intermediate products to be built into German products exported later to China. Unfortunately share of Slovene export to Germany is much less than in some other NMSs (19 per cent compared to 32 per cent in the case of the Czech Republic or 26 per cent in case of Hungary and Poland (Economist Intelligence Unit, July 16, 2010)).

31. See the list of 25 Slovene MNCs in appendix and changes in the list in the next chapter.
32. Survey ranking on Slovene multinationals in 2009, available at: http://www.vcc.columbia.edu/files/vale/documents/Slovenia_2009.pdf.
33. Very few Slovene investors on these markets report to benefit from local recession-related assistance. They have mostly relied on their own resources (see Bertoncelj and Tomažič, 2009: 2–3).
34. See details on the structure of Slovene investment abroad in Svetličič (2007: 67).
35. Acquisition of ECS GmbH from Essen (Germany) by Kolektor (June 2009) has been realized as a joint venture with a Chinese partner. Recent investments by Trimo were oriented toward investment hubs important for the Middle East and Africa (Turkey and North Africa).
36. Meaning that legal action has been initiated on the grounds of suspected privatization of benefits and externalization of costs of such MBOs by involved managers (alleged damage to shareholders and even criminal liability).
37. One among them is the higher share of foreign managers in top management of Slovene MNEs: Eight firms reported in 2008 participation of foreigners, while in 2009 already 15 out of 25 (Finance, November 30, 2009: 17).
38. The classification is based taking into account all the above aspects but mostly internationalization criteria (expansion or disinvestment), growth of sales, profits, employment, and R&D/training policies in the period 2006/2009. Only most representative cases are mentioned.
39. However most dinosaurs are in the textile and construction sector and among state-owned firms (see Domadenik *et al.*, 2010b; 110, 111) and not among top Slovene MNCs.
40. Equity now represents only 42 per cent of all sources of financing which is, on average, six percentage points less compared to firms in the Eurozone. Total debt to equity increased to 147 per cent compared to the Eurozone 105 per cent (Valentinčič *et al.*, 2010: 131, 132).
41. MBOs have also negative effect on performance. MBO firms were the most affected by the crises (Kneževič *et al.*, 2010: 100).
42. It is therefore not surprising that trust in Slovene managements has dramatically deteriorated. Only 13 per cent of respondents trust them while 48 per cent don't. Confidence index (0 no confidence, 100 total confidence) was assessed at 59 (see Sovdat and Toplak, 2009: 2).
43. Droga Kolinska and Kompas have been also facing difficulties and were 'fire sold' to foreign companies.
44. Tuš, the second largest retail chain in Slovenia having 13 trade units in BiH, six in Serbia, and three in Macedonia, although not on the list of top 25 Slovene MNCs, is planning to disinvest these foreign investments due to financial problems and inability to gain appropriate economies of scale due to dispersed network of trade units abroad (Finance, 23. July, 5).
45. TRIMO is in this group due to sector-specific effects, operating in a construction business which was hit by the crises severely. Otherwise, it could qualify in the Crabs/cheetah group keeping on its active internationalization expansion.
46. Their investments in Western Balkans reduced the capital of the company by one-fifth and caused losses of €220 million in 2010 (Lipnik, 2011: 9).

47. Hidria, Gorenje, and Trimo have some cheetahs characteristics in terms of a proactive response to the crisis and emphasis on new products and services, enhancing internationalization by new acquisitions abroad, but their revenues dropped significantly in 2009. Gorenje from the very beginning strategically aimed at richer customers in China. They entered the market with up scale Gorenje Pininfarina, and later on with Gorenje Ora-Ïto collection of household appliances. Out of 140 million of inhabitants of major provinces in China, 20–30 per cent are rich and demanding customers. They all the time demand newly designed goods and they do not buy in general stores for low and low-middle-income groups like Gome and Sunning. Therefore Gorenje sell in specialized stores (Petrov, 2009: 3).
48. The reason was poor performance of the firm in Brazil and lack of control in the China JV. In spite of majority ownership they had not been able to control the operations, which are obviously not crisis-related reasons for divestment.
49. Digital computers were born during the Great depression, IBM personal computers in the early 1980s (see Bughin *et al.*, 2009: 1).
50. Slovene MNEs still invest substantially and in many cases increased investments in 2010 and plan to do so in 2011. Out of 11 Slovene MNEs, five have invested more in 2010 than in 2009, two almost the same amount and only four less. The situation is similar in 2011 (two are increasing investment, one will invest the same amount as in 2010 and one less; see Bertoncelj and Pikon, 2010: 3).
51. According to Slovenian Statistical Office the share of innovation active enterprises (that introduced or improved products or processes) increased from 21 per cent to 52 per cent from 2006 to 2010. Large firms are relatively more active in innovation (75 per cent of surveyed firms) (SORS, 2004, cit in; Barlett and Bukvič, 2006: 341).
52. Some MNEs have cut also investments in education and training, although it is recognized as one among major source for lagging behind in competitiveness with leading firms in the world. Only 8.8 per cent of Slovene firms have, according to Ložar, similar program of the development of cadres as leading MNEs in the world (2008; 5).
53. Based on research of Kline and Partner (see Kline, Poslovni Dnevnik, May 24, 2010; May 21 and 23, 2011).
54. Some like Kolektor really substantially improved their position from the list of 2009 to 2011; Kolektor jumped from 89th to 34th place, Elan from 92nd to 42nd, Helios from 21st to 10th, Unior from 63 to 45th and Trimo from 28th to 15th place (Kline, 2011: 19).
55. This was in 2009, before the proclaimed insolvency. Now it is a dying star.
56. We see the ownership structure of the Slovene GDP formation in the future composed of 40 per cent contributed by foreign owned firms, 40 per cent by Slovene MNEs and the remaining 20 per cent by local market-oriented firms. Local firms, operating mostly in the domestic market, will eventually be in the minority.
57. Some tests about cross cultural knowledge have demonstrated rather poor results even in the case of knowledge about close markets.
58. The best illustration for delayed decision-making is the surprise by which the liberalization of textile products was taken. Although the decision in this respect was taken more than ten years before the liberalization took place, it

took managers by surprise. Recent increase in food prices is a similar example. One manger clearly indicated that this is a complete surprise for them although studies were alarming about the possibility of such developments in the last ten years.

59. Although risk management is not new, its importance substantially increased in face of more and more uncertainties and unpredictability in the global economic environment. Not least due to the very strong link between trust and international economic cooperation; more trust leads to more trade and FDI.
60. Pre-mortem analysis is an instrument which evaluates potential problems ex-ante. The precondition for effective application of such methods is to stimulate creative thinking as an instrument to get as much opinion as possible and not discussing only proposals stated in advance by leaders. Both, pre-mortem analysis and stimulation of creative thinking should become part of managers' mindset.

References

Altzinger, W., Bellak, C., Jaklič, A., and Rojec, M. (2003). Direct versus indirect foreign investment from transition economies: Is there a difference in parent company/home country impact? in M. Svetličič and M. Rojec (Eds.) *Facilitating Transition by Internationalisation: Outward FDI from Central European Economies in Transition*, Aldershot: Ashgate: 91–110.

Aykut, D. (2011). http://blogs.worldbank.org/prospects/outward-fdi-from-developing-countries-are-up-notably-south-south-flows, Accessed February 12, 2011.

Barlett, W. and Bukvič, V. (2006). Knowledge transfer in Slovenia: Supporting innovative SMEs trough spin-offs, technology parks, clusters and networks. *Economic and Business Review*, 8: 337–358.

Barrington, L., Hexter, E., and Mitchell, C. (2008). *CEO Challenge 2008: Top 10 challenges – Financial Crisis Edition*. The Conference Board.

Bertoncelj, M. (2011). Hidria v kitajsko naložbo milijon evrov, *Finance*, 133(12): 4.

Bertoncelj, M. and Pikon, R. (2010). Prihodnje leto novi val naložb, *Finance*, 224: 2–3.

Bertoncelj, M. and Tomažič, J. (2009). Podjetja se morajao v tujini znajti sama, *Finance*, 20(July): 2–3.

Bole, D. (2004). Dnevna delovna mobilnost v Sloveniji (Daily mobility of workers in Slovenia). *Acta Geographica Slovenica* 44–1. Ljubljana.

Bole, V., Prašnikar, J., and Trobec, D. (2010). *The Role of Intangible Assets in Exiting the Crisis*. Ljubljana: Časnik Finance: 117–130.

Bughin, J., Byers, H.A., and Chui, M. (2009). Using Technology to Turbocharge Innovation in a Downturn, McKinsey&Company, http://whatmatters.mckinseydigital.com/innovation/using-technology-to-turbocharge-innovation-in-a-downturn, Accessed May 2, 2011.

Burger, A., Jaklič, A., and Rojec, M. (2011). Poslovno *okolje za delovanje podjetij s tujim kapitalom v Sloveniji*. (Electronic bookseries Analize CMO, 7). Ljubljana: Fakulteta za družbene vede.

Calderon, C. and Didier, T. (2009). Severity of the crisis and its transmission channels, http://api.ning.com/files/18E7T4eYCsaDUED*PiP17ZGCAek6J3

aNUAiLdx1D5xT-L3tSOcCnWc0vsBiO10rhwJhl1E8n7sSoHxFWFnDRxBXFx VMZNAZS/SeverityoftheCrisis_Calderon_Didier_v2.pdf, Accessed January 29, 2012.

Chamber of Craft and Small Business of Slovenia. (2009). *Survey of Businesses in the First Half of 2009*, Ljubljana.

Cirman, A., Koman, M., Prašnikar, J., Valentinčič, A., and Voje, D. (2009). Slovenian exports in an economic crisis, in J. Prašnikar (Ed.) *How are Different Capitalist Systems Coping with the Current Crisis?* Ljubljana: Časnik Finance: 273–290.

Damijan, P.J. (2011). Izgubljena rast. *Objektiv*, 12(February): 14–15.

Delo FT (2009). Največje poslovne skupine, October: 20–21.

Domadenik, P., Czerny, B., Dobnikar, J., and Smolej, B. (2010b). Tangible investment in Slovene firms, in J. Prašnikar (Ed.) *The Role of Intangible Assets in Exiting the Crisis*, Ljubljana: 105–116.

Domadenik, P., Prašnikar, J., and Redek, T. (2010a). Intangible investment in Slovene firms in the 1990s, in J. Prašnikar (Ed.) *The Role of Intangible Assets in Exiting the Crisis*, Ljubljana: Časnik Finance: 79–94.

Economist Intelligence Unit. (2010). Eastern Europe Economy: Hitching its wagon to the Chinese. July 16.

Filipović, N. (2009). *Survey of Responses to Economic Crisis in Slovenian Companies* (internal report). IEDC – Bled School of Management.

Hill, H. and Jongwanich, J. (2009). Foreign direct investment and the financial crisis in developing East Asia, *Asian Development Review*, 26(2): 1–25.

Hymer, S.H. (1960). *The International Operations of National Firms: A Study of Direct Investment*, PhD Thesis, MIT Press.

Jaklič, A. and Svetličič, M. (2011). Multinationals from Slovenia – nano size, but giga important, in L. Brennan (Ed.) *The Emergence of Southern Multinationals*, Houndsmills: Palgrave Macmillan: 130–148.

Kalotay, K. and Filippov, S. (2009). The global crisis and FDI in new Europe, *Baltic Rim Economies*, 4: 32–33.

Kasahara, H. and Rodrigue, J. (2008). Does the use of imported intermediates increase productivity? Plant-level evidence, *Journal of Development Economics*, 87(1): 106–118.

Kline, M. (2009). Stare zvezde žarijo in nove se rojevajo, *Poslovni Dnevnik*, Ljubljana, 8(June): 27.

Kline, M. (2011). Kriza je močno spremenila lestvico, *Poslovni Dnevnik*, Ljubljana, 23 May: 18–19.

Kneževič, C.L., Koman, M., and Prašnikar, J. (2010). Productivity and ownership in Slovene firms, in J. Prašnikar (Ed.) *The Role of Intangible Assets in Exiting the Crisis*, Ljubljana: Časnik Finance: 95–104.

Kovač, S. (2011). Združenje manager je združenje svetih krav, *Finance*, 9(January): 14.

Lipnik, K. (2011). Škrjančkov let na Balkan je odpihnil petino kapitala, *Finance*, 29: 9.

Lowell, B. and Hulme, R. (2003). Managing for improved corporate performance, http://www.mckinseyquarterly.com/Organization/Strategic_Organization/Managing_for_improved_corporate_performance_1328, Accessed January 20, 2012.

Ložar, B. (2008). Slovenska podjetja nujno potrebujejo razvojni skok. http://www.zdruzenje-manager.si/storage/3197/BOSTJAN per cent20LOZAR.pdf, Accessed March 9, 2009.

Mrak, M., Rojec, M., and Silva-Jáuregui, C. (Eds.) (2004). *Slovenia: From Yugoslavia to the European Union*. Washington, DC: The World Bank.

OECD. (2011). *Economic Surveys of Slovenia*. February, Paris.

Petrov, S. (2009). Na Kitajski trg z najdražjimi izdelki, *Finance*, 26(164): 8.

Redek, T., Kopriva, G., Mihelič, N., and Simič, M. (2010). Investments in intangible Activities: Innovation in the Slovenian manufacturing sector, in J. Prašnikar (Ed.) *The Role of Intangible Assets in Exiting the Crisis*, Ljubljana: Časnik Finance: 149–160.

Repovž, E. (2009). Iskanje naložbenih možnosti, *DEO*, August 28.

Sauvant, K., Maschek, W.A., and McAllister, G. (2010). Foreign direct investment by emerging market multinational enterprises: The impact of the financial crisis and recession and challenges ahead, in K. Sauvant, G. McAllister, and W.A. Maschek (Eds.) *Foreign Direct Investment from Emerging Markets: The Challenges Ahead*, New York, NY: Palgrave Macmillan.

Simon, H. (2010). *Hidden Champions of the Twenty-First Century: Success Strategies of Unknown World Market Leaders*. Dordrecht; Heidelberg; London; New York, NY: Springer.

Skovgaard, L.P. and Hufbauer, G.C. (2011). *Foreign Direct Investment in Times of Crisis*. Working Paper 11–3, January, Peterson Institute of International Economics.

Smrekar, T. and Urbas, U. (2011). Dobiček Telekoma, ki je manjši od 100 milijonov, ni sprejemljiv, *Finance*, 31(February): 8–9.

Sovdat, P. and Toplak, S. (2009). Tako si lahko povrnete ugled, *Finance*. 11(December): 4.

Smrekar, T. and Weiss, M. (2011). Balkanska dilema: Oditi ali ostati, *Finance*, 2(January): 4.

SORS- Statistical Office of the Republic of Slovenia (2004). *Statistical Yearbook*, Ljubljana: SORS.

Sovdat, P. (2010). Grehi vredni 185 milijonov evrov, *Finance*, 3(December): 4.

Špacapan, O.B. (2010). Polletni rezultati mešano, *Kapital*, XX(503): 20–21.

Stergar, A. (2009). Podjetniki: Najhujše je mimo. *Delo*, 28(August): 11.

Stiglitz, J.E. (2010). Contagion, liberalisation, and optimal structure of globalization, *Journal of Globalisation and Development*, 1(2): 2.

Svenšek, K. (2011). Ukradeni milijono evrov, *Objektiv*, 12(February): 4–6.

Svetličič, M. (2007). Slovenian outward FDI, *Transnational Corporations*, 16(1): 55–81.

Svetličič, M. (2008). Reversed internationalisation path: The case of Slovenia, *AIB Insights*, 8(1): 3–9.

Svetličič, M., Rojec, M., and Lebar, S. (1994). Internationalisation strategies of Slovenian firms: The German market case, in K. Obloj (Ed.) *High Speed Competition in Europe*, Warsaw: University of Warsaw: 361–385.

Valentinčič, A., Marinšek, D., Mally, G.B., and Simoneti, N. (2010). Financial policies of manufacturing firms in Slovenia in 2006–2009, in J. Prašnikar (Ed.) *The Role of Intangible Assets in Exiting the Crisis*, Ljubljana: Časnik Finance: 131–140.

Varum, A. and Rocha, B.C.V. (2011). Do foreign and domestic firms behave any different during economic slowdowns? *International Business Review*, 20: 48–59.
Vuković, V. (2009). Tuš Bi Mercatorju Prodal Trgovske Centre Po Balkanu, *Poslovni Dnevnik*, Ljubljana, July 23.
Zupan, N., Farčnik, D., Fišer, J., Stančič, L.K., and Valenčič, G. (2010). Investment in people and organisational flexibility in Slovenian manufacturing firms in 2006–2009, in J. Prašnikar (Ed.) *The Role of Intangible Assets in Exiting the Crisis*, Ljubljana: Časnik Finance: 173–186.

12
Impact of the Global Crisis on the Internationalization of Estonian Firms: A Case Study

Tiia Vissak

Introduction

Although it is not possible to predict when economic crises may start and exactly how severe they will be, it is necessary to study their implications as they keep recurring (Caruana *et al.*, 2000; Grewal *et al.*, 2007). All firms face the impact of some economic crises, so, although it is not always possible to foresee them, it is important to be prepared (Dubrovski, 2007; Lee and Makhija, 2009) and to develop a clear strategy for dealing with them as companies without the ability to face economic difficulties due to crises may fail more frequently (Beaver and Ross, 2000; Grewal *et al.*, 2007).

The 2008/2009 global economic recession is believed to be the deepest since the 1930s and sometimes considered even more extreme. A crisis may be an important trigger for rebuilding a company and increasing its efficiency (Dubrovski, 2007) and thus, it can be seen as an opportunity, not an impediment (Beaver and Ross, 2000). Consequently, it is very important to study how the 2008/2009 economic crisis affected firms' international activities. This can help managers see a variety of approaches to preventing and alleviating the negative impacts of future crises or even to growing the business under such circumstances.

Although several articles on crisis-prevention and fighting measures and the impacts of economic slowdown on firms had been written already prior to the 2008/2009 crisis, there is still a need to study the situation, its consequences, and implications for managers from the perspective of a country experiencing a considerable recession (Latham, 2009). Moreover, it is necessary to study how an economic crisis affects internationalization because, according to some studies, internationalized firms may be affected considerably (Beaver and Ross, 2000; Hadjikhani and Johanson, 2000) while some others believe that crises may result in internationalization (Caruana *et al.*, 2000; Wennberg and Holmquist, 2008). The need to study this topic is especially evident in Estonia: In 2009, Estonia's GDP (in current prices) declined by 15.12 per cent and exports by 23.31 per cent compared with 2008. In 2010 they increased by 3.36 per cent and 34.00 per cent, respectively, while in 2011, GDP growth was approximately 8 per cent.

This chapter aims to investigate some positive and negative consequences of the economic recession on the international activities of four Estonian case companies. It starts with a literature review of the impacts of economic crises on firms' local and international activities. As the studies on the impacts of the 2008/2009 economic slowdown have not been extensively published yet, the chapter investigates what has been studied before. After a methodology section, case study evidence from four Estonian enterprises—two home textiles producers (Wendre and Krenholm) and two firms from the casino industry (Playtech Estonia and Olympic Entertainment Group)—is presented. Attention is paid to their actions and future plans, and also to other internal and external factors that led to their current situations. After presenting the case study evidence, the results are discussed. The chapter ends with managerial suggestions and future research implications.

Literature review

Economic crises are usually accompanied by a decrease in demand for products, services, or raw materials (Shama, 1993), and they may result in permanent changes in customer behavior (Latham and Braun, 2010). Firms do not suffer equally from an economic crisis: some may remain stable or even grow (Shama, 1993; Simon, 2010). It has also been noted that during crises, companies active in the same declining industry have different levels of success: some fail but some succeed (Dubrovski, 2007). The effect of a crisis may depend on a firm's age and activities. Latham (2009) suggests that younger firms fail more often than established ones. Beaver and Ross (2000) conclude that exporters and manufacturers are affected faster. Latham and Braun (2010), in turn, show that companies offering lower-cost products grow during crises while Simon (2010), Teece *et al.* (1997), Wu (2010), and Weerawardena *et al.* (2007) demonstrate that firms' success or failure may depend on the uniqueness and value of their resources and, especially, dynamic capabilities. The latter have been defined as 'the firm's ability to integrate, build, and reconfigure internal and external competences to address rapidly changing environments' (Teece *et al.*, 1997: 516).

Several studies have also shown how economic crises affect internationalization. Some authors have stated that de-internationalization—reducing operations or withdrawing completely from a specific market or switching to entry modes with smaller resource commitment (Calof and Beamish, 1995; Benito and Welch, 1997)—may occur as a result of radical changes in economic policies and industry conditions (Akhter and Choudry, 1993; Spence and Crick, 2009), increased perception of uncertainty (Figueira-de-Lemos *et al.*, 2011), and changes in advantages and disadvantages of operating abroad (Cuervo-Cazurra *et al.*, 2007) that often accompany economic crises. De-internationalization may later be followed by re-internationalization: Successfully renewed international operations (Welch and Welch, 2009).

It has also been stated that firms may internationalize much faster if their market conditions are stable (Johanson and Vahlne, 1990; Rhee and Cheng, 2002); thus, unstable market conditions may hinder internationalization as firms cannot fully use their previously acquired experiential knowledge (Hadjikhani and Johanson, 2000) and as it is not easy to react to changes in uncertain situations due to not understanding their causes (Figueira-de-Lemos *et al.*, 2011). In addition, economic slowdowns may reduce firms' ability to invest abroad (Buckley *et al.*, 2008). Moreover, economic crises may weaken network relationships (Grewal *et al.*, 2007), reduce trust between partners, and lead to lower expectations of foreign markets (Hadjikhani and Johanson, 2000).

It has also been shown that experiential knowledge can help an international firm during a crisis, and foreign ownership can be helpful, especially if the subsidiary remains relatively autonomous (Wang *et al.*, 2005). According to Teece *et al.* (1997), firms' global success also depends on their timely responsiveness, innovation speed, and management capabilities. Moreover, firms demanding less capital—like those active in services—may internationalize faster (Rhee and Cheng, 2002) and companies performing below expectations due to the economic crisis in the home market may also be interested more in internationalizing, especially in entering still growing markets (Caruana *et al.*, 2000; Wennberg and Holmquist, 2008).

From the above, it can be concluded that economic crises may hinder firms' local and international activities—even cause partial or full de-internationalization—but may also offer new opportunities. Some firms will speed up their internationalization and some (re)start it.

Methodology and case study evidence

The case study method was chosen as it enables one to conduct research in countries with a sample base too small for using statistical generalization (Chetty, 1996), investigating phenomena within their real-life contexts, combining previously developed theories with new empirical results, and developing new and empirically valid theoretical and practical insights (Eisenhardt, 1989; Ghauri, 2004; Gummesson, 2006; Yin, 1994). Moreover, Dooley *et al.* (2010), Grewal *et al.* (2007), and Hadjikhani and Johanson (2000) have emphasized the need for conducting case studies to assess the effects of dramatic economic changes and analyzing successful and unsuccessful firms' strategies and tactics during economic recession.

According to Eisenhardt (1989), there is no ideal number of cases in the case study approach, but a study of 4–10 cases should work well. Otherwise it is difficult to generate theory or cope with the volume of data. This chapter is based on four cases from two sectors. It was decided to select one traditional sector (home textile production) and one new segment of the service sector (the casino industry) to increase the generalizability of the results. Two firms were selected from each sector: In both cases, one company that had been growing successfully and another that faced serious problems.

The case stories were based on interview materials, annual reports, the case firms' homepages, business papers, and other publicly available data. As a company's ability to react to an economic crisis depends on its current strategies, and also on its earlier history, both aspects were studied. In the case of Playtech Estonia, its parent corporation's strategies were also investigated as this firm is strongly dependent on its parent, its only direct customer.

A home textiles company, Wendre (currently belonging to Peter Hunt through a Swedish firm Trade House Scandinavia AB), is one of Europe's largest bedding manufacturers. It mainly produces pillows and blankets, but also mattresses and bedspreads. Peter Hunt started co-operating with Wendre after its privatization to VELY&Co in 1993. In that year, the production of blankets and pillows started (before, it had produced carpets). Hunt began delivering fabrics and synthetic fibers after and selling the company's products in the West as the Soviet market had disappeared and the local market was too small. In 1996, Trading House Scandinavia AB acquired 26 per cent of Wendre. By 1999 (then the firm's turnover was €8.8 million), its share had increased to 67 per cent and by March 2002 to 100 per cent.

In 1998–2003, Wendre acquired four Swedish producers that were later merged with Wendre Scandinavia AB. As part of the Swedish concern, the enterprise achieved easier access to several European countries (receiving the ISO 9001 certificate in 2000, ÖKO-TEX 100 in 2003 and the ISO 14001 in 2005 was also helpful), but it has also exported to the US, Canada, Brazil, Colombia, Japan, China, Malaysia, and the United Arab Emirates (for export data, see Figure 12.1). In 2005, Wendre launched another plant in Estonia and, thereafter, its turnover doubled. In 2006, it established a joint venture Wenfom with an Austrian company Eurofoam GmbH to cut and treat foam and foam boards in Estonia (to produce foam-filled chair cushions) and acquired a plant in Poland. During the period 2006–2007, Wendre managed to increase its turnover from €44.0 to €62.9, net profits from €3.9 to €5.5 million and the number of employees in Estonia from 596 to 648. In 2008, the firm's turnover was €65.1 and net profits €5.5 million and it had 735 employees.

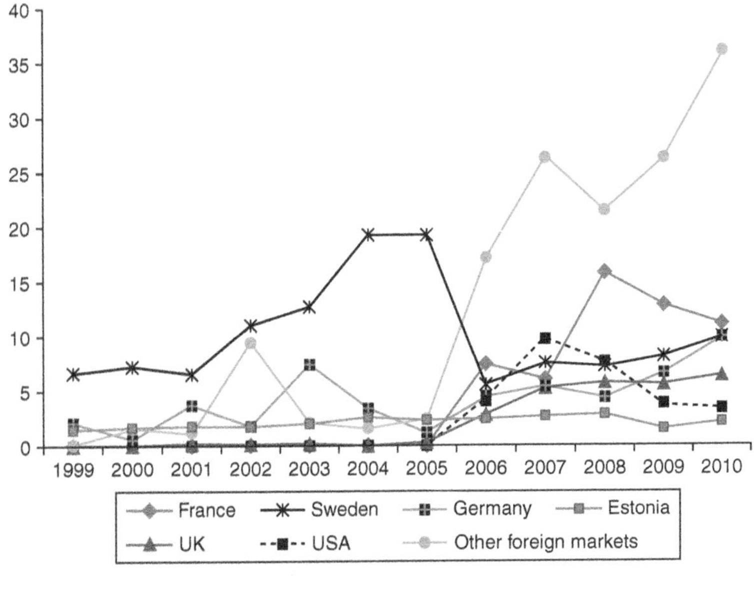

Figure 12.1 Wendre's turnover from selected markets (€ millions)

In 2009, its turnover fell to €64.8, net profit to €3.3 million and the number of employees to 656. In total, Wendre exported 97.6 per cent of its turnover. For 2010, a turnover of €70.3 million was expected (but reached €76.31 million) and export share remained almost the same (97.2 per cent) despite the increasing cotton and polyester prices. The number of employees increased to 744. The company announced its plans to invest considerably and double its turnover in the near future. In 2010, Peter Hunt was nominated Estonia's Entrepreneur of the Year and the firm received the title Exporter of the Year. Wendre had not suffered losses for 15 consecutive years. In 2011, the firm's turnover already reached €100 million and it expected growth for 2012 due to entering the furniture industry segment.

Peter Hunt and Wendre's CEO Vahur Roosaar stated that the owner's clear vision, ambitions (to become Europe's best home textile producer through flexibility, focusing on continuous education and innovation) and readiness to invest, generate ideas and to take risks have brought success. Moreover, the firm has been oriented at finding long-term and loyal co-operation partners and it has participated actively in trade fairs. In 2012, it plans to invest up to €1 million in its sales personnel's foreign visits and to developing its sales offices. The concern's subsidiaries in Sweden, China, Poland, and Germany form a strong supply chain; the owner has invested considerably in optimizing it, and also in increasing production efficiency, decreasing delivery times, and improving product quality (Wendre tests raw materials in Europe's largest independent labs). Wendre has also created a strong team of leaders and paid considerable attention to co-operation within the firm: Organized workshops and seminars for its employees so that they are informed of Wendre's current position and future plans and are motivated to work well. Moreover, its management periodically reviews employees' suggestions that could raise the company's efficiency (it has been the owner's strategy to earn €0.06 per blanket and sell a million blankets than earn €0.60 per blanket and sell 100) and make its working environment more pleasant. The firm is also very flexible in reacting to market environment changes.

Although the economic crisis affected several enterprises seriously, V. Roosaar has stated that it may be good in a long-term perspective as resources will be used more efficiently than during the past economic boom. Naturally, increasing profits became harder as customers asked for lower prices. Moreover, getting credit became more difficult and expensive and some suppliers started demanding advance payments. Still, Wendre managed to acquire a new plant in Estonia in April 2009 (it was launched in November; it employed 70 people and started producing folding beds) and it plans to develop new product groups, expand to Southern Europe and become listed at the stock exchange in the near future.

Krenholm did not manage to survive the 2008/2009 crisis as successfully as Wendre, but it also had a longer history and thus, more problems to cope with in the 1990s. From its foundation in 1857 until Estonia's independence in 1918, the firm sold textiles in the Russian Empire and China. In the 1920s, Krenholm concentrated on Scandinavia and Western Europe. After the second world war, its production was diverted mainly to the Soviet market, but it also exported (mostly to the Eastern Bloc). It had 13,000 employees. When Estonia regained independence and the former Soviet market collapsed because of low prices, unstable demand, high Russian import tariffs, the lack of an investment protection treaty, and lost contacts, Krenholm had to find new export markets again. In the 1990s, the shares of different markets changed considerably. In 2007, the firm ended exporting to the US. After that, it mainly concentrated on Sweden, Finland, and the three Baltic States (see Figure 12.2).

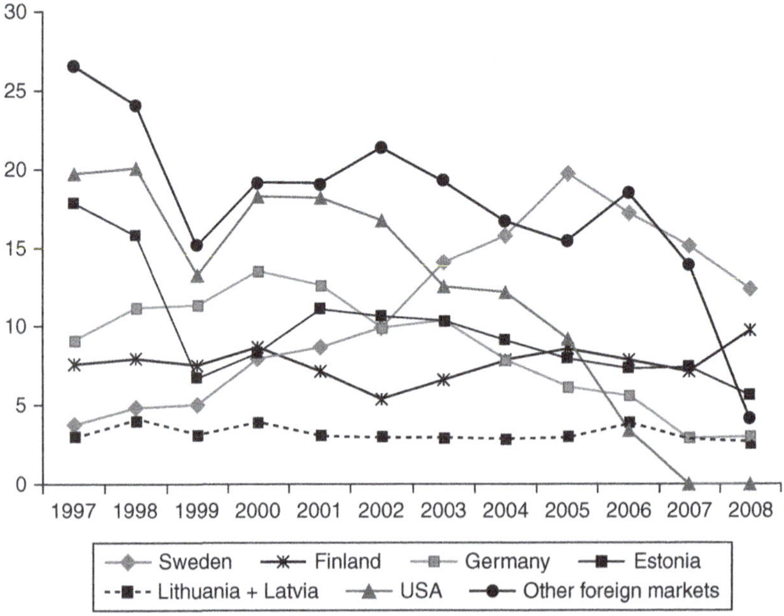

Figure 12.2 Krenholm's turnover from selected markets (€ millions)

Krenholm's turnover was €45.1 million in 1995, increased to €80.1 million in 1998 and fell to €49.6 million in 2007 and €37.6 million in 2008 while the number of employees fell to about 500. In 2008, it had a loss of approximately €6.4 million. In 2009, decline continued: The parent company had a loss of €4.40 million (a year earlier, €9.02 million) and its turnover decreased from €41.61 to €25.35 million (Krenholm's annual report for 2009 was not submitted to the Commercial Register). In the first half of 2010, the firm's turnover was €8.52 and net loss €2.42 million. It filed for bankruptcy in November 2010 as it could not cope with increased cotton prices and decreased demand. In September 2011, a new company—New Krenholm Holding—was created. They promised to rent a plant on Krenholm's previous production site, buy some Krenholm's finishing machines and start exporting to Scandinavia, Latvia, Lithuania, and Russia. However, these plans did not realize as they could not raise enough capital.

Several factors caused the big 'jumps' in the firm's development. The previous production system was not efficient any more. Estonia developed, and salaries increased much faster than the owners (since 1994, Borås Wäfveri AB from Sweden) had initially predicted. To achieve salary increases, Krenholm's strong trade union threatened with strikes. The firm also had to cope with Asian and Russian crises before the 2008/2009 crisis, and also with increasing cotton, water, and electricity prices and large fluctuations of the US dollar exchange rate as it bought most of its cotton in US dollar. Moreover, free trade agreements between the EU and its partners in the US in the beginning of the millennium and the opening up of the global textiles market in 2005 worsened its situation. As Krenholm could not compete with Asian low-cost producers, it had to concentrate on small, less profitable orders. Moreover, its customers demanded lower prices, not higher quality or shorter delivery times. Thus, Krenholm's turnover decreased and it was not profitable for several years.

In addition to the above, the firm's managers and owners did not react quickly enough to the changing economic environment. Only in 2005, they started producing wider fabrics; in 2006, opened a design house and in 2007, started ordering subcontracting from Asia. Also, they did not reduce the number of employees fast enough, did not close weaving and spinning departments until June 2008 (after that, they concentrated on sewing and finishing), did not renew all machinery (some were more than 50 years old), could not react to the US dollar exchange rate fluctuations fast enough and did not pay sufficient attention to marketing. Moreover, according to one of its previous

CEOs, Krenholm paid too much over the market price for raw materials, ordered subcontracting from other firms despite not fully using its own production capacity and sold some textiles for prices below production costs. Although Borås Wäfveri paid some of Krenholm's debts, invested in some machinery, brought know-how and helped the firm to get quality certificates (ISO 14001, ISO 9001, ÖKO-TEX, Nordic Swan and EU-Flower), opened an e-shop and tried to find strategic investors, Krenholm's financial indicators did not improve.

Playtech Estonia was established in 2001 in Tartu and its activities started in the autumn of 2002. It is one of Estonia's largest software developers. It has been growing fast (for export figures, equal to turnover, see Figure 12.3). It belongs fully to Playtech Software Ltd.: The world's largest publicly traded online gaming software supplier, established in 1999. The parent firm was registered in Cyprus because of a favorable tax environment. In 2002, it was incorporated in the British Virgin Islands as an offshore company with limited liability and then it moved to the Isle of Man that has a 0 per cent corporate tax rate

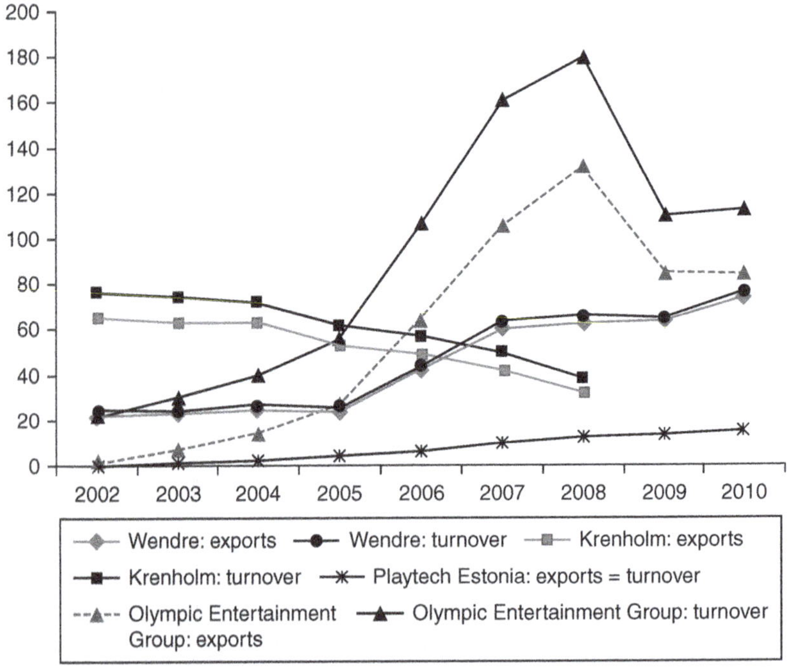

Figure 12.3 The exports and turnover of Wendre, Krenholm, Playtech Estonia, and OEG (€ millions)

(as subsidiaries are taxed according to their home countries' laws, the corporation's total effective tax rate was 2.1 per cent in 2010), while the marketing and advertising unit was located in Israel and the managing unit on the Isle of Man.

Playtech Software Ltd. designs, develops and manufactures software in different languages for online (internet casinos, poker rooms, and bingo sites; its service IPoker offers services to more than 30,000 players simultaneously) and land-based gaming and sports betting companies and mobile operators from Europe, Asia, the US. In total, it offers more than 500 games. Its unit in Tartu, Estonia, is the group's largest development center. All casino products are developed there. This unit is also responsible for quality assurance and product delivery. In 2011, Playtech Software Ltd. had 518 employees in Estonia and almost 600 in other countries including Israel, Bulgaria, the Isle of Man, and the UK.

Playtech Estonia hired its first employees in 2002. By the end of that year, their number increased to 52 and the company's turnover was €0.27 million. In 2004, the firm's turnover was already €2.63 million. By 2005, the number of employees increased to 200. In 2007, Playtech Estonia's turnover was €9.41 million and a year later €12.25 million (its only customer was the mother company; in 2007, its turnover was €65.7 million and in 2008 €111.5 million and net profit €40.7 million). In 2009, Playtech Software Ltd's total revenue was €114.8 million (Playtech Estonia's turnover increased to €14.04 million) and a year later it reached €142.3 million (Playtech Estonia's turnover was €15.83 million).

In 2009, Playtech Estonia opened a new development center in Tallinn, Estonia, with 15 employees (there, the mother company already had a daughter company Videobet with 90 employees; Playtech Estonia launched it in 2006, but it soon became its mother company's subsidiary; it develops software for fixed odds betting terminals and casino machines). By 2010, the unit's number of employees increased to 50.

The mother company focuses on forming stable customer relationships and co-operating with customers in developing new solutions. It tries to guarantee higher quality and flexibility than Asian low-cost competitors. It recognizes that its employees are its largest asset and tries to foster their co-operation. Playtech Estonia provides benefits for its employees: Offers training, supports their sports and other activities, pays for some dental care, home internet and even some vacation travel and it has special relaxation rooms. Most of its employees are also the mother firm's shareholders. To find new employees, the company grants scholarships to students of Tartu Art College and the University of Tartu.

The firm's salaries have been above the Estonian average and they are increasing. During the Estonian economic crisis, the firm retained all employee benefits.

According to the former CEO of Playtech Estonia, the strength of this firm is its ability to react fast to the changes in the outside environment, while at the same time, keeping management stable. Although the non-executive chairman of Playtech Software Ltd. Roger Withers stated that he was aware of the current global economic conditions and understood that no industry is escaping the effects of the slowdown, he promised that the group's market-leading position and diversified business model should ensure that its financial performance will remain sound. Moreover, the company will continue following its strategy of organic and acquisitive growth and plans to take full advantage of emerging opportunities. It will enter new markets, launch new products and make new acquisitions.

Olympic Entertainment Group (OEG) faced serious problems during the economic crisis. It opened its first casino in Estonia at Tallinn Olympic Yachting Centre in 1993. Currently it has casinos in Estonia, Latvia, Lithuania, Belarus, Poland, and Slovakia. This region was selected as its gambling market grew faster than that of any other region in the world. The firm's growth was relatively smooth at first, so it even did not have to take considerable loans and this made the firm's situation easier compared to some competitors. In 1997, it renovated Kungla Hotel in Tallinn into Baltic countries' first casino hotel. In 2001 the first foreign market—Lithuania—was entered and in 2002 Latvia followed. In 2004, OEG expanded to Ukraine and in 2006 to Belarus. In 2007 it entered Poland and Romania while Slovakia's turn came in 2008 (see Figure 12.4). Then, the firm's new vision was formulated: To be a global casino and resort operator with a passion for service excellence. In the third quarter of 2011, it had 1997 employees (about 21.7 per cent of them in Estonia) and 63 casinos. The firm's shares are listed in the main list of securities of the Tallinn Stock Exchange.

In 2007, the company reported a net profit of €23.4 million, but in 2008, it had a net loss of €29.2 and in 2009—€22.1 million. In 2008, the firm's turnover increased from €159.0 to €178.2 million (73.5 per cent of it came from abroad: 23.4 per cent from Latvia, 19.6 per cent from Poland, 14.8 per cent from Lithuania, 11.9 per cent from Ukraine, 1.4 per cent from Romania, 1.2 per cent from Slovakia, and 1.2 per cent from Belarus) and its market shares increased from 51 to 54 per cent in Lithuania, from 42 to 45 per cent in Estonia, and from 15 to 16 per cent in Latvia. In the fourth quarter of 2008, the Baltic gaming

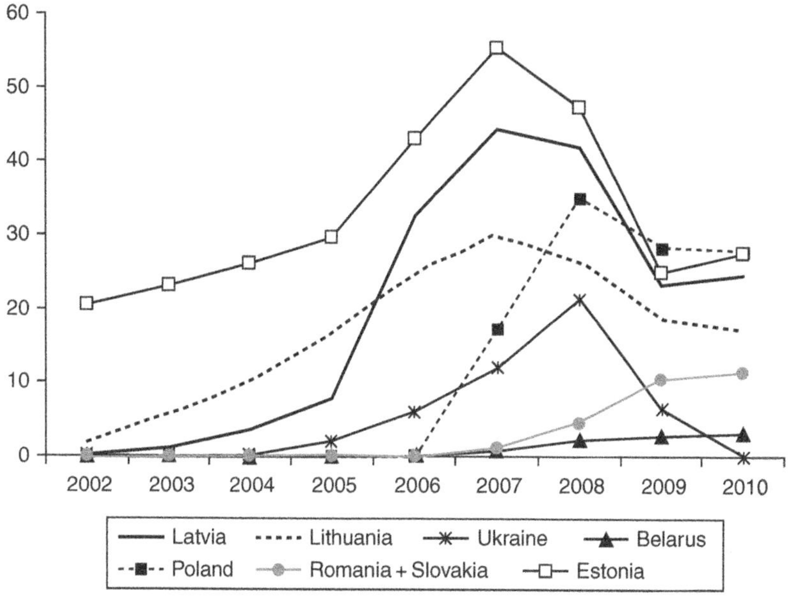

Figure 12.4 The turnover of OEG from selected markets (€ millions)

market contracted by 20 per cent and the Estonian market by 30 per cent. In 2009, Estonia's gaming market fell further by 52 per cent, Latvia's by 33 per cent and Lithuania's by 39 per cent. In 2009, the firm's turnover was only €108.8 million and it had a net loss of €21.5 million. Such losses and decreases in turnover can be partly explained by the weakening on the Polish, Ukrainian, and Romanian currencies toward the Euro (thus, OEG had to re-assess several investments), by the obligation of casino customers to register themselves in Lithuania and Estonia, smoking bans in these countries' casinos and also because the firm had to end activities in Ukraine as casinos were banned there (24 casinos were closed down and the firm lost approximately €11.6 million). In 2010, the turnover increased to €112.5 million and it managed to earn a net profit of €3.1 million. In January–September 2011, the turnover was €93.2 million.

To cope with challenges, OEG implemented an extensive efficiency program in 2008. It closed ten casinos with negative cash flows (but opened 21 new ones and renovated 15) and reduced the number of employees by 288 (by about seven per cent). In 2009, due to a large net loss, the group's salaries were reduced by 20 per cent and OEG closed down more casinos (in the end of 2009 it had 68 casinos while exactly a year earlier—131) and again reduced the number of employees. In 2008–2009, the number of employees was reduced by 1600, in total: about 40 per cent of its workforce. In 2010, OEG's salary costs decreased further by 11.5 per cent and the number of employees was reduced by 230. To cut costs, OEG also reduced the number of slot machines in 2009 (this decreased fixed costs as the gambling tax depends on the number of slot machines; in 2008, the firm's total gaming tax expenses were €30.9 and in 2009—€25.0 million; in 2010, the number of slot machines was slightly increased again and this resulted in gaming tax expenses of €25.5 million) and also shortened some casinos' opening times (before, all operated 24 hours a day). Due to the economic crisis, it also managed to save from rental costs (in 2008, the total rental costs were €20.0 million while in 2009 €14.5 million and in 2010, €10.8 million only) as it reached new agreements with the owners of some premises and some decreased the rent even by 50 per cent. OEG also saved some rental costs because it closed down some of the casinos. Marketing costs were reduced from €14.1 to €8.1 million in 2009 but increased to €9.5 million in 2010. In total, in 2009, OEG saved €42.2 million and in 2010, €21.0 million. Still, its market shares reached 53 per cent in Estonia, 68 per cent in Lithuania, and 20 per cent in Latvia.

The increases in market shares resulted from the firm's efforts to attract more customers: It transformed its casinos to casino lounges—increased the floor area for customers who wished to spend their leisure time without gaming, offered them free wireless internet and newspapers, organized events and campaigns and increased the variety of drinks and food in its bars. Although it closed down several casinos, it opened its second casino in Slovakia and new casinos in Poland, Romania, and Lithuania in 2009, and in 2010 the third casino was opened in Slovakia. In 2011, OEG sold both of its Romanian casinos and closed down one in Poland, but opened one in Slovakia and one in Lithuania. It also continued supporting employee training to retain high service quality. Moreover, as Russia decided to close down most of its casinos (except in four regions) in July 2009, the firm's casinos started attracting Russian tourists. OEG also participated in a tourism fair in China for introducing its casinos to Asian players and these tourists' share has already increased in its Polish casinos. It has also not excluded the possibility to re-enter Ukraine again if laws become more favorable. It also entered the internet casino segment in February 2010 in co-operation with Playtech and made its services available both in Estonia and abroad (before it was not possible as this area was not clearly regulated by Estonian laws and the firm was afraid that offering such services could threaten its other investments). As a result, it earned €1.3 million from these services in 2010.

OEG's managers have remained relatively optimistic: They expect that after the crisis, the company's turnover may increase considerably; not only because of its own changes for getting more customers, but also because of the close-down of some competitors as this has already increased the firm's market shares in all countries. In the future, OEG may also consider entering some countries' lottery market.

Discussion

According to Latham (2009) and Dooley *et al.* (2010) firms do not react to the recession similarly: Some respond rapidly and thus adapt better to the changed economic state, while some are too late and have to take more drastic measures. In principle, to survive during an economic crisis or even grow, companies have to decrease costs and/or increase revenues (Latham and Braun, 2010). Latham (2009) has stated that larger and older companies tend to prefer the former while smaller and younger firms the latter. Grewal *et al.* (2007) warned against excessive cost reduction as this could lead to lack of resources and harm firms' ability to react to the crisis. It is also possible to reduce assets—for example, sell equipment, a business line or a factory (Sudarsanam and Lai, 2001)—especially if the firm is near bankruptcy (Hofer, 1980) or is operating below capacity (Sudarsanam and Lai, 2001). This may help to achieve both cost reduction and temporary revenue increase. Some measures are introduced in Table 12.1.

The four case firms used different methods to cope with their problems: For example, they invested in new technologies and production techniques, decreased delivery times, moved some activities to lower-cost countries and paid attention to improving their working environments (see Table 12.2).

It can be said that two firms were more successful than others: While Wendre and Playtech Estonia continued growing, Krenholm and OEG (although active in the same sectors: Home textiles and the casino industry, respectively) had to reduce their number of employees considerably and close down some activities.

Krenholm went bankrupt in the autumn of 2010. Its problems were caused by several factors: Not only by its economic environment but also by its recent actions and previous development. It did not manage

Table 12.1 Actions for developing the firm and coping with the challenges of an economic crisis

The goal	Actions
Becoming more prepared (Beaver and Ross, 2000; Grewal *et al.*, 2007)	• Monitoring debt and finances • Minimizing risks in stock and credit management (using longer-term financing) • Examining business forecasts carefully • Building reserves • Taking care of important relationships with main buyers and suppliers • Trying to get a clear picture what is happening in the firm
Decreasing costs	• Reducing shipping, receiving or inventory procedure costs (Tuttle, 2003) • Dropping less successful products (Beaver and Ross, 2000) • Using outsourcing (Tuttle, 2003) • Decreasing labor costs through franchising, staff redundancy, two-tier wage rates, contracting out labor, using part-time and temporary employees (Alamdari, 1998; Schuler and Jackson, 1989) • Moving production to a low-cost country (Lee and Makhija, 2009)
Increasing revenues	• Becoming more flexible (Lee *et al.*, 2009) and faster than low-cost producers (Tuttle, 2003) • Improving design (Wang and Gupta, 2003) • Improving product quality (Tuttle, 2003) • Increasing promotion costs (Shama, 1993) • Providing additional services, such as benchmarking and training (Tuttle, 2003) • Creating strategic alliances with domestic and foreign firms—for example, with those offering complementary products or services (Wang and Gupta, 2003) • Increasing productivity through profit sharing, increased flexibility in work hours, facilitating innovation, letting employees to participate more in running their firm (Alamdari, 1998; Schuler and Jackson, 1989) and offering them incentives for innovation (Wang and Gupta, 2003).
Reducing assets (Sudarsanam and Lai, 2001)	• Selling equipment • Selling a business line • Selling a factory
Other methods (with mixed effects)	• Investing in R&D (Lee *et al.*, 2009; Lee and Makhija, 2009) • Making changes in top management (Sudarsanam and Lai, 2001) • Trying to get assistance—for example, export support—from governmental agencies (Caruana *et al.*, 2000) • Entering new business segments (Hofer, 1980)

Table 12.2 Actions taken by the four case firms

Firm	Actions
Wendre	• Expanding both in- and outside Europe • Exporting, but also establishing foreign subsidiaries • Participating actively in trade fairs • Co-operating with other firms belonging to the corporation • Fostering co-operation within and outside the firm • Having a clear and ambitious vision of its future • Investing in increasing flexibility, production efficiency and quality, developing new products, decreasing delivery times and optimizing the supply chain • Paying attention to long-term and loyal co-operation partnerships • Finding new production possibilities • Creating a strong experienced team of leaders • Increasing employee motivation • Reducing the number of employees
Krenholm (now bankrupt)	• Exporting to several European countries (drew back from the USA) and having sales subsidiaries in some of them • Ordering subcontracting from Asia (since 2007) • Concentrating on smaller orders • Increasing quality, improving design, and shortening delivery times • Closing down weaving and spinning departments • Reducing the number of employees • Opening an e-shop
Playtech Estonia	• Concentrating on its only direct customer: The mother corporation, but through it, exporting to Europe, Asia, and the US • Creating a favorable working environment • Fostering co-operation within the firm • Offering more benefits for long-term employees • Offering stock options for employees • Co-operating with educational institutions for getting new employees (offering scholarships for students) • Concentrating on higher quality and flexibility • Reacting fast to the changes in the outside environment • Keeping management stable • Launching new products
OEG	• Step-by step expansion to Central and Eastern Europe • Concentrating on fast-growing markets • Attracting more customers from Russia and other foreign countries • Closing down casinos with negative cash flows • Reducing the number of employees

Table 12.2 (Continued)

Firm	Actions
	• Reducing salaries • Reducing the number of slot machines (during the crisis, later increasing it) • Shortening some casinos' opening times • Saving from rental costs • Saving from marketing costs (during the crisis, later increasing them) • Transforming casinos to casino lounges • Investing into employee training and increasing its service quality • Entering additional market segments: internet casinos (in 2010) etc.

to react to the crisis quickly enough and it became more oriented at cutting costs rather than increasing revenues (although it also paid some attention to that: invested in some new technology and product design and tried to pay more attention to marketing). It also sold assets, including real estate and equipment. This firm was relatively slow at its restructuring in the 1990s: It could not foresee the changes in the overall business environment (like the opening up of the world textile trade, decreasing textile prices and increasing salaries and cotton prices) and thus, did not earn profit for several consecutive years. Frequent reductions in the number of employees had a negative impact on employee motivation. Several changes in the firm's top management did not result in considerable positive changes, either.

Wendre was more successful than Krenholm despite operating in the same sector and having almost the same size. It was more active in expanding its activities and entering foreign countries (in Europe and outside it, both through exporting and establishing joint ventures and foreign subsidiaries); moreover, its owner has a clear and ambitious vision of the firm's future development. The firm was more oriented at increasing revenues than decreasing costs although it also paid attention to the latter: For example, increased its production efficiency. Wendre invested considerably in new technology and paid attention to developing its human capital: It was active in increasing employee motivation and fostering co-operation in- and outside the firm: Between employees, with the owner's other enterprises, and also with other foreign suppliers and customers. As a result, its turnover did not drop considerably during the crisis and started increasing soon after: Moreover, it continued earning a profit. Still, changes in individual markets were relatively substantial: So, it experienced partial de- and re-internationalization.

OEG also faced serious problems: Its turnover decreased and share price fell during the crisis. The crisis reduced demand for its services and the changes in the regulatory environment—like smoking bans in casinos, the requirement to register customers, and a casino ban in Ukraine—worsened its situation further. As a result, the company had to cut down costs considerably: It reduced the number of casinos, slot machines and employees, shortened opening times, and reduced salaries during the crisis even after end of the slowdown in 2010 (then, only marketing costs and the number of slot machines were increased slightly). Still, the firm also tried to find new revenue sources: Rebuilt its casinos to casino lounges to attract more customers, attracted foreign tourists; entered the online games market in 2010 and has considered entering the lottery market in the future. Thus, although in 2009 its situation was problematic, the firm's situation started improving again in 2010 and it may become even more successful in the future.

Playtech Estonia has managed to grow despite the economic crisis. Its parent company is its only customer (the software is sold to others but the Estonian company does not have to do it itself) and it has managed to keep expanding fast, so Playtech Estonia has not felt the need to formulate a very clear strategy for coping with the effects of the crisis. Thus, its main focus is rather on increasing revenues, not cutting costs. Playtech Estonia has paid considerable attention to co-operation in and outside the firm, has tried to keep its management stable and focused on developing a favorable working environment. This has increased employee motivation and this, in turn, is very important for any company that is highly dependent on human capital.

From the above we can conclude that two firms continued growing despite the economic crisis, while the two others—although operating in the same sectors—had serious problems. Still, it cannot be said that certain actions would guarantee large and instant success to any firm: For instance, all four firms paid attention to cutting costs and increasing revenues, just the proportion of using these strategies differed: Krenholm and OEG paid more attention to the former, while Wendre and Playtech Estonia to the latter. So, there is some support to the conclusion of Grewal *et al.* (2007) that excessive cost reduction may reduce firms' crisis response possibilities.

We should also note that the overall economic environment has not been exactly the same for these firms: Although Krenholm and Wendre were both active in home textiles production, Krenholm was affected more by decreasing prices as its production segment was more vulnerable. Both Playtech Estonia and OEG are active in the casino industry; but Playtech does not have its own casinos, so it has not been affected by the same regulations. The success of Wendre and Playtech Estonia can be also partially explained by having strong and helpful (foreign) owners with a clear future vision. Although Krenholm was fully foreign-owned and OEG has both local and foreign owners (as portfolio investors), they received less assistance from them than the two more successful firms.

Conclusions and implications

The 2008/2009 economic crisis did not affect all enterprises similarly and such effects depended not just on outside factors (like decreasing demand in some sectors): Managers' actions also played an important role. As a result, two case enterprises—Wendre and Playtech Estonia—managed to continue growing, while the two others—Krenholm and OEG—faced problems despite being active in the same sectors as Wendre and Playtech Estonia. Still, the impact of the economic environment cannot be underestimated: The two more successful firms were not affected as strongly as the two less successful firms.

There are several ways for dealing with an economic crisis and even benefiting in the future: For instance, moving some activities to lower-cost countries, focusing on other countries and customer segments and co-operating more with local and foreign enterprises. Some firms have also made other changes: Increased their products' value-added, modernized technology and reduced delivery times, while some have paid considerable attention to improving their working environment and increasing employee motivation. Some of these methods could be also recommended to other companies. Still, it must be taken into account that these solutions are not universal (the success of a certain strategy also depends on other factors: For example, the specific conditions of the industry segment where the firm is operating—how important the price is for customers, where the lower-cost competitors are located, how good are their products and services, how quickly they can respond to customers' needs and so on) and the fact that the solutions depend also on the situation on each of its markets (the economic crisis does not affect each of them equally). So, before making any changes, the firm's and industry's situation and also the overall economic environment should be analyzed very thoroughly. Every firm should try to develop its unique crisis-prevention and fighting strategy rather than copy others.

Future research could develop in several directions. For example, it could study how the case firms will develop in the future on each of their markets. Also, more firms should be involved, especially those that ceased their local or international activities because of the crisis and those that managed to continue growing after radical changes: By reorganizing their production processes, concentrating on new markets or market segments, introducing new product lines or moving to completely new industries. In larger countries, some other data sources—for example, surveys and databases—could be also used as this increases generalizability. Then, it should become clear which methods are more efficient for coping with economic slowdowns. Further we will be able to understand how using or not using them affects firms in the short and long run, and if these effects differ in more and less advanced, small and large countries/companies and if the difference depends upon industries and industrial segments. Thus, a more longitudinal approach could be taken. This should help to make predictions and it must result in more detailed managerial advice.

Acknowledgment

The research was financed by the Estonian Science Foundation's Grant (No. 8546) and target financing of the Estonian Ministry of Education and Research (No. 0180037s08).

References

Akhter, S.H. and Choudry, Y.A. (1993). Forced withdrawal from a country market managing political risk, *Business Horizons*, 36(3): 47–54.

Alamdari, F. (1998). Trends in airline labor productivity and cost in Europe, *Journal of Air Transportation World Wide*, 3(1): 71–88.

Beaver, G. and Ross, C. (2000). Enterprise in recession: The role and context of strategy, *International Journal of Entrepreneurship and Innovation*, 1(1): 23–31.

Benito, G.R.G. and Welch, L.S. (1997). De-internationalisation, *Management International Review*, 37(Special Issue 2): 7–25.

Buckley, P.J., Cross, A.R., Tan, H., Xin, L., and Voss, H. (2008). Historic and emergent trends in Chinese outward direct investment, *Management International Review*, 48(6): 715–748.

Calof, J.L. and Beamish, P.W. (1995). Adapting to foreign markets: Explaining internationalisation, *International Business Review*, 4(2): 115–131.

Caruana, A., Ewing, M.T., and Ramaseshan, B. (2000). Effects of economic recession on export activity. The case of Australia, *Journal of Global Marketing*, 13(4): 93–106.

Chetty, S. (1996). The case study method for research in small- and medium-sized firms, *International Small Business Journal*, 15(1): 73–85.

Cuervo-Cazurra, A., Maloney, M.M., and Manrakhan, S. (2007). Causes of the difficulties in internationalisation, *Journal of International Business Studies*, 38(5): 709–725.

Dooley, K.J., Yan, T., Mohan, S., and Gopalakrishnan, M. (2010). Inventory management and the bullwhip effect during the 2007–2009 recession: Evidence from the manufacturing sector, *Journal of Supply Chain Management*, 46(1): 12–18.

Dubrovski, D. (2007). Management mistakes as causes of corporate crises: Countries in transition, *Managing Global Transitions*, 5(4): 333–354.

Eisenhardt, K.M. (1989). Building theories from case study research, *Academy of Management Review*, 14(4): 532–550.

Figueira-de-Lemos, F., Johanson, J., and Vahlne, J-E. (2011). Risk management in the internationalisation process of the firm: A note on the Uppsala model, *Journal of World Business*, 46(2): 143–153.

Ghauri, P. (2004). Designing and conducting case studies in international business research, in R. Marschan-Piekkari and C. Welch (Eds.) *Handbook of Qualitative Research Methods for International Business*, Cheltenham, UK: Edward Elgar: 109–124.

Grewal, R., Johnson, J.L., and Sarker, S. (2007). Crises in business markets: Implications for interfirm linkages, *Journal of the Academy of Marketing Science*, 35(3): 398–416.

Gummesson, E. (2006). Qualitative research in management: Addressing complexity, context and persona, *Management Decision*, 44(2): 167–179.

Hadjikhani, A. and Johanson, M. (2000). Expectation as the driving force for entry and exit in the turbulent Russian market, *Journal of East-West Business*, 5(1/2): 99–121.

Hofer, C.W. (1980). Turnaround strategies, *Journal of Business Strategy*, 1(1): 19–31.

Johanson, J. and Vahlne, J.-E. (1990). The mechanism of internationalisation, *International Marketing Review*, 7(4): 11–24.

Latham, S. (2009). Contrasting strategic response to economic recession in start-up versus established software firms, *Journal of Small Business Management*, 47(2): 180–201.

Latham, S.F. and Braun, M.R. (2010). Jilted? The manager's little book for keeping customers in a recession, *Journal of Business Strategy*, 31(1): 4–10.

Lee, S.-H. and Makhija, M. (2009). Flexibility in internationalisation: Is it valuable during an economic crisis? *Strategic Management Journal*, 30(5): 537–555.

Lee, S.-H., Beamish, P.W., Lee, H.-U., and Park, J.-H. (2009). Strategic choice during economic crisis: Domestic market position, organisational capabilities and export flexibility, *Journal of World Business*, 44(1): 1–15.

Rhee, J.H. and Cheng, J.L.C. (2002). Foreign market uncertainty and incremental international expansion: The moderating effect of firm, industry, and host country factors, *Management International Review*, 42(4): 419–439.

Schuler, R.S. and Jackson, S.E. (1989). Determinants of human resource management priorities and implications for industrial relations, *Journal of Management*, 15(1): 89–99.

Shama, A. (1993). Marketing strategies during recession: A comparison of small and large firms, *Journal of Small Business Management*, 31(3): 62–72.

Simon, A. (2010). Resources, dynamic capabilities and Australian business success, *Journal of Global Business and Technology*, 6(2): 12–31.

Spence, M. and Crick, D. (2009). An exploratory study of Canadian international new venture firms' development in overseas markets, *Qualitative Market Research: An International Journal*, 12(2): 208–233.

Sudarsanam, S. and Lai, J. (2001). Corporate financial distress and turnaround strategies: An empirical analysis, *British Journal of Management*, 12(3): 183–199.

Teece, D.J., Pisano, G., and Shuen, A. (1997). Dynamic capabilities and strategic management, *Strategic Management Journal*, 18(7): 509–533.

Tuttle, A. (2003). Can manufacturing make a comeback, *Industrial Distribution*, 92(6): 19–22.

Wang, J. and Gupta, V. (2003). Post-crisis management: A study of corporate restructuring in Asia, *Journal of the Academy of Business and Economics*, 2(2): 209–217.

Wang, H.-M., Huang, H., and Bansal, P. (2005). What determined success during the Asian economic crisis? The importance of experiential knowledge and group affiliation, *Asia Pacific Journal of Management*, 22(1): 89–106.

Weerawardena, J., Sullivan Mort, G., Liesch, P.W., and Knight, G. (2007). Conceptualizing accelerated internationalisation in the born global firm: A dynamic capabilities perspective, *Journal of World Business*, 42(3): 294–306.

Welch, C.L. and Welch, L.S. (2009). Re-internationalisation: Exploration and conceptualisation, *International Business Review*, 18(6): 567–577.

Wennberg, K. and Holmquist, C. (2008). Problemistic search and international entrepreneurship, *European Management Journal*, 26(6): 441–454.

Wu, L.-Y. (2010). Applicability of the resource-based and dynamic-capability views under environmental volatility, *Journal of Business Research*, 63(1): 27–31.

Yin, R.K. (1994). *Case Study Research Design and Methods*. London: Sage.

13
Servicing Local Customers for Entering Foreign Markets: Internationalization of Russian IT Firms

Marina Latukha and Andrei Panibratov

Introduction

Having recognized the positive impact of recent trends of technological developments on the rise of international activities of service sector companies (Vandermerwe and Chadwick, 1989), this chapter focuses on how the mode of entry correlates to the firm specifics. It also tries to address the particular characteristics of the service firm that define the necessity for a particular choice of strategy. We study to what extent and how the specifics of the home country and domestic market characteristics explain the international results of Russian IT companies.

The theoretical framework is based on two main concepts. First is Dunning's ownership, location, and internalization (OLI) paradigm that draws motivations for FDI. These are (i) resource-seeking investments aimed at accessing unique resources specific to foreign locations (e.g. natural resources), (ii) market-seeking investments aimed at entering new markets, (iii) efficiency-seeking investments pursuing an efficient specialization of firms, and (iv) strategic asset-seeking investments aimed at augmenting the set of proprietary resources of firms.

The OLI framework argues that there are three factors that contribute to the prevalence of FDI: Ownership advantages, location advantages, and internalization. With respect to 'ownership advantages', a firm engages in FDI if it has a competitive advantage over other firms, which it primarily uses to exploit in foreign markets (referred to as 'asset-exploiting FDI'). However, firms also engage in FDI to increase their competitive advantage: This behavior is known as 'asset-augmenting

FDI'. Second, if there is a desirable natural or created resource that is indigenous to a certain location but that is immobile, then a firm will engage in FDI to obtain the 'locational advantage'. The third factor, 'internalization', reveals that if the transaction costs of exploiting certain resources through traditional market instruments are high, a firm will opt for FDI (Dunning, 2000).

The second concept is firm-specific advantage (FSA) and country specific advantage (CSA) theory developed by Rugman. The key precondition to become engaged in foreign investments is that a firm must possess some unique competitive advantage, or firm-specific advantages (FSA). The multinational company needs to build on some type of FSA that, at the simplest level, is nonlocation-bound, that is, easily transferable across borders as an intermediate product. It can be a functional, production-related proprietary asset, typically technological, manufacturing, or marketing know-how; or an organizational capability to efficiently co-ordinate and control the multinational company's asset base (Rugman and Verbeke, 2003). Hence, the FSA concept covers a very broad set of unique company strengths (competencies and capabilities). The CSAs are the location-bound, exogenous factors in a multinational company's home market. The CSAs result from the home country's economic and institutional environments, such as labor force, factor endowments, government policies, national culture, productive reputation, or institutional framework. In fact, both FSA and CSA can be related to the ownership (O) and location (L) advantages of the OLI framework.

Internationalization of service companies and IT firms perspective

Nearly 50 academic studies for the period 1971–2007 were devoted to service companies—that is, 1.35 articles per year and 0.34 articles per journal (Kundu and Merchant, 2008). This proves that theoretical and empirical knowledge about the patterns and determinants of internationalization activities in the service sector are still limited (Castellacci, 2010).

Internationalization is considered to be the process when a company moves from operating in a domestic market to international markets (Andersen, 1993; Buckley and Casson, 1998). Some research acknowledges that theories described for manufacturing products are applicable to services (Boddewyn *et al.*, 1986; Katrishen and Scordis, 1998). Other scholars suggest that direct applicability is questionable (Johanson and

Vahlne, 1990). Majkgård and Sharma (1998) suggest that hard services, where production and consumption are decoupled, and soft services (e.g. IT), where production and consumption occur simultaneously, differ in the internationalization process. Hard services can be internationalized in the same way as manufacturing industries; soft services cannot. Hence, IT services should follow different strategies (Erramilli, 1990; Ekeledo and Sivakumar, 1998).

The fact that service companies from emerging markets are capable of growth and internationalization has been ignored (Pauwels and de Ruyter, 2005). Companies looking to expand internationally have access to a large range of different strategies, and potential modes of entry from exporting to establishing a subsidiary in foreign markets. Many scholars believe that companies go international in order to increase their market share (Johanson and Vahlne, 1977; Luostarinen, 1980; Cavusgil, 1980), and this requires greater resource commitment when the opportunities are available along with the investment being justified and managers' commitment being at an appropriate level (Johanson and Vahlne, 1990; Oystein and Servais, 2002). Higher involvement modes of entry are viewed as an instrument of help for generating knowledge in internationalization and knowledge of a foreign market: Language, habits, culture, foreign market behavior, and functioning of the market (Johanson and Vahlne, 1977). Besides the fact that many companies choose other modes of entry, the incremental expansion model dominates the theoretical literature relating to how companies implement internationalization.

Erramilli (1990) says that soft service producers face difficulties with exporting because exporting requires a separation of producer and consumer, and therefore they are limited by the choice of contractual relationship, licensing, foreign direct investment (joint venture or wholly owned subsidiary) or franchising. Such entry modes require substantial resource and managerial commitment, and do not allow the company to benefit from the experience accumulated through a more gradual approach (Carman and Lengeard, 1980).

Aharoni (1999) suggests that there are three ways of providing services abroad: (i) supplying the service from operations based in the host country to customers located abroad, (ii) supplying the services from operations based in the host country to indigenous customers, and (iii) foreign customers with services at the home country of the service provider (in the case of tourism).

According to Javalgi and Martin (2007), the resource-based view (RBV) of firms has emerged as a framework to examine suitable competitive advantage in the areas of service marketing and management. The authors state that the degree of control influences the choice of entry decision. Control determines risks, the success of strategic goals, the degree of intangibility of services, and the ultimate performance of the company.

Javalgi and Martin (2007) suggest a framework which can be adopted for an IT company as the obvious example of service firms. Important elements in this framework are company-level resources, management characteristics, firm characteristics along with competitive and international advantages, the degree of involvement/risk, and host country factors. Firm-level resources, management, and firm characteristics make a company generate unique competitive and international advantages which themselves generate the return. Company-related resources and characteristics lead to the choice of entry mode, taking into consideration host country factors, which also affect the decision on entry mode.

Sanchez-Peinado and Pla-Barber (2006) found that cultural distance did not significantly influence the choice of entry mode by service firms. Nevertheless, they found a negative relationship between international experience and the choice of higher-control entry modes, partially supporting Erramilli's results and contradicting Uppsala's predictions.

The influence of external and internal factors on service firms' choice of market entry mode was also studied by Erramilli (1990). He concluded that service firms tend to use more integrated (higher-control) entry modes—the larger the foreign market size, the greater the unavailability of host country suitable partners. The firm's corporate policy on keeping control over its overseas operations was also found to be important. These firms tend to use less integrated (lower-control) entry modes—the greater the restriction on foreign ownership, the stronger the firm's aversion to environmental risk, the greater the firm's desire to get rapidly established, and the greater its constraints on internal resources.

Service firms from emerging markets are increasing their efforts to integrate into the global economy and they have already started exporting abroad. Cardone-Riportella and Cazorla-Papis (2001) have suggested several drivers for the considerable growth of the services sector in the economies of both industrialized and developing countries. The most important reasons include tense competition in domestic markets, profit margin pressure, and the opportunity to develop business in foreign markets. These also best characterize the motives for internationalization of Russian IT companies.

Vernon-Wortzel and Wortzel (1988) state that the international expansion of companies from emerging markets is primarily accomplished by producing at home and exporting goods to foreign markets. These companies follow both the internationalization (Johanson and Vahlne, 1977) and the international product life cycle (Vernon, 1966) models. They first go overseas by exporting and then, when market knowledge is obtained, commit in the form of more investment-oriented entry modes. Aulakh *et al.* (2000) consider that the majority of firms from emerging markets are still in the early stages of the internationalization process where exporting is dominant. The exception is high-tech companies and particularly IT firms which internationalize 'virtually' without having the need to invest or export.

Research methodology

This chapter is not aimed at analyzing merely managerial perceptions but rather at determining the actual sources of competitive advantage of Russian firms. We were also interested in looking at the possible political influences on the impact of competitors when approaching the study. The case study method was chosen for several reasons. This lends itself better to investigating the significance of non-economic issues. A further reason is that the issue of internationalization of the core sectors of emerging economies still requires a more careful conceptualization and theory building. As Eisenhardt (1989) argued, the case study approach is especially appropriate in new topic areas. Given that the greatest activity of Russian MNEs is in forming partnerships and alliances abroad, we also refer to Halinen and Törnroos' (2005) discussions of the opportunities of a qualitative/case study approach to examine the international partnerships-based strategies.

Given our general interest in how Russian MNEs' success can be attained in both developed and developing economies, we aimed to study the process in which these firms strive to obtain market leadership via various investment decisions abroad. As our research focused on the process of foreign market entry and further development of overseas operations, we specified that our selected case studies had to be major firms which are said to have obtained a substantial competitiveness over local and other foreign players in a major Russian industry prior to internationalization.

We sought three case studies of about same time-span. Our case companies—Sitronics, Kaspersky, and Yandex—fit our initial sample specifications, coming from three major sectors of the IT industry in

Russia (electronic devices and IT solutions; software and anti-virus programs; internet services and search engines), and all three firms are said to have obtained substantial success in entering the respective markets in developed and developing countries. This sampling, although based on one sector, hopefully allows us greater generalizability of results due to the relatively large-scale international operations of these three MNEs.

The main sources of the primary data were the managers of Russian firms and of foreign companies' subsidiaries in Russia in the IT-related industries. The data were based on interviews of the top and middle management of the three firms and on information from experts in the selected industries.

The research questions were the following:

- How does the entry mode correlate with the service firm specifics in the IT industry?
- What important characteristics of the Russian IT firm define the entry mode selected?
- How do home country specifics and domestic market characteristics explain the international results of Russian IT companies?

Russia as a context

Despite the widespread perception that most Russian MNEs rise exclusively from the natural resource-based industries, the study of Elenkov (1995) helps us to understand the roots of technology-based internationalization of Russian companies. He investigated the importance of the military sector in the context of the coopetition of Russian and Western technologically developed firms in the airspace industry. While the non-military sector was technologically obsolete due to the lack of strong technical staff, close linkages with advanced R&D institutes and modern equipment, the strong Russian military industry was nurtured at the expense of the largely neglected civilian sector (Elenkov, 1995).

The Russian aerospace MNEs also introduced a new dimension of competition in their industry which was characterized by aggressive R&D development, effective implementation of new technology to produce advanced aircrafts and related products, and consistency in keeping the total cost down (Elenkov, 1995). With time, these features become typical for most Russian technology-based firms.

An international springboard perspective, provided by Luo and Tung (2007), generalizes several strategies adopted by emerging MNEs, which include cumulative benefits from inward investment before undertaking OFDI, leapfrogging trajectory, and coopetition with global players.

As the most common destinations for Russian OFDI are CIS and Eastern European countries, there is a possibility of Russian MNEs having an advantage of originating from a developing economy and operating in a familiar environment, hostile to developed countries' MNEs (Cuervo-Cazurra and Genc, 2008).

The strategies and features of emerging markets' MNEs on the example of Chinese companies were discussed by Child and Rodrigues (2005). According to the authors, emerging markets' MNEs have stronger catch-up capabilities than was expected. The features of Chinese companies, such as government involvement in large companies' business activities and the necessity to overcome latecomer disadvantages, can be recognized in the Russian economy as well.

Western MNEs that have invested in Russia within the last two decades have managed to achieve high quality production and services, an effective marketing policy that was adapted to the Russian conditions and developed local partnerships (Panibratov, 2009). Hence, benefits from their operations were not only financial but also created and gained knowledge.

The motives of MNEs' internationalization are considered to be the same as those of companies from developed economies with market, labor, resource, and technology seeking prevailing over the rest (Rasiah *et al.*, 2010), although again, in the case of Russia, resource and market seeking motives are most often stated as the main ones, but with little respect to industry specifics (Panibratov and Verba, 2011).

OFDI from Russia is both 'exodus' and 'expansion' in terms of the role of both home country factors that encourage firms to invest abroad and the attractiveness of foreign locations for Russian firms (Vahtra and Liuhto, 2006). Exodus was strong in the early 1990s (at the beginning of the transition), followed by a period of less escape in the mid-1990s. The crisis of 1998 prompted a rise in capital escape, which was followed by normalization again, and the crisis of 2008 increased the motivation of exodus once again.

International expansion of three leading Russian IT firms

Kaspersky

Kaspersky Lab (Kaspersky) is a Russian IT company, founded in 1997 in Moscow. It is the market leader in the development of anti-virus software. While Kaspersky offers anti-spyware, anti-spam, and anti-intrusion products, its most famous product is Kaspersky Anti-Virus, which is much praised within the industry as well as by the customer.

By 2005, Kaspersky Lab had grown into an international company, employing over 1,500 computer specialists. The company is present in more than 100 countries globally. It has headquarters in Moscow and regional offices in Europe (the Netherlands, Germany, France, the UK, Poland, Romania, Sweden), Asia (Japan, China, South Korea), and US.

While the majority of businesses in the IT industry grow through mergers and acquisitions, Kaspersky follows a path of organic development. As it aims for global growth, the main strategy remains to offer new enterprise-oriented solutions, regional expansion, and increased partners. In order to better serve its customers, Kaspersky established relationships with distributors in other countries, starting its international expansion with exporting.

One key step in the company's internationalization was engaging in partnerships in order to conquer the US market. In 2001, Kaspersky Lab announced a partnership with Itamigo, a developer of internet security services. This enabled it to launch the first Kaspersky anti-virus products to customers in the US. Exploring partnerships has the advantage of low costs and shared risk.

The European market was entered by launching European retail sales in 2001. The company made use of local retail and distribution networks in order to provide its products to the European market. These developments were followed by opening regional offices in Europe.

In 2003 a regional office in Beijing, China, was opened which was the beginning of its exploration of the less-developed markets. After the company established its presence in the East, it continued to expand into the African market.

Results explained

Kaspersky Lab has established multiple strategic partnerships with key players in the software industry. With partners all over the world, it was able to expand its presence in the global market and stay at the industry's lead. Among its strategic partners were Microsoft, Intel, IBM, Novell, Check point, and Linux Solutions.

For Microsoft, Kapersky Lab was a so-called Gold Certified Security Solutions Partner. Furthermore, the two companies were working on several joint projects. Kaspersky Lab has optimized its systems for Intel products.

Another partnership was the National Coalition Against Spam, of which Kaspersky Lab was one of the founders. Others included Microsoft. The coalition was formed in Russia and was aimed at fighting spam.

Kaspersky Lab focused on global expansion and penetrated through successful partnerships. This was an outstanding example for the international success of a Russian IT software company. The paradox is that global giants like Microsoft or Intel competed with much smaller Russian companies. The competition on the software market was mediocre in this decade in Russia.

Sitronics

Sitronics is one of the largest national players in the high-tech industry. Established in 2002, it was set up as a scientific center, directed at microelectronics and telecommunications equipment and software. In 2004 it established a business line related to IT services. The company gained stakes in several others, among which is Kvazar-Mirco, the largest IT company in Ukraine. Now, Sitronics is the largest high-tech company in Eastern Europe operating in the field of IT, telecommunications solutions, system integration and consulting, and development and manufacture of microelectronics products.

The company is a key partner for the states and governmental institutions in the field of infrastructural transformations in Russia and the CIS countries. It often implements the strategy of public-private partnerships, taking part in scientific research backed up by government.

The company has subsidiaries in over 30 countries and employs over 10,000 people. It is ranked as one of the top three Russian IT companies. Major international competitors are Microsoft, IBM, and SAP AG.

Having over 3,500 clients around the globe, the company exports to over 60 countries in Western and Eastern Europe, the Middle East, North America, North Africa, and Central and South-East Asia. Manufacturing is done in Russia, Greece, the Czech Republic, Romania, and China. The major enterprises of Sitronics are located in Prague and Athens for telecommunications solutions, in Kiev for IT, and in Zelenograd and Moscow for microelectronics solutions.

Sitronics has launched its operations in the fastest-growing ICT market in the world, India, adopting the name Sitronics India with its head office located in New Delhi. The group started to operate in the Indian market in May 2008, and it has had a permanent presence in India since November 2008. The formal registration of the new subsidiary was completed in April 2009. The main focus in India was on the telecommunications sector, transport industry, state organizations, and educational systems. The primary objective of the new subsidiary was to introduce the complete range of Sitronics' products and solutions to the Indian market.

Results explained

The expansion strategy of Sitronics is based on strong partnerships with key global and regional players. Sitronics has developed strategic alliances with Cisco Systems, STMicroelectronics, Infineon, and Giesecke and Devrient in relation to the most important products and services. Sitronics has vendor relationships with Siemens, Ericsson, Motorola, Oracle, Intel, Sun Microsystems, and Microsoft. Key customers are both local companies (MTS, Comstar-UTS, and MTT), and international firms (OTE, Cosmote, Vodafone, Ericsson, Arcelor Mittal, and TCL).

Expansion and development of services in India provided the firm with numerous opportunities for growth, even in such difficult times as the period after 2008. At the end of 2009, Sitronics announced that it had launched a billing platform for pan-Indian telecom operator Sistema Shyam TeleServices, which traded under the MTS-India brand. The new platform, after being implemented in Mumbai (India's financial capital) and the state of Maharashtra, was intended to be rolled out to other regions of the country.

An important deal of the company was a joint venture, established in the city of Hangzhou in the East of China. Sitronics held a 51 per cent stake with ZTE Corporation owning the remaining 49 per cent. The aim of the new enterprise was to enable the company to migrate its mass manufacturing and production capacity from Europe to South-East Asia, thereby improving efficiency and reducing costs.

Another part of Sitronics' strategy was the strategic partnership with Nokia Siemens Networks, a global enabler of communications services. Within this partnership, Nokia Siemens Networks has signed an initial framework purchase agreement with a Sitronics subsidiary, Sitronics Microelectronics. According to the agreement, Microelectronics became the official global supplier of analogue power management electronic components for Nokia Siemens Networks products.

Besides the few prominent examples above, Sitronics was engaged in aggressive international regional expansion by means of geographical, vertical, and product expansion strategies. It used strategic partnerships and IJVs in order to get inside new attractive markets, enjoying the benefits of the established networks, cheaper resources, and lower risks. The strategies Sitronics was using have been really successful and brought positive results in both market share and sales revenues.

Yandex

Yandex is the leading internet search engine and one of best-known brands in Russia with more than 15 million visitors and users. The name 'Yandex' appeared in 1993, when in a company named CompTek employees started with development of a program which allowed them to search and operate with a quantum of information of their own (Latukha, 2010). This product became one of the first search engines in Russia.

Yandex was separated from CompTek so that it can focus on providing services concerning web browsing. It was launched practically immediately after 'plugging' Russia into the internet—in 1997. Yandex appeared to be one of the first companies. During the same year the Rambler, Mail.ru, List.ru, and Apport companies were also launched.

On the Russian market, Yandex is a pioneer in context advertising. After the launch of this product in 2004, its share skyrocketed in all advertising sectors. In 2005, revenue from the advertising services of Yandex was US$100 million, 80 per cent of which was revenue from context advertisements. Yandex's major competitor in this field remains Google, which has a tremendous client base and worldwide experience.

Yandex, like any other internet company, was international from scratch—an advantage owing to the nature of the internet company itself. The only physical international asset of Yandex is its subsidiary company, Yandex Labs, which was founded in 2009 in Silicon Valley in California, but it is used for research and not to provide services in the US.

During 2009 two new domains were created: In Ukraine (yandex.ua) and in Kazakhstan (yandex.kz). Both work on a Russian language basis but are geographically reoriented in Ukraine and Kazakhstan in keyword search processes.

The internet markets of Belorussia and Poland were considered as the next important targets for Yandex. Most of the population of Belarus speaks Russian and uses it in daily life (along with Byelorussian). As for Poland, many obstacles were expected. The entire population of Poland uses predominantly the Polish language, and few of them know Russian. Besides, the aversion to all Russia-related things was noticeable in the country. Moreover, Yahoo and Google are very strong on this market. Both companies have their domains in Poland running in Polish language.

Western markets are highly attractive for internet companies as they can easily be entered without any significant spending on facilities or the labor force. At the same time, they are extremely competitive for all host firms. Though the meaning of entry barriers in the case of the internet industry is changing compared with the more 'physical' sectors, Yandex managed to open its subsidiary in the US to provide support for the Russian domain in the US for Russian expatriates living there.

One interesting part of the Yandex strategy is the permanent competition with Google in Russia. In many countries worldwide, Google has reached dominance on the search-engine market. However, by the end of 2010 a few countries remained where that was not the case. In these the local search engines still manage to get a larger market share than Google. The Russian market was top-ranked in this case and Yandex was mentioned as a local absolute leader with 46 per cent of market share.

Several explanations can be given for this. First, Yandex made investments in the Russian market long before Google. Second, the company technology was perfectly aligned with the language. Third, innovations were offered that Google has to copy to be able to compete. Fourth, strong brand awareness and loyalty from Russian customers was achieved. And, finally, Yandex successfully exploited the opportunity to establish partnerships and strategic alliances with local companies at an early stage.

Whereas Yandex has a strong brand in Russia, Google has one of the strongest brands in the world, and it is expanding into Eastern Europe with technology now optimized for the Cyrillic alphabet, which it previously lacked. Google and Yandex are now in direct competition in Russia, Belarus, and Ukraine. Although one of the founders of Google is Russian in origin, the US company was not looking for opportunities to enter the Russian market until 2005. Google's priority was entering the developed markets first. By the end of 2010 Yandex was among the top ten world search engines, but its world market share was only about 1.5 per cent. At the same time Google had 62.4 per cent of the market. This was the reason for the enormous difference in these companies' revenues: US$160 million vs. US$16 billion for Google and Yandex, respectively.

Results explained

Yandex is a software firm that develops and maintains an internet search engine primarily for the Russian market, where it has a strong brand. Yandex introduced innovations to the industry in the form of the pay-per click system of pricing for advertising. Furthermore, the company is a pioneer within context advertisements. These innovations made

Yandex's revenues soar by the end of 2005. However, competition with Google has stiffened in recent years, and that is a strong competitor to have indeed.

Does it make sense to study the process of internationalization of an internet company given that from the very beginning such a company operates (virtually) all over the globe? The key to understanding this phenomenon lies in essence on the internet—it is a supranational open environment that can barely be controlled. Internet companies provide their services to anyone who has access to the world Wide Web, so they are international right from their inception. This is one of the main advantages of internet companies which process search queries for anybody on the web. The same is true for advertising services—they are available to any company regardless of their country of origin.

Yandex is a company that has grown internationally through innovation. It has made some innovations in the field of online advertising pricing. However, this has not helped it to expand internationally. It might be that the barrier of the Cyrillic language was what kept Yandex from Google's clutches for a while, but now that it has been overcome, the US giant might swallow Yandex as it did most other search engines ten years ago. In any event, Yandex is more of an international company by the nature of its business than by managerial strategy.

Results and discussion

In the strategic sectors of the Russian economy (mostly natural resource based) the motives for internationalization of national firms may be explained with the fast growth of the local market, low cost opportunities, and home government incentives. Russian companies benefit abroad from the high level of staff education which provides for better manpower at relatively low cost. Russian IT enterprises develop their operations to become potential service providers for these national resource-based firms (Latukha *et al.*, 2011).

With regard to the geographical distribution of the international activities of the case companies, data show that despite strong interest in the markets of developed economies, Russian IT firms have generally targeted developing country firms, particularly in CIS and Asia, where Russian resource-based firms have been better placed.

From the standpoint of technology differences, the greenfield strategy can be advantageous only if the significant technological gap between key competitors exists. As the technological sophistication of both Russian and foreign firms in the high-tech sector is about equal (if compared with natural resource-based enterprises), the partnership oriented strategy is more appropriate.

When expanding internationally, Russian IT firms often acquire an equity stake in an existing local firm, the stake ranging from minority to equal ownership. At the same time, as most of the key industries in different countries are under high governmental protection and surveillance, the rise of the share in ownership up to 100 per cent may be difficult or even impossible.

Our chapter also has important implications for the strategies of Russian MNEs and their dependence on the Russian and host governments. The Russian state imposes ownership restrictions on foreign firms in the IT industry in order to protect the dominant position of local companies, which generate profits sufficient to finance acquisitions abroad. Host countries' governments are often interested in attracting Russian investments or serving Russian policy (some CIS countries both), which may facilitate the international expansion of Russian firms.

The generalization of the internationalization experiences of the case companies, presented in Table 13.1, may be of interest for any further studies of the phenomenon of Russian multinationals.

Our analysis shows that Russian natural resource giants are not the only leaders in internationalization, as companies which gained beneficial state support. The difference between them and Russian service companies is in the fact that companies from service industries are able to explore new foreign markets without any governmental support.

Table 13.1 International results of Russian firms in the IT sector

Major Foreign Destinations	**Entry Modes**	**Expansion Approach**	**Role of State**
Europe and Asia in antivirus and PC solutions, CIS in search engines	Strategic partnerships with the top of the software industry; 'virtual' entry more than physical as the core mode; exporting	Manufacturing in countries with a cheap labor force; opening regional offices in Europe and CIS	Despite support from government, the sector seems to be less dependent on the state than other high-tech industries (e.g. telecoms)

The markets of CIS are potentially very attractive to Russian IT companies. In most of the CIS countries, the local population and authorities speak Russian and seek Russian language services. Hence, Russian IT companies have obvious CSAs there. The effect of the country of origin helps them to internationalize naturally and essentially without using additional effort. The experience of their companies, while working in domestic markets, creates advantages in competition with local firms. The home country environment plays an important role in the process of the internationalization of Russian service companies.

Table 13.2 provides CSA and FSA for selected service industries while entering CIS countries. The third and fourth columns provide information about triggers in the home country environment which affected the firm's CSAs/FSAs.

The role of government is important in the process of internationalization not only in being included in one's shareholder structure but also in everyday work. As we can see, each country's government creates preconditions for companies' CSA and FSA. For some firms this is a disadvantage; in some, specific factors play a negative role, while internationalizing. In any case, possibilities of avoiding factoral disadvantages exist.

IT firms' internationalization is totally different in the whole sector internationalization path. The demand for high-quality software has been growing since the 1990s and continues to grow. For a Russian software company like Kaspersky Lab, it was difficult to compete with the Western giants, whose products originally tended to be of higher quality and image. Even Russian customers did not favor Kaspersky or Yandex

Table 13.2 Home country effects in evaluating CSAs and FSAs of Russian IT firms in the process of expansion in CIS countries

CSA	FSA	Macro-Level Influences (on CSA)	Micro-Level Influences (on FSA)
Still no positive image of Russian software companies	High-quality products and services. Possibility to sell services for relatively lower prices	Just recently Russian government decided to support innovation, including in software	Low level of economic prosperity means low level of wages; for high-tech companies cheap labor means cheap services

services if they were of low quality, as in that sector, customers have great choice, as all of the service products are easily accessible without the need for the provider firm to have a physical presence in the country. High-quality products allowed Kaspersky and Yandex to compete with world giants in software design and to establish long-term partnerships with the world's most famous computer software producers and resellers. While going abroad, Kaspersky has used a partnership entry model. It has its regional offices in various parts of the world: In Europe, Asia, and North America. Such distribution allows it to establish partnerships with local software distributors. Also the company has strategic partnerships with the leading operational system producers: Microsoft, Linux, IBM, and others. Creating such coalitions allows Kaspersky to sell its products as a PC starting package, which go together with a PC, like the operating system or office tools.

The approach of Kaspersky is highly dependent on the image of the company. Until the image is good and the products are uptodate and of high quality, the company will continue establishing partnerships. Such companies as Microsoft and IBM are checking twice before including new software in their package or announcing an application as the software of choice to be used together with their products.

The OLI (Ownership, Locational, and Internalize) paradigm asserts that the decision of whether a company should internalize its knowledge or not should be based on combining the effect of the 'O' (Ownership)-specific and 'L' (Location)-specific advantages. The most decisive factor for a company wanting to be multinational is that it should have some kind of ownership advantages that can give it competitive advantages over its local competitors in a particular location. These ownership advantages are internal and exclusive to the company, and it should have the possibility of enjoying their benefits at least over a certain period of time. These advantages can be abstract or concrete, which can put the company in a relatively advantageous position in a particular market. This can also help the company to become a market leader and be cost-effective vis-à-vis its competitors. This gives the company the ability and power to engage in FDI in foreign countries.

Analytical models which were used in the analysis show that they are relevant to the process of international expansion of the companies studied. Russian firms' CSA and FSA are forming their advantages/disadvantages in Ownership and Locational preferences. Such characteristics create internal modes, which fit in these conditions (Table 13.3).

Table 13.3 OLI framework application to Russian IT firms

OLI	Evidence
Ownership	Companies produce high-quality products and services. Employees are well educated and, because of cheap manpower, they are able to be competitive on the international market, especially on the US market, where costs are much higher. Companies have their shares on the Russian stock market, Kaspersky and Yandex performing best on the market. Financial implications allow companies to go abroad.
Location CIS	the market of CIS is differently important for case companies. The level of piracy and low level of intellectual rights protection will not allow such companies like Kaspersky Lab to benefit from reselling their services. Yandex or other search engines with a diversified number of free services can benefit from those markets as they are able to localize their services better than global players
Europe	For Kaspersky Lab, the European market is more favorable: European customers are taught to buy all software, so creating offices in Europe is a good idea in terms of being closer to distributors and resellers
	For Yandex, the European market is very competitive. The expansion of global search engines like Google restricts competition concerning marketing. Large investments must be made before entering the European market
Asia/US	Being closer to the main PC and software producers is vital for high-tech companies. As most products and services are produced in the US and some parts of Asia, companies need to organize local offices or even R&D centers to be closer to their partners
Internalization	While selling IT services abroad, companies need to establish strong partnerships with local distributors and local and global producers. In this context, establishing strategic alliances is the best option. All distribution work is done by the partners and there is no necessity to move production abroad. So joint ventures or wholly owned subsidiaries do not suit this industry and are possible only in cases of cheaper manpower.

It is possible to see that internal conditions and organizational structures as well as the approaches to internationalization differ between the analyzed IT firms. The biggest advantage, or in some cases limitation, lies in the government support for the company. If the difference between the IT firms internationalization can be explained by the nature of the industry and international market situation, the difference between the companies' choice of entry modes within one industry is very much affected by the role of government and its impact on a firm's decision-making.

Conclusion

To conclude, the fast development of the Russian IT sector has led to the rise of advanced technologies and highly skilled labor force; hence, the Russian IT MNEs are more focused on, acquisition of customers than on, acquisition of technologies when expanding abroad.

The greenfield strategy is preferred when a significant technological gap among major players exists. In the IT sector the sophistication of Russian and foreign firms is about equal, and the partnership-based strategy may be more appropriate. Moreover, as national high-tech industries are in most cases strongly protected by local governments, partnerships abroad become a core form of market entry strategy.

Although Russian MNEs are generally highly dependent on the home and host governments, Russian IT companies have been relatively less influenced by the home state. Rather, their international activities have been shaped more by economic factors. Hence they seem to be less 'escaping' and more 'investing' when compared with their natural resource-dependent counterparts.

References

Aharoni, Y. (1999). Internationalisation of professional services: Implications for accounting firms, in D. Brock, M. Powell, and C.R. (Bob) Hinings (Eds.) *Restructuring the Professional Organisation*, London: Routledge: 20–40.

Andersen, O. (1993). On the internationalisation process of firms: A critical analysis, *Journal of International Business Studies*, 24(2): 209–231.

Aulakh, P., Kotabe, M., and Teegen, H. (2000). Export strategies of service companies emerging markets, *The Academy of Management Journal*, 43(3): 342–361.

Boddewyn, J.J., Soehl, R., and Picard, J. (1986). Standardisation in international marketing: Is Ted Levitt in fact right? *Business Horizons*, November–December: 69–75.

Buckley, P.J. and Casson, M.C. (1998). Analyzing foreign market entry strategies: Extending the internalisation approach, *Journal of International Business Studies*, 29(3): 539–562.

Cardone-Riportella, C. and Cazorla-Papis, L. (2001). The internationalisation process of Spanish banks: A tale of two times, *International Journal of Bank Marketing*, 19(2): 53–68.

Carman, J. and Lengeard, E. (1980). Growth strategies of service firms, *Strategic Management Journal*, 1(1): 7–22.

Castellacci, F. (2010). The internationalisation of firms in the service industries: Channels, determinants and sectoral patterns, *Technological Forecasting and Social Change*, 7(3): 500–513.

Cavusgil, S. (1980). On the internationalisation process of firms, *European Research*, 8(6): 273–281.

Child, J. and Rodrigues, S. (2005). The Internationalisation of Chinese firms: A case for theoretical extension? *Management and Organisation Review*, 1(3): 381–410.

Cuervo-Cazurra, A. and Genc, M. (2008). Transforming disadvantages into advantages: Developing-country MNEs in the least developed countries, *Journal of International Business Studies*, 39(6): 957–979.

Dunning, J.H. (2000). The eclectic paradigm as an envelope for economic and business theories of MNE activity, *International Business Review*, 9: 163–190.

Eisenhardt, K.M. (1989). Building theories from case study research, *Academy of Management Review*, 14(4): 532–550.

Ekeledo, I. and Sivakumar, K. (1998). Foreign market entry mode choice of service firms: A contingency perspective, *Journal of the Academy of Marketing Science*, 26(4): 274–292.

Elenkov, D. (1995). Russian aerospace MNCs in global competition: Their origin, competitive strengths and forms of multinational expansion, *The Columbia Journal of World Business*, Summer: 66–78.

Erramilli, M.K. (1990). Entry mode choice in service industries, *International Marketing Review*, 7(5): 50–62.

Halinen, A. and Törnroos, J. (2005). Using case methods in the study of contemporary business networks, *Journal of Business Research*, 58: 1285–1297.

Javalgi, R. and Martin, C. (2007). Internationalisation of services: Identifying the building blocks for future research, *Journal of Services Marketing*, 21(7): 391–397.

Johanson, J. and Vahlne, J.-E. (1977). The internationalisation process of the firm: A model of knowledge development and increasing foreign market commitments, *Journal of International Business Studies*, 8(1): 23–32.

Johanson, J. and Vahlne, J.-E. (1990). The mechanisms of internationalization, *International Marketing Review*, 7(4): 11–24.

Katrishen, F. and Scordis, N. (1998). Economies of scale in services: A study of multinational insurers, *Journal of International Business Studies*, 29(2): 305–324.

Kundu, S.K. and Merchant, H. (2008). Service multinationals: Their past, present, and future, *Management International Review*, 48(4): 371–377.

Latukha, M. (2010). *Human Resource Management at Yandex*, The European Case Clearing House (ECCH). 2010-410-101-1.

Latukha, M., Panibratov, A., and Safonova-Salvadori, E. (2011). Entrepreneurial FDI in emerging economies: Russian SME strategy for Brazil, *International Journal of Entrepreneurship and Innovation*, 12(3): 201–212.

Luostarinen, R. (1980). *Internationalisation of the Firm*. Helsinki: Acta Academicae Oeconomicae Helsingiensis.

Luo, Y. and Tung, R.L. (2007). International expansion of emerging market enterprises, *Journal of International Business Studies*, 38: 481–498.

Majkgård, A. and Sharma, D. (1998). Client-following and market-seeking strategies in the internationalisation of service firms, *Journal of Business-to-Business Marketing*, 4(3): 1–41.

Oystein, M. and Servais, P. (2002). Born global or gradual global? Examining the export behaviour of small and medium-sized enterprises, *Journal of International Marketing*, 10(3): 49–72.

Panibratov, A. (2009). Internationalisation process of Russian construction industry: Inward investments perspective, *Journal for East European Management Studies*, 2: 210–228.

Panibratov, A. and Verba, C. (2011). Russian banking sector: Key points of international expansion, *Organisations and Markets in Emerging Economies*, 2(1): 63–74.

Pauwels, P. and de Ruyter, J.C. (2005). Research on international service marketing: A state of the art, *Advances in International Marketing*, 15: 75–91.

Rasiah, R., Gammeltoft, P., and Jiang, Y. (2010). Home government policies for outward FDI from emerging economies: Lessons from Asia, *International Journal of Emerging Markets*, 5(3/4): 333–357.

Rugman, A. and Verbeke, A. (2003). Extending the theory of the multinational enterprise – internalisation and strategic management perspectives, *Journal of International Business Studies*, 34(2): 125–137.

Sanchez-Peinado, E. and Pla-Barber, J. (2006). A multidimensional concept of uncertainty and its influence on the entry mode choice: An empirical analysis in the service sector, *International Business Review*, 15: 215–232.

Vahtra, P. and Liuhto, K. (2006). An overview of Russia's largest corporations abroad, in K. Liuhto (Ed.) *Expansion or Exodus – Why do Russian Corporations Invest Abroad?* New York, NY: International Business Press: 23–40.

Vandermerwe, S. and Chadwick, M. (1989). The internationalisation of services, *The Service Industries Journal*, 9(1): 79–93.

Vernon. R. (1966). International investment and international trade in the product cycle. *Quarterly Journal of Economics*, 80: 190–207.

Vernon-Wortzel, H. and Wortzel, L.H. (1988). Globalizing strategies for multinationals from developing countries, *Columbia Journal of World Business*, Spring: 27–55.

14
Longitudinal Internationalization Processes of Born Globals: Three Chinese Cases of Radical Change and the Global Crisis

Xiaotian Zhang and Jorma Larimo

Introduction

The research interests in SMEs' internationalization processes have increased rapidly in recent decades. Internationalization processes have been studied for many years through different theoretical approaches and many arguments have been discussed in order to give a clearer picture of what internationalization is and how a firm goes international (Welch and Luostarinen, 1988; Johanson and Mattsson, 1988; Mattsson and Hertz, 1998). In the past two decades, born global studies have been conducted mainly in high-tech industries, but born globals have also been identified in other fields, like the design sector and low-tech (e.g. food) industries. Both external and internal factors, such as the owner's background, orientation and commitment of the owners/key managers, networking, modern communication methods, firm's tangible and intangible resources, industrial clusters, and governmental influence have to be taken into account to analyze the reasons for driving born global firms' fast internationalization and to illustrate their development paths.

Even though the attention on the later stages of a firm's internationalization process is increasing, a gap still remains in previous studies of born globals: These studies focus on how a firm initially becomes born global and what drives such fast internationalization. Very few studies have concentrated on what is a firm's internationalization path after it has become international and its long-term development (Zettinig and Benson-Rea, 2008). The internationalization process may also involve radical changes, such as market exit and re-entry. Previous studies by Calof and Beamish (1995), Benito (1997), Johanson and Vahlne (2009) on 'de-internationalization' and the evidence from Welch and Welch (2009) on 're-internationalization' have clearly proved that a firm's internationalization process may often be depicted as a wavy line rather than a straight line or curve. Furthermore, Vissak's (2010b) work on nonlinear internationalization addressed various nonlinear processes, including re-/de-internationalization, born again global, etc., and it concludes that nonlinear internationalization is neither an irregular deviation nor an exception of linear internationalization, but linear internationalization is an exception of nonlinear internationalization.

The main aim of this chapter is to analyze the development of the international operations of born global firms in the long run, rather than over a short period of time. The objectives of the study are to:

- summarize the key features and operationalizations of born global firms;
- analyze born global cases and their international operation development in the long run with a focus on the changes in terms of foreign market exit and re-entry.

A qualitative case study research method is selected and three Chinese born global company cases are chosen to illustrate their long-term international development. The three cases demonstrate the features associated with born global firms as identified in previous research, the strategies that the case firms selected, and the kind of de-internationalization and re-internationalization as identified when their international operations were analyzed in the long run (over a period of 15 years). The cases also exhibit the reasons and motives for the changes in their operations during the global financial crisis.

The chapter sets out with a literature review, which clarifies the definitions of the internationalization process and explores internationalization forms and processes. The review focuses on the existing literature on born globals and their internationalization processes to indicate the gaps in research. Following this, three case studies from China are presented to demonstrate different kinds of development path. The chapter concludes with a discussion, conclusions, and suggestions for further research.

Literature review

This section presents some of the existing publications related to internationalization, internationalization process, and born globals. Its aim is to provide an overview of the previous studies and research in order to summarize the key features assumed to be linked to the born global firms, their existence, and international operations.

Internationalization theories

The internationalization processes of firms have been a popular subject of widespread research during the past several decades. As the concept of internationalization is still elusive even after several decades of studies (Kuivalainen and Sundqvist, 2006), the views on the internationalization process need to be re-conceptualized (Bell *et al.*, 2003). Welch and Luostarinen (1988) defined internationalization as 'a process of increasing involvement in foreign operations and commitment with international markets. A company becomes involved in international business when it sells its products to foreign markets, buys products from abroad or starts to cooperate in some area with a foreign firm. Internationalization is a process which starts with inward operations, continues with outward operations and finally is strengthened with co-operative models'. And later Luostarinen (1994) gave a clearer definition of internationalization as 'a step-by-step process of international business development whereby a firm becomes increasingly committed to and involved in international business operations through specific products in selected markets'. Meanwhile, Johanson and Mattsson (1988) defined internationalization as 'the number and strength of the relationships between the different parts of the global production network increase'. Korhonen *et al.* (1996) made the distinction between inward and outward activities. Johanson and Mattsson (1988), as well as Mattsson and Hertz (1998), developed the network approach to study internationalization. They consider the business networks as the relationships among the firm and its customers, suppliers, competitors, and government. They argue that in the business network the number and strength of the relationships between different parts increases as the internationalization of the firm develops. Ahokangas (1998) also argues that 'the internationalization process is a cumulative process in which relationships are continually established, developed, maintained, and dissolved in order to achieve the objectives of the firm'.

Born global studies

From the mid-1990s there has been an increasing number of studies focusing on the rapid internationalization of new ventures after their start-up in a fashion that cannot be explained by the slow process described by the Uppsala school (e.g. Lindqvist, 1991; Rennie, 1993; Oviatt and McDougall, 1994; Bell, 1995; Knight and Cavusgil, 1996; Madsen and Servais, 1997; Aspelund and Moen, 2001). Table 14.1 summarizes the key facilitating factors of the increasing prevalence of rapidly internationalizing firms, as well as the key distinctive features of these firms and triggers for their internationalization.

These rapidly internationalizing firms have received different titles. Lindqvist (1991) calls these types of firms infant multinationals. Oviatt

Table 14.1 Conditions and distinctive features of born global firms (based on Cavusgil and Knight, 2009)

Facilitating Factors	Globalization of markets Advances in communication and information technologies Advances in production technologies Global niche markets Global networks
Distinctive Features	Highly active in international markets from or near founding Characterized by limited financial and tangible resources Found across most industries Managers have a strong international outlook and international entrepreneurial orientation Often emphasize differentiation strategy Often emphasize superior product quality Leverage advanced communications and information technologies Typically use external, independent intermediaries for distribution in foreign markets
Internationalization Triggers	Export pull Export push Worldwide monopoly position Product-market conditions necessitating international involvement Superior product offerings Global network relationships Global niche markets

and McDougall (1994) classify them as international new ventures (INV), whereas Rennie (1993) gives them the name of 'born globals'. 'Born global' seems to be the most commonly adopted term (see, e.g. Rialp *et al.*, 2005).

In defining born globals, scholars focus on different aspects. The Born Global Model (McKinsey and Co., 1993; Knight and Cavusgil, 1996; Madsen and Servais, 1997) was coined in a survey for The Australian Manufacturing Council by the consultants of McKinsey (see McKinsey and Co., 1993; Rennie, 1993). It accepts that the firm should be internationalized during the first three years since establishment. It should enter culturally distant foreign countries and regions, and achieve at least a 25 per cent share of turnover from abroad during this period. In other studies the time frame from the establishment to the beginning of international sales has varied quite a lot—from two to six, and even nine years, but the most common view or condition for a firm to be called a born global seems to be that the international sales have to start within three years of establishment (see reviews by Rialp *et al.*, 2005). Furthermore, there appears to be significant variation in what should be the minimum share of exports and other conditions related to the international sales of born global. Some speculate that international sales in general are enough of an indicator, but most authors specify that in order to be called born global, the international sales of a firm should have reached at least 10 per cent (Zhou *et al.*, 2007). More common is the view that there should be at least a 25 per cent limit of international sales within three years (see Rialp *et al.*, 2005). However, some authors have set stricter conditions. Luostarinen and Gabrielsson (2004) argue that at least half of the sales should be outside the home continent of the firm. Meanwhile, Lummaa (2002) states that sales should be at least in five foreign countries and these should be located in at least two cultural clusters. A typical and commonly required feature for a firm to be called a born global seems to be that among the first target countries there are also geographically and/or culturally more distant countries from the home country of the firm, in contrast to the original Uppsala model (see, e.g. Bell, 1995).

Other issues related to born global firms are the background and other key features of the owners or the management team. Birley and Norburn (1987) noticed that the owners of the international new ventures (INVs) usually have more overseas travel, work, or education experience. Furthermore, these authors noted that in born global firms the global mindset of managers existed from the creation of the firms and these firms started their foreign businesses very quickly. Furthermore, Knight and Cavusgil (1996), McAuley (1999), and Freeman and Cavusgil (2007) consider that the entrepreneurial orientation, prior knowledge, commitment of the owner(s) of the firm to internationalization and global mindset of the owners give high value toward driving the firm's internationalization processes and its speed, because prior business experience leads to a better capacity to facilitate the acquisition of additional knowledge, which accelerates the entry actions toward the foreign market (Oviatt and McDougall, 2005).

Other features often attributed to born global firms are networking and establishment of alliances. For instance, Granovetter (1985), Ellis and Pecotich (2001), and Sharma and Blomstermo (2003) have studied the role of networks in born global firm's internationalization processes and their results give support to the importance of networking. Additional support for the importance of networking in internationalization focusing on the information technology sector is found in the studies by Hara and Kanai (1994), and Bell (1995). Gulati (1999) suggests that firms use networks to generate resources instead of developing them on their own. Finally, Coviello and Munro (1995) emphasize the importance of global social networks, which are described as 'the web of personal connections and relationships for the purpose of securing favors in personal and/or organizational actions'.

Concerning international cooperation, Chetty and Campbell-Hunt (2004) argue that born global SMEs enter world markets via the creation of strategic partnership, thus benefitting from the networks of their partners, their local knowledge and marketing capabilities. Alliances and partnerships can significantly accelerate the deepening of entry into existing markets or entry into new markets. Alliances and partnerships may be pivotal, especially in cases of market entry into new geographically and/or culturally more distant markets or into markets with intense competition.

In summary, the above section has explained that the key feature of born global firms is their very 'rapid' internationalization after establishment—but the views on what 'rapid' means have varied from one to even nine years, three years being a quite commonly used time period. The second feature is the level of international sales: some authors do not state any specific level, some refer to at least 25 per cent from total sales after three years, and some state that at least 50 per cent from total sales should come either from countries belonging to two or more cultural clusters or the share of sales outside the home continent should be over 50 per cent. However, but when this percentage is achieved they do not specify. The third feature is that the foreign sales of a firm has to expand rapidly to several target countries and the first target country may also be geographically more distant from the home market. The fourth feature is that the owners (or key managers) of the company have previous international experience, and are internationally oriented and committed to foreign operations. The fifth feature is that networking and strategic alliances are important to speed up internationalization (to speed up the process of building or compensating for a firm's resources or lack of them, to speed up entry into new markets, etc.). The sixth feature is that internationalization is not necessarily a gradual, smoothly developing process. Instead, there may be periods of very rapid expansion and also slower periods, and even periods of decreasing international operations.

Entry and re-entry of born global firms

Oviatt and McDougall (1994), Madsen and Servais (1997), and Fan and Phan (2007) highlight the importance of the firms' home market for internationalization. Although there are born global firms in large markets such as the US and Germany, and in emerging markets such as China and Brazil, several studies clearly show that firms in small domestic markets are under higher pressure to be born global and internationalize faster (see e.g. Rialp *et al.*, 2005). Zucchella and Scabini (2007) suggest that SMEs have better opportunities to internationalize faster if they locate and operate in regional clusters and industrial zones.

Even though the phenomenon of born global has been studied over two decades, it is still not well explained (Oviatt and McDougall, 2005). Most studies focus on how a firm becomes born global and the determinants of this process, and not enough studies have been devoted to the post-internationalization processes of a born global firm—that is, what happens to born globals after they become international and to what happens in their post-internationalization process. In the long run, the development of international sales and operations of born global firms is not necessarily a smooth and gradual expanding process. There may be radical changes in the role of international sales. Calof and Beamish (1995), Benito (1997), Freeman (2007), and Johanson and Vahlne (2009) have focused on 'de-internationalization', which shows a situation where a firm reduces or stops activities in all or some foreign markets. Also, Bell *et al.* (2003) found evidence from situations where an internationalized firm turned back to its domestic market, and even suspended all the cross-border activities, which have lasted more than ten years. Then some of these firms suddenly internationalized rapidly again and became highly international. The authors named them 'born-again globals'.

Welch and Welch (2009) use the term 're-internationalization' and define it as a 'process involving a period of international business activity, then exit from international operations, followed by a time-out period of some duration, then a process of international re-entry, concluding with successfully renewed international operations'. Recently, a group of scholars (Javalgi *et al.*, 2011) developed a framework of global market re-entry. This shows that both global environment (economic, political, and cultural factors) and host-country environment (changing economic, political, and cultural factors) influence a firm's re-entry decision. According to their model, the main objectives of a firm's re-entry are to achieve growth and diversification, salvaging sunk costs and capturing resources. The international knowledge and experience gained earlier gives the company a good basis for making the re-entry decision, selecting the markets and deciding about the operation strategies to be applied in the re-entry.

In the empirical part of this chapter we shall focus our analysis on the long-term development of international operations. We will analyze the features that are regarded to be typical of born global firms, which could be identified in the case of these firms and the type of links that could be identified between these features. Furthermore, we focus on the radical changes of the case firms' later stages of internationalization and discover the reasons for their foreign market entry, exit, and re-entry.

Methodology and case selection

Case studies have been chosen as the method of research, as these allow building, expanding, and generalizing theories by combining existing theoretical knowledge with new empirical insights (Dyer and Wilkins, 1991; Yin, 1994; Marschan-Piekkari *et al.*, 2010; Vissak, 2010a). In this chapter, a multiple case study approach (Miles and Huberman, 1994) was selected in order to illustrate development trends, to make improved generalizations and to reduce the risk of misjudging a particular situation (Leonard-Barton, 1990).

The three cases were selected from more than 200 Chinese firms which participated in a survey focusing on the internationalization of Chinese SMEs conducted in 2009. All selected firms were located in South and East China, because in these regions there are many export-oriented firms which started exporting a long time ago. This also makes it possible to see the changes that the process of their internationalization has undergone in the long term. The three companies selected were established at about the same time and had a similar number of employees and turnover, which facilitated comparative research. They fulfilled the criteria set as 'born global', but later, due to different circumstances, their internationalization processes became completely different.

In-depth interviews using structured questionnaires were used for data collection. With company A, face-to-face interviews were carried out with the three founders of the company, and later on an extra interview with the sales manager was conducted via internet phone. The total interview time for company A was five hours. With company B, a three-hour face-to-face interview with the two owners of the company took place, and another two-hour interview was conducted via the internet. The two founders of company C joined the interview via the internet and the total interview time was three and half hours.

All interviews were conducted in Chinese. The structured questionnaires were carefully prepared in Chinese and sent to all interviewees before the interviews. Several key informants were selected from the three firms to see multiple viewpoints and to reduce the likelihood of misinterpretation (Ghauri, 2004). The interviewer was a native Chinese speaker who was fluent in English. He ensured that the questions were clearly understood and answered. During the interviews, questions about the development histories of the firm, the business situation at the beginning, the first export performance, export strategies, reasons for success, future development, and so on. were asked and answered in full. Data from each firm's export and import records, the annual turnover, the annual income; and the net profit were collected via two channels: (i) each firm's financial department and (ii) the Trade and Industry Bureau and the Financial and Tax Department of the local government. We followed the recommended '24-hour rule' for completing the detailed interview notes and impressions (Yin, 1994).

Due to the requests of the owners and general managers, the firms' names and some financial data have not been disclosed. For the same reason and to retain anonymity, the interviewees are only referred to according to their occupational titles.

Case studies

Case one

Company A is a manufacturer of electronic chargers including travel, universal, hands-free phone chargers and mobile phone chargers. The factory is located in the industrial zone of Guangzhou city, Southern China. Currently, the company has 223 full-time employees including 12 managerial staff, 15 R&D staff, 19 quality control staff and 177 technical workers. The turnover of the company was US$14.83 million in 2010.

Company A was established in 1997 by three Chinese founders. Two had a postgraduate degree in business and worked in the US together, and the third founder is their mutual friend who worked in local government. All three of them have higher education degrees in business and are fluent in English. The idea of forming a new factory came from the first two founders. During their ten-year stay in the US, they were well connected with a few major electronic products sales chains there, and with a few wholesalers in Canada. The huge demand for electronic chargers in North the US gave them strong confidence and a desire to start production in China. The third founder joined the team and began preparatory work in 1995.

In 1997 the manufacturing enterprise was officially opened with capital of RMB8 million. The major financial investment came from the three founders and a bank loan. The factory started with 55 employees and the main targets were export to the US and production for the domestic Chinese market.

The first order came to the factory in 1997 from a company in Fujian province and the second order was from a manufacturer in Guangdong province. Company A received their first big order from the US at the beginning of 1998. Right after that, company A got an order for original equipment manufacturer (OEM) production for hands-free phone chargers from another US sales chain. The Canadian partner made the order at the end of 1998 of 50,000 universal chargers. Company A had an excellent start, and the two founders went back to the USA at the end of 1998 for an international exhibition and to strengthen the co-operation with their partners. During the exhibition, they established connections with one German and one British buyer. Both placed orders for travel chargers at the beginning of 1999. Also during their trip in 1998, the founders opened a small office in Chicago where two Chinese colleagues began to work on sales and marketing. As of mid-1999, company A already had more than 100 employees and exported to six partners in four countries. By the end of 1999, company A had also received orders from Singapore and Malaysia via the International Guangzhou Trading Exhibition.

In 2000, company A was awarded Self-Administrated Import and Export Certification and it expanded the factory by building two new production workshops with two modernized production lines. The period between 2000 and 2006 was characterized by growth. It exported products to 12 countries and participated in four international exhibitions each year in the USA, Germany, and Russia. Its branch office in Hamburg was opened in 2003 and the representative office in Moscow in 2004.

However, the company's growth strategy worked well only until 2007. As a result of the negative impact of the global financial crisis, company A started to lose orders from the US and later on from Western Europe. In 2009 orders from Canada, the USA, or European countries, and the offices in Chicago and Russia were closed temporarily. However, other partners still made orders, even though the quantities were reduced significantly. Different from others, the founders of company A decided to form an R&D department in 2009 with the purpose of designing and developing new models of chargers, such as solar mobile phone chargers. With this effort, the situation improved in 2010, and it got orders again from the former partners in the USA and Canada. Its new solar mobile phone chargers were welcomed in Italy and Spain. The company survived this crisis and bounced back. As suggested by the founder of company A, the crisis was somehow a test for Chinese export-oriented manufacturers. The ones that stood strong and knew how to innovate and move ahead survived (Table 14.2).

Case two

Company B is a manufacturer producing remote controls and flyback transformers. The factory is located in the 'Chinese Electronic Town'-Qinlan town, Tianchang city in Anhui province. Currently there are 185 full-time employees of which 15 are managerial staff, 22 R&D staff, 55 higher-level technical workers and 93 workers. The turnover of company B in 2010 was US$11.52 million.

Company B was established in 1996 by two Chinese founders. Both worked in the local government offices and in a trading company in Shanghai before they started the new business. They were educated in Shanghai, were fluent in English and had experience of foreign exhibitions and trade fairs. Company B was established with the financial resources of the founders and their families, and a small bank loan. In their previous jobs, the founders had established good connections with foreign partners, especially in the USA. They had also identified the demand for remote controls and flyback transformers from other manufacturers in the domestic market.

Table 14.2 Turnover of company A, 1997–2010 (US$ millions)

	CN	US	CA	GE	UK	NE	FR	RU	SIN	MA	IT	SP	Total
1997	0.52	–	–	–	–	–	–	–	–	–	–	–	0.52
1998	0.65	0.36	0.21	–	–	–	–	–	–	–	–	–	1.22
1999	0.81	0.45	0.22	0.10	0.09	–	–	–	0.05	0.09	–	–	1.81
2000	0.85	0.82	0.52	0.19	0.11	–	–	–	0.08	0.12	–	–	2.69
2001	1.05	1.32	0.61	0.33	0.12	0.10	0.11	–	0.10	0.15	0.33	0.29	4.51
2002	2.33	1.35	0.83	0.52	0.15	0.22	0.19	0.20	0.12	0.28	0.65	0.45	7.29
2003	3.00	2.53	1.23	0.68	0.33	0.33	0.36	0.25	0.09	0.33	0.73	0.85	10.71
2004	3.69	3.39	2.89	1.02	0.52	0.51	0.45	0.57	0.15	0.36	0.98	1.21	15.74
2005	3.12	3.45	2.92	1.95	0.88	0.75	0.72	0.89	0.16	0.39	1.12	1.56	17.91
2006	3.19	2.12	1.22	2.55	1.88	0.75	1.00	1.12	0.22	0.42	1.45	2.00	17.92
2007	3.23	1.22	0.85	1.92	1.03	0.32	0.85	1.33	0.18	0.29	1.65	1.92	14.79
2008	3.88	0.85	0.32	1.08	0.55	0.10	0.62	1.06	0.14	0.21	0.85	1.85	11.51
2009	4.12	–	–	1.05	–	–	0.33	0.95	0.18	0.24	–	1.68	8.55
2010	4.28	1.53	0.92	1.12	0.89	0.52	0.69	0.82	0.21	0.30	1.52	2.03	14.83
2011 till Nov	4.51	2.32	0.98	1.53	0.99	0.43	0.52	1.07	0.20	0.39	1.13	2.09	16.16

CN-China, US-the United States, CA-Canada, GE-Germany, UK-United Kingdom, NE-Netherlands, FR-France, RU-Russia, SIN-Singapore, MA-Malaysia, IT-Italy, SP Spain.

The first order of 50 thousand remote controls for air conditioners came very quickly from the local air conditioner producer. The first foreign order came in 1996 from the US partner with whom they had previously worked in Shanghai. In 1997, company B started to export to Canada and Mexico on the US partner's recommendation, plugging into their networks. In the same year, it got two important domestic clients who are large manufacturers of radio-controlled toys in mainland China. In 1998 local government started to promote their 'Chinese Electronic Town' by organizing a few exhibitions and promotional conferences. Many foreign buyers were invited to come to visit the electronic town and its industrial zone. From this platform, company B started to export to Germany and Sweden. To improve its performance in Europe, in 1998 it opened its representative office in Düsseldorf where two Chinese and one German colleague worked.

Company B received ISO9001 certification and Self-Administrated Import and Export Certification in 2000 which could be considered a milestone. By this time it already exported to seven countries: the USA, Canada, Mexico, Germany, the Netherlands, Sweden, and Finland. In the domestic market it produced remote controls for three major TV manufacturers and two major radio-controlled toys producers.

For the first time in 2002, the company joined an industrial exhibition in Moscow where it met one buyer from Russia and one from Belarus. Even though Eastern Europe was not its target market, company B welcomed orders from this growing market. However, another main target of company B was to supply major electronic producers in China. In 2004 it had more than eight stable major domestic partners.

During the financial crisis it became very difficult for many Chinese manufacturers to export, and the same applied to company B. After 2006, orders from the US and Western Europe shrank. By the end of 2008, company B lost almost all of its foreign orders due to the negative influence of the global financial crisis. The founders realized that the situation was dire and decided to focus on the major domestic partners. In 2009, company B supplied only the Chinese domestic manufacturers who made branded electronic products. Even though the turnover fell from 2007 to 2009, company B survived by relying on its domestic market which had considerable demand. In 2010, previous German partners visited company B again and made another order. At the end of 2010, one US company and one Dutch company also placed orders. The owner of company B explained that the domestic market would be its main focus but that it would still need to have more exports as the profit rates are much higher than those in the domestic markets. Company B has developed a new five-year strategy of exporting to the US, the EU, and Africa (Table 14.3).

Case three

Company C is a manufacturer producing clothes that include tights, leggings, legwarmers, socks, and pantyhose. It was established in 1997 and located in Yiwu city, Zhejiang province. Together with two local Chinese founders, there were 68 people working in the factory in the first year. Today, company C has more than 389 employees of whom 15 are managerial staff, 22 R&D staff, 6 light industrial engineers, 85 skilled workers and 261 workers. The turnover of company C in 2010 was US$18.58 million.

The two local Chinese founders had never been abroad, couldn't speak any foreign language, and their education was from high school only. The reason why they started the business was because they had a very close connection with a few local footwear enterprises. These usually ordered socks and sold them together with shoes in their own brand shops. As personal connections are one of the main success factors in doing business in China, the two founders started the new company and were promised orders from local partners.

Two of local footwear enterprises placed orders in the first year, another two footwear groups from Chengdu city, West of China, also placed orders. However, even though the leaders of company C didn't have a clear plan for internationalization, they met a few foreign buyers from the US via the local footwear enterprises. The US companies placed quite a large order of sports socks in 1998, and later on a Canadian company also placed an order through the recommendation of a local enterprise. The considerable export benefit increased the interests of two founders and they decided to send a sales manager to Los Angeles to open a sales office. In the same year, they got two Italian buyers from the US. Italian partners' visits and cooperation also opened the door to the European market. In 1999, buyers from France and Spain began to order OEM and original designed manufacturer (ODM) services from company C.

In 2000, the founders of company C decided to divide the sales department into a domestic sales division and an international sales division. The international sales division focuses on expanding sales networks abroad and increasing exports. The domestic sales division is focused on finding more clients who are stable larger footwear enterprises. Both divisions developed quite well between 2000 until 2006. The company exports to 8 foreign countries and supplies to 15 domestic enterprises.

Table 14.3 Turnover of company B, 1996–2010 (US$ millions)

	CN	US	CA	ME	GE	SW	FIN	NE	RU	BY	Total
1996	0.33	0.12	–	–	–	–	–	–	–	–	0.45
1997	0.45	0.23	0.09	0.05	–	–	–	–	–	–	0.82
1998	1.02	0.68	0.50	0.12	0.32	0.21	–	–	–	–	2.85
1999	1.65	1.35	0.58	0.18	0.45	0.22	0.10	–	–	–	4.53
2000	2.35	1.52	0.69	0.32	0.68	0.21	0.15	0.12	–	–	6.04
2001	4.00	1.65	0.73	0.35	1.23	0.18	0.16	0.15	–	–	8.45
2002	3.86	1.66	1.00	0.38	1.32	0.32	0.15	0.25	0.10	0.03	9.07
200e	4.52	1.83	0.82	0.32	1.33	0.28	0.21	0.28	0.15	0.07	9.81
2004	5.65	2.00	0.93	0.39	1.35	0.26	0.25	0.32	0.31	0.10	11.56
2005	5.59	1.65	1.01	0.42	1.82	0.28	0.18	0.33	0.52	0.07	11.87
2006	6.74	1.02	0.75	0.31	1.05	0.15	0.15	0.27	0.45	–	10.89
2007	6.89	0.83	0.51	0.23	0.85	0.10	0.10	0.19	0.31	0.05	10.06
2008	7.03	0.32	0.21	0.10	0.32	0.05	0.08	0.11	0.18	0.03	8.43
2009	6.55	–	–	–	–	–	–	–	–	–	6.55
2010	7.56	0.45	–	–	0.33	–	–	0.18	–	–	8.52
2011 till Nov	7.92	1.03	–	0.21	0.35	–	–	0.21	0.33	0.15	10.20

CN-China, US-the United States, CA-Canada, ME-Mexico, GE-Germany, SW-Sweden, FIN-Finland, NE-Netherlands, RU-Russia, BY-Belarus.

Company C got the Self-Administrated Import and Export Certification and ISO9001 Certification in 2000, which made it more convenient for it to develop the business.

However, due to the strict regulations and both European and US new anti-dumping policies for Chinese textile products, company C feels that it has become more and more difficult to export. During the previous financial crisis, it started losing its foreign clients one by one. At the end of 2009, company C stopped all export activities. The founders decided to continue focusing on the domestic market as their domestic sales division was still working effectively.

During the interview, both founders explained that supplying footwear for the big Chinese market is a lot easier and more predictable than exporting abroad. Even though the margin may be lower than when supplying foreign companies, it is still preferable to focus on the domestic market, as this has more than 25 per cent of the world's consumers. The founders also emphasized that the future strategy for the company is to become a leading OEM and ODM supplier for Chinese domestic brand footwear producers and thus the company is not planning to undertake any further international activities (Table 14.4).

Discussion

Characteristics of the born global firms

The case studies discussed so far show that the three case companies initially internationalized according to the traditional 'Born Global Model'. They are born global as per the definitions of Rennie (1993), Oviatt and McDougall (1994), Knight and Cavusgil (1996), and Lummaa (2002). Based on Cavusgil and Knight's (2009) suggestion of the characteristics of born global, here we test the three case firms for these features (see Table 14.5).

Company A was established in 1997, received the first domestic order in 1997 from a company in Fujian province, and the first foreign order came from the US at the beginning of 1998. In the same year, another US and a Canadian company placed their orders. In 1999, company A started to export to one German and one British buyer. From the second year of its establishment, its export share reached more than 25 per cent. Company B was established in 1996 and the first domestic order was from a local air conditioner producer. The first cross-border order also came in 1996 from the US partner. In 1997, company B began to export to Canada and Mexico, and in 1998 to Germany and Sweden.

Table 14.4 Turnover of company C, 1997–2011 (US$ millions)

	CN	US	CA	IT	FR	SP	PO	RU	TU	Total
1997	0.95	0.53	0.15	–	–	–	–	–	–	1.63
1998	2.56	1.02	0.56	0.12	–	–	–	–	–	4.26
1999	3.52	1.23	0.62	0.15	0.09	0.11	–	–	–	5.72
2000	5.55	1.55	0.65	0.23	0.11	0.23	–	–	–	8.32
2001	7.69	1.69	0.52	0.56	0.12	0.25	–	–	–	10.83
2002	9.12	2.35	0.25	1.00	0.15	0.31	0.05	0.07	–	13.30
2003	10.23	2.56	0.65	1.05	0.15	0.32	0.09	0.10	0.03	15.18
2004	10.25	3.03	0.68	1.10	–	0.40	0.12	0.12	0.05	15.75
2005	12.35	2.15	0.92	1.05	0.12	0.36	0.15	0.10	–	17.20
2006	13.89	2.00	0.75	0.89	0.15	0.28	0.18	0.15	0.08	18.37
2007	14.42	1.43	0.35	0.72	0.23	0.19	0.21	0.10	0.10	17.75
2008	15.99	0.75	0.21	0.32	0.10	0.12	0.10	0.05	0.06	17.70
2009	16.72	0.10	–	0.11	–	–	0.02	–	–	16.95
2010	18.58	–	–	–	–	–	–	–	–	18.58
2011 till Nov	20.15	–	–	–	–	–	–	–	–	20.15

CN-China, US-the United States, CA-Canada, IT-Italy, FR-France, SP-Spain, PO-Poland, RU-Russia, TU-Turkey.

Table 14.5 Born global features of case firms

		Firm A	Firm B	Firm C
Distinctive Features	Highly active in international markets from or near founding	HIGH	HIGH	MIDDLE
	Characterized by limited financial and tangible resources	HIGH	HIGH	HIGH
	Managers have a strong international outlook and international entrepreneurial orientation	HIGH	HIGH	MIDDLE
	Often emphasize differentiation strategy	HIGH	HIGH	MIDDLE
	Often emphasize superior product quality	HIGH	HIGH	HIGH
	Leverage advanced communication and information technologies	HIGH	HIGH	HIGH
	Typically use external, independent intermediaries for distribution in foreign markets	HIGH	HIGH	HIGH

Company B also had more than 25 per cent of export share since the second year of its foundation. Company C was founded in 1997 and received four orders from domestic firms. In 1998 it started to export to the USA and Canada, and in 1999 to France and Spain. Company C has had more than 25 per cent export share since the first year of its establishment. All three case firms' internationalization developments were smooth from their establishment until 2007.

Longitudinal internationalization processes

In this part we study the longitudinal internationalization processes of the three case companies in terms of international market entry (early stages of internationalization process), international market exit (de-internationalization), and international market re-entry (re-internationalization). The key drivers in the global and host-country environment are discussed, and the discussion focuses on re-entry objectives and re-entry decisions.

International market entry (early stages of internationalization processes)

Global environment drivers, as one of the world's major economies, China has continued its economic reform of 'opening up' since 1978

Table 14.6 The early internationalization processes of case firms

Firm	1st Export Country	2nd Export Country	3rd Export Country	1st Export Country in EU	Main Export Market
A	USA	Canada	Germany	Germany	USA
B	USA	Canada	Mexico	Germany	USA
C	USA	Canada	France	France	USA

and its central and local governments have been heavily promoting exporting toward major international markets such as the US, the UK, Germany, Australia and Japan.

The three case firms have similar internationalization processes in terms of export orders (see Table 14.6). All three firms first exported to the USA, then to the European Union in a very clear order: the US, Canada and the EU. During the interview, the managers of companies A and B explained that the reasons why they started exporting to the USA and the EU instead of exporting to Vietnam or India first was because of the owners' personal connection and networks in those regions. The reason for company C to export firstly to the USA and the EU is its home country local networks, which brought to it the basic trust and positive introduction from local partners to foreign buyers.

Considering the host-country environment, most Chinese entrepreneurs have a common mindset to start exporting to larger developed country markets to achieve better performance. The three case companies had the same international market entry mode: Exporting followed by establishing representative offices or branch offices.

International market exit (de-internationalization)

After almost ten years of growth in international markets, the three case companies started de-internationalization in 2007. The main reason for their exit actions was the global financial crisis, which changed the global and host-countries environment radically.

The de-internationalization speed of the three case companies was very fast: company B and C totally exited the international market within three years. This was possible because of their low commitment international market entry mode—that is, exporting. Their products were mainly low-tech with much less competitiveness in diversification and innovation.

International market re-entry (re-internationalization)

Re-entry objectives

Companies A and B decided to re-enter the international market and succeeded, whereas company C decided to stay in the domestic market. The objectives of companies A and B are mainly to focus on international growth and diversification. Since their establishment, companies they have wanted to benefit from their pre-existing network ties in the USA and export their products there based on speed of delivery and low cost of production. As none of the case firms made investments in plants or production and marketing facilities overseas, the salvaging sunk cost was not an objective. However, during the interview, the owners of companies A and B mentioned that for the long-term development of their firms they re-entered the previous international markets. This also shows their objectives to capture emerging opportunities in the markets of Russia, Ukraine, Brazil, India, and so on, and to access resources globally in order to reduce their increased production costs and to keep competitive pricing.

Company C decided to remain a domestic firm and focus on the Chinese mainland market without any action of re-entry because it acted as a supplier of large and growing domestic partners. The owner stated that it was much easier and less risky for them to do business just with trustworthy partners in mainland China.

Re-entry decisions

Companies A and B re-entered their previous markets. The mode and scope of re-entry were limited to exporting. However, during the exit period, company A founded its R&D department and started product innovation, which has made its re-entry much more effective and successful.

The companies' owners played a significant role in their internationalization processes. They had a major role in decision-making regarding whether or not to return to international markets after the financial crisis (see Table 14.7). Comparing the three case firms, owners (A, B) who had more knowledge of foreign markets, overseas experiences, and international networks were convinced that they had to return to international markets, which also shows their commitment to internationalization. One of the main purposes of the strategy of companies A and B is to export their products globally by engaging in OEM for foreign companies. Also, the reason why they successfully returned to

Table 14.7 Owners' internationalization factors of case companies

Owner	**Commitment to Internationalization**	**Knowledge of Foreign Market**	**Overseas Travel, Work and Study Experiences**	**Social Networks in China**	**Global Networks**	**Risk Taking Mindset**	**Learning Mindset**
Firm A	High	High	High	Middle	High	High	High
Firm B	High	Middle	Middle	High	Middle	High	High
Firm C	Low	Low	Low	High	Low	Low	Low

international markets is because of their willingness to learn and to take risks. Company A started its innovation during the crisis when it had low export performance. Company B's decision to return to global markets was driven by the considerable profit potential from foreign clients and the belief that joint manufacturing with foreign partners would reduce production and global logistics costs in the long run. Company C became born global mainly because of its good social networks in China with the help of some promotion by local government. However, with low commitment to internationalization, less knowledge of foreign markets and overseas experience, the owner of company C decided to stay in the domestic market as there was lower risk (lower risk-taking mindset), stable profits (strong social networks in China) and easier business (lower learning mindset).

Table 14.8 shows that companies A and B had re-entered most of their previous foreign markets but not expanded to any new markets.

Company A re-entered all of its previous foreign markets relying on of its previous partners, except for the USA, where company A also re-entered via some new partners. The re-entry methods were the same—that is, via exporting and establishing sales offices in their major foreign market (the USA). However, due to company A's R&D activities, the products it exported were innovative with new designs, which helped it to increase its export share in 2011. The re-entry happened naturally without any planning. The purpose of the re-entry was to increase the export share and profits of the firm, meanwhile based on R&D to export more innovative products for sustainable growth.

Company B re-entered only a few of its previous foreign markets as the owner still considered the Chinese domestic market to be the company's main focus and wanted to allocate limited resources to developing foreign markets. It re-entered all the previously targeted developed country markets using its contacts with its previous partners. The owner mentioned that it was more stable to work with previous partners as their previous cooperation could make re-entry much easier and of lower risk. However, in the emerging markets, company B re-entered via new partners as the previous partners were not very reliable and some of them had gone bankrupt. During the exit period, company B learned more about emerging markets and searched for long-term partners. Company B established a new strategy for overseas business development for the next five years in order to establish factories in emerging countries in order to ensure sustainable development by reducing production and global logistics costs. Therefore, the methods of company B's re-entry

Table 14.8 The re-entry of companies A and B

	US	CA	ME	UK	GE	NE	SW	FIN	IT	RU	BY
Exit	AB	AB	B	A	B	AB	B	B	A	B	B
Re-entry	AB	A	B	A	B	AB	–	–	A	B	B
Re-entry type of Company A	Exp,Sal	Exp	–	Exp	–	Exp	–	–	Exp	–	–
Re-entry type of Company B	Exp,Sal	–	Exp,Sal,JM	–	Exp,Sal	Exp	–	–	–	Exp,Sal,JM	Exp
Re-entry via same previous partners	AB	A	–	A	B	AB	–	–	A	–	–
Re-entry via new partners	AB	–	B	–	–	–	–	–	–	B	B
Order of re-entry of Company A	1	2	–	4	–	3	–	–	5	–	–
Order of re-entry of Company B	2	4	5	–	1	3	–	–	–	6	7

US-the United States, CA-Canada, ME-Mexico, GE-Germany, NE-Netherlands, SW-Sweden, FIN-Finland, IT-Italy, RU-Russia, BY-Belarus, Exp-Export, Sal-Sales Office, and JM-Joint Manufactures.

in emerging markets include exporting, establishing sales offices, and preparing future joint manufacturing projects with local partners.

Role of the global financial crisis

The global financial crisis had a strong impact on the three firms' internationalization processes (see Table 14.9).

The global financial crisis forced the three case firms' to de-internationalize and exit foreign markets. Company A exited from part of its foreign markets; Company B and C exited all foreign markets. This was possible as their international operation model was with low commitment. Moreover, in comparison to earlier years, companies

Table 14.9 The role of the global financial crisis in case firms' internationalization processes

Firm	Effects	Reasons for Effects	Actions During Crisis	Actions After Crisis
A	Lost part of foreign clients (de-internationalization)	Cross-border operation model was too simple; low-tech products; short of cost advantages	Establishment of R&D facilities; communication with previous foreign partners; seek new foreign partners	Re-enter all the previous foreign markets with innovative products
B	Lost all foreign clients (de-internationalization)	Cross-border operation model was too simple; low-tech products; short of cost advantages	Seek new foreign partners; strategy and communication for joint manufacturing abroad	Re-enter some previous markets; established joint manufacturing abroad with new partners
C	Lost all foreign clients (de-internationalization)	Cross-border operation model was too simple; low-tech products	Strengthen the co-operation with domestic partners	No re-entry; successful co-operation with domestic partners

A and B lost their advantage of having low production costs. Consequently, some of their previous partners changed their suppliers in China during and after the crisis.

Although all three firms were internationalized as born globals, following the crisis they have totally different operation models. In these cases, crisis could be considered as a learning and re-preparing period for the three case firms. Company A established its R&D facilities and started to produce innovative products. It communicated with previous partners to introduce its new products and also seek new foreign partners to increase its foreign sales. Company B focused more on the strategy of reducing the production cost. Hence, it became the joint manufacturers with new foreign partners in the emerging markets. Company C transferred all of its resources to focus on the domestic market, which so far has proved to be a successful decision.

Three types of internationalization process changes

To get an overview, we put the longitudinal internationalization processes of the three case companies together. Figure 14.1 shows that there were three types of internationalization process changes.

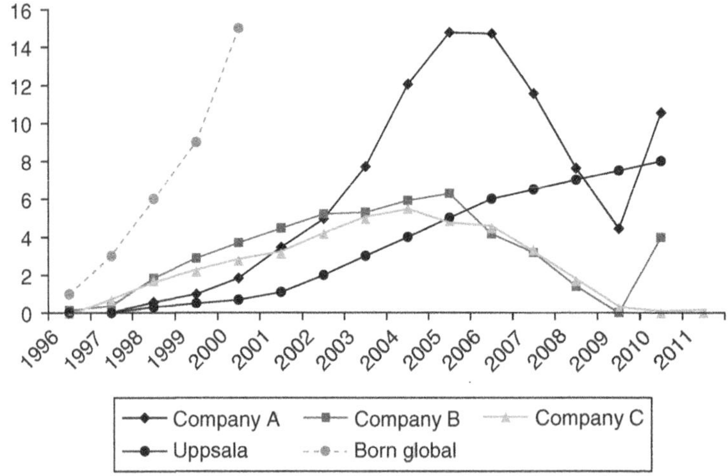

Figure 14.1 Internationalization process lines of the three case firms (formed according to their turnover)

Type 1: company A

Internationalized according to the born global model with almost ten years of international growth, then de-internationalized due to the impact of the global financial crisis. As soon as the economic situation improved, it started to re-internationalize into international markets.

Type 2: company B

Internationalized according to the born global model. It had almost ten years international growth, which was then followed by de-internationalization. The de-internationalization made the company become a completely domestic firm without any 'cross-border actions' or 'inward internationalization activities'. After a certain period of domestic development, the firm returned to international markets and continued its internationalization.

Type 3: company C

Internationalized according to the born global model. Had ten years of international growth followed by de-internationalization. This de-internalization made it become a domestic firm without any 'cross-border actions' or 'inward internationalization activities'. However, it remains focused on the domestic market and does not plan to go back to the international market.

Generalization

To generalize our longitudinal studies, we use Table 14.10, which shows the time outline and reasons for the changes.

From the above data we could conclude that there were common reasons for the changes in the three firms' internationalization behavior. First, the firms successfully became born globals because of the owners' good connections and previous contacts with either foreign or domestic partners. The industrial networks played a significant role in the first three years of international growth and business expansion.

All three firms experienced remarkable international growth from 1998 to 2007 due to high demand in the international market for lower-cost Chinese low-tech products and local governments' promotion that supported local enterprises to build up connections with foreign partners. However, the global financial crisis forced the companies to de-internationalize. Company A had stronger connections

Table 14.10 Timeline and reasons for the changes in international market entry, exit, and re-entry of the three case companies over time

	Become Born Global	Growth of Internationalization	De-internationalization	Become/Didn't Become Domestic Firm	Re-/not Re-internationalization
Company A	1997–1999 Owners have pre-contact in the USA; good connection with local government	1999–2007 Export-oriented strategy, huge demand in international market	2007–2009 The impact of global financial crisis and lack of product innovation	N/A New partners in emerging markets; strong previous co-operation relations	2009–2010 Owners' decision; export is always in the strategy; economic situation improves; innovation
Company B	1996–1998 Owners have contact in the USA; prior experience in business and government	1998–2006 Local government's promotion; export-oriented strategy, huge demand in international market	2006–2008 The impact of the global financial crisis	2008–2009 Owners' decision; firm has good partners and demand in domestic market	2009–2010 Owners' decision; economic situation improves; former client relations; huge demand in international market and better profit
Company C	1997–1999 Owners have good connection with local partners; recommendation by local partners; higher profit	1999–2008 Successfully using international networks; higher profit drives its speed of internationalization	2008–2009 Strict regulations and policies from both the European Union and the USA; the impact of the global financial crisis	2009–2011 Owners' decision; too difficult to export; export is not in the strategy; firm has very strong co-operation with a domestic firm and very profitable	N/A Owners' decision; too difficult to export; export is not in the strategy; the firm has very strong co-operation with a domestic firm and very profitable

and partnerships abroad, so it still had export opportunities in difficult times. Companies B and C had fewer connections abroad and better connections in the domestic market, so both turned to the domestic market only.

When we analyze the return of the three firms to international markets, we realize that the owners' decisions and their original strategy had a major impact. If the firm's owner had no clear purpose and strategy for foreign market growth at the beginning of establishment, then the export gains were more like an extra income for the firm. Hence, it was much easier for the firm to re-focus on the domestic market when it lost its foreign clients and connections during the crisis. The firm which did not re-internationalize received stable orders from its domestic market clients, which implied lower risk. However, this might be the case only in a country with a big enough domestic market.

Conclusions and implications

We could conclude that there are three types of change that could happen to the born global SMEs, as follows: (1) internationalize as born global, continue internalization and de-internalize, then re-internationalize; (2). internationalize as born global, continue internalization and de-internalize until it becomes a fully domestic firm, after that start to re-internationalize; (3) internationalize as born global, continue with internalization growth and de-internalize until it becomes a fully domestic firm and do not return to the international market in the future.

The unexpected external reasons, such as the global financial crisis, policy changes, international trade distractions and limitations, partnership changes, and so on all influence the 'de-internationalization part' of a firm's internationalization process. However, the owners' decision, the firm's strategic planning and any better opportunities in the domestic market are the main determinants of a firm's decision to return to the global market.

This chapter has certain limitations because the number of cases is not large enough to make a decisive generalization. However, it still offers new evidence for internationalization studies and fills the gap in the existing literature by discovering the three possible types of process changes in the internationalization of born global firms and the reasons behind them.

Future studies could certainly explore other aspects of the process studied in this chapter. For example, they could

- find more evidence that provides a more reliable basis for generalizations concerning the development of the internationalization process of born global firms and the reasons for changes during the process;
- develop additional case studies of companies in which the degree of internationalization was continuously increasing during the financial crisis, in order to cover all possible changes and paths of born global firms;
- conduct similar research as presented above of more traditionally internationalizing companies to compare their process changes and analyze the reasons for any changes.

Acknowledgments

This research was financed by the Estonian Science Foundation's Grant No. 8546.

Publication of this article is granted by the Doctoral School of Economics and Innovation created under the auspices of the European Social Fund.

References

Ahokangas, P. (1998). *Internationalisation and Resources. An Analysis of Processes in Nordic SMEs*. Doctoral dissertation, Vasa: Vaasan Yliopisto.

Aspelund, A. and Moen, Ø. (2001), A generation perspective on small firm internationalization: From traditional exporters and flexible specialists to born globals, *Advances in International Marketing*, 11: 197–225.

Bell, J. (1995). The internationalisation of small computer software firms – A further challenge to 'stage' theories, *European Journal of Marketing*, 29(8): 60–75.

Bell, J., McNaughton, R., Young, S. and Crick, D. (2003). Towards an integrative model of small firm internationalization, *Journal of International Entrepreneurship*, 1(4): 339–362.

Benito, G. (1997). Divestment of foreign production operations, *Applied Economics*, 29(10): 1365–1377.

Birley, S. and Norburn, D. (1987). Owners and managers: The Venture 100 vs the Fortune 500, *Journal of Business Venturing*, 2(4): 351–363.

Calof, J.L. and Beamish, P.W. (1995). Adapting to foreign markets: Explaining internationalization, *International Business Review*, 4(2): 115–131.

Cavusgil, S.T. and Knight, G. (2009), *Born Global Firms: A New International Enterprise*. New York, NY: Business Expert Press.

Chetty, S. and Campbell-Hunt, C. (2004). A strategic approach to internationalisation: a traditional versus 'born global' approach. *Journal of International Marketing*, 12(1): 57–81.

Coviello, N.E. and Munro, H.J. (1995). Growing the entrepreneurial firm: Networking for international market development, *European Journal of Marketing*, 29(7): 49–61.

Dyer, W.G. Jr. and Wilkins, A.L. (1991). Better stories, not better constructs, to generate better theory: A rejoinder to Eisenhardt, *Academy of Management Review*, 16(3): 613–619.

Ellis, P. and Pecotich, A. (2001). Social factors influencing export initiation in small and medium sized enterprises, *Journal of Marketing Research*, 38(1): 119–130.

Fan, T. and Phan, P. (2007). International new ventures: Revisiting the influences behind the 'Born global' firm, *Journal of International Business Studies*, 38(7): 1113–1131.

Freeman, S. (2007). An integrated framework of de-internationalisation strategies for smaller born-globals. *The 23rd Industrial Marketing and Purchasing (IMP) Group Conference*, Manchester Business School, United Kingdom.

Ghauri, P.N. (2004). Design and conducting case studies in international business research, in R. Marschan-Piekkariand C. Welch (Eds.) *Handbook of Qualitative Research Methods for International Business*, Cheltenham: Edward Elgar: 109–124.

Granovetter, M.S. (1985). Economic action and social structure: The problem of embeddedness, *American Journal of Sociology*, 91(3): 481–510.

Gulati, R. (1999). Network location and learning: the influence of network resources and firm capabilities on alliance formation, *Strategic Management Journal*, 20(5): 397–420.

Hara, G. and Kanai, T. (1994). Entrepreneurial networks across oceans to promote international strategic alliances for small business, *Journal of Business Venturing*, 9: 489–507.

Javalgi, R.G., Deligonul, S., Dixit, A. and Cavusgil, S.T. (2011). International market re-entry: A review and research framework, *International Business Review*, 20: 377–393.

Johanson, J. and Mattsson, L.-G. (1988). Internationalisation in industrial systems – A network approach, in N. Hood and J.-E. Vahlne (Eds.) *Strategies in Global Competition*, London: Croom Helm: 287–314.

Johanson, J. and Vahlne, J.-E. (2009). The Uppsala internationalisation process model revisited: From liability of foreignness to liability of outsidership, *Journal of International Business Studies*, 40(9): 1411–1431.

Knight, G.A. and Cavusgil, S.T. (1996). The Born Global firm: A challenge to traditional internationalisation theory, *Advances in International Marketing*, 8: 11–26.

Korhonen, H., Luostarinen, R. and Welch, L. (1996). Internationalisation of SMEs: Inward – outward patterns and government policy, *Management International Review*, 36(4): 315–329.

Kuivalainen, O. and Sundqvist, S. (2006). Profitability of rapid internationalisation: The relationship between internationalisation intensity and firms' export performance, *Journal of Euromarketing*, 16(1): 59–69.

Leonard-Barton, D. (1990). A dual methodology for case studies: Synergistic use of a longitudinal single site with replicated multiple sites, *Organisation Science*, 1(3): 248–266.

Lindqvist, M. (1991). *Infant Multinationals: The Internationalisation of Young, Technology-Based Swedish Firms*, Doctoral Dissertation, Stockholm School of Economics, Stockholm.

Luostarinen, R. and Gabrielsson, M. (2004). Finnish perspectives of international entrepreneurship, in L.-P. Dana (Ed.), *Handbook of Research on International Entrepreneurship*. Cheltenham: Edward Elgar Publishing: 383–403.

Lummaa, J. (2002). *Internationalisation Behavior of Finnish-Born Global Companies*, Unpublished Master's Thesis, Helsinki University of Technology, Helsinki, Finland.

Luostarinen, R. (1994). *Research for Action: Internationalisation of Finnish Firms and their Response to Global Challenges*. Forssa: UNU Wider.

Madsen, T.K. and Servais, P. (1997). The internationalisation of Born Globals: An evolutionary process? *International Business Review*, 6(6): 561–583.

Marschan-Piekkari, R., Plakoyiannaki, E. and Welch, C. (2010). Good case research in industrial marketing: Insights from research practice, *Industrial Marketing Management*, 39(1): 109–117.

Mattsson, L.-G. and Hertz, S. (1998). Internationalisation of small and medium sized firms-network process and network strategies. *Work-in-Progress Chapter Presented at the 14th Annual IMP Conference*, Turku 3–5.9.

McAuley, A. (1999). Entrepreneurial instant exporters in the Scottish arts and crafts sector, *Journal of International Marketing*, 7(4): 67–82.

McKinsey and Co. (1993). *Emerging Exporters. Australia's High Value-Added Manufacturing Exporters*. Melbourne: McKinsey and Company and the Australian Manufacturing Council.

Miles, M.B. and Huberman, A.M. (1994). *Qualitative Data Analysis: An Expanded Sourcebook*. London: Sage.

Oviatt, B.M. and McDougall, P.P. (1994). Toward a theory of international new ventures, *Journal of International Business Studies*, 25(1): 45–64.

Oviatt, B.M. and McDougall, P.P. (2005). Defining international entrepreneurship and modeling the speed of internationalization, *Entrepreneurship: Theory and Practice*, 29: 537–553.

Rennie, M.W. (1993). Global competitiveness: Born global, *McKinsey Quarterly*, 4: 45–52.

Rialp, A., Rialp, J., Urbano, D. and Vaillant, Y. (2005). The born-global phenomenon: a comparative case study research. *Journal of International Entrepreneurship*, 3(2): 133–171.

Sharma, D.D. and Blomstermo, A. (2003). The internationalisation process of Born Globals: A network view, *International Business Review*, 12(6): 739–753.

Vissak, T. (2010a). Recommendations for using the case study method in international business research, *Qualitative Report*, 15(2): 370–388.

Vissak, T. (2010b). Nonlinear internationalisation: A neglected topic in international business research, in T. Devinney, T. Pedersen and L. Tihanyi (Eds.) *The Past, Present and Future of International Business and Management*, Bingley, UK: Emerald: 559–580.

Welch, L.S. and Luostarinen, R. (1988). Internationalisation: Evolution of a concept, *Journal of General Management*, 14(2): 34–55.

Welch, C.L. and Welch, L.S. (2009). Re-internationalisation: Exploration and conceptualization, *International Business Review*, 18(6): 567–577.

Yin, R.K. (1994). *Case Study Research Design and Methods*. London: Sage.

Zettinig, P. and Benson-Rea, M. (2008). What becomes of International New Ventures? A co-evolutionary approach, *European Management Journal*, 26(6): 354–365.

Zhou, L., Wu, W. and Luo, X. (2007). Internationalisation and the performance of born-global SMEs: The mediating role of social networks, *Journal of International Business Studies*, 38(4): 673–690.

Zucchella, A. and Scabini, P. (2007). *International Entrepreneurship. Theoretical Foundations and Empirical Analysis*. London: Palgrave Macmillan.

Index

The names of all authors are not listed in the index; readers wanting the names of all authors and titles of all sources are advised to refer to the references after each chapter.

The manufacturer's authorised representative in the EU is Springer Nature Customer Service Centre GmbH, Europaplatz 3, 69115 Heidelberg, Germany. If you have any concerns regarding our products, please contact ProductSafety@springernature.com

Printed and bound by CPI Group (UK) Ltd, Croydon, CR0 4YY
10/10/2026
02231221-0011